UNDERSTANDING SCIENTIFIC REASONING

Fourth Edition

UNDERSTANDING SCIENTIFIC REASONING

Fourth Edition

Ronald N. Giere
Department of Philosophy
Minnesota Center for Philosophy of Science
University of Minnesota—Twin Cities

Harcourt Brace College Publishers
Fort Worth • Philadelphia • San Diego • New York • Orlando • Austin • San Antonio
Toronto • Montreal • London • Sydney • Tokyo

Acquisitions Editor David Tatom
Developmental Editor J. Claire Brantley
Project Editor Jim Patterson
Art Director Lora Knox
Production Manager Diane Gray
Product Manager Steve Drummond
Marketing Coordinator Carol Wadsworth

Copyeditor Donna Regen
Proofreader Jody St. John
Indexer Sylvia Coates
Compositor World Composition Services
Text Type 10/12 Bembo

Address for orders:
The Dryden Press
6277 Sea Harbor Drive
Orlando, FL 32887-6777
1-800-782-4479, or 1-800-433-0001 (in Florida)

Address for editorial correspondence:
The Dryden Press
301 Commerce Street, Suite 3700
Fort Worth, TX 76102

ISBN: 0-15-501625-3

Library of Congress Catalog Card Number: 96-83003

Printed in the United States of America
6 7 8 9 0 1 2 3 4 5 066 9 8 7 6 5 4 3 2 1

Harcourt Brace College Publishers

PREFACE

Understanding Scientific Reasoning was originally motivated by a desire to make some aspects of the philosophy of science relevant to the needs of all students. It now also serves the widely recognized goals of improving critical thinking skills and contributing to general scientific literacy. It is explicitly directed toward first-and second-year college students. Its specific purpose is to help these beginning students acquire cognitive skills useful for *understanding* and *evaluating* scientific material as found in college textbooks and in a wide variety of both popular and professional printed sources. The introductory chapter presents scientific reasoning as a cognitive skill whose acquisition requires considerable practice.

The text has three main parts. Part One (Chapters 2, 3, and 4) develops techniques for understanding and evaluating *theoretical* hypotheses of the sort typically found in the physical sciences as well as in the more theoretical parts of biology and the cognitive sciences. Part Two (Chapters 5 through 8) develops techniques for understanding and evaluating *statistical* and *causal* hypotheses typically found in the social and biomedical sciences. Part Three (Chapters 9 and 10) explains how scientific knowledge may be combined with individual or social values to reach personal or public policy *decisions*.

Chapter 2, "Understanding and Evaluating Theoretical Hypotheses," begins with a case study of the discovery of the structure of DNA. In my own courses, this discussion is supplemented by having everyone read J. D. Watson's *The Double Helix*. This provides all students in the course with a common point of reference. The chapter continues with an analysis of this case which develops a basic format for all the evaluations that follow. The analysis begins with a discussion of ordinary maps as models of spatial relationships among things like streets, buildings, rivers, and mountains. This introduces the crucial distinction between a model and the things modeled—a distinction not often made in everyday life, but absolutely crucial for understanding science. *Understanding* a bit of science, then, is presented as being mainly a matter of understanding the relevant models. *Evaluating* scientific hypotheses is presented as a process of deciding whether given data provides evidence for regarding a particular model as a tolerably good representation of some real world objects or processes. Understanding the decision process requires distinguishing between *data* resulting from a causal interaction with the world (observation or experimentation) and a *prediction* arrived at by reasoning about a proposed model. It is the agreement or disagreement between data and predictions that provides the basis for a decision as to how well a proposed model "fits" the real world.

Chapter 2 concludes with a simple six-point program for evaluating theoretical hypotheses. There is also a corresponding summary diagram. The program is easy to apply. Most students can internalize the program to the extent that they can analyze short, unedited articles with no prompting questions. The instructions for my examinations simply say: "Analyze these reports following the program we have developed in class." So the students are learning a useful skill that will stay with them for a long while.

Chapter 3, "Historical Episodes," applies the standard program to a variety of historical cases: Galileo's observations of the phases of Venus, Newton's mechanics and Halley's comet, Lavoisier's oxygen theory, Darwin's theory of evolution by natural selection, Mendel's genetics, and the 1960s revolution in geology. Instructors may pick and choose among these cases, perhaps even substituting some of their own favorites.

Chapter 4 focuses on classic *marginal sciences*: Psychoanalysis, Astrology, Extraterrestrial Visitation, Reincarnation, and Extrasensory Perception. Rather than emphasizing simple fallacies, it shows how marginal claims, like those of astrology, fare poorly when subjected to the same program for evaluation developed for understanding and evaluating more standard scientific cases. Moreover, it is made clear why these claims fare poorly: the data do not provide a sufficient basis for a clear decision between the proposed models and other plausible alternatives. This chapter is important because it brings home, in a dramatic fashion, the distinctive features of modern, experimental, science.

Part Two, "Statistical and Causal Hypotheses," begins by introducing statistical and probabilistic models as special cases of theoretical models. Chapter 5, "Statistical Models and Probability" is restricted to simple statistical models, including models for statistical correlation. Chapter 6, "Evaluating Statistical Hypotheses," presents judgments of support for statistical hypotheses as following a pattern similar to that used for theoretical hypotheses, but complicated by the need to deal explicitly with probability. There is a corresponding six-step program for evaluating statistical hypotheses. The emphasis is on survey sampling (as used, for example, in public opinion polls) and the estimation of statistical parameters.

I have tried to provide techniques for evaluation that for the most part can be used without resorting to written calculations. Students should be able to apply the programs as they read reports of scientific findings, doing any needed calculations in their heads. My experience has been that what people cannot immediately do in their heads, they are unlikely to do at all. It is only for homework exercises and examinations that things must be written down.

Chapter 7, "Causal Models," develops a model for simple *causal* relationships. The model is presented not as an "analysis" or "definition" of causality, but merely as the least complex model in a whole family of related causal models. Most examples, however, are treated in terms of the simpler model. The difference between causation and correlation is emphasized throughout. Chapter 8, "Evaluating Causal Models," is structured around the three types of experimental designs standardly used to evaluate causal hypotheses. There is, of course, an additional six-step program for evaluating causal hypotheses. Many instructors have thought that Chapter 8 is the most useful and engaging chapter in the whole book.

Part Three, "Knowledge, Values, and Decisions," presents some standard models of decision making which can be used to understand how scientific knowledge may be brought to bear on both personal and public policy decisions. It emphasizes the doctrine that decisions do not follow from scientific knowledge alone, but require a value input as well. Chapter 10 contains a six-point program for evaluating decisions.

This fourth edition contains many new exercises, some of which are reproduced with only minor editing from actual sources. These will be found mainly in Chapters 2, 6, and 8. The text itself contains no answers to the exercises, although it does contain many examples worked out in detail, several of which are new in this edition. Instructors can, therefore, use some of the exercises for homework and others for examinations. However, using examples published on topics of the day while the course is in progress increases student interest. An instructor's manual is available that contains answers to all exercises as well as enlarged versions of important diagrams which can be turned directly into overhead slides using an ordinary photocopying machine.

As originally conceived, the underlying framework of *Understanding Scientific Reasoning* was that of justification by logical argument. This has been a standard framework for logic texts, both formal and informal, for many years. My original strategy was to introduce some simple deductive forms, particularly *modus tollens*, and then to develop inductive adaptations for scientific contexts.

I had reasons for dissatisfaction with this approach long before I conceived a workable alternative. From the student's perspective, representing scientific reasoning in terms of simple argument forms seemed not to contribute much to their understanding of the scientific context. Reconstructing the reasoning as an explicit argument was often a burdensome, and frequently mechanical, exercise. Faculty, particularly those with some expertise in the area of probability and induction, were not always happy with my simple inductive forms, no matter how pedagogically expedient they were compared with available alternatives. But being dissatisfied is one thing; having a comprehensive, coherent alternative is quite another.

The third edition of *Understanding Scientific Reasoning* developed one such alternative. To that end, it was substantially rewritten, with the old introductory chapters on deductive argument forms completely eliminated. This made possible considerable simplification and streamlining of the whole text. The present, fourth edition refines and updates the approach developed in the third edition.

The earlier editions of this text have been used by a number of people outside of philosophy, in general science programs, for example, or in programs in science, technology, and society. The present edition is even more congenial to such uses. Its overall approach is much closer to the way scientists themselves think about science.

The majority of instructors, however, have been philosophers. Among philosophers, philosophers of science who emphasize historical development over logical form should find the present approach quite congenial. So will those philosophers who have been impressed by recent developments in the cognitive sciences. Those interested in critical thinking should also be quite comfortable with this approach. The book's emphasis on useful critical techniques fits in well with the ethos of the critical thinking movement.

Those who are apt to be most critical of the approach are philosophers who have always worked in the framework of justification by arguments, whether formal or informal. I understand full well that others may not share my dissatisfaction with traditional logical reconstructions of scientific reasoning. I would ask those instructors who have simply assumed a parallel with deductive reasoning at least to examine the new approach and to consider whether the gains do not outweigh the losses. The fact

ACKNOWLEDGMENTS

Many people, both students and teachers, have contributed to the development of this text over the years. In preparing the fourth edition, I am particularly indebted to Randy Maynes and Doug Stalker, both of whom used earlier editions in their own classes and passed along to me many useful hints, and even some materials for exercises. Many other users of the earlier editions have also made helpful suggestions. I hope those to whom I have not directly responded will accept this acknowledgment of their help. I also greatly appreciate the efforts of my editor for the past several years, Claire Brantley, and the project editor, Jim Patterson, for helping to bring this edition to fruition. Thanks also to David Tatom, acquisitions editor; Diane Gray, production manager; Lora Knox, art director; Steve Drummond, product manager; and Carol Wadsworth, marketing coordinator.

My main debt, once again, is to the principal secretary of The Minnesota Center for Philosophy of Science, Steve Lelchuk. Steve prepared the original electronic versions of all the diagrams, handled all the correspondence regarding the numerous required permissions, and assisted in hundreds of other little ways that made the task far easier than it otherwise would have been. Without his help it would have been very difficult for me to keep my promise to my wife, Barbara Hanawalt, that I would never again allow work on this text to intrude unduly on our life together.

Ronald N. Giere
Minneapolis
May 1996

Contents

Understanding Scientific Reasoning

Fourth Edition

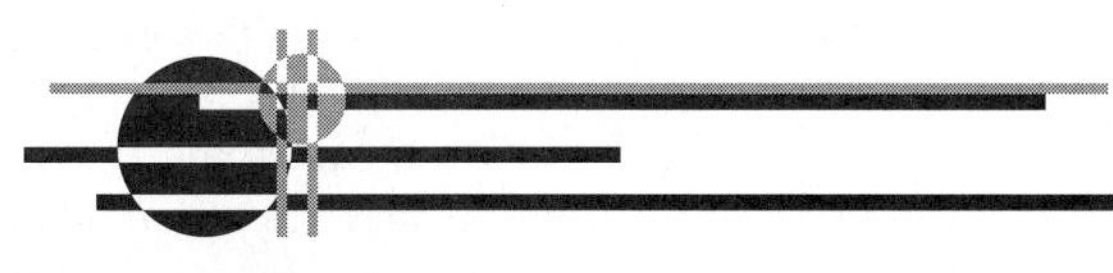

CHAPTER 1
WHY UNDERSTAND SCIENTIFIC REASONING?

Before undertaking any course of study, one should pause to ask, "Why am I doing this?" "What benefits can I expect to receive for my efforts?" This chapter provides you with some answers to these questions.

We begin by examining some general reasons why it is important for anyone to understand scientific reasoning. These general reasons are then illustrated with several examples. Having considered some reasons why it is important to understand scientific reasoning, we examine the general strategy of the text. The chapter concludes with some tips as to how you can master this subject most effectively.

1.1 WHY STUDY SCIENTIFIC REASONING?

We live in a world that is increasingly influenced by developments in science and technology. Even within the lifetime of most readers of this text, whole new fields of science and whole new technologies have come of age. Think, for example, of molecular biology and bio-engineering, space technology, and computers. At the middle of this century, shortly after World War II, there were no jet airliners, and most of the drugs now used in the treatment of disease had not yet been invented. As recently as 1925, the automobile had just become a prominent part of modern life, and much of what is now taught in departments of physics, chemistry, biology, and geology was unknown. Even the Gallup poll did not exist.

Of course, many things have become more and more influential during the past half century. Professional sports, television programs, and recorded music are prominent examples. But most things, such as spectator sports, you can take or leave as you wish. With science and technology, you do not have that luxury. The impact of scientific and technological developments on our day-to-day lives is so great that no one can afford to be ignorant of these developments.

In one respect, there is little danger of anyone remaining uninformed of new trends in science or technology. The amount of publicly available information about science and technology is overwhelming. Recent trends in science and technology are regularly reported on television news programs. Most major newspapers now carry at least a weekly science section. And there are several news magazines devoted exclusively to science and technology. If, as has been proclaimed, we are now living in an "information age" (like the "iron age" or the "automobile age"), much of the available information concerns science or technology. But therein lies the difficulty.

To take advantage of any sort of information, you need to know something about the activity involved. Baseball statistics mean little to someone who does not understand the game of baseball. Information about new recordings of classical music means little to someone unfamiliar with classical composers or modern performers. The same is true of science. Assimilating scientific information requires some conception of what science is all about and some special skills in evaluating the information we receive.

Here, then, is a general reason why anyone should develop some understanding of scientific reasoning. This skill is necessary if you are to take full advantage of the scientific information that is increasingly important for functioning effectively in both your professional and your personal life. Correspondingly, the aim of this text is to provide you with the required understanding of the scientific process and the necessary reasoning skills.

Scientific reasoning is best taught by carefully mixing general principles with concrete examples. Thus, having given you a general reason for studying this subject, I now present a few examples.

1.2 SOME PRELIMINARY EXAMPLES

Scientific subjects lie on a spectrum from those of primarily *intellectual* interest to those with immediate *practical* implications. Thus, reading about research on the structure of the universe or the evolution of mammals may have profound implications for how you *think* about the world, but it will probably not have much impact on anything you *do* tomorrow or even next year. On the other hand, learning about research into the causes of cancer or heart disease may not do much to change your views of the universe, but it may change your choice of what to have for breakfast tomorrow morning. The following examples range along the spectrum from intellectual to practical.

THE EXPANDING UNIVERSE

One of the most interesting scientific findings of the twentieth century was the discovery, in the 1930s, that the universe is expanding. That is, the galaxies that make up the universe (of which our Milky Way is only one) are all moving away from each other. Most astronomers now think that the present phase of expansion began with all the matter in the universe exploding in one big bang. The question remains, however, whether the present expansion will continue forever or whether it will eventually stop, with all the galaxies then coming back together for another big bang.

New scientific results are sometimes reported in the popular press even before they are published in professional scientific journals. It is not surprising, therefore, to find a newspaper article with the headline "Scientists Expect New Clue to Origin of Universe." According to this article, whether the universe will continue to expand or undergo a never-ending series of expansions and contractions depends on whether the density of atoms in the universe is greater or less than one atom for every 88 gallons of space. If it is greater, gravitational attraction will be strong enough to pull everything back together again. If it is less, gravitational attraction will not be strong enough to pull things back together, and the expansion will go on forever. The reason this article appeared when it did was that some scientists have claimed that new measurements of the strength of extragalactic x-rays by earth-orbiting satellites may soon provide a good estimate of the actual density of atoms in the universe.

This type of scientific information has few immediate practical implications for anyone. By the time the next contraction would occur, our sun will have long since died or exploded. But such findings may excite your curiosity. They may even influence your views about the universe as a whole and about your place in it. Moreover, because these findings are being written up for the general public, one ought to be able to understand the reported results without being an astrophysicist.

Can you identify the theories in question? Can you distinguish the theories from the facts? Do you know the difference between a theory and a fact? Can you tell which facts are relevant to which theories? Which results of the proposed experiments would support which theory? When you have finished Part One of this text, "Theoretical Hypotheses," you should be able to answer such questions. Moreover, you should be able to understand and evaluate reports of similar scientific episodes in a variety of sciences all the way from astronomy to zoology.

GLOBAL WARMING

As the decade of the 1980s came to an end, there was much talk about global warming and the "greenhouse effect." Indeed, in the United States, the 4 hottest years of the twentieth century occurred during that decade. Prominent scientists argued that the climate of the earth is indeed warming and, moreover, that the cause of the warming is primarily the burning of hydrocarbons, such as oil and coal, by humans. The increasing density of carbon dioxide and other "greenhouse gases" in the atmosphere, they argue, is causing the warming trend we have experienced.

Other scientists disagree. They argue that our recent experience of abnormally warm weather may well just be a fluctuation in the earth's overall climate. So there may not even be a genuine warming trend at all. Moreover, it is claimed, there are other mechanisms involving ocean currents and atmospheric winds that could produce the warm years we have experienced recently.

Does the recent unusually warm weather provide evidence of global warming? Does it provide evidence of a greenhouse effect? If not, why not? Here again, Part One of this text provides you with the resources to answer questions such as these.

Meanwhile, agencies of the United Nations and other international organizations have publicly urged the major industrial nations, which are responsible for most of the greenhouse gases, to take stringent measures to reduce the production of these gases. But many governments, including that of the United States, have argued that such measures would be very costly. They cite disagreements within the scientific community over the existence of global warming and its supposed causes as evidence that more study is needed. While the debate goes on, not much is being done to reduce hydrocarbon emissions. Is the lack of action by major industrial nations understandable in the light of the existing scientific controversy? Part Three of this text, "Knowledge, Values, and Decisions," should help you answer this sort of question.

CIGARETTE SMOKING AND CORONARY HEART DISEASE

It has been roughly 35 years since the Surgeon General of the United States first issued an official warning that cigarette smoking can be dangerous to your health. Its role in causing coronary heart disease, the number one cause of death among men over 50 years old, was particularly emphasized. Since that time, cigarette advertising has been banned from television, and warning labels have been placed on cigarette packs and printed advertisements. Airlines have banned smoking on all domestic flights. The Surgeon General continues to issue yearly reports focusing on such topics as smoking among teenagers and the effects on newborn babies of smoking by pregnant women. Yet the Tobacco Institute, the research arm of the tobacco industry, still maintains that the connection between smoking and coronary heart disease, or any other disease, is merely statistical. No causal connection, they say, has been proven. Moreover, millions of people continue to smoke, and the federal government itself continues to subsidize both the growing and the exporting of tobacco.

If you are not a statistician or a medical researcher, what are you to conclude? Who are you to believe? Is it true that all the data are merely statistical? What is the difference between a statistical correlation and a genuine causal connection? Could any statistical data prove the existence of a causal connection? If not, why not? What kind of evidence could establish the existence of a causal connection? You should be able to answer these sorts of questions after studying Part Two, "Statistical and Causal Hypotheses."

Suppose the Surgeon General is correct and smoking does cause coronary heart disease. Does it follow that you should not smoke or that you should give it up if you already do? How do you determine the risks? Can you balance the risk of getting heart disease against the pleasure of smoking or the discomfort of trying to give it up? Are the concerns of public health officials necessarily relevant to individuals who may be concerned only about their own chances of contracting smoking-related diseases? Here again, strategies for answering these sorts of questions are developed in Part Three, "Knowledge, Values, and Decisions."

SUMMARY

The primary answer to the question "why study scientific reasoning?" is that it will help you to understand and evaluate scientific information in both your personal life and your work. In an increasingly scientific and technological society, these abilities can literally be a matter of life and death for you, your family, and if you should achieve a position of power in business or government, for many others as well.

I have stressed the practical value of studying scientific reasoning because this is most readily appreciated by most people. But other motives are also important. One other motive is simply being able to understand and appreciate scientific findings as they are reported in the popular media. This can be a valuable ability even if the findings have no practical implications. Science is an increasingly important part of modern culture. Having some ability to understand and evaluate the latest scientific findings makes you a more literate and cultured person.

Finally, learning something about scientific reasoning provides insight not only into particular scientific findings but also into the general nature of science as a human activity. It is an activity that engages an increasing proportion of our population, consumes an increasing fraction of our resources, and impinges on an increasing number of our other activities. The better we all understand it, the better off we all will be.

1.3 How To Study Scientific Reasoning

I hope you are now convinced that studying scientific reasoning is a worthwhile undertaking. But you may well be wondering how this is possible without having to study a great deal of science. In answer to this question, I propose both a general strategy and some particular tactics for learning how to reason scientifically.

How Should We Understand Scientific Reasoning?

Most people think of scientific reasoning as the kind of reasoning that scientists use in the process of making new scientific discoveries. The obvious examples of scientific reasoning would then be the reasoning that led to the great discoveries in the history of science: Newton's discovery of the law of gravitation, Darwin's discovery of natural selection, Mendel's discovery of the laws of inheritance, Einstein's discovery of relativity theory, the discovery of the DNA double helix by Watson and Crick, and so on.

If this is what one means by scientific reasoning, it is difficult to see how anyone could learn how to do it without a great deal of training in science and perhaps a touch of genius as well. Those of us who are not specialists in a scientific subject could not hope to reason scientifically about that subject. Even specialists in one area would find it difficult to reason scientifically about subjects other than those in their own specialty. Our understanding of what constitutes scientific reasoning must be somewhat different.

Figure 1.1 pictures some relationships between scientists in their laboratories and most of the rest of us. Science is performed in laboratories. The results are communicated informally to other scientists and then published in technical scientific journals such as *The Physical Review, Science,* or *The New England Journal of Medicine.* Some of these results are picked up by more popular journals such as *Scientific American* or *Discovery.* Some are written up in news magazines such as *Time* or *Newsweek,* and some appear in local or national newspapers such as *The New York Times* and *USA Today.* Others appear on television newscasts or special programs such as "Nova." A few results eventually find their way into science textbooks for high school and college students.

For the purposes of this text, then, learning to understand scientific reasoning is a matter of learning how to understand and evaluate *reports* of scientific findings we find in popular magazines, national newspapers, news magazines, and some general professional publications. This requires very little knowledge of what really goes on in scientific laboratories. And it does not require the kinds of skills that are necessary actually to do laboratory research.

FIGURE 1.1

How information gets from scientific laboratories to the average citizen.

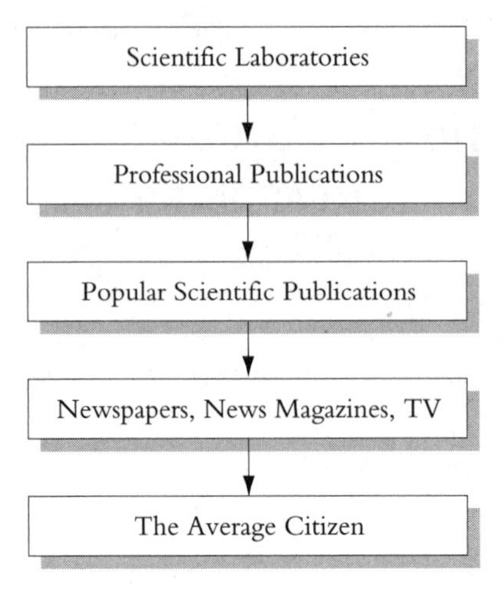

GENERAL STRATEGY

Now that we have a better idea of what we mean by scientific reasoning, we can begin to ask how one should approach learning about such reasoning. The obvious way to learn about scientific reasoning is by learning to be a scientist. But this is not necessary for our purposes. Nor is it even the best way. We could not hope to learn more than one or two scientific subjects, and although there is a general pattern to all scientific reasoning, different subject matters lead to great differences in emphasis. So studying physics would not prepare you to deal with biomedical issues, and studying sociology would not prepare you to deal with new findings in physics. We want to be able to deal with all these subjects and more.

The tools we will use have been borrowed from several subjects that deal with reasoning in general: studies into the nature of science by philosophers of science; the study of logic by philosophers; the study of human reasoning by cognitive scientists; the study of probability and statistical inference by mathematicians and statisticians; and the study of decision making by all the above. We will not ourselves, however, be examining any of these areas in their own right. The borrowed pieces have been knit together for one purpose: to help you learn to understand and evaluate the reports of scientific findings that you will meet in your everyday life and work.

A COMPUTER ANALOGY

A computer analogy may help you better to grasp the general strategy of this text. In thinking about the operation of a computer, we can distinguish three basic components. First, there is the *hardware,* which includes the circuit boards containing the central processing unit and memory, the disk drives, keyboard, and so on. Then, there is

FIGURE 1.2

Scientific reasoning as a computer program for processing information.

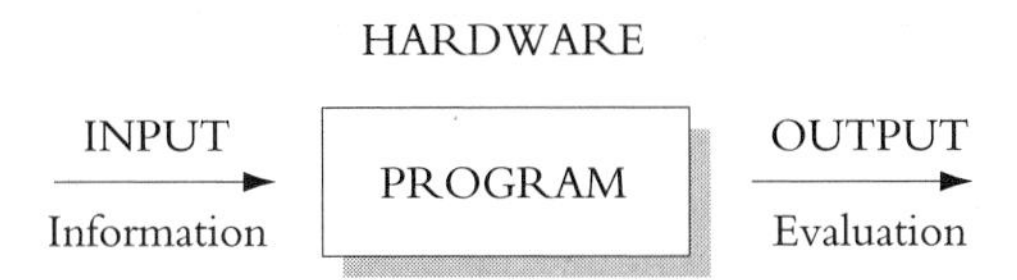

software, the programs that tell the machine what to do with various inputs. Finally, there is the *information* that is fed into the machine for processing. These components are pictured in Figure 1.2.

Now, thinking of yourself (briefly!) as a computer, you can be fairly sure that the purpose of this text is not to change your *hardware.* I assume that people differ somewhat in their native intelligence,which is a function of the hardware (or wetware) they have inherited. This text, however, is designed not to require any special hardware. Any average off-the-shelf hardware will do.

More surprising, perhaps, it is not my purpose to feed you new *information,* at least not in the usual sense. You will not be required to learn new facts, for example, about chemistry or biology—there are no formulas or parts of animals to memorize.

The information presented in this text is really part of a new *program* that is intended to improve the way you process ordinary scientific information. My objective, then, is to help you to reprogram the way you assimilate, organize, and evaluate everyday scientific information.

TACTICS

Now that you have a better idea of the general aims and strategy of the text, we can turn to the *tactics* of how the subject is presented and how it should be studied.

The text itself proceeds on three levels. First, I present some **general ideas** about the nature of science and such things as probability and causality. You should not regard this as material to be memorized. Rather, it forms the *background* for learning how to process scientific information. To assimilate these general ideas, you must read actively and critically, even skeptically. If you do not understand something, do not just reread it, although that may be necessary. Try to formulate explicit questions about what you do not understand. Then look for answers to your questions in the text—or ask your instructor.

Accompanying all the general ideas are **examples,** some of which are discussed in great detail. The purpose of the examples is to help you grasp the general ideas in such a way that you can use them in dealing with new cases. What you are trying to acquire is the ability to deal with new cases.

Finally, there are **exercises** for you to work out on your own. Most of the exercises consist of reports of some scientific finding that you are to analyze using the techniques explained and illustrated in the text. Very few questions focus on the background ideas themselves. Your goal is to learn to *use* these ideas in real life.

REASONING AS A SKILL

I suggest that you think of learning scientific reasoning as being like learning a new skill such as playing the piano or playing tennis. Learning a new skill is something that cannot be done simply by reading about it. You have to practice actually doing it. The point of the exercises, then, is to provide you with an opportunity to practice your reasoning skills.

The correct way to approach the exercises is as follows. First, study the relevant sections of the text and any related lecture notes until you think you understand the general principles. Pay particular attention to the examples that are worked out in the text itself. Then, try working the assigned exercises without looking back at the text or your notes. If you get stuck while doing a problem, spend 5 to 10 minutes thinking about it, but not longer. Go on to the next problem. Maybe it will give you a clue how to solve the previous one. If, after a while, there are still some problems you cannot figure out, go back to the text and your notes to see if you can discover for yourself what you are doing wrong. If, after an honest effort—that is, another 10 or 15 minutes of hard thinking—you still do not see what is wrong, it is time to consult with someone, perhaps a classmate or your instructor. Remember that the material within a given part of the text tends to be cumulative. If you miss something important at the beginning, you will probably be confused all the way through.

Keep in mind that the object of doing the exercises is not simply to get the right answer down on a sheet of paper. The object is to develop the skills that will enable you to do the exercises without having the text at hand. You will most likely not have access to the text during quizzes and examinations. More important, you will not have it when you need to evaluate scientific reasoning in day-to-day situations. That is where the real payoff from developing reasoning skills should be.

Another implication of thinking of reasoning as a skill is that you must practice *regularly*. Do the exercises to each chapter as they are assigned. Do not let things go and then try to cram the night before a test. No one would dream of staying up all night practicing before a tennis match or a piano recital. Staying up all night studying for a test of reasoning skills is almost as silly. Believe me, it will not work.

Finally, as in music or sports, becoming *very* good at scientific reasoning requires both practice and talent. Becoming *tolerably* good, however, requires mainly practice and only a little talent. For most people, tolerably good is good enough. So work at developing your skills little by little. By the time you have to face a quiz, you will just be doing what comes naturally. And you will be able to do it naturally in real life, too.

Part One

Theoretical Hypotheses

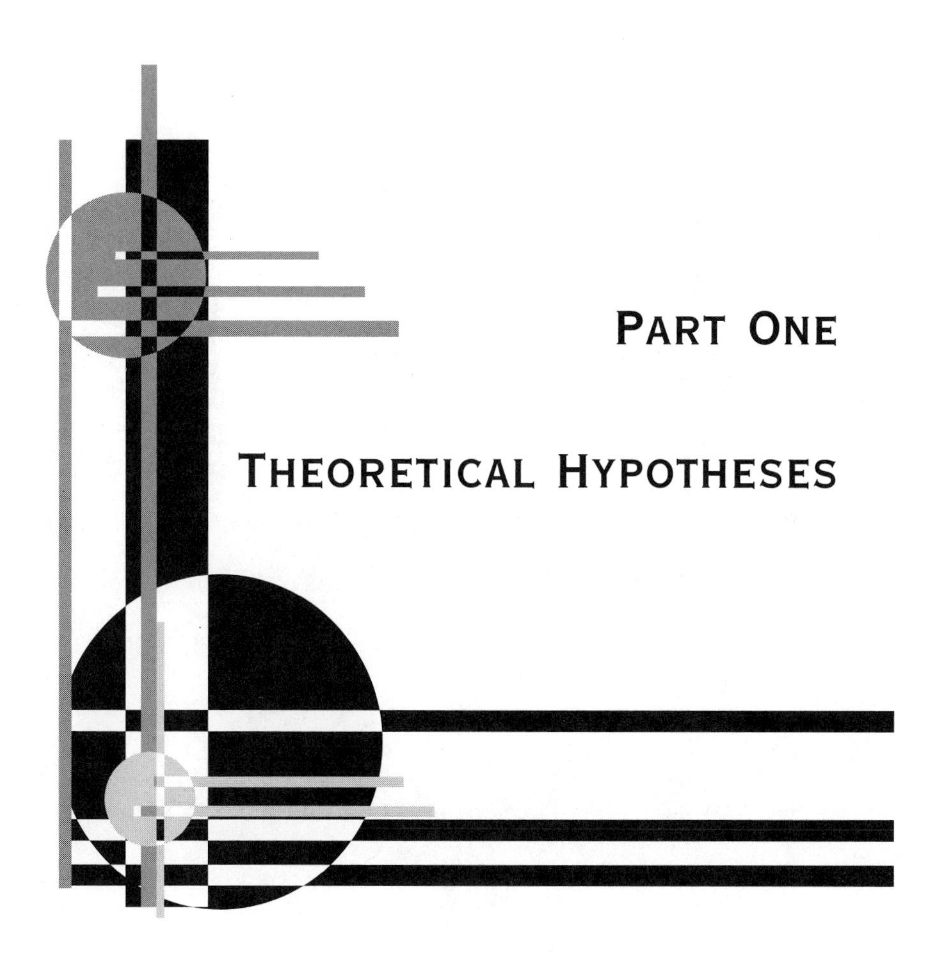

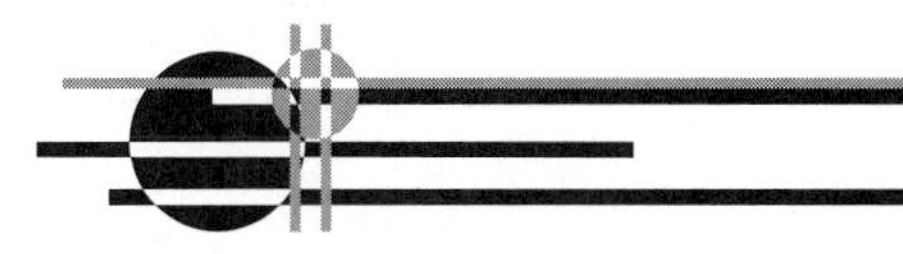

CHAPTER 2
UNDERSTANDING AND EVALUATING THEORETICAL HYPOTHESES

In this chapter, we develop a framework for understanding and evaluating a wide range of scientific cases. The chapter begins with a case study, the discovery in 1953 of the structure of *deoxyribonucleic acid (DNA).* The case study provides enough background so that this particular episode can be used as an example throughout most of the chapter. After the framework is in place, it is applied to a variety of other examples.

2.1 THE DOUBLE HELIX: A CASE STUDY

In the fall of 1951, a 23-year-old American named Jim Watson arrived at the Cavendish Laboratory of Cambridge University in Cambridge, England. He had come in pursuit of his personal scientific quest to discover the physical structure of DNA, a discovery he was sure would bring him fame. Why DNA?

The idea that human inheritance is transmitted from parents to offspring by identifiable bits of matter in germ cells (sperm and eggs) has a long history. Since about 1900, there had been slow but steady progress in determining the chemical structure of these particles, now called **genes.** By 1950, it was well known that germ cells contained both DNA and proteins, which are large chains made up of amino acids. Despite Oswald Avery's 1944 experiments, which strongly suggested that genes were made of DNA, in 1950 most biologists and chemists still thought that genes were made of proteins rather than DNA. One of the relatively few people who took Avery's work seriously was Salvador Luria, an Italian-born geneticist teaching at Indiana University. Watson, after completing his B.A. in Zoology at the University of Chicago in 1947, went on to study for his Ph.D. with Luria. When Watson finished his Ph.D. in 1950, he and Luria decided that the best route to further progress in genetics would be through detailed knowledge of the chemical structure of DNA. Watson received a grant for further study in biochemistry with an expert in Copenhagen.

The state of knowledge in 1951 concerning the makeup of DNA is summarized in Figures 2.1 and 2.2. A DNA molecule was thought to consist of one or more chains of nucleotides, called **polynucleotides.** Each individual nucleotide consists of a sugar molecule (deoxyribose), a phosphate molecule, and a base. There are four different possible bases, two each of two kinds: purines (adenine and guanine) and pyrimidines

FIGURE 2.1

A short section of DNA as represented by organic chemists in 1951. Note that this representation omits any reference to the three-dimensional arrangement of the atoms.

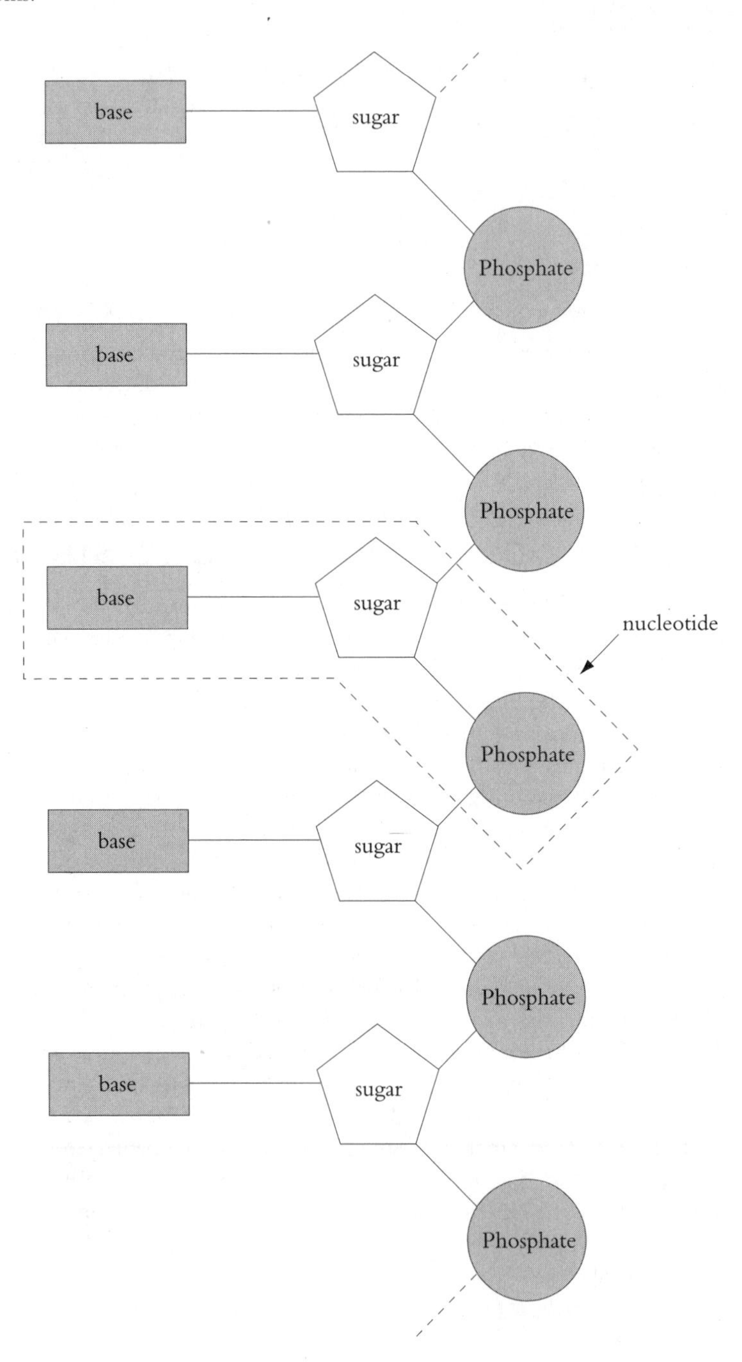

FIGURE 2.2

Representations of the four bases known in 1951 to be present chemically in DNA.

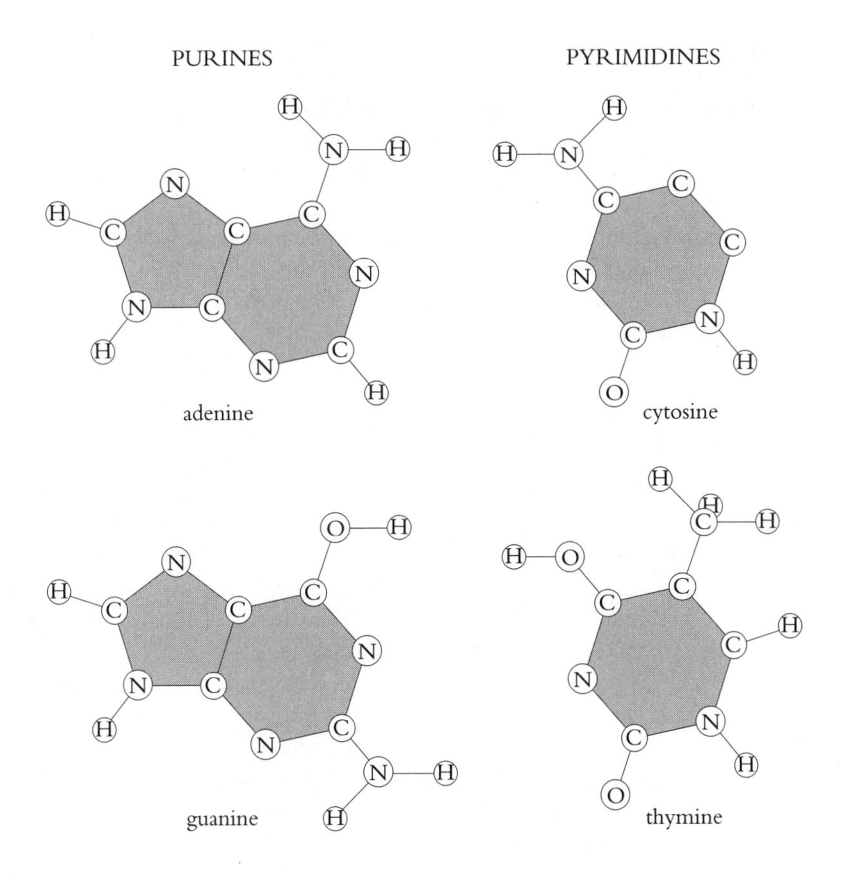

(cytosine and thymine). Such chains of nucleotides were thought of as consisting of a **backbone,** composed of the sugar and phosphate, which supports the **sequence of bases.** What Luria and Watson wanted to know was how all these pieces fit together in three-dimensional space. They believed that such structural knowledge would make it clear how genes function in the process of inheritance.

Watson found the work in Copenhagen a waste of time. The following spring, he went off to Naples, Italy, for 2 months, where he spent his time reading articles from the early days of genetics and daydreaming about discovering the secret of the gene. While in Naples, he attended a small scientific meeting concerning the structure of large molecules in living organisms. One talk excited him. Maurice Wilkins, an Englishman working at Kings College in the University of London, showed a photograph taken by focusing x-rays on a small amount of chemical DNA. The picture indicated that DNA had a fairly regular crystal-like structure. That meant that there was a reasonable chance of actually figuring out some details of the structure. Watson was delighted and began to think that x-ray methods were a better route to the structure of DNA than the biochemistry he had vainly been trying to master. He tried to make friends with Wilkins but without success.

While visiting a friend in Geneva on the way back to Copenhagen, Watson learned that the world's greatest living physical chemist, Linus Pauling, had just discovered the structure of a significant protein molecule, α-kerotin. The structure was a **helix,** and Pauling had discovered it by building a physical model of the molecule, using information obtained from x-ray photographs. Now Watson was sure this was the way to proceed. But where could he go to pursue his quest? He had been put off by Wilkins, and he was sure Pauling would pay little attention to someone with so poor a knowledge of physical chemistry. The only place he could think of was the Cavendish Laboratory, where he knew that some people were using x-ray techniques to study large molecules. He wrote to Luria for help. By good fortune, shortly after receiving Watson's letter, Luria saw one of the Cavendish scientists at a meeting in the United States and arranged for Watson to begin work there the following fall. In science, as in other endeavors, it helps to have influential friends.

THE THREE-CHAIN MODEL

It was at the Cavendish Laboratory that Watson first met Francis Crick. Although a dozen years older than Watson, Crick was still working on his Ph.D. He kept getting distracted by other interesting theoretical problems. Crick, however, shared Watson's belief in the importance of DNA and his hunch that the best strategy for discovering its structure was to build models as Pauling had done in discovering the α-helix. They speculated that DNA also possessed a helical structure.

One possible embarrassment was that Wilkins was already working on the problem, and, unlike Americans, English scientists tended to respect such territories. However, Wilkins' own work was going very slowly because he did not get along with another person in his laboratory also engaged in x-ray studies of DNA, Rosalind Franklin. Partly because of his conflicts with Franklin, Wilkins voiced no objections to Watson and Crick's fiddling with models of DNA.

Crick soon provided a major contribution to the project by developing a theoretical account of how x-rays are diffracted by helically shaped molecules. If one is going to use x-ray pictures in building models of helically shaped molecules, one needs to know what an x-ray picture of such molecules should look like.

They still needed more information about existing x-ray photographs of DNA. Luckily, Franklin was scheduled to give a talk in London concerning her recent work. Watson was dispatched to attend the talk to learn what he could. The day after Franklin's talk found Watson and Crick on the train to Oxford for a weekend visit with a friend. Crick was excited. His theory of x-ray scattering, together with the data Watson related from Franklin's talk, indicated that there could be only a few possible helical structures for DNA molecules. It should consist of at least two, but not more than four, polynucleotide chains. They decided to try a model with three chains.

The next big question concerned the position of the sugar phosphate backbones relative to the bases. There were only two major alternatives: put the intertwined backbones in the center and let the bases hang out on the outside, or put the backbones on the outside and try fitting the bases inside. Fitting the bases inside seemed too complicated, so they decided to try building a model with the bases on the outside.

On returning to Cambridge, they set about building a model using pieces of wire and specially fabricated metal plates to represent the various components of the polynucleotide chains. In this task, their major reference work was Pauling's book *The Nature of the Chemical Bond*. This book provided the best available information about the distances and angles between the various groupings of atoms held together by chemical bonds. A good model had to reflect these basic features of atoms.

In less than a month, they had completed what they regarded as a quite satisfactory model. They invited Wilkins and Franklin up from London to inspect their handiwork. It took Franklin only a few minutes to discover a major flaw in the model. Natural DNA is surrounded by water, which is loosely bound to the molecule. Watson and Crick's three-chain model left far too few places for water molecules to hook onto the DNA molecule. In fact, real DNA accommodates ten times the amount of water permitted by the model. Indeed, Franklin had given the correct information in her talk the previous month. Watson had misremembered what she had said!

In the aftermath of their humiliation by the group from London, the director of the Cavendish Laboratory, Sir Lawrence Bragg, forbad Watson and Crick to engage in any more DNA model building. Watson went off to spend Christmas with the family of a friend in Scotland. His dreams of fame and glory seemed far from being realized.

THE TWO-CHAIN MODEL

Returning from vacation, Watson took up learning how to take x-ray pictures of the tobacco mosaic virus (TMV). He was not wasting his time because TMV should have a helical structure. And, indeed, several months and a new x-ray tube later, he obtained good pictures clearly indicating a helical structure. But neither Watson nor Crick stopped thinking about DNA, even though they were officially forbidden to work on it.

Meanwhile, two scientists at Cold Spring Harbor Laboratory in Massachusetts reported an experiment that strongly supported the idea that the primary genetic material is DNA, not proteins. In 8 years, the scientific climate had changed. Unlike Avery's work, these new experiments were being taken very seriously by many other geneticists. For Watson, news of these results was both good and bad. It confirmed that he was right to focus on DNA. But now a lot of other people would start working on DNA. His advantage was slipping away.

Another new result aroused their interest. An Austrian-born biochemist at Columbia University, Erwin Chargaff, had carefully measured the base contents of DNA from several different biological species. The relative amounts of the pyrimidines, cytosine and thymine, varied from species to species. But, remarkably, the amounts of adenine and thymine were the same in all samples, as were the amounts of cytosine and guanine. Like Chargaff, Watson was sure these results were highly significant, but no one seemed to have any idea just what the significance might be. Crick, too, became increasingly preoccupied with the Chargaff results.

September 1952 found Watson turning his attention to the idea that bacteria come in male and female pairs. If true, this meant that the genetics of bacteria are much more like that of higher organisms than had earlier been thought. Crick was once more back at work on his still-unfinished Ph.D. dissertation. One new aspect of their lives was that Linus Pauling's son, Peter, had joined their group at the Cavendish Laboratory. Through Peter they were able to keep abreast of the news from Pasadena.

The first ominous word was that Pauling was working on α-coils. A little later came word that he was working on DNA, but no details. Then, in the middle of January, came a draft of a paper in which Pauling outlined a model of DNA. To their great relief, Watson and Crick found that Pauling had come up with a model superficially resembling their own ill-fated three-chain model. In addition, it had several other features that they felt sure had to be mistaken. They figured they had at most 6 weeks before Pauling discovered his mistake and turned the full power of his genius to rectifying the blunder. Nevertheless, they were determined to turn all their energies to the problem once again. The serious prospect that Pauling, an American, might beat his British group to the solution was enough to convince Bragg to let them try again.

Watson journeyed down to London to show Pauling's paper to Wilkins and to enlist his support for their new effort. Not finding Wilkins immediately, he went around to Franklin's laboratory. Citing Pauling's paper, he tried to convince her of the urgency of the situation and to enlist her, and her carefully acquired x-ray data, in the effort. She chased Watson out of her laboratory, reportedly insisting that she would have no part of their "little boys' games."

Wilkins consoled Watson by showing him a picture Franklin had taken of what she called the "B form" of DNA, which contained much more water than the then-standard "A form." The pattern, as shown in Figure 2.3, was incredibly simpler than any Watson had seen before. The strong black crosses could only come from a helical structure. That followed immediately from Crick's theory about how x-rays are diffracted by helixes. Watson returned to Cambridge more excited than ever.

FIGURE 2.3

A schematic rendering of the pattern revealed by Rosalind Franklin's 1952 x-ray photograph of the B form of DNA.

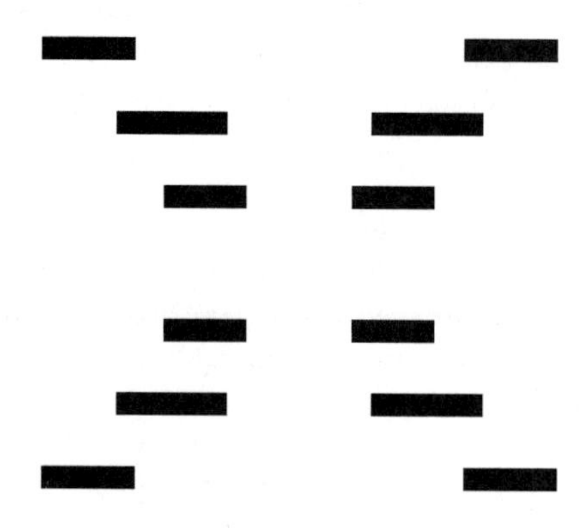

They still did not have enough information to answer the big questions that had faced them the year before: how many chains are there? are the bases outside or inside? and if the bases are inside, how are they arranged? This time Watson decided they should try two-chain models, appealing to the general idea that important biological entities come in pairs. The decision whether to put the bases outside or inside was more difficult. They had always worried that there would be too many different possible ways of arranging the bases on the inside, thus making it difficult to decide which is correct. But seeing that they were getting nowhere with base-outside models, they decided to have a go at models with the bases inside.

The idea was that a base attached to one sugar phosphate backbone should bond with a base on the opposing sugar phosphate backbone, thus forming a kind of miniature spiral staircase. An immediate problem was that, although the distance between the two strands, the diameter of the spiral, should be constant, the bases are all of different sizes. Hooking up any two bases across the inside would either deform the bases or make bulges in the spiral backbone. Nevertheless, despite deformations and bulges, Watson proceeded to build a model with bases bonded like-with-like (i.e., adenine with adenine, and so on).

He was shortly set straight by an American crystallographer, Jerry Donohue, who had once worked with Pauling. Watson had taken information about the hydrogen bonds from a standard textbook. Donohue informed him that the standard textbooks were wrong. The bases could not possibly bond the way Watson's like-with-like model required. Crick voiced still other objections. Watson reluctantly gave up on the like-with-like scheme.

The machine shop at the Cavendish Laboratory was late in producing the little tin plates they needed to represent the bases. Being impatient to get on, Watson cut his own set of bases out of stiff cardboard. Playing around with his cardboard models, Watson discovered that the combination adenine-thymine has a very similar shape to the combination guanine-cytosine. With these "steps," one could build a spiral staircase with a uniform diameter. Donohue confirmed that the required hydrogen bonding would work. Moreover, this scheme provided an immediate explanation for the Chargaff results because each pair consists of one purine and one pyrimidine, and only these particular combinations would bond in the required manner. Crick, who later claimed independently to have come to the same conclusion without benefit of Watson's cardboard models, was quick to proclaim that they had found "the secret of life."

But there was still work to do. When the shop delivered the metal cutouts, they took a plumb line and measuring stick to the model, carefully aligning all the pieces to make sure that they did fit together in a configuration consistent with knowledge of the relevant chemical bonds. It seemed to be in order. Even Sir Lawrence Bragg was pleased. More important, Wilkins and even Franklin agreed that the proposed structure was confirmed by a detailed examination of their own x-ray data.

"We wish to suggest a structure for the salt of deoxyribose nucleic acid (D. N. A.)." So began the 900-word paper by Watson and Crick published in *Nature,* March 25, 1953. Figure 2.4 shows a schematic rendering of the structure of DNA as it appeared in this first paper. By prior arrangement, Watson and Crick's paper was followed by papers by Wilkins and Franklin, respectively. These papers set the direction

FIGURE 2.4

A schematic representation of the double helical structure of DNA as shown in Watson and Crick's 1953 paper in *Nature*.

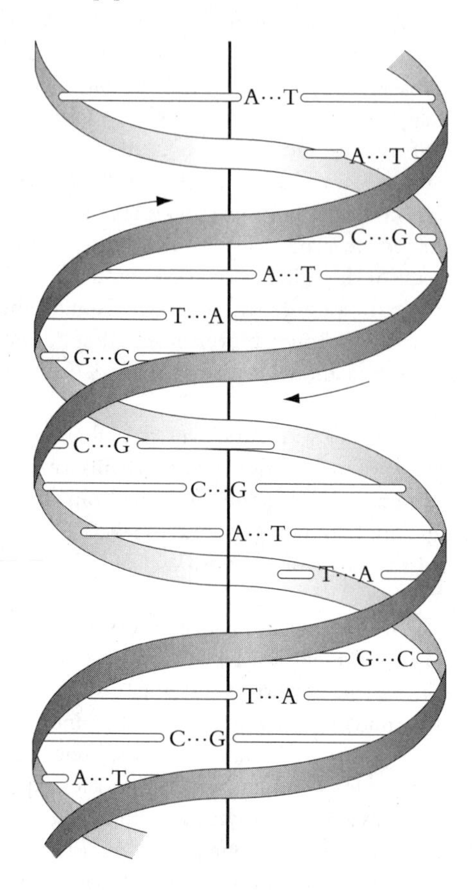

for work in molecular biology that continues as we traverse the final decade of the twentieth century.

2.2 UNDERSTANDING EPISODES IN SCIENCE

Now that we know the basic story of how the structure of DNA was discovered, let us go back over the case to develop a few general analytical tools for understanding this and similar episodes in science. We first survey some general features of such episodes and then go on to examine a few of these features in more detail.

THE HUMAN CONTEXT OF SCIENCE

The Double Helix, Watson's own personal account of the discovery, was first published in 1968, 15 years after the event. Many people objected that the book was too personal.

In particular, it exposed the all-too-human foibles and weaknesses of the participants. Prominent among these, of course, were the conflicts between Rosalind Franklin and Maurice Wilkins. But also there were the sometimes unflattering characterizations of Francis Crick as talking too much, Sir Lawrence Bragg as being too stiff, and Linus Pauling as being too much the showman. And, of course, there is the picture of Watson himself as obsessively pursuing a Nobel Prize in active competition with Wilkins, Franklin, and Pauling.

Why did people object to the personal nature of *The Double Helix?* Some, such as Crick and Wilkins, objected that Watson had distorted the story. But others objected mainly because they wished to preserve an image of science as a "rational," "objective" activity. Besides being flattering, this image often serves scientists well in dealings with people outside science. Watson showed that the official image of science is simply not correct.

Of course, no one should ever have been taken in to start with. Science is a human activity, and scientists are ordinary human beings. Thus, among scientists, as among members of any other profession, one should expect to find a full range of human strengths and weaknesses. So, one general lesson from this episode is that the successes of science are not due to scientists being unusually blessed with virtues such as objectivity, modesty, or honesty. We must look elsewhere for an explanation of why science works as well as it does.

A more practical lesson is that, behind every episode you read or hear about, there are many typically human stories. People's reputations and careers are on the line. The standard report of new scientific findings you see in newspapers or magazines, however, reveals only snatches of these stories, if anything at all. We can only imagine what the real flesh-and-blood scientists were doing. Nevertheless, in trying to understand an episode, it always helps to remember that real people were there behind the scenes all along.

EXPLORING HOW THE WORLD WORKS

Let us grant, then, that science is a human institution run by people with a wide range of interests and motivations. Still, there must be some things that distinguish science from other institutions such as commerce, the military, the arts, politics, or religion. The most general claim we can make is this: in so far as they participate in science as an institution, scientists are engaged in *exploring how the world works*. Whatever their differences in personal motivation and style, Pauling, Watson, Crick, Wilkins, and Franklin were all engaged in trying to figure out the structure of DNA. This was part of the larger project of figuring out how genes replicate and, thus, how parents pass on characteristics to their offspring.

We can also say something in general about how scientists explore the workings of the world. They engage in careful and deliberate interactions with the world. They do experiments and make observations, some of which are designed to help them decide which of several possible ways the world *might work* is most like the way it *really does work*. This activity distinguishes a scientific tradition, for example, from a religious tradition that seeks understanding of the world through the interpretation of sacred texts or from a literary tradition based on a particular literary form, such as the novel.

It is often said that science is distinguished by the use of something called "the scientific method." This claim is doubtful, at best, because the methods scientists actually use are as varied as the subjects they study. Most of what we can say, in general, about the methods of science, about experimentation, for example, cannot be specific enough to be of much use to any scientist engaged in actual research. Some things can be said, however, that can be of use to an onlooker seeking to understand, and to some extent to evaluate, the goings-on in particular scientific inquiries.

FINDING A PROBLEM

No scientist is simply engaged in the general pursuit of discovering how the world works. Every scientist focuses on some particular aspect of the world, and they all have special problems they seek to solve. Watson, for example, set for himself the problem of determining the three-dimensional structure of DNA.

How an individual scientist comes to focus on a particular problem is largely a matter of the accidents of personal history. Watson was apparently interested in biology from an early age. He had been an avid bird watcher and later claimed that he first developed an interest in the nature of genes as a senior in college. His interest in DNA, in particular, seems to have been sparked by his Ph.D. superviser, Salvador Luria.

The lesson for us is that knowing about how a particular scientist came to work on a problem is not likely to be of much use in understanding or in evaluating specific scientific results. It may be interesting as biography and useful for understanding why particular avenues of inquiry were pursued when they were, but that is not our concern here.

CONSTRUCTING MODELS

Watson and Crick spent a lot of time thinking about, talking about, and actually building *models* of DNA. Not all scientists literally build scale models like the wire and metal plate models Watson and Crick constructed. In a more abstract sense, however, most scientists can be said to be engaged in constructing models of some aspect of the world, if only in their minds. Understanding episodes in science requires some understanding of the particular models being developed. Learning to analyze reports of scientific episodes also requires an appreciation of the nature and role of models in science. Acquiring such an appreciation is one of our first tasks.

DECIDING WHETHER A MODEL FITS

Scientists do not construct models just for the fun of it. Constructing models is part of the process of figuring out how the world works. While working on their models, scientists are always trying to decide whether these models actually exhibit a reasonably good fit to the real world. In making such decisions, scientists obviously consider all sorts of facts, particularly the results of careful experiments. But their decision-making process is influenced by many other factors as well. Among these may be the desire to be the first to make an important discovery or the fear of being shown to be wrong. Watson's desire for success clearly outweighed his fear of making mistakes, as demonstrated by his initial enthusiasm for the disastrously ill-fitting three-chain model.

To understand episodes in science, we have to learn more about how scientists decide whether a model really does fit the world.

CONVINCING OTHERS

It is not enough for an individual scientist to decide that a model fits. Other scientists must be persuaded to make the same decision. This requires data and arguments that will appeal to scientists approaching the subject with a wide variety of different interests, backgrounds, and skills. Franklin, for example, came to agree that DNA has a helical structure long after Watson, Crick, and Wilkins were quite convinced it must. Pauling fairly quickly agreed that the double-helix model was correct after seeing both the model and the x-ray data in London. Other scientists in the field quickly agreed after hearing about it or reading the papers by Watson, Crick, Wilkins, and Franklin.

SPREADING THE WORD

Once most of the scientists directly involved in a scientific area decide that a model fits, a much slower process begins by which that conclusion spreads to the general nonscientific public. Scientists may be involved in this process, as Watson has been, but so are many others, particularly teachers, journalists, and even filmmakers. It is at this stage of the game that the rest of us learn most of what we know about science. To understand and evaluate scientific information as presented for the general public requires learning how to use what is presented to reconstruct features of the models and the decision-making processes that went into producing the information in the first place. We turn now to this task.

2.3 MODELS AND THEORIES

Scientists often describe what they do as constructing **models.** Understanding scientific reasoning requires understanding something about models and how they are used in science. In fact, there are at least three different types, or uses, of models to keep in mind.

SCALE MODELS

Watson and Crick were helped greatly by actually trying to construct a physical model of DNA. This was a model in the ordinary sense in which model airplanes and dollhouses are models. They are all **scale models**. The big difference between Watson and Crick's model and more familiar scale models is the extreme nature of the scale, which, in the case of the DNA model, was roughly a billion to one. That is, an inch in the model represented roughly one one-billionth of an inch in an actual DNA molecule.

Scale models are widely used in science and even more widely used in engineering. We can learn a lot about the wind resistance of various automotive designs, for example, by testing scale models of automobiles in small wind tunnels. This is much easier, and cheaper, than building wind tunnels large enough to hold full-sized cars. Nevertheless, when you find scientists talking about models, they most likely are not talking about scale models.

ANALOG MODELS

In *The Double Helix,* Watson talks about noticing spiral staircases and thinking that the structure of DNA might be like a spiral staircase. He also had the example of Pauling's α-helix. Here we would say that Watson was using a spiral staircase and the α-helix as **analog models** for the DNA molecule. He was suggesting that the DNA molecule is analogous to the α-helix or to a spiral staircase. One might also say that he was *modeling* the structure of DNA on that of the α-helix or a spiral staircase.

The most famous analog model in modern science is that of the solar system as an analog model for an atom. The nucleus of an atom, containing protons and neutrons, is said to be analogous to the sun. The electrons are said to be analogous to planets circling the sun. There is no doubt that this analogy between the solar system and atoms was extraordinarily fruitful during the first half of the twentieth century. It suggested all sorts of questions that formed the basis of much research (e.g., How fast are the electrons moving around in their orbits? Are the orbits circular or elliptical?). In investigating such questions, scientists learned much about atoms. In particular, they learned about many respects in which atoms are not like the solar system. In the end, a good analogy often leads to its own demise.

Analog models are typically most useful in the early stages of research when scientists are first trying to get a handle on the subject. At this point, almost any suggestion as to how they might construct a new model may be helpful. At later stages, when the question turns to *evaluating* how well the new model fits the real world, the original analog model is less useful. In trying to convince Wilkins and Franklin that they had the right structure for DNA, Watkins and Crick did not appeal to features of spiral staircases. Nor did they simply appeal to Pauling's success with the α-helix. Similarly, facts about the orbits of the planets were not used as evidence that the solar system model of the atom is correct. For these evaluations, other evidence was needed.

In sum, thinking about analog models may be very useful in attempting to *understand* a proposed new model. Analog models are much less useful when attempting to *evaluate* a proposed new model.

MODELS AND MAPS

The models most commonly referred to in scientific contexts are *theoretical models.* In attempting to understand what theoretical models are, it is helpful to invoke an analogy between theoretical models and maps (i.e., to use maps as analog models for theoretical models). Maps are more abstract than scale models but still less abstract than typical theoretical models.

Before proceeding, you are encouraged to produce a map of your own. This could be a map showing a trip between home and school, between a dormitory and a classroom building, or between home and work. Figure 2.5, for example, is a map that depicts part of my own university campus, including the main library and the building housing my department.

On my map, as shown in Figure 2.5, there is a solid arrow. What is the object to which the arrow is pointing? Stop and answer this question before reading any further.

FIGURE 2.5

A partial sketch of the Twin Cities campus of the University of Minnesota.

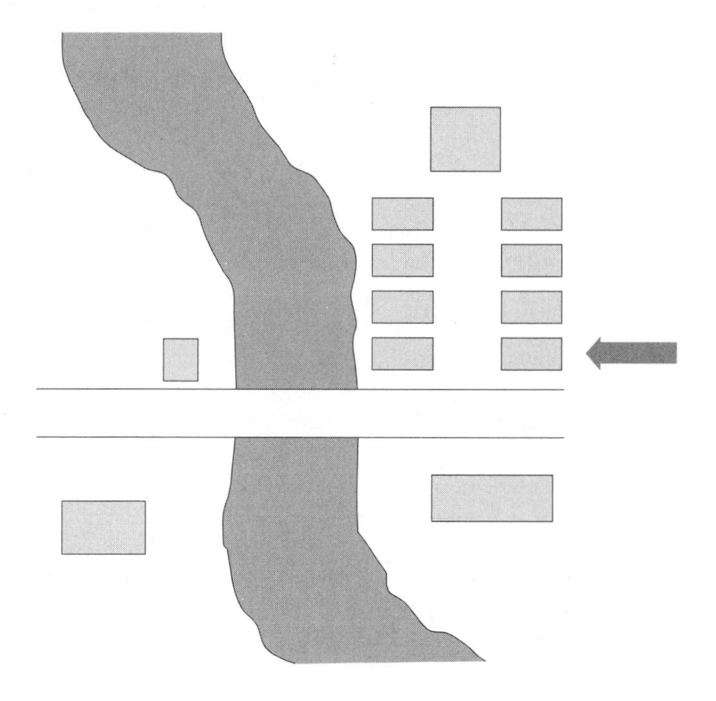

The usual answer is that the arrow is pointing to a building, presumably the university building in which my office is located. What would you think if I were to tell you that your answer is mistaken? Not only is it mistaken, it is not even close to being right. It is totally off base. No doubt, you would begin to suspect that there is some trick being played on you. You would be right. But the trick has an important point.

The correct answer is that the arrow is pointing to a rectangle drawn on the page. That is, quite literally, what the arrow is pointing to. The reason one is inclined to say the arrow points to a building is that it is pretty clear from the map and accompanying text that the rectangle *represents* a building. One therefore *interprets* the arrow as pointing to what the rectangle represents rather than to the rectangle itself.

The point of this exercise is that *a map is not the same thing as what it represents.* In the case of maps, no one is likely to make this mistake. After all, you can fold up a street map and put it in your pocket; you cannot fold up the city and put it in your pocket. Nor are you likely to mistake a scale model for the thing modeled. Surely no one was in danger of confusing Watson and Crick's wire and tin scale model for a real molecule of DNA. Theoretical models, as we shall see, are another matter.

Granting that a map is distinct from what it maps, what is the relationship between the two? It is true, but not very informative, to say that the map "maps" the area mapped. It is somewhat more informative to say that the map *represents* the area mapped. The next question is, How does a map manage to represent a particular space?

The first part of the answer is that a map exhibits a particular *similarity of structure* with the space mapped. In the case of maps, the particular similarity of structure is spatial. The spatial relationships among marks on a street map, for example, correspond to the spatial relationships among the streets in the city represented by the map.

The second part of the answer as to how a map manages to represent the area mapped is that we have a whole set of fairly well understood *social conventions* for constructing and reading maps. Without these conventions, a map would be just a piece of paper with lines drawn on it. The conventions for street maps are so well known that most people are not even aware of them. But this is a special case. Few people knew the conventions for interpreting Watson and Crick's scale model of DNA. One had to know a lot of physical chemistry to be able to interpret a particular tin plate as representing a purine base. Franklin could do it easily and quickly recognized that the three-chain model did not have enough places to attach water molecules.

The analogy between maps and models suggests further interesting questions. One is, Could there be a perfect map (e.g., a perfect map of Chicago)? The answer depends on what one means by a "perfect map." Suppose it means a map that contains a perfectly accurate representation of every feature of the city. Is that possible? Hardly. To represent every feature would mean representing every alley, house, garage, tree, bush, broken sidewalk, and abandoned car. It would mean representing not just the locations of buildings but their height as well. That is an impossible task. So, one way in which maps are not perfect is that they are *incomplete* in the sense that they represent only *selected features* of their subject, such as streets, and ignore others such as heights of buildings.

Restricting our attention to those features that are represented, there remains the question of how *accurately* those features are represented. For example, does our map of Chicago accurately portray the distance between the Water Tower and the Chicago River or between Michigan Avenue and Halsted Street? And is it accurate to the nearest 10 yards? yard? foot? inch? Clearly, no map is going to be perfectly accurate down to a fraction of an inch.

In summary, a map can be used to represent a place because there exists a set of social conventions that allow us to interpret features of the map as representing features of the place. All maps are incomplete in that they do not represent all features of the place represented. And no map gives a perfectly accurate account of the features that are represented. Nevertheless, there remains a similarity of structure between the map and the place represented. They are similar in some specifiable respects and to some specifiable degree of accuracy. All these things hold as well for the relationship between theoretical models and the parts of the world they represent.

THEORETICAL MODELS

A theoretical model is part of an imagined world. It does not exist anywhere except in scientists' minds or as the abstract subject of verbal descriptions that scientists may write down. When Watson was building the three-chain model, for example, he could have written down a description of what a DNA molecule would be like, if it were like this model. His description could have begun: "The model has three sugar phosphate backbones that twist in a helical structure with bases arranged. . . ." This description obviously could not describe a real DNA molecule, because we now know that DNA has only two chains, not three. What it describes, rather, is a *possible* molecule that turned out not to exist at all.

Watson and Crick did build a scale model with three chains. What is the relationship between that scale model and the corresponding theoretical model? The scale model can be used in place of words to characterize the theoretical model. One simply says, "The theoretical model has three sugar phosphate chains with bases arranged like this" and, then, points to the scale model. This strategy works because there is a similarity of structure between the scale model and the theoretical model. We can understand that similarity if we know the conventions used in building the scale model (e.g.,that red wires stand for hydrogen bonds).

Why can we not just stick to scale models and dispense with the notion of theoretical models? Because not all theoretical models have corresponding scale models. Watson, for example, never completed a scale model of the two-chain molecule with like bases bonded together. But this model existed as a theoretical model. Watson even described it in a letter to Max Delbrück. More fundamentally, scientists construct theoretical models of a whole variety of complex processes for which it would be difficult, if not impossible, to build working scale models.

To keep the idea of a theoretical model from becoming too mysterious, it helps to realize that we all frequently create things like theoretical models. For example, we can imagine giving a party, including imagining who comes with whom and who says what to whom. Here, we are constructing a theoretical model of a complex social event. The party may never occur, or if it does, it may be nothing like originally imagined. In the process of doing science, scientists imagine all sorts of complicated things and processes, including large molecules such as DNA. Some of these imagined possibilities turn out to have counterparts in the real world; others remain mere possibilities.

THEORETICAL HYPOTHESES

The most important question we can ask about a theoretical (or scale) model is whether it is, indeed, similar to the world in the intended respects and to the intended degree of accuracy. By way of shorthand, we often simply ask, "Does the model fit the world as intended?" Even more simply, "Does the model fit?"

There is another way of talking about the fit between models and the world that is often used by scientists, journalists, and other commentators on science. To accommodate this way of talking, we must introduce some additional terminology.

When scientists make the claim that their model is, in fact, similar to the world in the desired respects, we can say that they have formulated a *theoretical hypothesis* and that they are claiming that this theoretical hypothesis is *true.* A **theoretical hypothesis,** then, is a statement (claim, assertion, conjecture) about a relationship between a theoretical model and some aspect of the world. It asserts that the model is indeed similar to the world in indicated respects and to an implied degree of accuracy. If the model is similar to the world, as claimed, then the theoretical hypothesis is **true.** If the model is not similar to the world, as claimed, then the theoretical hypothesis is **false.**

FIGURE 2.6

A picture of the relationship between a model and the real world. The hypothesis that the model fits the real world may be either true or false depending on whether or not the model actually fits.

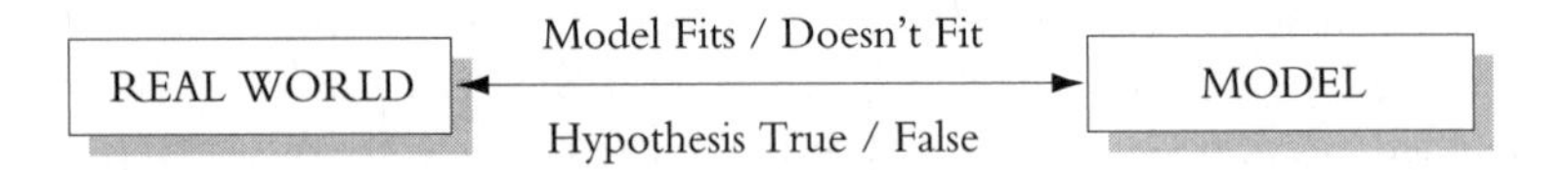

For example, early in the story, Watson and Crick formulated the theoretical hypothesis that DNA has a helical structure with three polynucleotide chains. That hypothesis was shown to be false. They later formulated the theoretical hypothesis that DNA has a two-chain structure. That hypothesis turned out to be true. In general, asking whether a specified theoretical hypothesis is true or false is just another way of asking whether the corresponding theoretical model fits the real world. This relationship is pictured in Figure 2.6.

"Truth" is a heavy-duty concept whose meaning has been debated by philosophers and others for 2,000 years. Theories of the nature of truth are normally discussed in courses in logic and philosophy. The above discussion of the truth or falsity of theoretical hypotheses falls into the category of what is usually called *the correspondence theory of truth*. But there is no need to enter these troubled waters here. For the practical purposes of understanding and evaluating reports of scientific findings, it is sufficient to think in terms of the fit between a model and the world. And here the analogy of the fit between a street map and the streets of the corresponding city provides a useful guide. If that is not enough, we can always fall back on the more restricted relationship between a scale model and the real thing. If that does not work, an abstract inquiry into the nature of truth is unlikely to be of much help.

Finally, in everyday speech, the word *hypothesis* often carries the connotation of a claim that is highly speculative—a conjecture without any real support. Thus we may reply to a claim we dispute by saying, "Well, that is one hypothesis." Here, the implication is that there are other equally plausible hypotheses that we might propose.

For the purpose of developing a systematic framework for understanding and evaluating scientific findings, it is best to ignore this way of talking. For us, the claims made on behalf of both the three-helix model and the two-helix model are both hypotheses. Indeed, in our preferred terminology, all general scientific claims are "hypotheses." The difference is that some hypotheses are well supported by the evidence and others are not. The important thing is to learn to distinguish between those hypotheses that are well supported and those that are not. That tells you which hypotheses it is reasonable to regard as true and which not.

THEORIES

Everyone knows that scientists produce *theories*. Yet up to now, we have not explicitly talked about theories as such. The reason is that *theory* is a quite vague and often ideologically loaded term. The main reason for calling something a theory may be to give it honorific status or, alternatively, to call it into question. Which function is served by using the word *theory* depends largely on the intentions of the speaker and the nature of the audience. Here we use a more neutral analysis. We already have in hand all the elements of such an analysis.

For our purposes, a **scientific theory** has two components: a **family of models,** which may include both scale models and theoretical models, and a **set of theoretical hypotheses** that pick out things in the real world that may fit one or another of the models in the family.

In 1953, there was basically just one model, the double helix, and one chemical substance, DNA, to which it was applied. But several years later, when people began talking about "the theory of molecular biology," there was a whole family of similar models and a range of other substances to which they were applied, including ribonucleic acid(RNA). We will encounter other theories that clearly include many distinct, but similar, models.

Like the word *hypothesis,* the word *theory* often carries the common meaning of something speculative. Those who question the theory of evolution, for example, commonly claim that evolution is "merely a theory" and not a "fact." Here again, we shall reject this common usage. For our purposes, the theories of molecular biology and the theory of evolution are all theories. Whether they are *also* facts depends on whether the corresponding models fit the world or, alternatively, whether the corresponding theoretical hypotheses are true. If so, they are facts; if not, they are not facts.

The important question is, How well is each theory supported by the evidence? Here, the relevant distinction is not between theory and fact but between theory and *data,* a distinction that is crucial for evaluating theoretical hypotheses and, thus, theories.

2.4 DATA FROM THE REAL WORLD

Everybody knows that to determine whether a proposed model fits the world some information is needed about the part of the world in question. But not all information is relevant. We use the term ***data*** (singular, *datum*) to refer to all the special information that may be directly relevant to deciding whether the model in question does fit. There are several general characteristics that such data must have.

The first feature that information must have to function as data is that it be obtained through a process of **physical interaction** with the part of the real world under investigation. The interaction may be *active,* as when one does experiments on the materials in question. Or, the interaction may be *passive,* as when radio astronomers measure radio frequency signals from distant galaxies. In either case, the data result from a physical interaction with the relevant part of the real world.

A second general feature of data, as opposed to mere information, is that relevant differences can be **reliably detected.** Detection may be a simple matter of looking, as when we observe a chemical solution change from blue to green. More often, detection requires elaborate instruments that produce outputs among which a scientist can discriminate just by looking. Often, these outputs are computer printouts of tables of numbers or of graphs. Figure 2.7 provides a schematic picture of the relationship between the real world and some data.

FIGURE 2.7

A picture of the relationship between the real world and data generated through a physical process of observation and experimentation.

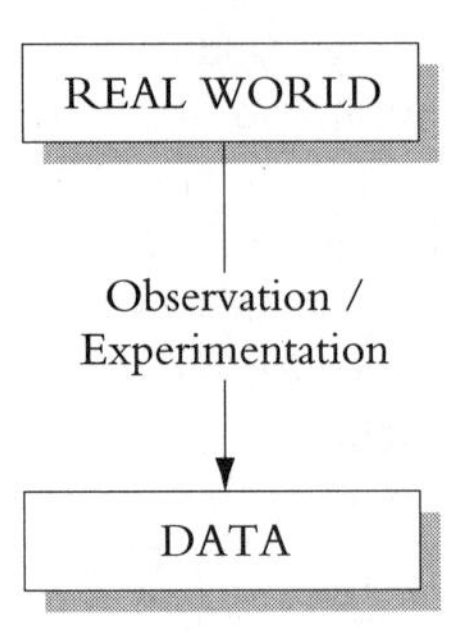

Among important bits of data in the story of the double helix were Chargaff's results on the one-to-one ratio of purines to pyrimidines in DNA, Franklin's results on the amount of water in DNA samples, and of course, Franklin's x-ray pictures of DNA. In each case, these data were obtained by actually working with samples of DNA.

Among information used by Watson and Crick that did not count as data in favor of their model of DNA was Pauling's discovery of the helical structure of α-kerotin. This information was influential in the decision by Watson and Crick to investigate helical models of DNA. Acquiring this information, however, required no physical interaction with samples of DNA. It could not, therefore, play a role as data for their hypothesis that DNA fits a helical model.

Here is one respect in which the analogy between maps and theoretical models breaks down. We can discover that a street map is deficient simply by finding a street that is not on the map. That requires no special skills or instruments. We can just look and see. Most models in modern science are not like that. Modern science typically investigates things that are very small (DNA), very large (our galaxy), very far away (distant stars), or otherwise inaccessible (the center of the earth). In all these cases, we cannot just look to see whether a proposed model fits. This fact has profound implications for how we might *evaluate* whether a model fits the real world.

2.5 PREDICTIONS FROM MODELS

The fact that we can only interact indirectly with the objects of a scientific investigation means that we can only investigate the fit between parts of the objects and some limited aspects of a proposed model. It is important, therefore, to be able to figure out what kind of data an object that did fit the proposed model would produce in the circumstances of a particular experiment. Scientists often speak of using a model to make **predictions** about what kind of data would be produced. This requires some explanation.

Sometimes, scientists use a model to make predictions in the literal sense of trying to say ahead of time what the data will be like. Often, however, predicting the data simply means being able to use the model to determine what the data should be like

FIGURE 2.8

A picture of the relationship between a model and a prediction obtained by reasoning about the model in the given experimental context.

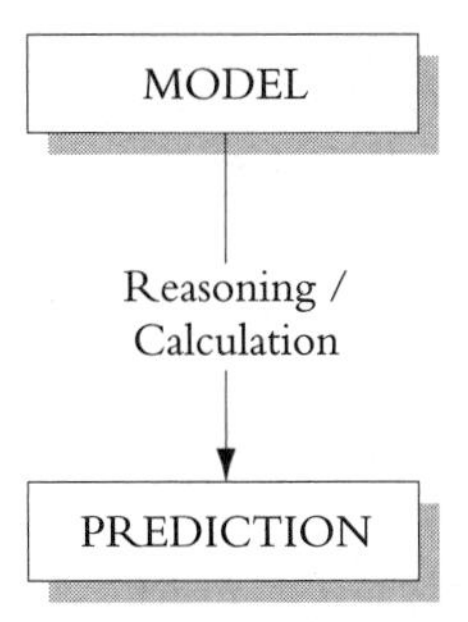

if the proposed model does fit the real world, even though the experiment has already been done. For example, the double-helix model was said to "predict" the Chargaff ratios even though Chargaff's experiments were done several years earlier. Similarly, the model allowed Crick to calculate the kind of x-ray pattern a double helix would produce and thus, in this respect, "predict" the kind of picture that Franklin, at that point unbeknownst to Watson and Crick, already had in her possession.

The example of Crick's prediction of the x-ray pattern exhibits another important feature of making predictions from models. It requires more than just the model in question. It also requires that one have a well-attested model of the experimental setup. Thus, Crick had also to have a good model of how x-rays are diffracted by atoms. Otherwise, he could not calculate what the pictures should look like if the x-rays were being diffracted by a helically shaped molecule.

Figure 2.8 provides a schematic picture of the relationship between a model and a prediction derived from the model. Note that here the arrow represents not a physical interaction with the world but a process of reasoning or calculation based on our understanding of the theoretical model under consideration.

2.6 THE COMPONENTS OF A SCIENTIFIC EPISODE

We are now in a position to construct our own model of a scientific episode in which data are used to evaluate whether a particular theoretical model fits the real world. Our model has four components: (1) a **real-world** object or process under investigation; (2) a **model** of the real-world object or process; (3) some **predictions,** derived from the model, describing what the data should be like if the model does, in fact, fit the real world; (4) some **data** generated through the sorts of interactions with the real world assumed in the predictions derived from the model. It is helpful to arrange these components as shown in Figure 2.9. This arrangement reveals four important relationships among the four components.

FIGURE 2.9

The four elements of an ideally complete report of a scientific episode involving a theoretical hypothesis.

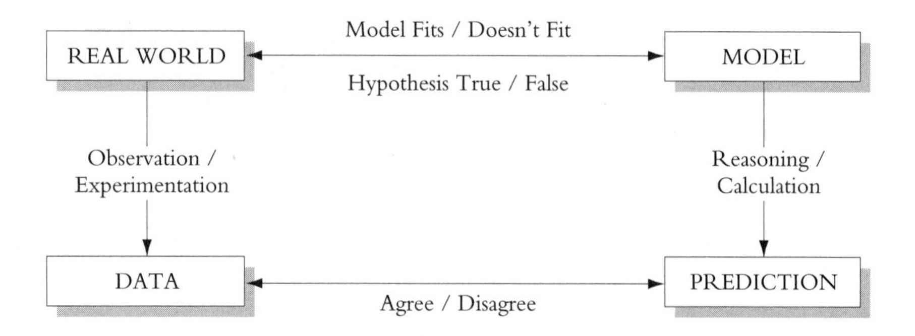

First, the relationship between the real world and the model is expressed by a *theoretical hypothesis* asserting that the model fits the real world. It is understood that the model fits only in some respects and then only to some specified degree of accuracy. If the model does not fit accurately in the intended respects, then the theoretical hypothesis is false.

The model and the prediction are related by *reasoning* or calculation. The real world and the data are related by a *physical interaction* that involves observation or experimentation.

Figure 2.9 also contains a relationship not previously noted, namely, one between the data and the prediction. If what is going on in the real world, including the experimental setup, is similar in structure to the model of the world, including a model of the experimental setup, then the data and the prediction should *agree.* That is, the actual data should be as described by the prediction. On the other hand, if the real world and the model are not similar in the relevant respects, then the data and the prediction may *disagree.*

To understand the relationships pictured in Figure 2.9, it is helpful to contrast the top part of the figure with the bottom and also the left side with the right. The top part of Figure 2.9 pictures the relationship between the real world and the model in question. Are the model and the real world similar in the respects under study and to an appropriate degree of accuracy? This relationship is typically not open to direct inspection. We cannot look at DNA in a test tube and see the helical structure. The bottom part of the figure, by contrast, pictures a relationship that can be evaluated by relatively direct inspection. Scientists can examine the data and see whether they agree with the predictions derived from the model.

The left side of Figure 2.9 pictures relationships existing in the physical world. The data are generated through physical interactions with bits of the real world. The right side of the figure, by contrast, pictures relationships that are mainly symbolic. The model exists mainly as a description of a possible type of object. This is so even if in giving the description we refer to a physical model such as Watson's scale model of DNA. Predictions derived from the model are likewise just descriptions of results that would be obtained in specified circumstances, circumstances that might not ever be realized.

It is important to keep these relationships in mind because *evaluating* hypotheses regarding the fit between models and the world turns out to depend crucially on whether the data and the prediction agree. That is, agreement at the bottom of the diagram is used to evaluate fit at the top. As we shall soon see, however, there is more to evaluating the fit between a model and the world than just agreement between data and predictions.

Finally, it should be realized that Figure 2.9 provides a model of fully developed scientific episodes that contain all four components arranged to make possible an evaluation of how well the model fits the real world. Many episodes, and thus many reports of scientific findings, do not include all four components. It is common, for example, to find reports that describe only the part of the real world under investigation together with some new data. There may be no mention of models or predictions. Similarly, we often find discussions of new models of real-world entities or processes with no mention of data or predictions. Occasionally, we find accounts of models of real-world things that include predictions but no discussion of data. We can learn a lot from such reports. Unless all four components are present, however, there may be nothing we can subject to an independent evaluation.

2.7 EVALUATING THEORETICAL HYPOTHESES

We are now ready to begin developing a general scheme that can be used by nonspecialists to evaluate scientific hypotheses as reported in various popular and semitechnical sources. We will continue with examples from the story of the double helix. Later in this chapter, we work through several completely different examples.

The basic idea behind the evaluation of hypotheses is to use the agreement or disagreement between data and predictions, information that is relatively accessible, to evaluate the fit between a model and the real world, something that is not directly accessible. Ideally, there are only two possible cases: either the prediction and the data agree or they do not agree. We will treat these cases separately, beginning with the case in which the prediction and data disagree. That turns out to be the simplest of the two cases.

In less than ideal situations, it may not be clear whether the prediction and data agree. Agreement may be a matter of degree. In such cases, it is difficult for a nonspecialist to make any independent evaluation of whether the model in question fits the world. Here, the best we can do is rely on the informed judgment of specialists. Unfortunately, when agreement between data and predictions is unclear, specialists often disagree among themselves about how well the model might fit the real world. In such cases, the only safe course for the nonspecialist is to regard the data as inconclusive and to suspend judgment about the model until more decisive data become available. If use of the model in question is relevant to some practical decision that needs to be made, the problem, then, is to make that decision in a manner that takes proper account of the uncertainty as to whether the corresponding theoretical hypothesis is true. This latter sort of situation is treated in Part Three of this text.

EVIDENCE THAT A MODEL DOES NOT FIT THE REAL WORLD

The story of the double helix provides a clear example of a model that was judged not to fit the real world—the three-chain model of DNA. Here, the decisive data were provided by Franklin's experimental measurements of the amount of water contained in samples of DNA. The three-chain model yielded a prediction as to how much water such a DNA molecule would accommodate. This prediction could be made simply by examining the scale model as long as one could interpret the model and knew enough physical chemistry to judge where water molecules might fit into the structure. The trouble was that the prediction from the model gave a value for the amount of water that was only one-tenth the amount Franklin had measured. So there was a clear *disagreement* between the experimental data from real samples of DNA and the prediction based on the three-chain model of DNA. This situation is pictured in Figure 2.10.

In this case, we are tempted to conclude without further ado that the hypothesis is false (i.e., real DNA molecules do not closely resemble the proposed three-chain model). Franklin immediately drew that conclusion, although Watson and Crick took a little longer to come around. As nonspecialists reading about this episode, we could just follow their lead. But if we are attempting to reach an *independent* evaluation, we cannot be quite so decisive. There are two possibilities that militate against so hasty a conclusion, neither of which tend to be accessible to a nonspecialist.

One possibility is that *the data were mistaken.* That is, Franklin's experiment yielded a mistaken value for the amount of water. There are all kinds of things that, unbeknownst to anyone, might have gone wrong with the experiments to yield a value for the amount of water ten times greater than the actual amount. Only people experienced

FIGURE 2.10

The elements of the episode involving Watson and Crick's three-chain model of DNA.

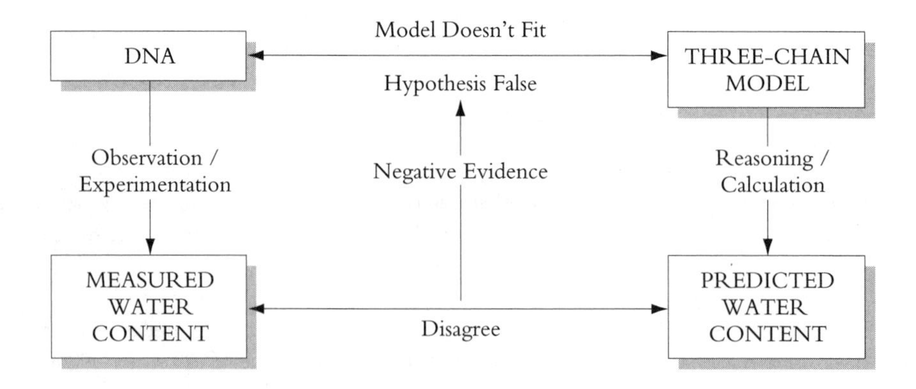

with the actual apparatus and experimental techniques can reliably judge how likely it is that something was seriously wrong with the experiment.

A second possibility is that, through misunderstanding of the model itself or because of a mistaken model of the experimental apparatus, *the prediction was mistaken.* A proper understanding of the model or the experiment might have yielded a predicted value in agreement with the actual data. Again, this is something for which a nonspecialist must rely on the judgments of the experts.

For these reasons, we will take reports of clear disagreement between data and predictions only as a basis for concluding that there is *good evidence* that the hypothesis is false. That is, there is a good reason, although not necessarily a conclusive reason, for believing that the model does not adequately represent the real world.

EVIDENCE THAT A MODEL DOES FIT THE REAL WORLD

One nice feature of the double-helical model for DNA is that having the sugar phosphate backbones on the outside left a lot of room for water molecules to attach themselves. So the double-helix model yielded a prediction for the amount of water in agreement with Franklin's data. Should we take that as evidence for thinking that the double-helix model adequately represents the physical structure of DNA?

As a matter of fact, Watson and Crick did not treat the agreement between the amount of water predicted by the double-helix model and the measured amount of water as a basis for arguing in favor of the double-helix hypothesis. Why not? Because they knew of many possible ways to build models with the required places for water. It could be done with a variety of three-helix models, for example, so long as one put the backbones on the outside. Thus, predicting the measured amount of water provided no basis for distinguishing the two-helix model from a variety of three-helix models. There was, therefore, no basis for regarding this agreement between prediction and data as evidence that the two-helix hypothesis, rather than some three-helix hypothesis, was true.

This explains why the x-ray data were regarded as being so important. According to Crick's calculations, a double helix should produce a quite distinctive pattern (i.e., a pattern unlikely to result from molecules with a significantly different structure). Thus, agreement between the predicted x-ray pattern and actual x-ray pictures provided a reliable basis for distinguishing between a double-helical structure and a variety of other structures. In this case, therefore, agreement between the prediction and the data did provide evidence in favor of the double-helix hypothesis. The components of this case are pictured in Figure 2.11.

The moral of this story is that mere agreement between a prediction and relevant data is not enough to provide a basis for thinking that a theoretical hypothesis is true. *Agreement counts only when such agreement would have been very unlikely if the hypothesis were clearly false,* which is to say, if some significantly different model provided a better fit to the real world. Ignoring this moral puts us in great danger of thinking that we have evidence in favor of what is, in fact, a false hypothesis.

At this point, we might have the following worry. No matter what the data happen to be and no matter what model is being considered, is it not always possible at least to imagine there being some completely different model that, nevertheless, just happens

FIGURE 2.11

The elements of the episode involving Watson and Crick's two-chain model of DNA.

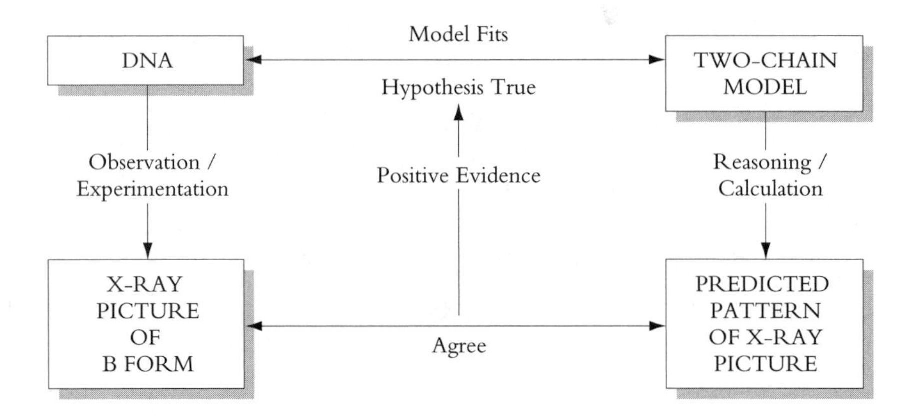

to yield the same prediction as the model under consideration? Does this not mean, therefore, that agreement between a prediction from a model and observed data can never provide any basis for thinking that the model fits the world?

This sort of difficulty has been voiced by scientific skeptics since the development of Greek astronomy nearly 2,000 years ago. The reply is that it is never enough for an alternative hypothesis to be imaginable in the abstract. It must be plausible relative the general scientific understanding of the kinds of models being used at the time by scientists working in the same general area. In the typical case, there will not be more than a few such plausible alternatives. We can, therefore, have good evidence that the model in question is the best fitting among all plausible alternatives. We cannot expect more from any scientific investigation.

The above theoretical worry has a more practical consequence. It is often difficult for a nonspecialist to judge independently whether there are very many other plausible models that would also yield predictions in agreement with existing data. In many cases, therefore, all the nonspecialist can do is rely on the reported judgments of specialists as to whether there are any such alternative models. These judgments, unfortunately, are often more implicit than explicit. We must read very carefully to determine whether there is any consensus on the availability of other plausible models yielding the same predictions. With experience, however, we can learn to recognize the kinds of hints from which we can infer the existence of the relevant consensus.

Finally, as in the case of disagreement between predictions and data, we cannot take even initially unlikely agreement between a prediction and data as a definitive basis for deciding whether a proposed model fits the real world. The most we can conclude is that there is *good evidence* for thinking that the model fits. The possibility of serious experimental errors or of mistakes in determining what prediction the model yields precludes a definitive conclusion on the basis of any single experiment. Even for cases in which it seems to the nonspecialist that scientists themselves reach a definitive conclusion on the basis of a single experiment, they may be relying in part on knowledge of other experiments, as well as on their considerable experience with the experimental and theoretical techniques involved.

2.8 A PROGRAM FOR EVALUATING THEORETICAL HYPOTHESES

In this section, we reduce the process of evaluating reports involving theoretical models to six easy steps. This does not require learning anything new. It is just a matter of organizing what we already know into a kind of "program" for doing an analysis. The advantage of developing such a program is that we can have in our heads a simple, uniform scheme for the evaluation of all sorts of scientific reports, a scheme that is easy to remember and to apply.

The program has two parts. The first four steps instruct us to identify the four basic components in a complete episode. These steps provide a basis for *understanding* the episode. If all four components are reported, we can go on to the final two steps, which constitute an *evaluation* of the associated theoretical hypothesis. If not all four components are identifiable, it may not be possible to perform an evaluation.

The Program

Step 1. Real World. Identify the aspect of the real world that is the focus of study in the episode at hand. These are things or processes in the world that can be described mostly in everyday terms together with a few widely used scientific terms. Do not use terms introduced to characterize particular models to be evaluated.

Step 2. Model. Identify a theoretical model whose fit with the real world is at issue. Describe the model, using appropriate scientific terminology as needed. A diagram may be helpful in presenting a model.

Step 3. Prediction. Identify a prediction, based on the model identified, that says what data should be obtained if the model actually provides a good fit to the real world.

Step 4. Data. Identify the data that have actually been obtained by observation or experimentation involving the real-world objects of study.

Step 5. Negative Evidence? Do the data agree with the prediction? If not, conclude that the data provide good evidence that the model does not fit the real world. If the data do agree with the prediction, go on to Step 6.

Step 6. Positive Evidence? Was the prediction likely to agree with the data even if the model under consideration does not provide a good fit to the real world? This requires considering whether there are other clearly different, but also plausible, models that would yield the same prediction about the data. If there are no such alternative models, the answer to the question is "No." In this case, conclude that the data do provide good evidence that the model does fit the real world. If the answer to the above question is "Yes," conclude that the data are inconclusive regarding the fit of the model to the real world.

Figure 2.12 summarizes the above program in diagrammatic form. The diagram may be easier to remember than the verbal instructions and may help you recall the details of the written program.

Although the first four steps in the diagram are numbered in the order given in the program, the diagram itself suggests that there is nothing sacred about this particular

FIGURE 2.12

A summary in diagramatic form of the program for analyzing reports involving theoretical hypotheses.

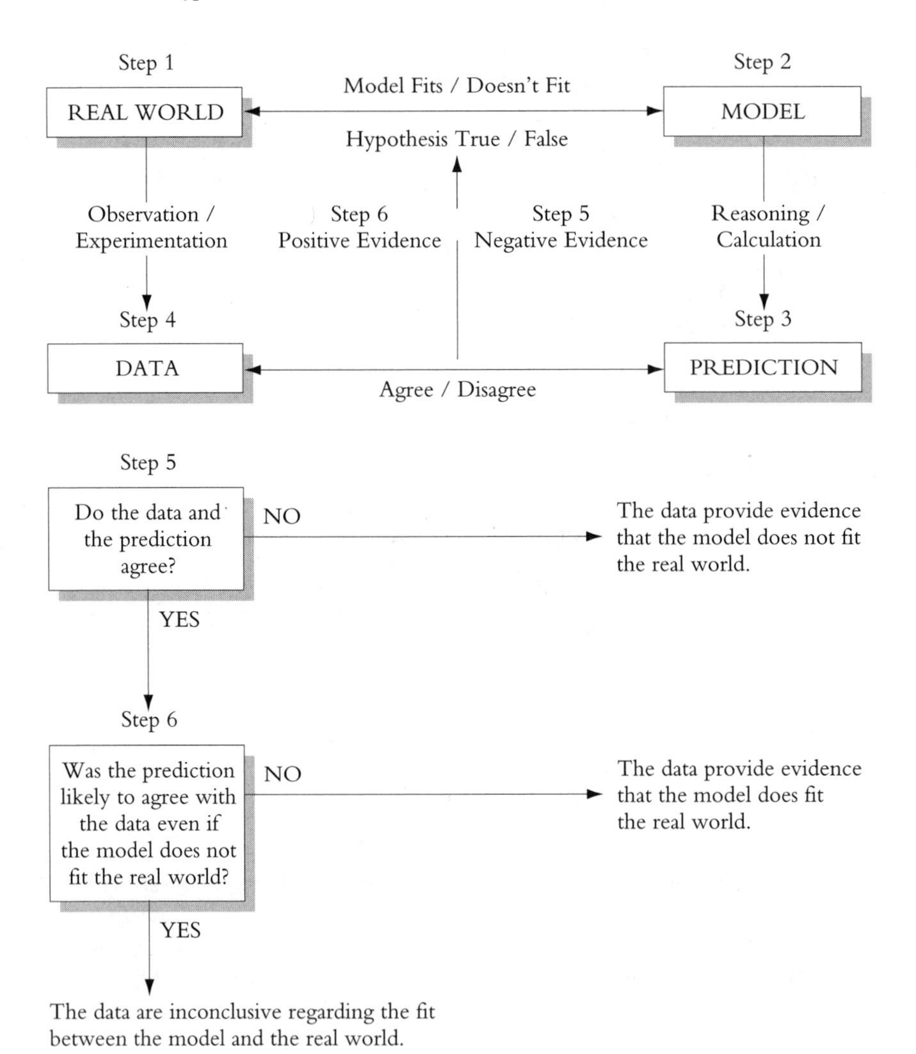

ordering. What is important is that one identify all four components before proceeding to the evaluation in Steps 5 and 6, in which the order is important. As a general rule, it is advisable to begin with the real-world objects. This tells you what the whole episode is about. But the order in which you identify the remaining three elements may vary. The structure of a particular report, particularly the order in which information is presented, may make one order seem to you more natural than another. It is fine for you to follow that order, as long as you clearly identify the components in the episode.

Finally, the program is only a guide, an outline to help you evaluate reports of scientific findings. Learning to use it effectively requires experience. The only way of acquiring that experience is to perform many evaluations.

2.9 WHY THE PROGRAM WORKS

Why should you use the suggested program for evaluating theoretical hypotheses? Because, by following the program you will have a good chance of reaching the right conclusion, whatever the right conclusion happens to be. There are three possibilities: (1) the data may provide evidence that the model does not fit the world; (2) the data may provide evidence the model does fit the world; or (3) the data may be inconclusive. In each case, the program will lead you to the appropriate conclusion.

CASE (1). When the data and the prediction *disagree,* that is typically because there are some respects in which the model does not adequately represent the real world. Steps 4 and 5 of the program are particularly relevant to this case. Step 4 is relevant because it requires you to consider whether there is a prediction that is clearly derived from the model. That is important because, if the prediction has little to do with the model, the relationship between the prediction and the data would not be much of an indicator of any similarity, or lack of similarity, between the model and the real world. Step 5, then, asks you to consider whether the data and the prediction agree. If they do not, that is an indication that something is wrong with the model, and the program directs you to the appropriate conclusion.

CASE (2). If the data and prediction *agree,* the program directs you to Step 6. It asks you to consider the question, Was the prediction something that would be likely to agree with the data, even if the model under consideration does *not* adequately fit the real world? This question forces you to seek information in the report regarding other plausible models that could yield the same prediction. If there seem to be no other such models, then agreement between the prediction and the data is a pretty reliable indicator of adequate fit between the model under consideration and the world. The program directs you to conclude that the data provide evidence of such a fit.

CASE (3). What if the agreement between the data and the prediction was quite likely even if the model in question does not fit the world? That is, what if there are other models that yield the same prediction and whose fit to the world is, initially, as plausible as the model under investigation? In this case, the agreement between the data and the prediction provides little basis for thinking that the model under investigation fits the world better than any of the other models. However, the existence of other possible models provides no basis for thinking that the model under investigation does not adequately fit the world. So the agreement between prediction and data turns out to be inconclusive regarding any fit between the model in question and the world. The program directs you to that conclusion.

In sum, whatever the appropriate evaluation happens to be, the program will lead you to draw the right conclusion.

2.10 HOW THE PROGRAM WORKS: THREE EXAMPLES

We will now work through three examples that together illustrate each of the three possible results of applying the program for analyzing reports involving theoretical hypotheses. Each example begins with an actual report that has been only slightly edited and shortened for the purpose of these illustrations. Readers are strongly urged to attempt their own analyses by applying the program to the reports before going on to read the analyses in the text. We always learn more from seeing how something should be done if we have already tried it for ourselves.

A CASE OF NEGATIVE EVIDENCE

Gene Analysis Upsets Turtle Theory

Researchers have concluded from genetic analyses that a widely accepted theory explaining why green turtles migrate 1,250 miles to an island in the middle of the Atlantic Ocean to lay their eggs and then swim back to Brazil is invalid.

According to the popular theory, the turtles started coming to the island more than 40 million years ago, when it was close to the shore of South America, and just kept coming as the island moved farther and farther away. But the new research concluded that the turtles had been using the island for only a few tens of thousands of years.

The now-invalid explanation was advanced 15 years ago by Archie Carr and Patrick J. Coleman. It was a bold idea, based on knowledge that the Atlantic Ocean was born 70 million years ago and began spreading. This gradually increased the isolation of Ascension Island, formed by volcanic activity on the ocean's centerline.

As long as the Atlantic was narrow, according to this hypothesis, remote ancestors of today's green turtles had no trouble reaching the island and laying their eggs in its beaches. They then returned to the shallow waters along the Brazil coast to feed on its marine grasses. After 40 million years, the ocean had grown to substantial width, but, according to the hypothesis, the turtles continued to reach the island by some mysterious form of navigation that still enables them to find it.

Now three scientists have examined the extent to which genetic material in the Ascension Island turtles has changed from that of the same species elsewhere. The difference, they believe, is far too small to have evolved over 40 million years. But it is sufficient to show that the Ascension Island turtles are a distinctive group from those nesting at other Atlantic sites, having probably used the island for not more than a few tens of thousands of years.

A comparison was made of a specific locus (the mitochondrial DNA) in the genetic material of turtles from four widely separated regions of the earth. Earlier work had indicated how fast, in a particular population, subtle changes in this material occur over centuries or millions of years. In the 1987 nesting season, eggs, or turtle hatchlings, were taken from twelve nests on French Frigate Shoal in the Hawaiian Islands, ten on Hutchinson Island off Florida, eight on Aves Island off Venezuela, and sixteen on Ascension Island in the mid-Atlantic.

The turtles in Hawaii had presumably been isolated from the other locations since the Isthmus of Panama formed about 3 million years ago. Their DNA, as expected, was most distinctive and provided an index of how fast turtle DNA becomes modified.

Analysis

Step 1. Real World. The real-world subject matter is the population of turtles that has been found to migrate between the coast of Brazil and Ascension Island 1,250 miles out into the middle of the Atlantic Ocean. The question scientists have asked about these turtles is how they ever came to make such a long and difficult trip to lay their eggs.

Step 2 Model. According to the previously accepted "standard" model, the members of this species of turtles began visiting the island roughly 40 million years ago when it was quite near the coastline of Brazil. But over the next 10 to 20 million years, the island moved farther out to sea as the floor of the Atlantic Ocean spread out, moving South America farther and farther from the middle of the ocean. The turtles, in this model, kept going to the island, even though the trip got longer and longer.

Step 3. Prediction. The model predicts that any measurements of the age of this population of turtles should yield an age of roughly 40 million years. According to the standard model, that is how long ago the turtles would have had to begin migrating to Ascension Island.

Step 4. Data. Examination of parts of the DNA of turtle eggs taken in 1987 from four different groups of turtles around the world provides a measure of how long a particular population of turtles has existed as a distinct population. By this method, it was determined that the Ascension Island turtles have existed as a distinct population for only a few tens of thousands of years.

Step 5. Negative Evidence? The data and the prediction clearly disagree. The prediction is that the age of the population should be measured at roughly 40 million years. The data put the age at more like 40 thousand years. That makes the prediction roughly 1,000 times greater than the data indicates! The data, therefore, provide clear evidence that the model fails to fit the real world. As the headline says, the gene analysis upsets the turtle theory.

Note that the analysis has only five steps. The program makes it clear that whenever the data and prediction disagree, your analysis will terminate at Step 5. Note also that, strictly speaking, the prediction is not that the turtle population is 40 million years old. Rather, the prediction must be about the kind of data that would be expected if the model fit the world. So the prediction is that the data obtained by examining DNA samples from turtle eggs would be of the type that is known to indicate an age of 40 million years.

A CASE OF POSITIVE EVIDENCE

New View of the Mind Gives Unconscious an Expanded Role

For decades, mainstream research psychologists suppressed the notion that crucial mental activity could take place unconsciously. But now, in the wake of exciting new studies, experimental psychologists are taking the unconscious more seriously. Among the most influential of the new studies are investigations into the role of the unconscious in the visual perception of objects and words.

One of the main researchers in this new area is Dr. Anthony Marcel of Cambridge University. He has developed a model of unconscious perception in which the unconscious mind perceives and remembers things of which the conscious mind is unaware. One of the most impressive tests of this model involves what is called "unconscious reading."

In these experiments, Dr. Marcel flashes a word on a screen for a very short time. In addition, the word of interest is "masked" by being surrounded with other nonsense words such as *esnesnon*. When asked directly, the subjects were unable to say what real word appeared on the screen. Dr. Marcel then asked his subjects to guess which of two words looks like the masked word. For example, the masked word might be *blood* and the two choices for look-alikes might be *flood* and *week*. The subjects were correct in their guesses an astonishing 90 percent of the time.

Analysis

Step 1. Real World. The aspect of the real world being investigated is the human mind, particularly human perceptual abilities.

Step 2. Model. The model is not described in much detail. The important thing is that, in Dr. Marcel's model, the human mind has an unconscious component that "perceives and remembers things of which the conscious mind is unaware."

Step 3. Prediction. The model, as reported, does not yield any very precise predictions. It suggests, however, that the subjects might be able unconsciously to perceive and remember the masked words that they could not consciously identify. If so, then it would be expected that their guesses about the word should be right more often than not.

Step 4. Data. The data come from the "unconscious reading" experiments. In these experiments, the subjects "guessed" the correct word "an astonishing 90 percent of the time," even though they could not consciously report what word they had seen flashed on the screen.

Step 5. Negative Evidence? No. The prediction and the data clearly agree. The subjects guessed the correct word far more often than not.

Step 6. Positive Evidence? That the data are described as "astonishing" is a good indication that these sorts of results are thought not to be very likely in the absence of something like unconscious perception. The only obvious alternative model is that the subjects were just guessing. It is very unlikely, however, that mere guessing between two alternatives would produce 90 percent correct answers. So, the data do support the hypothesis that a model including unconscious perception does fit the human mind.

In this example, the model is only vaguely described. It is difficult to see a clear connection between the model and the prediction. Such cases often result in an inconclusive evaluation. What saves this case, however, is that the data are quite dramatic. It is difficult to imagine another plausible model that could explain the data.

A CASE OF INCONCLUSIVE DATA

Was That a Greenhouse Effect? It Depends on Your Theory.

The memorably uncomfortable summer of 1988 left many Americans with a suspicion that nature is at last getting even for mankind's wanton pollution of the atmosphere. From California to the Carolinas, the summer's heat wave and drought took a sobering toll. Electric power faltered, vast forests went up in flames, river navigation was throttled, and crops failed.

The "greenhouse effect"—the trapping of solar heat by pollutant gases in the atmosphere—became a household phrase. Some climatologists warned that unless we quickly mend our ways, the world's grain belts will turn to dust bowls, coastal regions will be flooded, forests will die, and countless species will become permanently extinct. On June 23, Dr. James A. Hansen of the National Aeronautics and Space Administration caught the nation's attention when he told a Senate committee that the warming trend almost certainly stems from the greenhouse effect. A crisis, he warned, may not be long in coming.

But forecasting climate has never been as straightforward as scientists could wish. Many are not even sure that the summer's weather was really symptomatic of any trend at all. According to the Climate Analysis Center of the National Weather Service, July 1988, when the heat wave was at its peak, was only the eleventh hottest July in 58 years of recordkeeping. And while China also suffered a heat wave and a drought, Ireland and parts of western Europe were unusually chilly and wet.

A. James Wagner, an analyst at the Weather Service, acknowledges that during this decade the world has seen the four warmest years of the past century—1980, 1983, 1986, and 1987. "But I do not feel that the evidence is overpowering that this is anything more than a normal fluctuation," he said.

Climatologists have invented several models in an attempt to understand fluctuations in the weather. One such model, which seems to mimic the real climate quite realistically, was devised by Dr. Edward Lorenz of the Massachusetts Institute of Technology. This model, which does not take carbon dioxide into account but does reckon on the interactions of the atmosphere with the ocean, exhibits large variations.

"The Lorenz model was run backward on a computer for the equivalent of about 400 years," Mr. Wagner said, "and the large fluctuations it sometimes produced, which were not entirely random but were not cyclical either, were quite startling." The swings, he said, were as much as ±3.6°F in global temperature from one year to the next. The model sometimes produced clusters in which several years close together were unusually hot—a pattern imitating the real climate of the 1980s.

Analysis

Step 1. Real World. The real-world object of study is the climate of the earth.

Step 2. Model. The model is the "greenhouse model." According to this model, the earth's atmosphere acts like the windows in a greenhouse, trapping light and heat under the atmosphere. Carbon dioxide increases the efficiency with which the atmosphere traps heat.

Step 3. Prediction. The prediction is that the earth's temperatures should be increasing. However, the model is not developed in sufficient detail to permit precise predictions of how much the temperature should increase by specified dates or whether the increases would be uniform around the world.

Step 4. Data. The data include the drought that covered much of the United States during the summer of 1988. Also included is information about temperatures during other years, both recent and in the more distant past.

Step 5. Negative Evidence? No. The data and the prediction seem to agree. The summer of 1988 was unusually warm, and for most of this decade, at least in the United States, the weather has been quite warm relative to earlier years.

Step 6. Positive Evidence? The data, however, seem to be relatively likely to have occurred even in the absence of any "greenhouse effect." Some climatologists have even developed an alternative model, the Lorenz model, which predicts relatively large fluctuations in the earth's temperature. These past few years could be one of those fluctuations. The data, therefore, are inconclusive regarding the applicability of the greenhouse model to our current climate. That does not mean, however, that the greenhouse effect is not operative or that it will not show up with more dramatic force in the future.

2.11 CRUCIAL EXPERIMENTS

There is one special experimental situation that has fascinated scientists since the seventeenth century. This is an experimental setup that allows one to make a clear choice between two rival models. If the experiment is well designed, one model will come out the winner and the other the loser. The fate of both is settled in one stroke. Following the terminology of the seventeenth-century scientist, philosopher, and statesman Francis Bacon, experiments of this type are called **crucial experiments.** So powerful are crucial experiments, that scientists, and even historians of science, often reconstruct the past to make it seem that a particular experiment was a crucial experiment—even though, in fact, no one at the time thought of it that way!

THE STRUCTURE OF CRUCIAL EXPERIMENTS

Figure 2.13 provides a schematic picture of a crucial experiment. Some bit of the real world is put through the apparatus, which produces a reading on a scale. The reading is the data. There are two rival models of the material under investigation. For the moment, we will simply call these $\mathbf{M_1}$ and $\mathbf{M_2}$, respectively. The experiment is cleverly designed so that if $\mathbf{M_1}$ fits the material in the apparatus, it is very likely that the apparatus would produce a reading in region $\mathbf{R_1}$ of the scale and very unlikely that it would produce a reading in region $\mathbf{R_2}$ of the scale. Similarly, the design ensures that if $\mathbf{M_2}$ fits the material in the apparatus, it is very likely that the experiment would yield a reading in the region $\mathbf{R_2}$ of the scale and very unlikely it would produce a reading in region $\mathbf{R_1}$. So, $\mathbf{M_1}$ predicts a reading in region $\mathbf{R_1}$, and $\mathbf{M_2}$ predicts a reading in region $\mathbf{R_2}$.

The beauty of this design comes across when we consider that the result of the experiment is to be used to decide which model best fits the world. The strategy is that if the experiment produces a reading in region $\mathbf{R_1}$, then we choose $\mathbf{M_1}$ as the best-

FIGURE 2.13

A schematic representation of a crucial experiment.

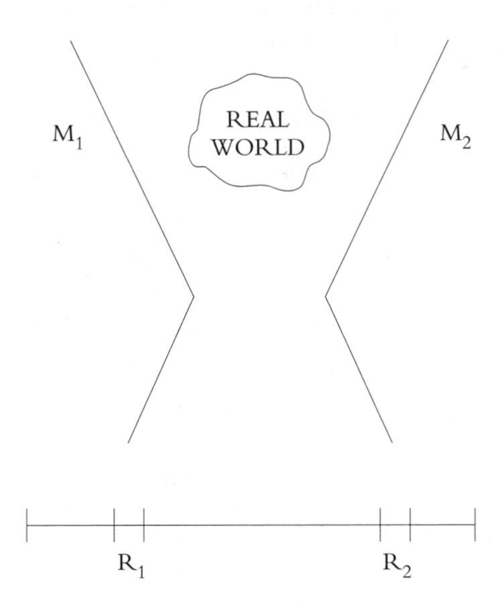

fitting model. Likewise, if the reading is in region $\mathbf{R_2}$, we choose $\mathbf{M_2}$ as the best-fitting model.

To see why this is an effective strategy, consider the matrix shown in Figure 2.14. Because there are two models to choose between and two different choices that can be made, the whole experiment has four, not just two, possible final results. Two of these results are *correct* choices: choosing $\mathbf{M_1}$ as the best-fitting model when, in fact, $\mathbf{M_1}$ is the best-fitting model, or choosing $\mathbf{M_2}$ as the best-fitting model when, in fact, $\mathbf{M_2}$ is the best-fitting model. The other two possible results are clearly *incorrect:* choosing $\mathbf{M_1}$ as the best-fitting model when, in fact, $\mathbf{M_2}$ fits best, or choosing $\mathbf{M_2}$ as the best-fitting model when, in fact, $\mathbf{M_1}$ fits best.

The experiment is designed with the presumption that one of the models provides an adequate fit and the other does not. So, initially, there are two possibilities. We can consider each in turn. Suppose, first, that $\mathbf{M_1}$, in fact, provides the better fit. The design ensures that the likely result of the experiment will be a reading in region $\mathbf{R_1}$. In this case, we correctly choose $\mathbf{M_1}$ as the best-fitting model. On the other hand, suppose that $\mathbf{M_2}$, in fact, provides the better fit. The design ensures that the likely result of the experiment will be a reading in region $\mathbf{R_2}$. In this case, we correctly choose $\mathbf{M_2}$ as the best-fitting model. Either way, we are very likely to make a correct choice and very unlikely to make an incorrect choice. The only open question is which of the two possible correct choices we will make. That depends on the data.

In actual practice, experiments that are designed to be crucial experiments often do not work out. The data obtained turn out to be a reading in neither of the regions predicted by the two models. Unless there was some mistake in the execution of the experiment or in the derivation of the predicted readings, we can only conclude that neither of the two models adequately represents the real-world material. The initial presumption that one of the two models fits has to be rejected.

Even though definitive crucial experiments are relatively rare, the possibility of devising such experiments provides a clear, even though idealized, model of scientific reasoning at its best. Understanding this model of scientific reasoning can help us evaluate the less than ideal cases we meet every day.

ANALYSIS OF A CRUCIAL EXPERIMENT

You should attempt to evaluate the following report before reading the sample analysis that follows.

Mutations

It has long been known that changes in the genes of organisms can occur. Such changes are commonly called "mutations." In the 1940s, it was not yet known how mutations occur. Part of the answer to this question was given by a famous experiment performed by Max Delbrück and Salvador Luria. It had recently been learned that some types of viruses (bacteriophages, or phages) can attack and kill some types of bacteria. It is relatively easy to "grow" bacteria in covered dishes containing nourishment in which bacteria generally thrive. These are called "bacteria cultures."

FIGURE 2.14

A matrix representing the choice between two theoretical models in a crucial experiment.

	$\mathbf{M_1}$ Best Fits the Real World	$\mathbf{M_2}$ Best Fits the Real World
Choose $\mathbf{M_1}$ as the Best Fitting Model	CORRECT	INCORRECT
Choose $\mathbf{M_2}$ as the Best Fitting Model	INCORRECT	CORRECT

Delbrück and Luria discovered that, in some bacteria cultures, a few of the bacteria survive attacks by phage viruses. Moreover, descendants of the surviving bacteria tend also to survive phage attacks. This shows that the genes of some of the bacteria had undergone mutations that made them resistant to the phage virus and that these resistant bacteria passed their mutant genes on to their offspring.

The question remained as to whether the mutations that made the bacteria resistant were caused by the attacking virus itself or whether they merely happened by chance. The experiment at issue was designed to answer this question regarding the cause of the mutations. Delbrück and Luria considered what would happen if a number (say, twenty) of bacteria cultures, each with a similar small number of bacteria, were allowed to grow for a short time, then injected with the same quantity of phage virus, and then allowed to grow some more. If the phages were producing the mutations, they argued, then all the bacteria cultures should end up with roughly the same number of resistant bacteria.

However, if the mutations were arising by chance, it follows that those bacteria cultures in which the chance mutation happened to occur early in the experiment would end up with many more mutant bacteria than those cultures in which the mutation happened to occur late in the experiment. The earlier mutant bacteria would have a longer time to multiply. Those cultures in which the chance mutation happened to occur at some intermediate time would end up with an intermediate number of mutant bacteria. If it is a matter of pure chance when the mutation occurs, one would, therefore, expect that, by the end of the experiment, there would be a large variation in the numbers of mutant bacteria in the different bacteria cultures.

Delbrück and Luria prepared some bacteria cultures, then introduced the phage virus, and later found that the actual number of resistant bacteria differed widely from one bacteria culture to the next.

Analysis

One way to evaluate this report would be to run through our standard program twice, once for each model. It is quicker, and more enlightening, however, to do just one analysis. In this case, many of the steps have two parts.

Step 1. Real World. The real-world object of study is the process by which mutations arise in bacteria.

Step 2. Models. There are two models: (1) according to the *causal* model, the mutations are caused by the action of the phage virus on the genes of the bacteria; and (2) according to the *chance* model, the mutations in the genes of the bacteria occur by chance, independently of any action by the phage viruses.

Step 3. Predictions. There are two predictions, one for each model: (1) the *causal* hypothesis yields the prediction that the number of resistant bacteria will be roughly the same in all the bacteria cultures, and (2) the *chance* hypothesis yields the prediction that there will be a large variation in the numbers of mutant bacteria in the different bacteria cultures.

Step 4. Data. They found that the actual number of resistant bacteria differed widely from one bacteria culture to the next.

Step 5. Negative Evidence? The data (1) agree with the prediction derived from the chance hypothesis and (2) disagree with the prediction derived from the causal hypothesis. The data, therefore, provide good evidence that the causal hypothesis is mistaken.

Step 6. Positive Evidence? The only rival to the chance hypothesis mentioned in the report is the causal hypothesis, which yields a different prediction from the chance hypothesis. It is difficult even to imagine another hypothesis. So it does not appear likely that there would have been a large variation in the number of resistant bacteria if the chance hypothesis were false. The data, therefore, provide good evidence that the chance hypothesis is correct.

• EXERCISES

Analyze these reports following the six-point program for evaluating theoretical hypotheses developed in the text. Number and label your steps. Be as clear and concise as you can, keeping in mind that you must say enough to demonstrate that you do know what you are talking about. A simple "yes" or "no" is never a sufficient answer. Some of these reports are taken directly from recent magazine or newspaper articles and are presented here with only minor editing.

EXERCISE 2.1

EINSTEIN'S IMPOSSIBLE RING: FOUND

A phenomenon first predicted by Albert Einstein in 1936, and then dismissed by him as something that would be hopeless to look for, has now been found. Astronomers conducting a survey of radio sources at the Very Large Array [VLA] radio telescope near Socorro, New Mexico, have discovered an object in the constellation Leo that has been imaged into a complete ring by the gravitational lensing effect.

"Of course, we'd all heard of Einstein rings," says team member Jacqueline Hewitt of the Haystack Observatory in Massachusetts. "But when I saw it come up on the computer screen, I thought at first it was a problem with the [VLA's image analysis] software."

It was not. Yet her skepticism was understandable. According to Einstein's general theory of relativity, gravitational lensing would happen when light or radio waves from a distant galaxy or quasar pass by a massive foreground object on the way to earth. The object's gravity would deflect the radiation and thus produce one or more distorted images of the source. A number of such images have actually been found during the past decade. As Einstein himself pointed out, however, the image can only form a complete ring if a source and the lensing object are precisely lined up with the earth—which seems absurdly improbable.

Except that there it was on Hewitt's computer screen—radio source MG1131 + 0456, a tiny oval about 2 arc seconds across with elongated bright spots at either end. In subsequent observations, Hewitt and her colleagues were able to rule out the possibility of its being a supernova remnant or any other such ring-like structure. Moreover, using a regular optical telescope, they obtained optical images of a candidate for the imaging mass: a 22nd magnitude object whose shape and other characteristics are those of a large elliptical galaxy.

EXERCISE 2.2

WHY IS THE WORLD FULL OF LARGE FEMALES?

Animals come in a vast range of sizes, from the tiniest zooplankton to the largest whale. Absolute body size has a crucial influence on a species' life history, affecting such factors as metabolic rate, longevity, and territorial range. And, within a species, relative body size—females compared with males—is important in behavioral ecology terms, too. In most species in the world, females are larger than males, although this rule applies more to groups such as insects, fishes, amphibians, and reptiles than it does to mammals and birds. Nevertheless, the largest animal that has ever lived is a female: the female blue whale.

Why females should attain a larger body size than males has long fascinated biologists. Darwin had an explanation for it, namely: "Increased size must be in some manner of more importance to the females . . . and this perhaps is to allow the production of a vast number of ova." This so-called fecundity-advantage model "has achieved the status of conventional wisdom," says Richard Shine of the University of Sydney, Australia. The model appeals through its simplicity and its consistency with many empirical observations. However, it has not been formally tested, says Shine, a deficiency he has recently repaired. He finds that even though the model may apply in some species, it is by no means universal.

It is no easy task, of course, to solve the question of why one sex may be bigger than the other in a particular species, not least because there are two partners in the game. Specifically, the female might be the bigger of the sexes because of the kind of selective advantage that Darwin proposed; but it is equally true that if males evolve small body size for some different adaptive reason, then the same pattern of body size dimorphism would apply. Several biological factors are likely to be operating in any particular case, and this should always be born in mind when looking for "the" factor.

Shine elected to test the model in something of a roundabout fashion, thereby hoping to avoid confounding variables that might affect body size in different directions. He measured male-female body size differences in a series of lizard species, some of which produce variable clutch sizes while in others the clutch size is constant. "If the main selective pressure for large female size is an associated increase in fecundity," says Shine, "the species with invariant clutch sizes would have no such advantage and females should tend to be smaller (relative to males)."

It turns out that in anoline iguanids, which produce a single egg, the proportion of species in which the female is larger than the male is about the same as in other iguanids in which clutch size is variable. "The same tends to be true for other lizards with invariant clutch sizes," says Shine. "These data, involving at least seven separate phylogenetic lineages of lizards, appear to falsify the main prediction of the fecundity-advantage model."

EXERCISE 2.3

PRIONS

In the mid-1970s, biologists generally believed that infectious agents must contain genetic material made of nucleic acid (DNA or RNA) to multiply in their victims. Over the next decade, this belief was challenged by research into the causes of rare degenerative diseases of the brain called "spongiform encephalopathies" because they produce holes in the brain, leaving it looking somewhat like a sponge. The most common such disease, which occurs in sheep and goats, is called "scrapie" because its victims sometimes become so disoriented that they scrape off pieces of their own wool before they die. The most well-known recent outbreak of these diseases was an epidemic of "mad cow disease" in Great Britain in the late 1980s and early 1990s, an outbreak traced to the existence of ground-up sheep heads in commercial feeds. There are four known *human* varieties of the disease, including one, Kuru (laughing death), which existed only among a tribe in Papua, New Guinea, and was apparently transmitted by the (now discontinued) practice of eating the brains of one's deceased relatives.

Suspicions that scrapie was transmitted by proteins alone, without accompanying genetic material, arose first among researchers in Britain. Extracts from the brains of scrapie victims were subjected to ionizing radiation and injected into the brains of normal animals. Ionizing radiation should break down any DNA or RNA present in the extract. Yet, these irradiated extracts produced scrapie in the previously healthy experimental animals. Other researchers then subjected similar extracts to procedures known to break up proteins. These treated extracts had a greatly reduced ability to produce scrapie in healthy animals. Some researchers in both Britain and the United States concluded that, somehow, proteins alone were able to produce scrapie in healthy animals. An American researcher, Stanley Prusiner, suggested the name *prions* for these infectious agents to distinguish them from agents such as viruses and bacteria. [For more information, see the articles "Prions," *Scientific American,* October 1984; and "The Prion Diseases," *Scientific American,* January 1995, both by Stanley B. Prusiner.]

EXERCISE 2.4

IDENTIFYING THE SCRAPIE PRION

Having shown that proteins can produce scrapie, the next task was to isolate the particular protein that produces scrapie. This search led to a particular protein named PrP, for "prion protein." Surprisingly, however, PrP turned out to be produced naturally in a great many mammals, including mice, with no harmful effects whatsoever. Had they made a mistake? Was PrP not the infectious agent after all? Prusiner suggested that there might be two forms of PrP, one common and harmless, the other rare and deadly. Having identified PrP, it became possible to isolate the particular genes responsible for its production. Moreover, it was discovered that victims of scrapie and related diseases had a slightly mutated version of the gene that produces normal PrP. With these discoveries, it became possible selectively to breed mice that produced normal PrP, others that produced low levels of the deadly PrP, and still others that produced high levels of the deadly version. It was then possible to construct a persuasive experiment showing that the mutant PrP can indeed transmit scrapie-like infections from one animal to another.

Mice producing high levels of the deadly PrP start out healthy but eventually die of a scrapie-like disease. Those producing low levels of the deadly PrP remain healthy. However, if extracts from the brains of a dead high-level producer are injected into the brain of a low-level producer, it too dies of the disease. If, moreover, extracts from the brain of this second victim are injected into still another low-level producer, it too dies of the disease. Without the injections, neither of the low-level producers would have contracted the disease.

EXERCISE 2.5

HIV VERSUS THE HUMAN IMMUNE SYSTEM

One of the many mysteries surrounding the human immunodeficiency virus (HIV), the cause of AIDS (Acquired Immuno-Deficiency Syndrome), has been how, despite great variability, it almost always manages to defeat the immune system of its host. Some victims succumb within a few years of infection. Many others survive with few symptoms for as many as 10 years before the disease takes over. A few have survived without overt symptoms for as long as 15 years. How can this be?

One hypothesis, described in the August 1995 issue of *Scientific American,* is that the population of viruses actually evolves in the environment of the immune system of its individual victims. The means by which the virus replicates is known to produce relatively large numbers of mutations. While retaining their ability to attack the agents of the immune system, these mutated viruses would become invisible to those agents until they themselves become sufficiently numerous to induce production of new immune system agents designed specifically to attack the new mutants. All the viruses, however, could attack any immune system agent, whereas the immune system agents could only attack those particular mutant viruses that they were designed to recognize. Thus, the forces of the immune system would become more and more specialized and divided. The total size of the virus population would continue to increase. Eventually, the immune system gets overwhelmed, and the virus population takes over. Evolution, however, depends on chance mutations and the environment (in this case the immune system), which varies greatly from individual to individual. So, one would expect a wide variation in the length of time it takes for the virus to take over.

The genetic structure of the viruses can now be ascertained in the laboratory. It is thus possible to assess the genetic variability of the virus population in an individual victim as the disease progresses. For the few patients for which this has been done, the results follow the suggested evolutionary pattern. Immediately after infection, there are few variants of the virus. Later, before there are manifest symptoms of the disease, there are more varieties of mutated viruses. Finally, when the disease becomes manifest, a few variant viruses predominate.

EXERCISE 2.6

A HERESY IN EVOLUTIONARY BIOLOGY

As anyone with even a passing knowledge of evolutionary biology knows, natural selection is a twofold process: the generation of genetic mutations followed by the fixation of variants that are favored by prevailing conditions. And in the world of evolutionary biology, one thing has seemed certain: the generation of genetic mutations is a continuous and random process, uninfluenced by external circumstances. However, if John Cairns, Julie Overbaugh, and Stephen Miller of the Harvard School of Public Health are correct in their interpretation of certain experiments with the bacterium *Escherichia coli,* that certainty may be on shaky ground.

In a paper published in the current issue of *Nature,* Cairns and his colleagues aim "to show how insecure is our belief in the spontaneity (randomness) of most mutations." The Harvard researchers describe the results of a handful of experiments that, they suggest, demonstrate that "bacteria can choose which mutations they should produce." Anything more heretical can hardly be imagined. They do add, however, that "this is too important an issue to be settled by three or four rather ambiguous experiments."

One of the experiments involves taking colonies of *E. coli* that are incapable of metabolizing lactose and exposing them to the sugar. If the lactose-utilizing mutants simply arise spontaneously in the population and are then favored by prevailing conditions, then this would lead to one pattern of new colony growth. A distinctly different pattern is produced if, under the new conditions, the rate of production of lactose-utilizing mutants is enhanced. The observation is something of a mixture of patterns, indicating that directed mutation appears to be occurring. "This experiment suggests that populations of bacteria . . . have some way of producing (or selectively retaining) only the most appropriate mutations," note Cairns and his colleagues. They cite two other types of experiments that can also be interpreted in this way.

Because the randomness of mutation has been so fundamental to evolutionary biology since the 1940s, few researchers have cared to test the notion directly. There are therefore no data beyond those from this handful of experiments that might indicate how general a phenomenon directed mutation might be. Nevertheless, Cairns suspects that it might well turn out to be rather widespread, at least in bacteria. Kent Holsinger, a theoretical population geneticist at the University of Connecticut, says that "if it is general and not just confined to *E. coli* and other bacteria, it could have major implications for evolutionary biology. At the very least, he notes, "there is something going on here that we haven't considered."

EXERCISE 2.7

DISCOVERY SUPPORTS THEORY THAT METEOR CAUSED DINOSAUR EXTINCTION

Researchers say they have strong new evidence that the age of dinosaurs ended 65 million years ago when a giant meteorite or comet slammed into the earth with the energy of a billion atomic bombs. Scientists with the U.S. Geological Survey office in Denver said last week that microscopic particles of quartz found in Europe, New Zealand, the Pacific Basin, and elsewhere contain structural cracks associated with the impact of a large body hitting the earth. The mineral debris indicates that a single catastrophic event, and not a series of volcanic eruptions suggested by other scientists, ended the 150-million-year reign of the great lizards, they said in a new report. The microscopic fracturing found in the quartz is more like that associated with the pressures of a massive impact than what would have resulted from volcanic activity, they say in a study published in the May 8, 1987, issue of the journal *Science*.

Bruce Bohor, Peter Modreski, and Eugene Foord said that the "shocked quartz" is found in the same sediment layers that contain unusually high levels of iridium, a metal common in asteroids, meteors, and comets. The researchers said the latest findings bolster the controversial 10-year-old theory of Nobel Prize-winning physicist Luis Alvarez and his geologist son, Walter, that a single catastrophic event led to a great extinction of life on earth. Geological evidence appears to show a massive extinction of dinosaurs beginning about 65 million years ago, but scientists have been unsure of the reason why.

The Alvarez theory says the impact of the extraterrestrial body released energy equivalent to that of 6 billion Hiroshima atomic bombs and threw up a giant cloud of debris that encircled the globe and diminished sunlight for months, if not years. Climate cooling resulting from the dust blocking sunlight resulted in the death of dinosaurs and many other types of animal and plant life, according to the theory.

The theory is based on finding up to 600 times normal levels of iridium in clay deposits from the period, and Bohor said in a telephone interview that the same iridium concentrations have been found at every site of the telltale quartz particles. The even distribution of the shock quartz and certain minerals combined with it point to a big comet or meteorite striking a continental area in the Northern Hemisphere, he said. A body 6 miles wide hitting the earth at 45,000 miles per hour, as calculated by the Alvarez theory, could have blasted debris high enough into the atmosphere to account for the worldwide shock quartz distribution, Bohor said.

High pressure associated with volcanic activity can fracture quartz crystals, and proponents of the volcanic theory of dinosaur extinction say this is the source of the shock crystals found in sediments from the period. However, Bohor and his colleagues said quartz fractures caused by impacts are distinct from those resulting from other pressures. "When a meteorite strikes the earth, the mass and speed of impact cause a shock," Bohor said. "This shock wave bounces around in different directions as it hits other objects and comes back into the crystal to produce multiple sets of fracture features unique in impact shocks."

The report said multiple sets of fractures were evident in quartz particles found at several sites: Stevns Klint and Nye Klov in Denmark; Petriccio and Pontedazzo in Italy; Caravaca in Spain; Woodside Creek in New Zealand; and a core taken from the north central Pacific Ocean basin. The samples matched those previously found in Montana and Wyoming, Bohor said, and Soviet scientists recently found the same type of quartz on the east side of the Caspian Sea in the Soviet Republic of Turkmen.

EXERCISE 2.8

THE EXPANDING UNIVERSE

One of the most interesting discoveries of the twentieth century is that the universe is expanding (i.e., the galaxies are all moving away from each other). This discovery stimulated the creation of many models of kinds of systems in which such expansion would take place. Two of these models were widely regarded as possibly representing the structure of the real universe. One was an "explosion model" (the "Big Bang" theory) in which all matter is originally concentrated in one place and explodes outward. The other is a "steady-state model," in which subatomic bits of matter are created out of nothing and eventually move outward, leaving each region of space with the same total amount of matter for all time.

If the universe is an exploding system, it follows that the density of matter (the number of galaxies per cubic light-year) gets less and less the farther away from the original explosion one gets. If the universe is a steady-state system, however, the density of matter should be exactly the same everywhere. This remains true wherever in the universe one happens to be. Whichever direction one looks, the density of the most distant galaxies should be less if the explosion model is correct.

To decide which of these two models best fits the real universe, what we need to do is measure the density of matter in the most distant regions of space. In recent years, radio telescopes have made it possible to make such measurements. These measurements show a clear decrease in the density of the most distant observable galaxies.

EXERCISE 2.9

NEW OBSERVATIONS REVEAL COSMIC MYSTERY

In the 1920s, it was discovered that the stars exist in large spiral or platter-shaped clusters we now call galaxies. Each galaxy contains millions of stars, with most near the center and fewer out toward the edges. Our sun and solar system are now thought to be roughly one-third the way in from the edge of the galaxy we call the Milky Way.

Since the discovery of galaxies, astronomers and astrophysicists have naturally wondered how they work and, in particular, what keeps them together. The standard idea has been that a galaxy is held together by the force of gravity. If this is right, then it is possible to calculate the motions of various stars within the galaxy. Unfortunately, it has not until now been possible to measure the motions of stars with sufficient accuracy to determine whether the calculated motions are correct or not.

Recently, however, computers have been used to sharpen the images of stars produced by large telescopes. This new technique has revealed that the stars on the outer edge of the Milky Way are moving much faster than they should according to the standard calculations.

The result has scientists baffled. They have not yet been able to come up with an alternative model that might explain this surprising result.

EXERCISE 2.10

SCIENTISTS PUT A NEW TWIST ON CREATION OF THE UNIVERSE

A "Great Wall" of galaxies stretching hundreds of millions of light-years across the known universe has been discovered by two Harvard astronomers and threatens long-held fundamental theories of how the universe came into existence.

The wall, some 500 million light-years long, 200 million light-years wide, and 15 million light-years thick, consists of more than 15,000 galaxies, each with billions of stars. Described as the "largest single coherent structure seen so far in nature," the image of the wall emerged after about a decade of effort to map the structure of the universe in three dimensions. Correspondingly, there are large areas of relative void, containing comparatively few galaxies.

The astronomer's findings were published November 17, 1989, in the journal *Science*. Although the area surveyed is huge, it is only a small piece of the known universe. The astronomers involved said the survey area is to the universe what Rhode Island is to the earth, a small percentage. The survey was performed by mapping the "red shifts," or motions, of a large group of galaxies some 200 to 300 light-years from the earth.

The survey, using the 60-inch telescope at the Whipple Observatory in Arizona, was conducted by dividing an area of the universe into thin slices, then noting the position of galaxies within the slices. As more of the slices were completed and layered together, a three-dimensional portrait of the area emerged and slowly revealed the massive wall of galaxies.

If this map of the universe proves to be a reality, it means the long-held theories of a universe evolving from a smooth, super-hot plasma following a Big Bang some 15 billion years ago might be wrong. The concentration of galaxies around voids filled with either mysterious "dark matter" or nothing points to a very uneven, lumpy universe that apparently could not evolve out of the smooth beginnings described by current theories.

What, if anything, is in the voids, remains unknown and could be a key to understanding the universe. Many scientists believe that 90 to 99 percent of the matter in the universe is dark and has yet to be detected. Whether the huge voids, some as large as 150 million light-years in diameter, contain dark matter is not known.

But given their vast size, said Margaret Geller, one of the two Harvard astronomers to make the discovery, "it may make more physical sense to regard the voids as the fundamental large-scale structures of the universe."

The fundamental theory most threatened by the discovery is known as the "standard model." It holds that the universe originated in a "Big Bang" and has expanded in a fairly uniform manner for the past 15 billion years. It calls for a homogeneous universe that is very much the same in every direction. But the new findings raise questions about how such an uneven system of voids and galaxies could have developed out of a uniform, homogeneous beginning in 15 billion years.

"In my opinion, something is fundamentally wrong in how (scientists believe) the structure of the universe formed," she said. "Maybe the universe isn't homogeneous." Geller said the work is important philosophically because "mapping the universe is about finding its origins. If we can't understand where the universe came from, then we can't understand where we came from."

In their paper detailing the discovery of the "Great Wall," Geller and her colleague, John Huchra, hinted that the wall may be much larger than they have measured. The "most sobering" result of their discovery, they said, is that the size of the largest structures they have found "is limited only by the extent of the survey." If the structures and the voids are larger still, then scientists may have to abandon entirely the fundamental idea of a homogeneous universe.

"There is no theory that even comes close to explaining what we are seeing," said Michael Kurtz, also an astronomer at Harvard.

EXERCISE 2.11

GRAVITY WAVES

Newspapers around the world recently carried reports of a striking new experimental test of Einstein's General Theory of Relativity. According to Einstein's theory, a large rotating mass should give off "gravity waves" that travel at the speed of light. Several scientists have previously claimed to have detected gravity waves, but none of these claims was very well substantiated. The new experiment was made possible by the discovery of a unique "pulsar"—a very dense star that emits powerful radio waves in distinctive pulses. This particular pulsar appears to be rotating in orbit around another large but invisible mass (perhaps a "black hole"). The discovery of this unique pulsar was made using a radio telescope 1,000 feet in diameter—the world's largest.

If the observed system indeed fits an Einsteinian model, it should give off gravity waves. Moreover, according to the model, because gravity waves carry off energy from the system, the rate of rotation of the pulsar around its companion body should be slowing down by about one ten-thousandth of a second a year. Using the large radio telescope and "clocks" accurate to 50 millionths of a second a year, the rate of rotation of the system was measured over a period of 4 years. The most recent measurements show that the system has indeed been slowing down by just about one ten-thousandth of a second a year—as predicted. Even scientists who had previously doubted the existence of gravity waves had to admit that finding the system to have slowed down by the predicted amount was quite remarkable.

EXERCISE 2.12

COMET SOURCE: CLOSE TO NEPTUNE

Comets have been considered outsiders, visitors from an enveloping cloud of inactive comets on the far fringes of the solar system. But new computer simulations of how comets can be drawn into the inner solar system eliminate a far-distant spherical cloud of comets as the source for a major class of comets. The only practicable source in these simulations for the comets that now follow small, quick orbits near the planets is a flat disk of comets lying just outside the orbit of Neptune. That is a distance of little more than 30 times the distance between the sun and the earth (30 astronomical units) compared to the tens of thousands of astronomical units to the distant comet cloud.

Martin Duncan of Lick Observatory and Thomas Quinn and Scott Tremaine of the University of Toronto ran their computer model of the solar system to see how some of the peculiar characteristics of the short-period comets, those having orbital periods of 200 years or less, might have originated. Could the cloud of comets, called the Oort cloud, supply objects that behaved like these? It clearly is the source of the 589 known long-period comets, the ones rarely seen from the earth as they loop by the sun on circuits that require 200 to millions of years to complete. Everything about their motion is consistent with their having been jostled out of the Oort cloud by a passing star and into an orbit that passes near the sun.

But the short-period comets do not behave like typical Oort cloud comets gone astray. Most strikingly, the orbits of the short-period comets tend to lie within about 30 degrees of the plane of the earth's orbit, called the ecliptic. And only 4 of the 121 known short-period comets have their orbits tilted more than 90 degrees so that they are orbiting in the direction opposite to that of the earth. By contrast, half the comets in the Oort cloud must have such retrograde orbits.

Duncan and his colleagues first checked to see if, as reported 15 years ago, the four giant planets could select from comets falling in from the Oort cloud only those having low-inclination orbits typical of short-period comets. Using a mathematical model that included the sun, the four giant planets, and 5,000 comets falling into the vicinity of massive Jupiter from the Oort cloud, they ran a simulation on their own souped-up Sun-3 microcomputer for a total of several months of computer time. They speeded up the calculation of millions of years of orbital evolution by increasing the mass of the giant planets by a factor of up to 40 in the simulation.

To their surprise, these modelers found that the planets are not selective at all when they deflect comets into new smaller orbits. The comets from the Oort cloud that achieved periods of less than 200 years formed a cloud of their own, with no preference for orbiting in a disk near the ecliptic. In addition, three-quarters of them had periods greater than 15 years; only 21 of the 121 observed short-period comets had periods greater than 15 years.

Ruling out the Oort cloud, the modelers next tried a belt of low-inclination comets near Neptune's orbit. The idea dates back to a suggestion by Gerard Kuiper in 1951 that it would be only natural to find some debris from the formation of the solar system beyond Neptune. Comet-sized objects would not have formed planets there, but neither the giant planets nor passing stars could easily dislodge them or even smear their disk into a cloud. In fact, an absence of comets there would imply an oddly abrupt outer edge to the original solar system disk.

When the simulation was run with a disk of comets orbiting between a distance of 50 and 20 to 30 astronomical units, or well inside the orbit of Neptune, the comparison with reality was impressive. The mean orbital distances of both simulated and observed short-period comets cluster around 3 astronomical units with a lesser tendency to be near 5 astronomical units, the orbital distance of gravitationally influential Jupiter. That is also where the preponderance of maximum orbital distances lies for both sets of comets. Comets in each set also have a tendency to be passing the ecliptic when they are closest to the sun.

Most crucially, about half the simulated comets, which started out with inclinations of 0 degrees to 18 degrees, retained inclinations of less than 30 degrees. More than 80% of observed short-period comets are confined to such a disk. About 8% of the simulated comets had their orbits tilted so much as to be in retrograde motion, compared with 3% of observed comets and 50% of Oort cloud comets. As is the case with observed comets, simulated retrograde comets tended to have periods longer than 15 years.

"You can't get good agreement," says Tremaine, "if you start off with inclinations far out of the ecliptic. It works if and only if the source is in the plane of the ecliptic." That moves the hypothesis of a comet belt lying beyond Neptune from being "very plausible to being the only plausible hypothesis." The Oort cloud as a significant source for short-period comets "is now ruled out," he says.

EXERCISE 2.13

THE GENETICS OF CANCER

Most people are familiar with the model of a chromosome as a string of beads, where the beads represent different genes. Since the early 1970s, it has been possible to identify sequences of genes along a chromosome. This led to the discovery that the chromosomes in cancer cells differ from normal cells in their sequences of genes. It was also known that some cancers run in families and thus must be inherited genetically. Yet, even though every cell of a person contains a complete copy of all its chromosomes, not all members of such families get cancer, and those who do exhibit it in only a few sites in their bodies. Moreover, most people who get cancer seem not to be members of a cancer prone-family.

One proposal for explaining these diverse findings, first developed in the early 1970s, has recently achieved broad acceptance. The idea, as explained in the March 1995 issue of *Scientific American,* is that it requires more than one change in the genetic structure of a chromosome to make it produce cancer cells rather than normal cells. People in cancer-prone families start off, so to speak, with one strike against them. They are thus more likely than others to accumulate the required set of mutations but still have some chance of never doing so. This proposal became known as the "two-hit" (or "multiple-hit") theory of cancer.

It was not until 20 years later that it became possible to devise a direct test of this proposal. Several researchers at different locations had fortunately preserved samples of brain tumors from patients who suffered repeated onsets in the same site. If the multiple-hit account is right, the cells of the later, more aggressive tumors should exhibit more mutations than the cells of earlier tumors. The earlier mutations, however, should be preserved in the cells of later tumors. To the delight of proponents of the multiple-hit account, that is just what they found.

EXERCISE 2.14

PROJECT

Find a report of the results of some experiment that is relevant to a theoretical hypothesis. You may find an example in a newspaper or news magazine. The Sunday supplement to your local newspaper is a good bet. The weekly science section of *The New York Times* is particularly good. Or you might try some popular sources that specialize in scientific findings, such as *Scientific American, Psychology Today,* or *Science.* When you have found something that you find interesting and substantial enough to work on, analyze the experiment following the standard program for theoretical hypotheses.

This exercise may be turned into a longer project by looking for other sources of information on the same theory. You might be able to uncover a whole history of experiments relating to the theory, each of which can be analyzed. You may discover other experiments bearing on hypotheses using similar theoretical models. Or you may discover cases in which such hypotheses were refuted. Perhaps more elaborate models of the same type were then developed to replace the discarded models. You can then look to see whether later evidence supported these new hypotheses, and so on.

One of the side effects of this project is that you may get an idea of the different levels of science reporting in various popular sources. Some sources tell you everything you need to know to evaluate the reported hypotheses. Others give so little information that you cannot tell whether the evidence supports the hypotheses. You are forced to take their word for it. Most sources fall somewhere between these two extremes.

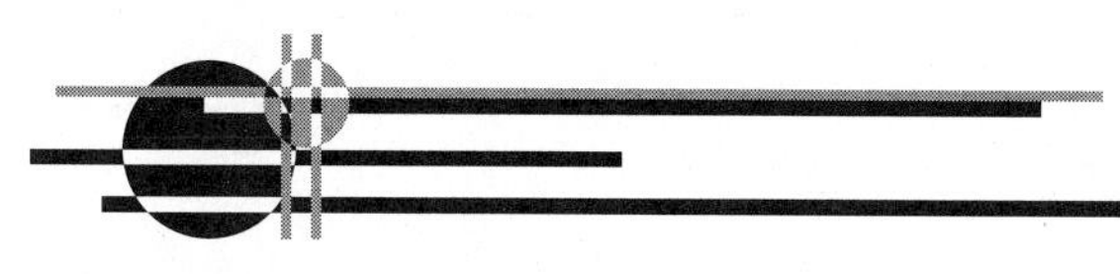

CHAPTER 3
HISTORICAL EPISODES

In this chapter, we examine several historical episodes involving theoretical hypotheses. These examples serve several purposes. The most important is to provide a set of *analog models* that may be useful in analyzing reports of new cases. That is, when meeting a new case, we can often find analogies between the new case and one or another of the historical cases. Exploiting such analogies can often help us understand and evaluate the new case quickly. This requires having an analysis of the historical case carefully stored in long-term memory for easy access.

There is a second, more general reason for studying these historical episodes. The conception of science found among scientists and other educated members of the society at large has to a great extent been shaped by the history of science as embodied in episodes such as those we shall be examining. These cases are part of our cultural heritage. Having at least some familiarity with that heritage is part of being a member of the culture. Of course, the sketches that follow are no substitute for a genuine introduction to the history of science. But even an oversimplified understanding of these episodes is better than no understanding at all.

3.1 THE PHASES OF VENUS

One of the founders of modern science was Galileo Galilei, universally known simply as Galileo. He was born in Pisa, Italy, in 1564 and did most of his scientific work in the years 1590 to 1640. To put Galileo in historical perspective, note that Shakespeare was born the same year, Martin Luther had died in 1546, and of course, Galileo's countryman Christopher Columbus first traveled to the New World in 1492. When the *Mayflower* landed at Plymouth Rock in 1620, Galileo was doing the research that led to his famous *Dialogue on the Two Chief Systems of the World,* first published in 1632. He died in 1642.

When Galileo was born, most people thought that the earth was literally the center of the universe. As a student, Galileo was taught the astronomy of the Greek astronomer Claudius Ptolemy, first published in 140 AD. In Ptolemy's system, the sun, moon, planets, and stars all revolve about the earth every 24 hours. Figure 3.1 is a sketch of the universe according to Ptolemy.

In 1543, the Polish astronomer Nicolaus Copernicus published his book *On the Revolutions of the Heavenly Spheres,* expounding the view that the sun is the center of

FIGURE 3.1

The Ptolemaic model of the universe.

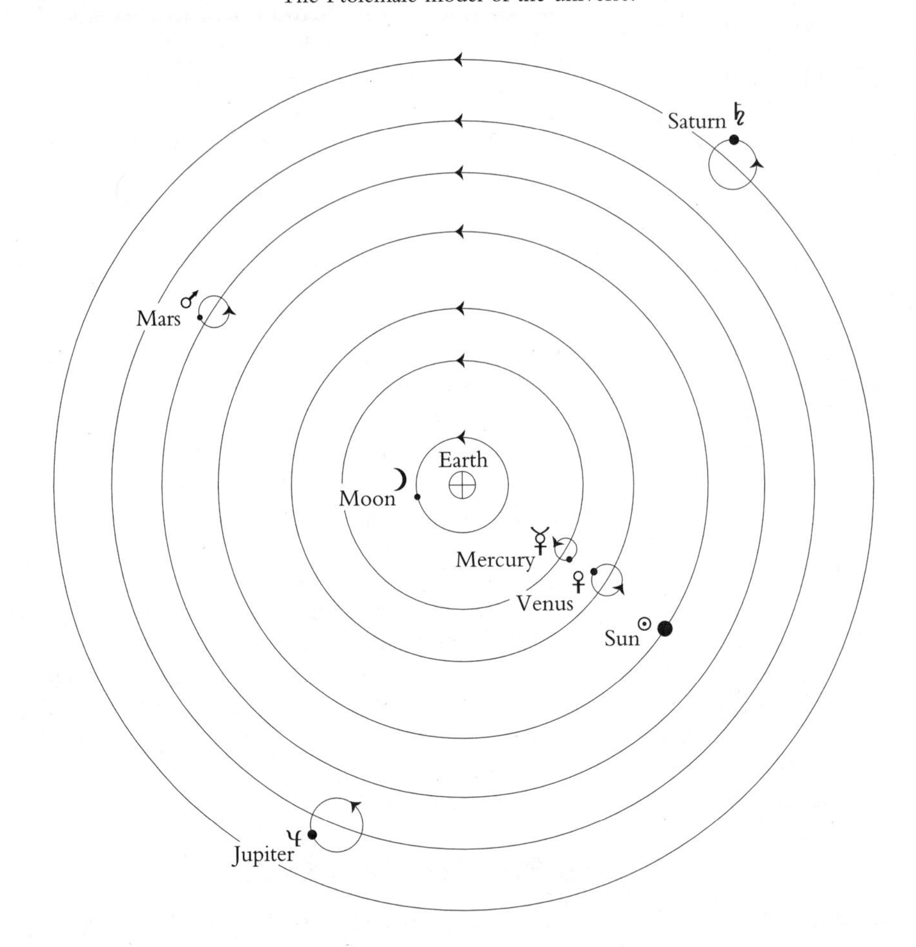

the universe and that the planets, including the earth, revolve in circular orbits around the sun. On Copernicus' view, the apparent motion of the rest of the universe is due to the earth itself spinning on its own axis once each day. Copernicus lived just long enough to see his book in print. Figure 3.2 is a sketch of the universe according to Copernicus. It is, of course, similar to our current picture of the solar system.

Galileo came to accept the Copernican system early in his life but for a long time kept his opinion largely to himself. In 1589, he became a lecturer in mathematics at the University of Pisa. He studied the properties both of floating bodies and falling bodies and investigated the motions of pendulums. There is a widely believed story about his dropping two bodies of the same material, but of different weights, from the top of the Leaning Tower of Pisa to prove that they would fall at the same rate. This story is most likely not true.

FIGURE 3.2

The Copernican model of the universe.

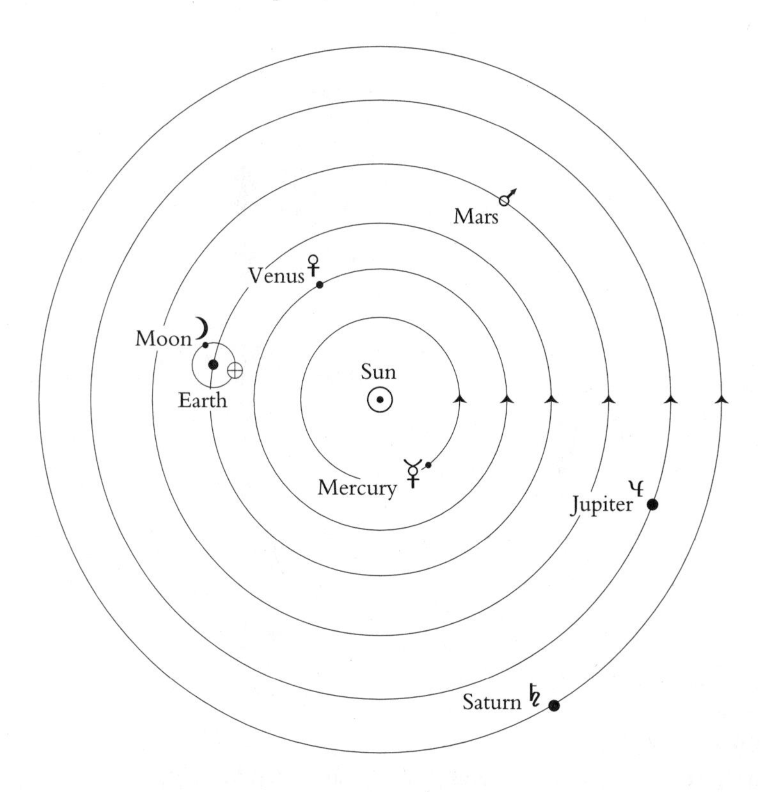

In 1602, Galileo became a professor of mathematics at the University of Padua. In 1604, a new star, which we now take to have been a supernova, appeared in the sky. Galileo studied it intensively. Sometime in 1609, he heard about the invention of a telescope and set out to build one for himself. A year and several telescopes later, he had a fairly good quality instrument with a magnification of about ×33. He turned it to the skies, becoming the first astronomer to use a telescope. He was the first person to see sunspots, mountains on the moon, and the moons of Jupiter.

Recent scholarship indicates that one of Galileo's students first suggested how the telescope might be used in an attempt to determine whether the Ptolemaic or Copernican picture of the universe is correct. In the Ptolemaic picture, Venus revolves in a small orbit (an epicycle) centered on a line connecting the earth and the sun, as shown in Figure 3.3. It follows that, when viewed from the earth, Venus is mostly dark because it is always illuminated from behind by the sun. At most, only a small crescent-shaped part of Venus will be illuminated. In the Copernican picture, by contrast, there will be times when Venus is almost fully illuminated. This would happen whenever Venus is on the opposite side of the sun from the earth, as shown in Figure 3.4. One cannot detect these differences with the unaided eye. With a telescope, however, one might

FIGURE 3.3

The Ptolemaic model predicts that one cannot observe Venus fully illuminated.

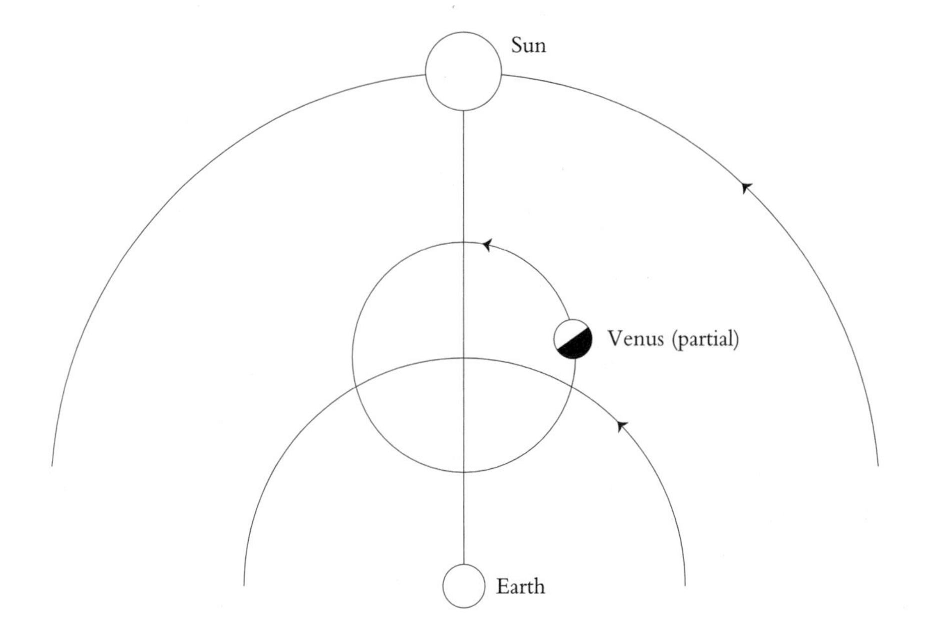

be able to see whether Venus ever exhibits a full Venus the way the moon exhibits a full moon.

There is some historical evidence to the effect that, when the theoretical significance of using his telescope to study Venus was first suggested to Galileo, Venus was, in fact, below the horizon for several weeks. Being anxious to claim the discovery for his own, Galileo, nevertheless, reported having made the requisite observations. He did not acknowledge the help of his student. Only later, in the latter part of 1610, did he, in fact, observe Venus go from a relatively dark sphere, to a crescent, to a fully lighted sphere, then back through a crescent phase (pointing the opposite direction from before), and finally returning to the original dark phase. James Watson was hardly the first major scientist to go out on a limb in pursuit of an important discovery.

Analysis

This episode sets up quite nicely as a prime example of a crucial experiment. There are two rival models with opposed predictions. The data clearly favor one model over the other.

Step 1. Real World. The real-world objects are the known heavenly bodies near the earth (i.e., the sun, moon, and known planets). The theoretical issue is how they are arranged and move relative to one another.

Step 2. Models. There are two models: (1) the Ptolemaic model, in which the sun, moon, and planets revolve about the earth (as shown in Figure 3.1); and

FIGURE 3.4

The Copernican model predicts that one can observe Venus fully illuminated.

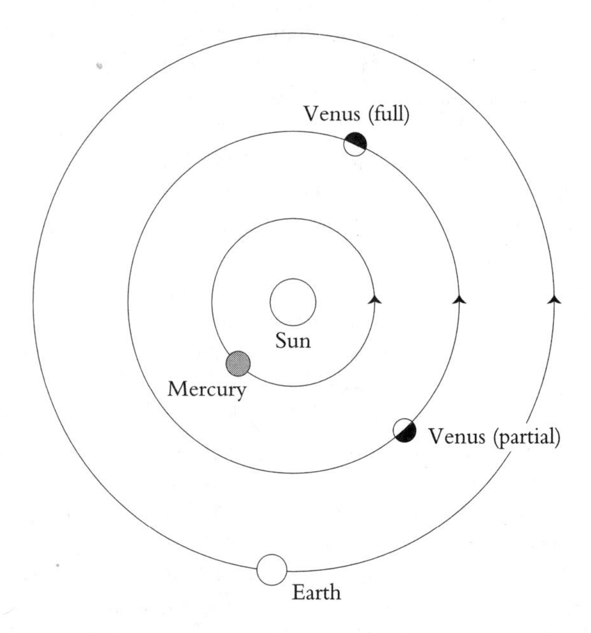

(2) the Copernican model, in which the planets, including the earth, revolve about the sun while the moon revolves about the earth (as shown in Figure 3.2).

Step 3. Predictions. There are likewise two predictions: (1) the Ptolemaic prediction that Venus can never be seen fully illuminated (as shown in Figure 3.3); and (2) the Copernican prediction that Venus can be seen going through a complete set of phases, including being fully illuminated (as shown in Figure 3.4).

Step 4. Data. The data are that Venus exhibits a complete set of phases and is sometimes fully illuminated.

Step 5. Negative Evidence? The data (1) disagree with the Ptolemaic prediction and (2) agree with the Copernican prediction. The data, therefore, provide evidence that the Ptolemaic model does not adequately represent the actual universe.

Step 6. Positive Evidence? The data would be impossible on the Ptolemaic model, and no other plausible models have been mentioned. So the data must be taken as providing positive evidence that the Copernican model provides a good fit to the actual universe.

Popular folklore often portrays Galileo as having slain the dragon of the Ptolemaic system with a single shot from his mighty telescope. Nothing could be further from the truth. Some people were initially convinced of the superiority of the Copernican system, but many more were not. Many questioned whether what Galileo reported seeing were not just reflections in his telescope. Few other people had access to any telescope at all, other than those built by Galileo himself. Again, many people wondered why Venus did not appear to the unaided eye to vary as much in its distance from the earth as required by the Copernican picture. These people were often unimpressed with Galileo's explanation that, because Venus is more fully illuminated when it is on the other side of the sun, it appears closer than it really is. Finally, many people continued to find it unimaginable that the earth really could be both revolving around the sun and spinning on its axis at what had to be tremendous speeds. Why do we not feel any such motion? Indeed, why are we not simply thrown off into space by the rapid spinning motion? For these and similar reasons, "The Scientific Revolution" was not completed for nearly 100 years after Galileo first turned his telescope to the heavens.

In conclusion, something must be said about the opposition of the Catholic Church to Galileo's views. Here again, popular folklore portrays Galileo as the valiant defender of free scientific inquiry against religious dogmatism. The truth is far more complex. Galileo was a deeply religious man. With his blessings, his favorite daughter spent her life in a religious order. For a long time, Galileo thought his work supported the power of the church. Initially, many religious scholars and authorities of the church welcomed his findings. Only later, partly because of the continuing threat of the Reformation begun by Luther and others, did the church attempt to prevent Galileo from teaching or publishing his views. Nor did Galileo do all that he might have to escape the power of the church. In 1610, he used his growing fame to secure a position in Florence, where the influence of the church was much greater than in Padua, which was part of the Venetian Republic. He could later have sought safety and freedom to publish in Venice, or even in Germany, but chose to remain in Florence.

3.2 ISAAC NEWTON AND HALLEY'S COMET

Isaac Newton was born in 1642, the year Galileo died. He brought together the scientific work of the previous century by creating a set of theoretical models that could be applied both to terrestrial objects, such as cannon balls and swinging lamps, and to celestial objects, such as the moon and the planets. So successful were these models that Newtonian science became one of the main inspirations for "The Age of Enlightenment," which lasted for most of the eighteenth century.

NEWTONIAN MODELS

The objects in Newtonian models are called "bodies." Bodies have several important properties, some more familiar than others.

POSITION. At any moment of time, every body is said to be located at some point in space. That point is its position at that moment in time.

VELOCITY. Velocity is change in position per unit time. One part of velocity is what we commonly call speed (e.g., 50 miles per hour). The other part of velocity is direction. A body moving 50 miles per hour heading north and a body moving 50 miles per hour heading south would have the same speed but opposite velocities because they are moving in opposite directions.

ACCELERATION. Acceleration is change in velocity per unit time. A body going from rest to 60 miles per hour in 1 minute would be accelerating at an average rate of 1 mile per hour per second. A body standing still has zero acceleration. So does one moving at a constant 50 miles per hour. A body slowing down has negative acceleration.

MASS. Newton was among the first to realize that there is a distinction between mass and weight. Mass is a property that a body possesses all by itself, no matter where in the universe it might be. Newton called it "quantity of matter." The weight of a given body, by contrast, depends on what other body it happens to be near.

MOMENTUM. Momentum is defined as the product of mass times velocity. Whatever amount of mass a body has, its momentum is that number multiplied by its velocity. A body standing still has no velocity and thus no momentum, even though it may have a large mass.

FORCE. This is the most difficult concept in classical physics. Whole books have been written just on Newton's conception of force, and many others on the concept of force in general. For the moment, we will just say that bodies can produce forces and that force is what makes bodies change their motion.

Having acquired some idea of the kinds of properties bodies exhibit, we turn now to Newton's three *Laws of Motion* and his *Law of Universal Gravitation*. These laws summarize much of what Newton had to say about how bodies behave.

FIRST LAW OF MOTION. If there is no force acting on a body, the momentum of that body will remain constant.

This law tells us that if any body is moving with a constant velocity (i.e., at a fixed speed in a straight line), then it will just keep moving at that velocity as long as no force interferes. A special case of this law occurs if a body is at rest (i.e., not moving at all). According to the first law, it must just stay at rest until some force acts on it.

SECOND LAW OF MOTION. If there is a force acting on a body, that body will accelerate by an amount directly proportional to the strength of the force and inversely proportional to its mass.

This law tells us that the more force you apply to a body, the faster it will accelerate. It also tells us that a given force will accelerate a lighter mass more than a heavier one.

THIRD LAW OF MOTION. If one body exerts a force on a second, then the second exerts a force on the first that is equal in strength but in the opposite direction.

This is the famous law of action and reaction: for every action there is a reaction, equal in force but opposite in direction.

Notice that these laws all tell us what a body should do if it is acted on by various forces, but none of them tells us what the forces themselves would be. The law of gravitation, then, describes one kind of force that is produced by every body and acts on all other bodies.

LAW OF UNIVERSAL GRAVITATION. Any two bodies exert attractive forces on each other that are directed along a line connecting them and are proportional to the product of their masses divided by the square of the distance between them.

This law tells us that all bodies generate a gravitational force and that the gravitational force between two bodies is greater for larger masses and smaller the greater the distance between them. Dividing by the square of the distance means that doubling the distance between two masses will reduce their mutual force to only one-fourth of what it was. Figure 3.5 illustrates these relationships (insofar as they can be pictured) for the simple case of a system consisting of only two bodies.

The above description of Newtonian models makes no explicit reference to any real objects in the world. There is no presumption that anything we would ordinarily call a "body" behaves like a "body" in Newton's models. So, we have here a description of a fairly elaborate set of theoretical models, probably the most famous theoretical models in the whole history of science.

As a matter of fact, many things in the world do behave like systems of Newtonian bodies: the motions of falling weights, the paths of cannon balls, the swings of a pendulum, the revolutions of the moon, and the motions of the planets. Indeed, because Newtonian models apply to so many things, their use has become part of our everyday understanding of the world. Since the advent of space flight, for example, most people are aware of the difference between mass and weight. Astronauts in orbit around the earth are weightless but obviously not without mass. Similarly, most people know that,

FIGURE 3.5

A Newtonian model for two bodies with gravitational attraction.

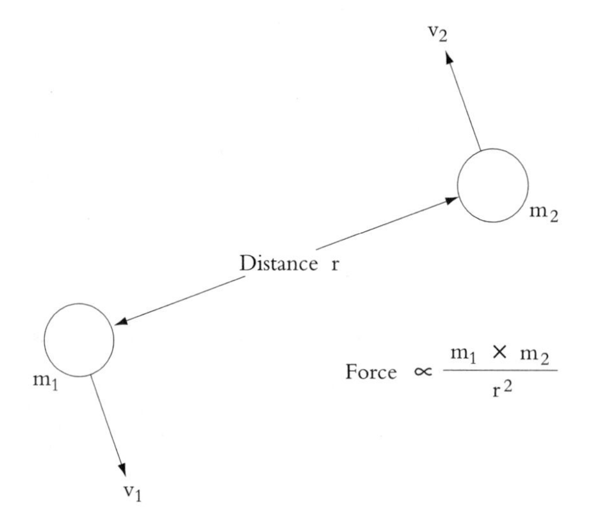

although astronauts have the same mass both on earth and on the moon, they weigh less on the moon. This is because the moon has less mass than the earth and thus generates a smaller gravitational force.

Finally, you should make special note of the fact that the above renditions of Newton's laws are given totally in words. No mathematical symbols were used. Yet everyone knows that physics is highly mathematical. How can this be? The answer is that, in fact, there is nothing that can be said using mathematical symbols that cannot be said in words. What matters are the underlying relationships, and these can be described in either words or special symbols. The difficulty is that the use of words is so cumbersome that by merely using words it would be practically impossible to do the calculations required to solve particular problems. For example, all the steps in a simple problem in long division could be written out in words, but you could hardly imagine actually figuring out the answer that way. It takes a special symbolism, really a special language, to do that easily. To achieve a fairly good intuitive understanding of the fundamental relationships, however, a special symbolism is rarely necessary. An intuitive understanding of what is going on is generally enough to be able to evaluate the relevance of new data to any set of models.

HALLEY'S COMET

Newton's work, *The Mathematical Principles of Natural Philosophy,* or *Principia,* an abbreviation of its original Latin title, was first published in 1687. Around 1695, Edmond Halley, an English astronomer and friend of Newton, began applying Newtonian models to the motions of comets. He was probably acting on Newton's own suggestion that comets may be like small planets with very large elliptical orbits. In any case, comets were very interesting objects because they had always been viewed as mysterious, even ominous. Their appearances certainly exhibited no apparent regularity. If Newton's suggestion was correct, however, the behavior of comets would exhibit a great deal of underlying regularity.

Halley began investigating a comet that he himself had observed in 1682. His observations of 1682 provided a quite precise location for the comet's path relative to the background stars. However, because the comet could be observed only during that small part of its orbit taking it near to the sun, it was not possible to determine how big the whole orbit might be and, thus, how long it would take for the comet to return. Indeed, it was impossible to determine from those observations whether the orbit was an ellipse, as Newton suggested, or a parabola. Newton's theory allowed the possibility of a parabolic orbit, but such an orbit would mean that the comet would come by only once and then leave the solar system forever. If, however, the orbit was elliptical, the comet should have traveled that same path many times before.

Halley began digging into the records of observations of previous comets. He found 24 recorded observations, going back roughly 150 years, for which the records were precise enough to compare with the observations of 1682. For two of these, one in 1606–1607 and one in 1530–1531, the recorded orbits were very close to that of the 1682 comet. Halley argued that it was extremely unlikely that three different comets should have such similar orbits and concluded that these were three appearances of the same comet in an elliptical orbit with a period of roughly 76 years. He speculated but could not prove that the slight discrepancies in the three orbits were due to gravitational influences from the planets, particularly Jupiter.

But Halley did not stop here. Using the data from all three cases, together with the hypothesis that he was dealing with a system represented by a Newtonian model, Halley calculated the time of the next return. He boldly predicted that the comet should be seen again in the latter part of December 1758. Figure 3.6 will help you to keep in mind the relevant details of this example.

Halley published his work on comets in 1705. It was well received by Newton and the growing band of English Newtonians. It did little, however, to convince the French. Halley himself died, a respected scientist, in 1743, 15 years before the predicted return of the comet. By this time, even the French were coming around to the Newtonian way of thinking, and Halley's prediction was remembered. In 1756, the French Academy of Science offered a prize for the most accurate calculation of the time the comet would return. The comet reappeared, as predicted, near Christmas 1758 and was officially named "Halley's comet."

Analysis

As presented above, the episode involving Halley's comet includes two different sets of data. It is instructive to do two analyses because, although both sets of data provide evidence for Halley's hypothesis, the evidence provided by the second set of data is superior.

Step 1. Real World. The real-world object of most direct interest was the comet observed in 1682. Halley was, of course, interested in other comets as well.

Step 2. Model. The model was a Newtonian model for two bodies in an elliptical orbit attracting one another by the force of gravity. The two bodies were identified with the sun and the comet, respectively.

FIGURE 3.6

Halley's comet.

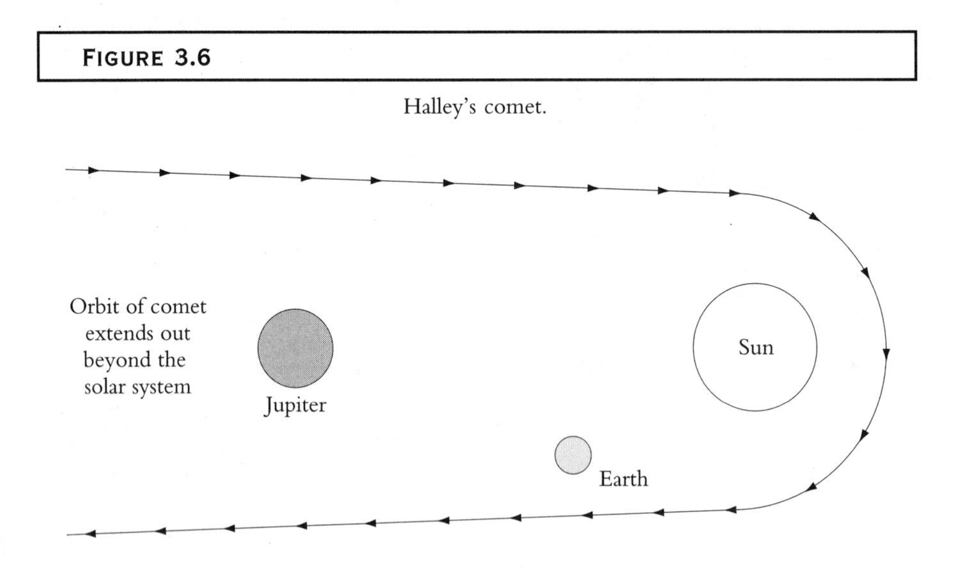

Step 3. Prediction. The first "prediction" was that one would be able to find records of comets with orbits similar to the comet of 1682 and occurring at roughly equal intervals.

Step 4. Data. Among 24 records of comets, those for comets in 1530–1531 and 1606–1607 had recorded orbits similar to the comet of 1682 and were spaced at about 76-year intervals.

Step 5. Negative Evidence? No. The data clearly agreed with the prediction.

Step 6. Positive Evidence? The only alternative hypothesis was that there were three different comets with similar orbits at 76-year intervals. Halley himself claimed that this was unlikely. Given that the documented incidence of similar comets was only 24 in 150 years, Halley's claim seems plausible. The data did provide evidence that the comet of 1682 fits a Newtonian model.

Before commenting on this analysis, let us analyze the data from the return of the comet in 1758.

Step 1. Real World. The real-world object of most direct interest is the comet observed in 1682.

Step 2. Model. The model was a Newtonian model for two bodies in an elliptical orbit attracting one another by the force of gravity. The two bodies were identified with the sun and the comet, respectively.

Step 3. Prediction. The second prediction was that the comet would return near the end of 1758.

Step 4. Data. A comet with the requisite orbit did appear as predicted.

Step 5. Negative Evidence? No. The data clearly agreed with the prediction.

Step 6. Positive Evidence? The only alternative hypothesis was that another comet with the same orbit just happened to appear right around the predicted time, 76 years later. That seemed to everyone extremely unlikely. So, the data provided very good evidence that the Newtonian model fits.

The main difference in the two sets of data is that, in the second case, it was far less likely that one should have found data agreeing with the prediction if the suggested model did not, in fact, fit the real world. In the first case, Halley predicted only that there might be some record of comets like the comet of 1682 with equally spaced intervals between them. To satisfy this prediction, it was sufficient to find records of two equally spaced comets with roughly the orbit of the observed comet of 1682. The time interval was originally left open. It could have been 10 years or 100. In the second case, the prediction restricted the return of the comet to a specific 1- or 2-week period 76 years later. That was much less likely to happen if what they were seeing were, in fact, different comets. So, the evidence that the Newtonian model fits was better in the second case than in the first.

3.3 THE DOWNFALL OF THE PHLOGISTON THEORY

In science, as in everyday life, one tends to remember the winners. The losers are usually forgotten. Some losers, however, are remembered, if only because they had a period of considerable success before their downfall. A famous loser is the phlogiston theory.

Fire, like the motions of the heavens, has always fascinated people. In the Western world, recorded speculation about the nature of fire goes back to the Greeks. We owe to them both the myth of Prometheus and the view that the world is made up of a few separate elements: earth, air, fire, and water. All four are present in the process of combustion. The common-sense view of combustion is that something is driven out of the burning object, leaving only ashes behind.

By the eighteenth century, this something had a well-established name, *phlogiston*—the fire stuff. Assuming that combustible material contains phlogiston explains most of the obvious facts about combustion. Heating drives off the phlogiston into the air; cooling makes it less volatile; smothering holds it in. The well-known fact that a burning candle placed in an enclosed container soon goes out was explained by saying that the enclosed air gets saturated with phlogiston, so that the phlogiston remaining in the wax has nowhere to go.

Phlogiston accounts not only for combustion but also for the very important process of smelting. This is the process by which crude ores are turned into more refined metals. Generally, this is done by carefully heating the ores, together with a measured amount of charcoal, to a controlled temperature. It was claimed that the charcoal contains an excess of phlogiston, which, at moderately high temperatures, leaves the charcoal and combines with the ore to form the metal. This hypothesis was substantiated by the fact that further heating at higher temperatures returns the metal to its original state. The phlogiston is driven out of the metal by the higher temperature. Even rusting was explained as the result of phlogiston slowly escaping from the metal.

These claims may be taken as characterizing *phlogiston models.* Such models lay behind many hypotheses about systems undergoing combustion, rusting, or the process of smelting. The *phlogiston theory* included the general hypothesis that this sort of model fits most cases of combustion, smelting, rusting, and so on. In what follows, we concentrate on combustion.

Combustion is very difficult to study. Most things we commonly burn are made of many different substances and give off many different gases when burned. Moreover, combustion generally is rapid and violent. Progress in such studies required finding some simple, well-controlled subjects for experimentation. In the 1770s, chemists developed a number of techniques for performing such experiments. The leaders were Joseph Priestly in England and Antoine Lavoisier in France. Priestly supported the phlogiston theory; Lavoisier led the revolution that overthrew it.

In the 1770s, using techniques first developed by Priestly, Lavoisier performed several careful experiments with mercury. In one of these experiments, he floated a precisely measured amount of mercury on a liquid and covered it with a glass jar, thus enclosing a known amount of air (Figure 3.7). The mercury was then heated through

FIGURE 3.7

Lavoisier's experiment.

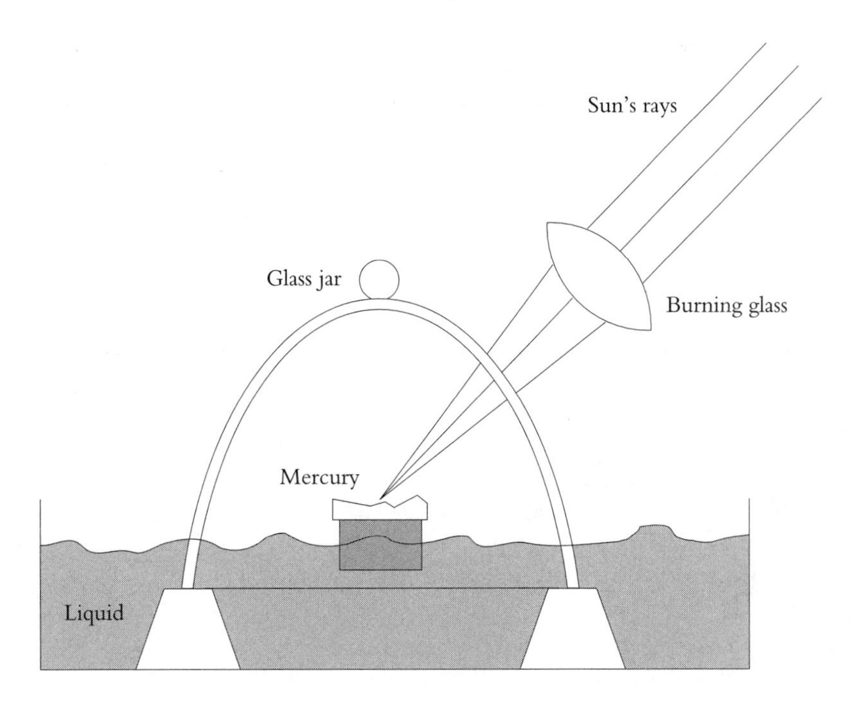

the glass using the rays of the sun focused by a powerful magnifying glass (a burning glass). In such circumstances, as Lavoisier well knew, a red powder, or ash, forms on the surface of the mercury. Some of the mercury undergoes a controlled burning.

Applying a phlogiston model to this experiment, we would expect two things. First, the resulting mercury plus red ash should weigh less than the original sample of mercury alone. This is because some phlogiston must be driven off, leaving the ash behind. And the volume of air inside the jar should increase because it now contains the phlogiston that was driven out of the mercury. This means that the level of the liquid inside the jar would drop to make room for the additional "air." When Lavoisier completed the experiment, the water level had gone *up*, and the mercury/ash combination weighed *more* than the original mercury alone.

Analysis

Step 1. Real World. The real-world phenomenon under investigation is the process of combustion. The specific case investigated is the controlled combustion of mercury.

Step 2. Model. The model is a phlogiston model according to which an invisible substance, phlogiston, is given off by various materials, including mercury, when they are appropriately heated.

Step 3. Predictions. The predictions, based on a phlogistion model, are (1) that the water level under the bell jar should go down (because of the phlogiston added to the air) and (2) that the mercury/ash combination should weigh less than the original mercury alone (because phlogiston has been driven out of the mercury, which became ash).

Step 4. Data. The data are (1) that the water level under the bell jar went up and (2) that the mercury/ash combination weighed more than the original mercury alone.

Step 5. Negative Evidence? The data and the prediction disagree. The data, therefore, provide evidence that the phlogiston model fails to represent the controlled combustion of mercury as carried out in this experiment.

Note that this analysis has only five steps. This happens whenever the analysis ends with evidence against a suggested hypothesis and there is no mention of any alternative supported by the data. Many readers will realize, of course, that there is an obvious alternative to the phlogiston model. According to this alternative model, there is something in the air that combines with the mercury to produce the ash. The water level goes up because the amount of air decreases, and the mercury/ash combination weighs more than the mercury alone because of the added weight of whatever it is in the air that combines with mercury to produce the ash. Lavoisier called this something "oxygen." That is another story.

3.4 DARWIN AND EVOLUTION

The scientific revolution of the seventeenth century changed biology as well as physics. But the real revolution in biology did not take place until the middle of the nineteenth century, with Charles Darwin's discovery of evolution by natural selection and Gregor Mendel's investigations into the mechanisms of inheritance. We look first at Darwin's achievement and then consider Mendel's research.

SPECIAL CREATION

Until the middle of the nineteenth century, throughout Europe and the Americas, the primary account of the origin of various life forms on earth was provided by the Judeo-Christian religious traditions. Regardless of other major differences in beliefs, Catholics, Jews, and Protestants all agreed that life, particularly human life, was the product of a special creative act by a supreme being acting outside the natural order of things. One reason for the widespread belief in special creation was the lack of alternative models that might account for both the great diversity of life forms and the seemingly exquisite fit between organisms and their environment. Fish have gills for living in water, birds have wings to fly, and humans have hands and eyes for finding food and shelter. How could this all have come about without the actions of a divine providence? Darwin provided an alternative model.

DARWIN'S FINCHES

Charles Darwin was born on the same day as Abraham Lincoln in 1809. His was a wealthy British family of physicians and manufacturers. At the age of 16, he was sent off to study medicine at the University of Edinburgh. Failing at that, he was sent to Cambridge University to study Divinity, where he was only slightly more successful. His real passion was geology and natural history. In 1831, through the influence of his naturalist friends, he obtained the (unpaid) position of naturalist aboard a British Navy ship, H.M.S. Beagle, which was then setting out on an expedition to survey South America and various Pacific islands. The voyage, which took him around the world, lasted 5 years.

One of the more fascinating stops was at the Galapagos Islands, remote Pacific islands roughly 600 miles west of Lima, Peru. Darwin argued that these islands were the relatively recent product of undersea volcanoes. There is one largish island, Albemarle, surrounded by three somewhat smaller nearby islands, and ten or so much smaller outlying islands, a few of these being 100 miles away from the central islands. Figure 3.8 shows the geography of the Galapagos Islands.

The islands exhibited a strange array of plant and animal life, including crabs, iguanas, giant tortoises, mockingbirds—and finches. Darwin and his shipmates collected samples, particularly the birds, which could be fairly easily preserved for the long trip back to England. But neither Darwin nor his companions were completely systematic about noting which birds came from which islands, an oversight he would later regret.

Arriving back in England in 1836, Darwin began what would turn out to be years of work of sorting through his specimens and trying to make sense of all that he had seen. Gradually, he realized the potential importance of the finches. There were, overall, fifteen to twenty different species of finches on the islands. Most of these were to be found on the inner islands. The outlying islands typically exhibited only two or three species each. All the species, however, bore a resemblance to species of finches back on the South American mainland.

The main difference among the various species of finches is the size and shape of their beaks. Moreover, the character of the beaks for different groups of species corresponds to the type of food it eats. For example, members of *Geospiza* have relatively short, sturdy beaks, well adapted for crunching seeds, which are their main diet. Members of *Platyspiza* exhibit a somewhat parrot-like beak suitable for eating leafs, buds, blossoms, and fruits. Again, finches belonging to the group *Cactospiza* possess a woodpecker-like beak, which they use to bore into wood to find insects such as beetles. Members of the group *Certhidea*, by contrast, have only a medium-strong beak suitable for eating smaller, softer insects. Finally, members of *Cactornis* have longish beaks suitable for probing flowers to feed on the nectar or poking into the body of a prickly pear cactus to eat the pulp. Figure 3.9 sketches the differences between these five groups. Both Darwin and later naturalists discovered many more differences of a similar sort.

DARWIN'S MODEL OF EVOLUTIONARY DEVELOPMENT

Although Darwin's family belonged to the more wealthy establishment in British society, it had a tradition of antiestablishment freethinking. Darwin's grandfather,

FIGURE 3.8

The geography of the Galapagos Islands.

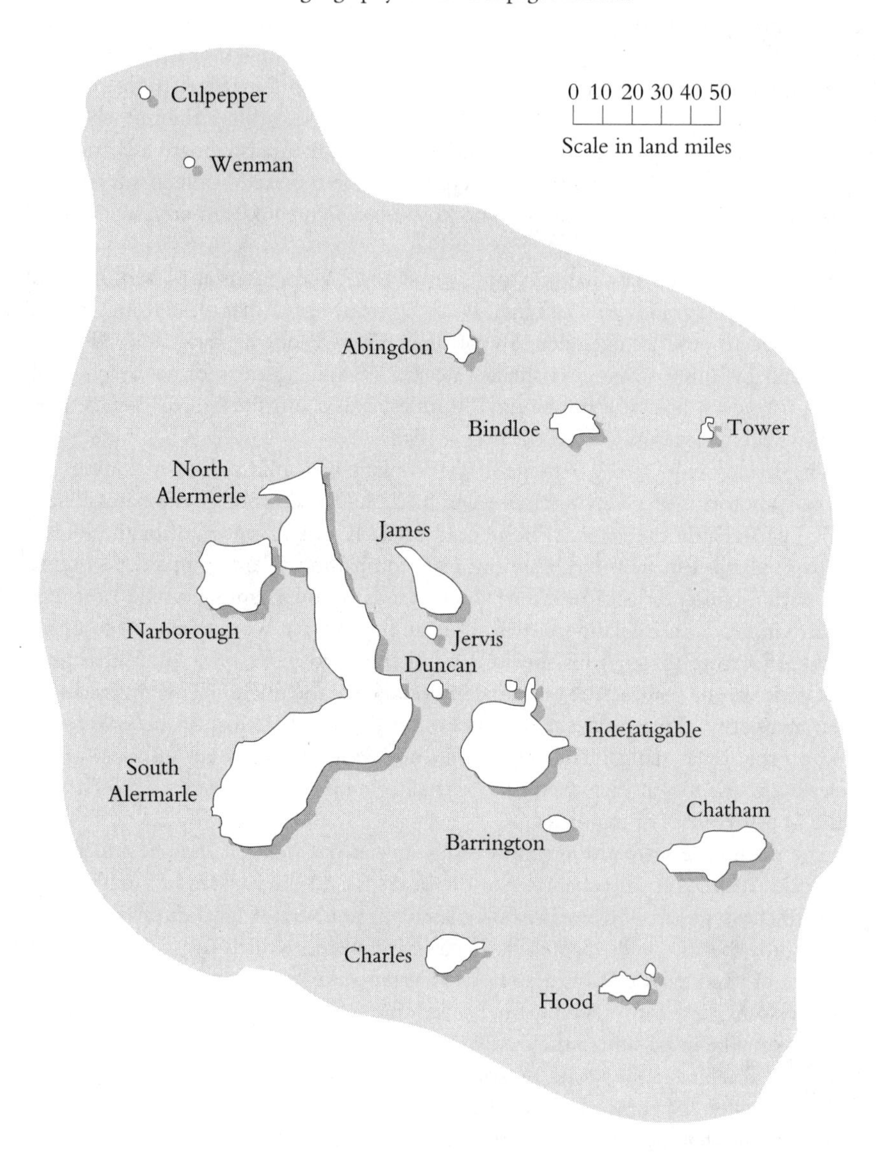

Erasmus Darwin, had even published works expounding the view that humans somehow evolved from lower forms of life. At Edinburgh and Cambridge, Darwin himself associated with several radical thinkers. It was not so surprising, then, that he would seek a *natural,* not a supernatural, explanation for his many empirical findings. What was novel in Darwin's work was the particular model of evolution he developed.

FIGURE 3.9

Differences among the beaks of five groups of Galapagos finches.

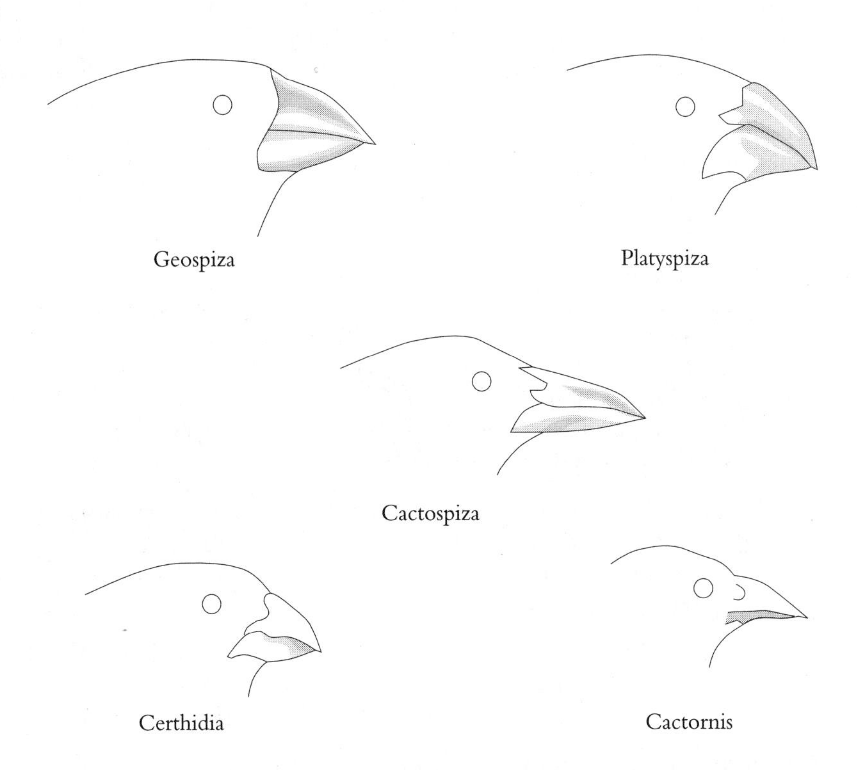

Darwin began thinking about the evolution of life forms at a time when, especially in Britain, ideas of competition in the marketplace were prominent. The idea was that the most successful businesses, and individuals, were those that were most competitive. Darwin was also impressed by the views set out in Thomas Malthus' *Essay on the Principle of Population.* According to Malthus, human populations naturally keep growing to the point where they outstrip the means for their survival. So there are always more people than there is adequate food and shelter. Only the stronger among them can survive.

Darwin applied these ideas to animal populations in general. At any time, he thought, there will be some variation in the traits exhibited by different members of a population. Some of these variations, depending on the particular environment, could be expected to give the individuals possessing them a competitive advantage in securing mates and leaving offspring for succeeding generations. If these traits are inherited, they would be relatively more prevalent in succeeding generations, eventually being shared by most members of the corresponding later population. In this way, a population might, over time, evolve into a different species. That, at any rate, was the model of evolution developed in Darwin's 1859 masterpiece, *The Origin of Species,* published more than 20 years after the voyage of the Beagle.

Evolution, on Darwin's model, is a very slow process. Significant changes in the prevalence of specific traits in a population might take many generations to observe. There was, however, one example of change in organic populations known to all—plant and animal breeding. Darwin had been familiar with the breeding of plants and animals such as dogs and pigeons since his childhood. By deliberately mating animals with desired traits, pigeon breeders, for example, regularly produced highly distinctive variations. If humans could artificially select traits they wished exhibited in their animals, why could not something similar—**natural selection**—happen in nature?

Analysis

Now let us apply Darwin's model to his data on the Galapagos finches. Here, the presentation of the case makes it natural to consider the data before the prediction.

Step 1. Real World. The specific facts to be explained are the correspondences between the character of their beaks and the diet of the various species of finches on the Galapagos Islands. How did the beaks of the various types of finches come to be so well adapted to the food they eat?

Step 2. Model. The model in question is Darwin's model of evolution, according to which inherited variations in traits make some individuals more fit than others to reproduce in the given environment. This leads to an increased prevalence of the favored trait in the population.

Step 4. Data. The data are the facts about the character of the beaks of various species of finches, together with information about the type of food most common to each species. The beaks are typically well adapted to the diets of each species.

Step 3. Prediction. The data are what one could expect if Darwin's model applied to the Galapagos finches. Suppose that a few finches managed to migrate from the mainland to the islands after these became habitable. Over time, one could expect that some individuals would be better adapted than others to different environments and different types of food. Those with shorter, stronger beaks, for example, would be better at chewing seeds lying on the ground. Those with longer beaks would be better at digging beetles out of tree bark. In many generations, the descendants of these different individuals could come to exhibit the differences in beak characteristics Darwin observed.

Step 5. Negative Evidence? No. The data and the prediction agree.

Step 6. Positive Evidence? Were the data and prediction likely to agree even if Darwin's model does not really account for the correlation between beak type and the diet of finches on the Galapagos Islands? Is there another model that accords equally well with the data? Here, more discussion is required.

At the time, as noted above, the main alternative model that might account for various life forms was special creation. Now, surely, if there were indeed a creator like the one proclaimed in the Judeo-Christian tradition, such a creator could have arranged for the finches on the Galapagos Islands to exhibit the differences in beak characteristics just as Darwin found them. Of course, if the islands themselves are of relatively recent origin, this would have to have been done in such a way that the islands became populated long after the original creation of the earth. Nevertheless, the envisioned creator could surely have arranged that. Does this possibility leave the case for Darwin's hypothesis inconclusive?

Here, much depends on how seriously one takes special creation as an alternative model of the origin of species. Even though a Judeo-Christian creator could have created Darwin's finches, there is nothing in the basic teachings of that tradition that directly bears on the question. The size and shape of the beaks of birds on volcanic islands in the Pacific Ocean is just not something that had ever been of concern to that tradition. Darwin's model of evolution, however, was designed for just such situations. So, one might argue, the two models are not really competitors at all. They deal with different things. This was a standard view among British establishment theologians after publication of the *Origin*. Indeed, some went so far as to argue that natural selection was the creator's way of creating human life on earth. Darwin had merely discovered another aspect of the creator's grand plan.

Of course, Darwin's finches were only a very tiny part of the evidence presented in the *Origin*. He also provided evolutionary models for hundreds of other examples from his voyage and from his next 20 years of research and correspondence with naturalists around the world. The collective weight of all this evidence was considerable. But none of this provides direct evidence *against* the hypothesis of special creation. No specific prediction of that hypothesis fails to agree with any data. What Darwin does provide is a well-developed alternative to special creation. On Darwin's alternative model, the fit between organisms and their environment that had been taken to be evidence of supernatural design is only evidence for the workings of natural selection. Thus, even just the plausibility of Darwin's model renders all the data from the apparent design of organic life inconclusive as evidence for the hypothesis of special creation. Here is an analysis of the evidence for the hypothesis of special creation after Darwin's work.

Step 1. Real World. The object of study is the origin and development of life forms on earth.

Step 2. Model. Life forms have been purposely created by a supreme being operating outside the normal course of nature.

Step 3. Prediction. Individual life forms should be well adapted to their environments.

Step 4. Data. Existing life forms are indeed well adapted to their environments.

Step 5. Negative Evidence? No. The data and prediction agree.

Step 6. Positive Evidence? The data are, nevertheless, inconclusive as evidence for the hypothesis of special creation because there is an alternative model, Darwin's model of natural selection, which accounts equally well for the data.

3.5 MENDELIAN GENETICS

We turn now to the second major development in biology during the nineteenth century. Although Mendel's life largely overlapped Darwin's, his work, in a monastery in central Europe, was lost until the beginning of the twentieth century. As a result, genetics became a twentieth-century science.

MENDEL'S ORIGINAL EXPERIMENTS

Mendel did most of his experimentation on a type of garden pea *(Pisum sativum)*. Mendel noted that pea plants exhibit several characteristics that come in pairs, called **traits.** The texture of the peas (which are the seeds of the plant) may be either smooth or wrinkled. Also, the color of the peas can be either yellow or green, and the height of the plants themselves may be either tall or short. To keep things simple, we shall concentrate on only one characteristic, the height of the plants.

Mendel discovered that when short plants are cross-pollinated with other short plants, the resulting seeds always yield short plants. Tall plants, however, seem to come in two types. Some pairs of tall plants produce seeds that yield only tall plants, but other tall plants produce seeds yielding a mixture of tall and short offspring. The short plants, as well as the tall plants that yield only other tall plants, are called **true-breeding** plants, whereas the other tall plants are called **hybrids.**

Experiment showed that if you cross-fertilize the true-breeding tall plants with the short plants (which are also true-breeding), the result is all tall plants. These tall plants, however, are all hybrids. If these hybrid plants are then self-fertilized, the result is a mixture of both tall and short offspring. So, whatever is responsible for determining whether a plant is short or tall seems to be transmitted through a generation of plants that are themselves all tall. The short plants show up again only in the following generation.

Mendel's unique contribution was to isolate the different characteristics of his plants and, then, actually to count the plants exhibiting the different traits. He discovered that the ratio of tall to short in the second generation was roughly 3 to 1. This ratio occurred again and again and with other characteristics besides height. Figure 3.10 shows Mendel's results.

MENDEL'S MODEL

Mendel sought to explain how a trait could be transmitted by plants that did not themselves exhibit that trait. Moreover, the explanation must account for the fact that the "hidden" trait appears in only one-fourth of the members of the succeeding generation. In an attempt to explain these things, Mendel constructed the following model.

Suppose that there are two things that determine which traits associated with any characteristic are actually exhibited. Mendel called these things **factors.** (Factors correspond very roughly to what we now call genes.) Suppose, further, that one factor is associated with being tall and the other with being short. Also, suppose that each individual possesses some combination of two of these two types of factors. Let **H** stand for the factor associated with tall plants and **h** for the factor associated with short plants. Then there are really three different types of individuals: those with two tall-

FIGURE 3.10

Mendel's original experiments.

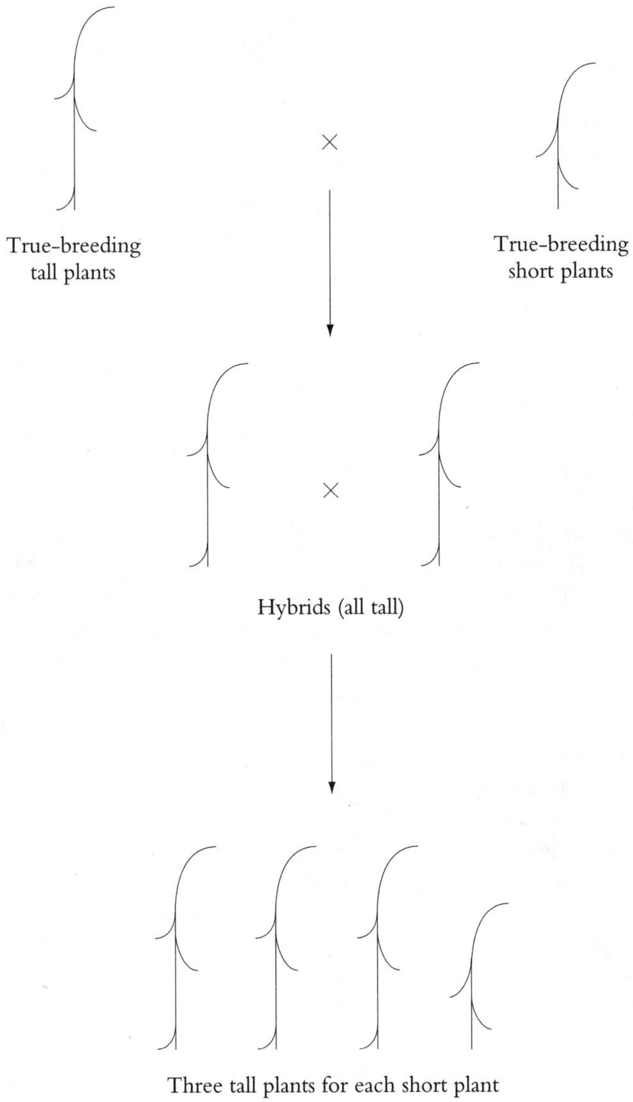

True-breeding tall plants

True-breeding short plants

Hybrids (all tall)

Three tall plants for each short plant

producing factors, those with two short-producing factors, and those with one of each. These three possibilities are shown schematically in Figure 3.11.

Next, assume that on pollination ("mating"), the seeds for the next generation get one factor from each parent. Moreover, assume the selection of a factor from either parent is the result of a **random** process. This is the crucial part of what is usually called **Mendel's Law of Segregation.** In the formation of the seed that becomes a

FIGURE 3.11

How Mendel's model classifies individuals by combinations of factors.

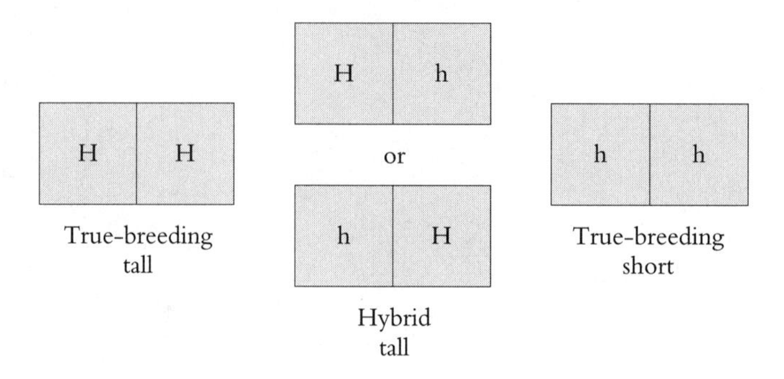

plant in the next generation, the four original factors (two from each parent) "segregate" themselves randomly into groups of two, one from each parent.

Finally, suppose that those individuals that have one factor of each type (the hybrids) exhibit the trait associated with only one of the two factors. This trait is called the **dominant trait.** The factor associated with this trait is called the **dominant factor.** That one of the factors should be dominant in this sense is known as **Mendel's Law of Dominance.** The other trait and its corresponding factor are called **recessive.**

Now let us take a new look at Mendel's experiment as pictured in Figure 3.10. This time, however, let us represent each individual by its factors alone. The result is shown in Figure 3.12. Let us go through this diagram carefully. The original parents consist of true-breeding tall and true-breeding short plants. Their union must produce hybrids because the offspring must get one factor from each parent and each parent has only one type to give.

When both parents are hybrids, however, there are four different ways the offspring can get its two factors: a tall from each parent, a tall from the first and a short from the second, a short from the first and a tall from the second, or a short from each. Because, by the law of segregation, these combinations are selected randomly, there should be equal numbers of each of these four types of offspring. However, by the law of dominance, only one of these four types will actually be short. The other three—the one true-breeding tall and the two hybrids—will all be tall. We thereby obtain the observed result that tall and short plants occur in the third generation in a ratio of 3 to 1.

THE BACKCROSS TEST

Mendel's model suggests another experiment. Why not try crossing the second-generation hybrids with the true-breeding short plants of the parental generation? A quick review of Figure 3.12 reveals what kind of mating this backcross represents. It seems that no one had ever performed this experiment before. Even if it had been

FIGURE 3.12

Mendel's model applied to his original experiments.

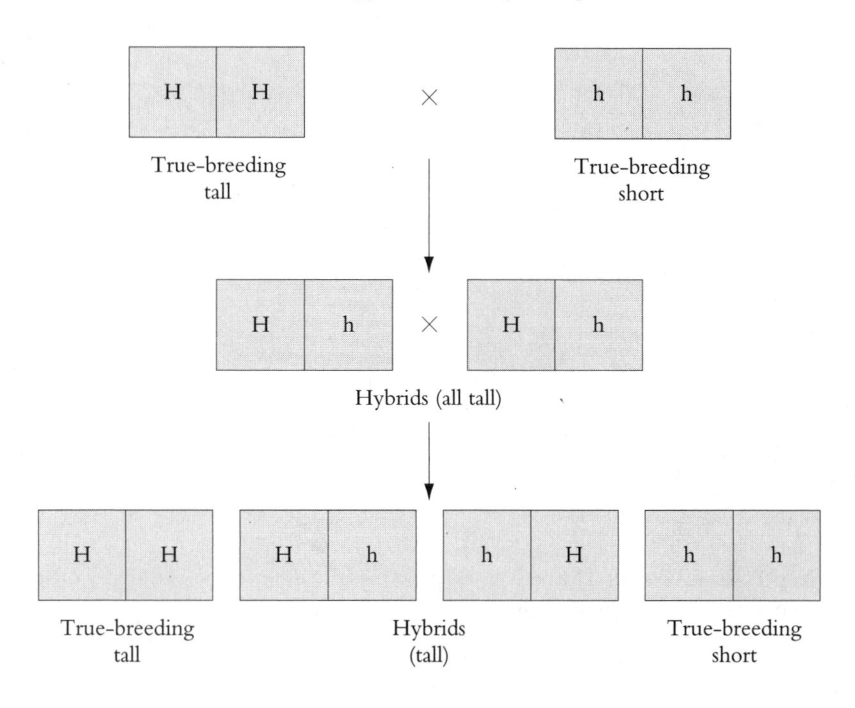

performed, no one seems ever to have reported actually counting the resulting plants to see what ratio of tall to short plants would occur.

Let us figure out what ratio Mendel's hypothesis predicts. The experiment is represented symbolically in Figure 3.13. The numbers 1, 2, 3, and 4 are attached to help keep straight the various possible combinations of factors in the offspring.

According to Mendel's model, there are four different possible ways an offspring could get its complement of two factors. According to the law of segregation, each of these possibilities is equally likely. So, on the average, there should be equal numbers of each type. Now, as you can see, two of the possibilities yield hybrids, which, by the law of dominance, would be tall. The other two are true-breeding short plants. So the ratio of tall to short plants in this sort of experiment should be 1 to 1. That is, on the average, half should be tall and half short. Mendel reported producing 208 plants by this type of cross-pollination. Of these, 106 were reported to be tall and 102 short. That is surely close enough to call the prediction true.

Analyses

There are two sets of data to consider: one set from the original experiments and one set from the backcross experiments. We will do two separate analyses.

FIGURE 3.13

Mendel's model applied to the backcross experiment.

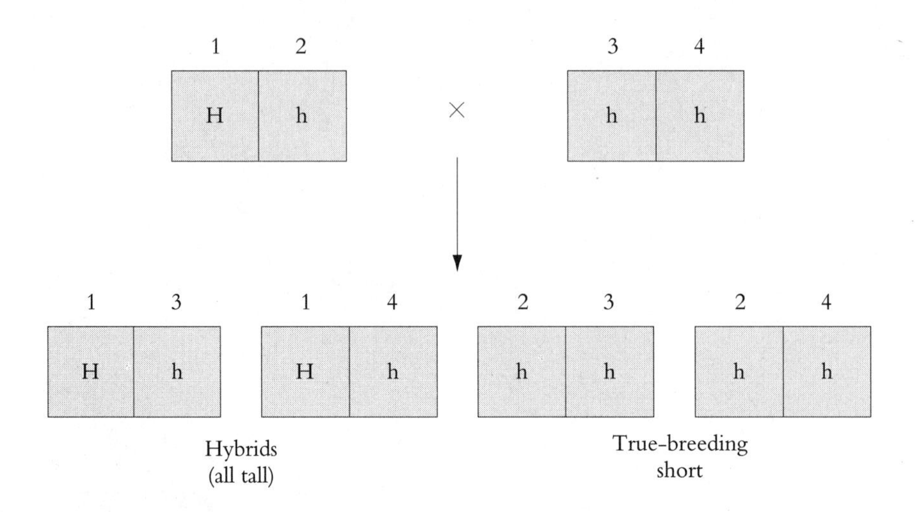

Step 1. Real World. The real-world process is the inheritance of traits by offspring from sexually reproducing parents.

Step 2. Model. The model is Mendel's two-factor model incorporating the law of segregation and the law of dominance.

Step 3. Prediction. The prediction is that the ratio of dominants (tall) to recessives (short) should be 3 to 1.

Step 4. Data. The data are the 3-to-1 ratios of tall to short plants in the original plant breeding experiments.

Step 5. Negative Evidence? No. If being tall is identified as a dominant trait and being short as a recessive trait, then the data and the prediction agree.

Step 6. Positive Evidence? Was the prediction likely to agree with the data even if Mendel's model did not provide a good fit to the real world? Answering this question requires further consideration.

Standard presentations of Mendel's theory, as found in college textbooks, for example, do not explicitly refer to alternative models that might equally explain the data. And none were mentioned in the above presentation. Nonspecialists coming to this subject for the first time are thus left to wonder just how likely observing a 3-to-1 ratio would be if Mendel's model *did not* fit the case. There are two general points to consider.

One point is that 3 to 1 is a fairly simple ratio. So, even without knowing much at all about genetics, we might suspect that there are other fairly simple mechanisms that could produce that ratio. To the extent that this is so, taking the agreement between Mendel's prediction and the data as evidence for his hypothesis could lead us to support a false hypothesis.

A second point concerns the procedure Mendel used in constructing his model. He clearly discovered the 3-to-1 ratio *before* he constructed his model. That means he was searching for a model that would yield a prediction of three tall to one short. It is very difficult to say how likely it is that such a search process should lead to a well-fitting rather than a poorly fitting model. The only thing we know for sure is that the procedure Mendel followed was very likely to lead to a model that yields the correct prediction, regardless of how well the model fits. That is because Mendel set out to find a model that would yield the 3-to-1 ratio and would clearly have rejected any model that did not do so. We do not know how many, if any, such models there were. Nevertheless, whatever model he ended up presenting for public scrutiny would be sure to yield the correct prediction, even if it did not fit the case in other respects. The net result is that it is very difficult to assess how much the agreement between the prediction from the model and the original data support a belief in the general correctness of the model.

The backcross experiment is significantly different. For completeness, we will run through the whole analysis.

Step 1. Real World. The real-world process is the inheritance of traits by offspring from sexually reproducing parents.

Step 2. Model. The model is Mendel's two-factor model satisfying the law of segregation and the law of dominance.

Step 3. Prediction. The prediction is that ratio of tall to short offspring in the backcross experiment should be 1 to 1.

Step 4. Data. The data were 106 tall plants and 102 short plants out of a total of 208 offspring.

Step 5. Negative Evidence? No. The data are in close agreement with the prediction.

Step 6. Positive Evidence? Was the prediction likely to agree with the data even if Mendel's model did not provide a good fit to the real world? Here again, the question requires extra thought.

The worry that the model was itself selected especially because it "predicted" the data is here eliminated. It is clear from all accounts that the model was developed before the backcross experiment. But we still face the fact that there might well be different but equally plausible models that would predict a simple 1-to-1 ratio for the backcross experiment. The case for Mendel's hypothesis is somewhat strengthened by the fact that the model must correctly predict *both* the original 3-to-1 ratio in the standard breeding experiment and the 1-to-1 ratio in the backcross experiment. And that it does. So, lacking any other suggestions of models yielding the correct prediction for both sorts of experiments, we can take the agreement between prediction and data as providing at least moderate support for Mendel's hypothesis.

Mendel worked on *Pisum* from roughly 1856 to 1866. At the time, he was a monk in a monastery in the city of Brno, in what is now the Czech Republic. His account of his discoveries was published in an obscure journal which mailed out 115 copies. Mendel corresponded with one renowned scientist who understood his work. But this scientist was studying another species of plant that, for complex reasons, did not yield Mendel's simple ratios. Indeed, few traits with which we are familiar exhibit such simple patterns of inheritance. In 1868, Mendel was appointed Abbot of his monastery. His official duties so absorbed his energies that by 1871 he was no longer able to continue his experiments. His work was largely forgotten until 1900 when several different people rediscovered his results. Then began the chain of discoveries that led up to the work of Watson and Crick in the 1950s.

3.6 THE REVOLUTION IN GEOLOGY

At the beginning of the twentieth century, the generally accepted hypothesis about the overall structure of the earth was that it was formed as a molten sphere that gradually cooled and formed a crust—on which we now live. As the sphere continued to cool, it contracted. As the whole sphere contracted inward, the crust cracked and deformed, yielding continents, mountain ranges, and the other major geological features now observed. This is the **contractionist hypothesis.** It is a consequence of contractionism that the continents have always remained more or less stable in their present positions. Once the crust solidified, there seemed no way for oceans or land masses to move around on the surface. This latter hypothesis came to be known as **stabilism.**

We can describe this situation by saying that geologists had developed a *theoretical model* of the earth using an analogy with a molten sphere suspended in space. Physicists and geologists had a fairly good idea of what such a sphere would do. The question was just how similar our actual earth is to such a model.

Until about 1950, most of our knowledge of the earth's geology could be pretty well explained using contractionist models. But there were some difficulties. For example, (1) there are remarkable similarities in the coastlines and other geological features of widely separated land masses. The fit between the coastlines of eastern South America and western Africa is particularly striking. It is difficult to see why, on a contractionist model, this should be so. (2) There are relatively new mountains running all along the west coast of North and South America, from Chile to Alaska, but only relatively old and less extensive mountains on the east coast. There are also volcanoes and earthquakes along the west coasts but not the east coasts. Why the asymmetry? (3) There are many similar species of plants and animals in places separated by oceans, as in Africa and South America. How could this have come to be?

It was not that contractionists lacked possible answers to these and similar difficulties. The addition of no-longer-existing land bridges to contractionist models, for example, would allow animals and plants to have migrated from one continent to another. But why, then, are there no remaining traces of these bridges?

MOBILISM

In 1915, a German scientist, Alfred Wegener, developed an entirely different model of the earth in a book later given the English title *The Origins of Continents and Oceans*. In contractionist models, the major movements are up and down—oceans sinking and mountains being pushed up. In Wegener's model, the major motions are horizontal. In particular, Wegener argued that the original cooling resulted in one large land mass, which he called Pangea. This mass, he claimed, subsequently broke up into continents that then drifted to their present positions—and they may still be drifting, although very slowly. This view came to be known as **mobilism.** Wegener was by no means the first person to advocate a mobilist hypothesis, but at the time, his was the most elaborate and systematic treatment of this view.

Using a mobilist model, we can easily account for many of those features of the earth that troubled stabilists. (1) The match in the coastlines and general geology of Africa and South America would be the natural result of South America having split off from what is now Africa and drifted to its present position. (2) The mountain ranges on the west coast of North and South America would be the natural result of the two continents pushing their way west. (3) The similarities in plants and animals now on different continents would be due to their having originally all been together on Pangea before it broke up. Wegener, therefore, regarded these observations as providing good evidence for a mobilist hypothesis.

Very few scientists in 1915 regarded Wegener's hypothesis as even remotely plausible. The main reason was simply that it seemed impossible that the continents really could move. In the first place, there seemed to be no horizontal forces to push them. Second, the continents are composed of softer material than the ocean floors—the lighter materials having floated to the top when the earth was still molten. How could this softer material push through a harder material? Thus, even if there were something pushing the continents, they would just break apart, crushed against the edges of the more solid ocean floors. If geologists were to be convinced that the continents move, they would have to be given both a better model and more powerful data than Wegener had provided. In fact, better models were devised by the time of Wegener's death in 1930, but it took until the 1960s before convincing data could be found.

SEAFLOOR SPREADING

One key to understanding the structure of the earth was the discovery of radioactivity by Marie and Pierre Curie in the 1890s. Radioactivity is due to the spontaneous decay of atoms of a few heavy elements such as uranium. When this happens, energy is given off and transformed into heat. If there were a reasonable amount of radioactivity taking place within the earth, the inside of the earth would be much hotter than contraction models generally assume. This heat could produce more molten material much closer to the surface than was previously thought possible. And this, finally, allows the possibility of large-scale horizontal movement driven by slow-moving convection currents of molten rock. These implications of radioactivity for drift models were recognized by the late 1920s, but there was no way then to test such speculative ideas. The secret to testing them lay at the bottom of the oceans.

FIGURE 3.14

Schematic cross section of an oceanic ridge.

It was not until the development of nuclear submarines in the 1950s that oceanographers obtained detailed knowledge of large ridges running along the ocean floor. One such ridge runs roughly north and south down the center of the Atlantic Ocean. Another lies off the coast of the United States in the eastern Pacific. These ridges were discovered to have a number of special characteristics. For example, there is a depression running down the middle of the ridges. The area within the depression, and along the ridge generally, is warmer than the surrounding areas. Also, the magnetism of the floor material alternates as one moves at right angles away from the ridge. Figure 3.14 is a schematic cross section of a ridge showing these features. What could have produced such ridges?

In 1960, Harry Hess, a respected geologist with a reputation for having a good scientific imagination, proposed a model that he called "geopoetry." In Hess' model, there are convection currents of molten material (produced by radioactive heating) under the ocean floors. In this model, ridges are produced by a rising convection current that then spreads out, forming the ocean floor. The spreading floor then descends back into the core at a trench that might be several thousand miles away (Figure 3.15). This model immediately accounts for the existence of ridges, their central depression, and the observed temperature differences.

Hess was aware from the beginning that his model fell into the mobilist tradition. An easy elaboration of the model makes possible the horizontal movement of the continents. We need only assume that the continents ride along on a piece of the earth's crust that is pushed by the expanding ocean floor. This model eliminates the need to explain how the continents could plow through the harder ocean floors. They do no such thing. Rather, they ride along on top of the moving harder material.

As an anonymous reviewer of a later paper by another drift supporter put it, this is the kind of thing one might talk about at a cocktail party, but it should not be published in a respectable scientific journal. Most scientists regarded Hess' hypothesis as being utterly implausible. How, indeed, could one ever test such a model? The secret lay in the alternating magnetic zones lying along the ridges.

MAGNETISM, GEOMAGNETISM, AND PALEOMAGNETISM

That the earth itself is a large magnet was known during the scientific revolution in the seventeenth century. In the 1950s, many scientists were studying the magnetism of the earth (geomagnetism), including the *history* of the earth's magnetism (paleomagne-

FIGURE 3.15

Hess's model of sea floor spreading.

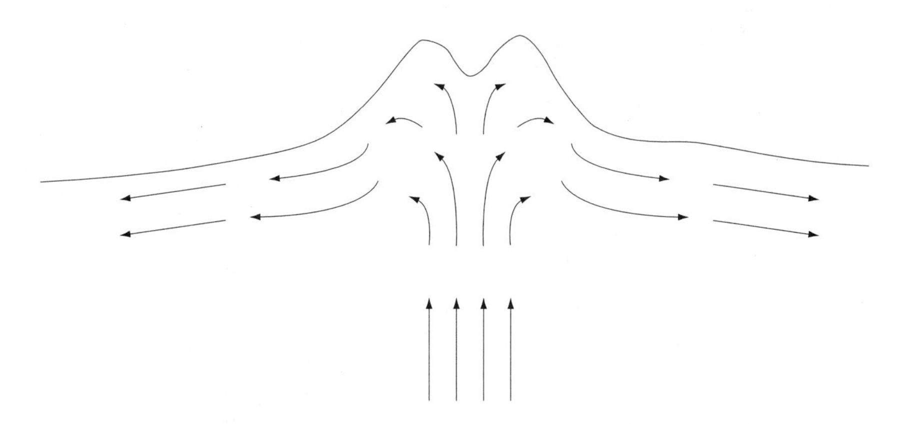

tism). Magnetic material, such as iron, which was originally free to move but then solidified into position, maintains the orientation it had when it solidified. By examining material formed over long periods of time without being disturbed, it is possible to determine how the magnetic field of the earth has changed over millions of years. Samples of such materials (e.g.,around volcanoes) seemed to exhibit a complete (180 degree) reversal of orientation at various times. This indicated that perhaps the earth's magnetic field itself had actually reversed poles several times (i.e., the north magnetic pole became the south magnetic pole and vice versa).

What does this have to do with seafloor spreading and continental drift? It took several years for anyone to see the connection. Then, in 1963, and working completely independently, a geologist in Canada (Lawrence Morley) and a geology graduate student in Cambridge, England, (Fred Vine) came up with a model for explaining the alternating strips of differently magnetized materials along the ridges. In their model, the iron in the rising molten material is free to orient itself with the earth's magnetic field at that time. When it reaches the surface, it cools, and the magnetized material gets locked into place. If the earth's magnetic poles reverse, then material coming along later will be oriented in the opposite direction.

If this model is correct, the history of the earth's magnetic field, for millions of years, would be laid out on the ocean floor in strips parallel to the ocean ridges. Moreover, there should be a correspondence between these alternating magnetic stripes and the alternating magnetic layers found in lava flows near volcanoes (Figure 3.16). All would provide records of the same sequence of global magnetic pole reversals.

Vine (together with his supervisor Drummond Matthews) and Morley published their views in 1963 and 1964, respectively. (Morley actually had the idea first, but his paper was turned down by two journals before it was finally published.) The reception by most geologists and geophysicists ranged from complete disinterest to outright hostility. That there should actually be such a pattern was generally regarded as fantastically improbable.

FIGURE 3.16

Predicted correspondence between magnetic records on land and along the ocean floor.

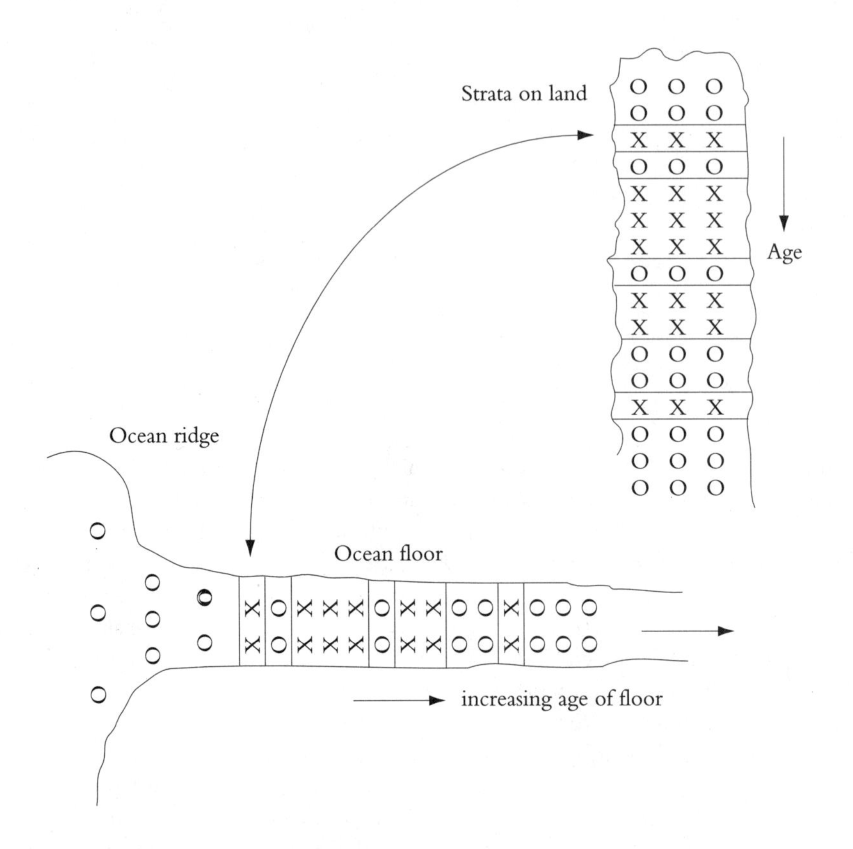

In the fall of 1965, an oceanographic research ship operated by the Lamont Geological Observatory at Columbia University was recording magnetic effects across the Pacific-Antarctic Ridge in the southeastern Pacific Ocean. By dragging a magnetometer near the ocean floor, they measured the changes in magnetic intensity in the floor as one moves perpendicularly across and away from a major ridge. When the data were analyzed early in 1966, they revealed a pattern of increasing and decreasing magnetic intensity matching the pattern of magnetic reversals found in minerals on land.

At the same time, other researchers at Lamont began to study the magnetism in core samples earlier drilled into the sediment layer at the bottom of the ocean near the southern tip of South America. Sediment is formed by soft material piling up on the bottom of the ocean and compressing the material underneath, which eventually solidifies. Because such sediment contains traces of magnetic materials, it too should exhibit the reversals in the earth's magnetic field. And, indeed, they found the same pattern of alternating magnetic orientation in the sediment.

The reaction of the geological community was immediate and dramatic. Nearly everyone embraced mobilist models. During the next few years, geologists developed the idea of seafloor spreading into what is now called **plate tectonics.** According to the theory of plate tectonics, the earth's surface consists of several "plates" that slowly move about the surface, constantly changing the configuration of continents and oceans. Much of geological research now involves working out the details of this general theory.

Analyses

There are two analyses to consider. One focuses on the data Wegener used to support his model of continental drift in the 1920s. The second focuses on the magnetic data first gathered in the 1960s. In the first episode, the data came before the predictions. In the second episode, the predictions came before the data. We, therefore follow that ordering of steps in these analyses.

Step 1. Real World. The real-world object is the structure and history of oceans and land masses on the surface of the earth.

Step 2. Model. The model is Wegener's model in which an original large land mass broke into pieces that, over millions of years, drifted to their current locations.

Step 4. Data. The data include (1) the matching coastlines of Africa and South America, (2) the mountain ranges on the western edges of North and South America, and (3) the similarities among plants and animals in places such as Africa and South America.

Step 3. Predictions. Wegener's model implies just the sort of data noted above.

Step 5. Negative Evidence? No. The data and the predictions agree.

Step 6. Positive Evidence? Were these predictions likely to agree with the data even if Wegener's model did not provide a good fit to the real world? As supporters of stabilist models argued, the data Wegener cited could plausibly be accounted for either by chance or by versions of a contractionist hypothesis. The matching of the coastlines and the location of mountain ranges were generally ascribed to chance. The similarities in plants and animals were said to have resulted from the existence of large land bridges that have since sunk or washed away. So Wegener's data were not regarded as very improbable if his model did not fit the actual history and structure of the earth's surface. The data were, therefore, widely believed to be inconclusive regarding the applicability of Wegener's mobilist model to the actual history of the earth.

The situation in the 1960s was significantly different.

Step 1. Real World. The real-world object is the structure and history of oceans and land masses on the surface of the earth.

Step 2. Model. The model is that, developed by Hess, Vine, and others, in which rising convection currents cause the seafloor to spread. The continents, in this model, move by riding on the top of the moving crust caused by the spreading seafloor.

Step 3. Prediction. The prediction, assuming the earth's magnetic field has indeed reversed directions several times in the past, is that alternating strips of normally and reversed magnetic material will be found parallel to oceanic ridges. Moreover, the pattern formed by the varying widths of these strips will match the pattern of magnetism found in successive layers of solidified lava near volcanoes. It would also match the pattern of magnetic materials in deep-sea sediments.

Step 4. Data. The data consist of measurements of magnetic materials on land, along oceanic ridges, and in sediment cores.

Step 5. Negative Evidence? No. The data and the predictions agree in great detail.

Step 6. Positive Evidence? Were these predictions likely to agree with the data even if Hess' and Vine's model did not provide a good fit to the real world? No. Even proponents of contractionist models regarded it as extremely unlikely that any such data could ever be found. There were no plausible contractionist models that predicted such data. So the data provided very good evidence that the new mobilist models do fit the actual structure and history of the earth's crust.

• EXERCISES

Analyze these reports following the six-point program for evaluating theoretical hypotheses developed in the text. Number and label your steps. Be as clear and concise as you can, keeping in mind that you must say enough to demonstrate that you do know what you are talking about. A simple "yes" or "no" is never a sufficient answer. Some of these reports are taken directly from recent magazine or newspaper articles and are presented here with only minimal editing.

EXERCISE 3.1

THE TYCHONIC SYSTEM OF THE WORLD

Most popular descriptions of the scientific revolution of the seventeenth century, like that in this text, follow Galileo's own presentation in concentrating on the conflict between the Ptolemaic and Copernican systems. Yet, at the time, there was a third alternative, which had been proposed by the equally famous Danish astronomer, Tycho Brahe (1546–1601). In the Tychonic system, the earth remains at the center of the universe and the sun revolves around the earth. The other five planets, however, revolve around the sun, not the earth.

Evaluate the evidence for the Copernican system provided by Galileo's observations of the phases of Venus, this time taking into account Tycho Brahe's alternative model. Does your analysis provide any help in understanding why it took so long for the Copernican hypothesis to become widely accepted?

EXERCISE 3.2

THE DISCOVERY OF NEPTUNE

During the first half of the nineteenth century, astronomers were still working out tables and charts giving the positions of the various planets. In this, they were aided by Newtonian theoretical models. But then the outermost planet, Uranus, caused some difficulties. Its observed orbit differed from what it should have been according to the then best-fitting Newtonian models. And the difference was much too great to be attributed solely to inaccuracies in measurement. They were forced to conclude that their current models were not correct. But they did not give up Newton's theory of celestial mechanics. By that time, there had been so many successful predictions using Newtonian models that they were reluctant to conclude that the general theory could be wrong. Around 1843, the English astronomer J. C. Adams and, somewhat later, the French astronomer Leverrier independently calculated that the observed orbit of Uranus could be explained if there were an additional planet beyond Uranus whose gravitational force produced the deviations from the earlier Newtonian predictions—which, of course, assumed no such planet. Using this more elaborate Newtonian model, Adams and Leverrier were able to calculate just where the new planet should be at any particular time. The planet, named "Neptune" by Leverrier, was observed in 1846, just where it was predicted to be.

EXERCISE 3.3

THE MISSING PLANET: THE STORY OF VULCAN

Like the orbit of Uranus, the observed orbit of the innermost planet, Mercury, failed to fit Newtonian models by amounts that could be reliably measured. Fresh from their discovery of Neptune, many astronomers immediately assumed that there must be yet another planet, closer to the sun than Mercury. Leverrier even named the new planet Vulcan and calculated just where it should be. Although several people claimed to have seen Vulcan, these reports were never substantiated.

EXERCISE 3.4

THE WAVE THEORY OF LIGHT: 1818

After a century in the shadow of Newtonian ideas, according to which light is composed of small particles, wave models of light were revived about 1800, first by an Englishman, Thomas Young, and then by a Frenchman, Augustin Fresnel. Fresnel's model was submitted for a prize offered by the French Academy of Sciences. One of the judges for the academy, S. D. Poisson, deduced that according to Fresnel's model, the shadow of a small circular disk produced by a narrow beam of light should exhibit a bright spot right in the center of the shadow. Poisson and the other judges are reputed to have thought that this refuted Fresnel's hypotheses because they had never heard of there being such a phenomenon and regarded it as highly unlikely to exist. No known particle models predicted such a spot. But when the experiment was carried out in carefully controlled circumstances, there was the spot, just as required by Fresnel's model. Fresnel received the prize in 1818.

EXERCISE 3.5

THE WAVE THEORY OF LIGHT: 1849

During the first half of the nineteenth century, there was a long controversy over the nature of light. According to Newtonians, light consists of small particles moving at high velocities, so that what we call light rays are really Newtonian particles. The competing theory, advocated mainly by French physicists, was based on the idea that light is really an example of a system of waves, like waves on the surface of a calm lake, in a bowl of jelly, or on a vibrating stretched string.Using standard Newtonian models, it was calculated that light should travel faster in water than in air and by a precisely determined amount. Similarly, using wave models, it was calculated that light should travel slower in water than in air, also by a precisely determined amount. It took until 1849 for anyone to design instruments that could measure the velocity of light accurately enough to detect the predicted differences. When the experiment was finally done, it was found that the velocity of light is lower in water and by the amount claimed by the wave theorists.

EXERCISE 3.6

THE OXYGEN THEORY

Lavoisier was not only interested in refuting the phlogiston theory, he sought also to establish his own oxygen theory. In many respects, oxygen models have just the opposite structure of phlogiston models. According to Lavoisier's oxygen model, when combustion occurs a component of normal air (about one-fifth by his measurements) combines with the combustible material. This component of air came to be called oxygen. Analyze Lavoisier's experiment with mercury as a crucial experiment applied to both phlogiston and oxygen hypotheses. It may help you to know that the red powder that formed on top of the mercury is mecuric oxide.

EXERCISE 3.7

CHILDBED FEVER

During the nineteenth century, many women died from what was then called "childbed fever." The first person who had any success in discovering the cause of this disease was a young Viennese physician, Ignaz Semmelweis. In the years 1844 to 1846, the death rate from childbed fever in the First Maternity Division of the Vienna General Hospital averaged roughly 10 percent. Curiously, the rate in the Second Division, in which women were attended by midwives rather than physicians, was only about 2 percent.

Semmelweis tried in vain for 2 years to discover why the rate should be higher in the "better" division. Then one day a fellow physician received a small cut on the finger from a student's scalpel during an autopsy. The colleague died exhibiting symptoms very much like those of childbed fever. Semmelweis wondered whether the disease might be caused by something in "cadaveric matter" that was being transmitted to the women during childbirth on the hands of the physicians and medical students, who spent every morning in the autopsy room before making their rounds.

Semmelweis reasoned that if this idea were right, the death rate could be cut dramatically simply by requiring the physicians and students to wash their hands in a strong cleansing agent before examining their patients. He then insisted that no physicians enter the maternity ward without first washing their hands in a solution of chlorinated lime, which he assumed must be strong enough to remove whatever it was that caused the disease. It worked. The death rate in the First Division for 1848 was less than 2 percent.

EXERCISE 3.8

THE DIGESTIVE SYSTEM

At the beginning of the twentieth century, it was known that the pancreas (a small organ near the stomach) secreted digestive juices into the duodenum (which connects the stomach with the small intestine). This happened whenever partially digested food entered the duodenum from the stomach. The question was whether the signal that started the pancreas working was transmitted by the nervous system or by a chemical substance carried by the blood. At the time, there were known examples of both nerve-stimulated organs and chemical-stimulated organs. No other stimulating mechanism was known. To decide the issue, two physiologists, W. M. Bayliss and E. H. Sterling, cut all the nerves going to and from the duodenum of an experimental animal. All blood vessels to and from the duodenum were left in place. They also inserted tubes to detect flow of digestive juices from the pancreas to the duodenum. The result of this experiment was that, when food entered the duodenum of the experimental animals, the pancreas secreted digestive juices in the normal way.

EXERCISE 3.9

PASTEUR AND ANTHRAX

Louis Pasteur, who died in 1895, is best remembered as inventor of the process we now call pasteurization. For example, carefully heating milk to about 63°C for 30 minutes and then cooling it rapidly allows the milk to be stored below 10°C for several weeks rather than several days. Pasteur's explanation for why the process works is that the heating debilitates the small organisms, "microbes," that produce the substance that causes milk to go sour.

By 1800, the English physician Edward Jenner had shown that innoculation with relatively harmless cowpox provides humans with immunity to deadly smallpox. Pasteur theorized that smallpox and many other diseases are produced by microbes. He suspected that debilitating, but not killing, the microbes would allow one to generalize Jenner's process of "vaccination" (from *vacca*, meaning *cow*) to other diseases.

In 1880, nearly 10 percent of the sheep, cows, and goats in France were dying of anthrax. From dead animals, Pasteur extracted material containing the anthrax bacillus and experimented with ways of attenuating it. Eventually, he discovered that heating for 8 days at between 42°C and 44°C would do the trick.

To convince the general public of his result, Pasteur arranged a public demonstration experiment. On May 5, 1881, at a farm near the town of Pouilly-le-Fort, 24 sheep, 6 cows, and 1 goat were inoculated with an attenuated anthrax bacillus. On May 31, all 31 inoculated animals, plus a similar assortment of 29 other healthy animals that had not been inoculated, were injected with fully active anthrax bacilli. By the end of the day on June 2, all the unvaccinated sheep were dead and all the unvaccinated cows very sick. All the vaccinated animals were still perfectly healthy. Pictures of healthy animals surrounded by the corpses of those that had not been inoculated made very good press.

By June of the next year, roughly 300,000 animals, including 25,000 cows, had been vaccinated with Pasteur's vaccine. And the mortality rate from anthrax had dropped to nearly 0.5 percent.

EXERCISE 3.10

ISLAND BIOGEOGRAPHY

In addition to the Galapagos Islands, Darwin and the Beagle also visited the Cape Verde Islands, which lie in the Atlantic Ocean roughly 300 miles west of the coast of what is now Senegal. The two sets of islands are very similar, being geologically relatively young archipelagoes of volcanic origin. Yet the bird species on the two sets of islands are very different. The bird species on the Cape Verde Islands, however, are similar to species on the nearby African continent. In his later work, Darwin took his less extensive observations on the Cape Verde Islands as additional evidence for his theory of evolution by natural selection.

EXERCISE 3.11

A CONFIRMATION OF CONTINENTAL DRIFT

Some of the best tests of hypotheses involving continental drift have become possible only since the development of accurate methods of determining the age of rocks, methods based on the examination of the products of radioactive decay. The following is taken from an article ("The Confirmation of Continental Drift") that appeared in *Scientific American* for April 1968. The particular hypothesis at issue is that Africa and South America are part of the system of land masses that have broken up and drifted apart. The investigators write:

> Of special interest to us at the start was the sharp boundary between the 2,000-million-year-old geological province in Ghana, the Ivory Coast and westward from these countries, and the 600-million-year-old province in Dahomey, Nigeria and east. This boundary heads in a southwesterly direction into the ocean near Accra in Ghana. If Brazil had been joined to Africa 500 million years ago, the boundary between the two provinces should enter South America close to the town of Sao Luis on the northeast coast of Brazil. Our first order of business was therefore to date the rocks from the vicinity of Sao Luis.
>
> To our surprise and delight the ages fell into two groups: 2,000 million years on the west and 600 million years on the east of a boundary line that lay exactly where it had been predicted. Apparently a 2,000-million-year-old piece of West Africa had been left on the continent of South America.

EXERCISE 3.12

CLUES TO THE DRIFT OF CONTINENTS AND THE DIVERGENCE OF SPECIES

In 1910, Alfred Wegener, a German meteorologist and explorer, began a long quest for evidence supporting the seemingly preposterous notion that the continents drift hither and yon. He eventually found it in a strange guise—the global distribution of marsupials, animals such as kangaroos and opossums that carry their young in a pouch. Marsupials, Wegener pointed out, are largely confined to Australia and South America, which are separated by thousands of miles of ocean. Yet, "even the parasites of the Australian and South American marsupials are the same," he wrote. The phenomenon, he concluded, "dates back to the time when Australia was still joined to South America via Antarctica." That Antarctica provided the link between the Americas and Australia 65 million years ago, long after the great southern continent of the era, Gondwanaland, began breaking up to form Africa, South America, India, Australia, and Antarctica, has now been dramatically confirmed by the discovery of fossil marsupial bones in the one-time land bridge. When Antarctica linked Australia and South America 80 million years ago, it lay in a more hospitable latitude than now, facilitating passage of temperate-zone animals. In 1989, search for fossil evidence of the link, financed by the National Science Foundation, focused on Seymour Island off the Antarctic Penninsula, famous for the fossils of giant penguins. In February, a party led by Dr. William J. Zinsmeister of the Institute for Polar Studies at Ohio State University spent 4 weeks combing the area. They found nothing until the end of their stay, when they returned to a site rich in penguin remains. Michael O. Woodburne of the University of California at Riverside spotted a marsupial jaw bone. The scientists soon found four fragments from two animals, which resembled a species living during the same era—40 million years ago—at the southern end of South America. The teeth characterize berry-eating marsupials, says Zinsmeister. He believes the animals, about 7 inches long, lived in vegetation near what was then shoreline.

EXERCISE 3.13

PROJECT

Look up an historical account of a scientific episode involving some theoretical hypothesis or theory. You might begin with an account in a standard textbook for a science course. Then you could look up the same episode in an encyclopedia or in a book on the history of science. There may even exist a whole book on the episode in question. Analyze the case following the six-step program developed in the text. Depending on how extensive an example you have uncovered, you may have to do several analyses involving different sets of data or different experiments.

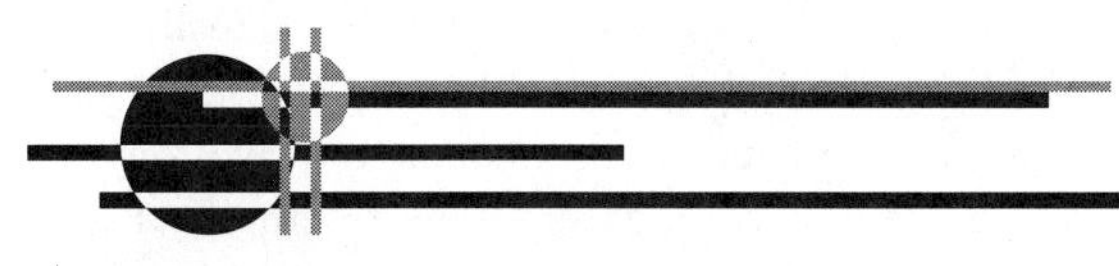

CHAPTER 4
MARGINAL SCIENCE

Up to now, the examples we have studied all belong within the mainstream of the Western scientific tradition. In this chapter, by contrast, we examine several examples whose very status as science would often be questioned. It is important to gain experience in evaluating such examples because the popular media contain many instances of purportedly scientific reports whose conclusions are, in fact, highly questionable. Often no indication is given that these instances are any different from cases clearly within the mainstream practice of modern science.

Many textbooks on philosophy, logic, or science attempt to provide simple criteria that we could use to distinguish genuine science from **pseudoscience.** I will not follow this strategy because I think it is impossible to devise the required criteria. For example, it is often said that science involves experimentation and pseudoscience lacks experiments. However, there are no experiments in astrophysics, which everyone admits is a genuine science. On the other hand, parapsychologists do perform experiments, and many people would regard parapsychology as a pseudoscience. I suspect there are similar counterexamples for any simple criterion that might be proposed to sort the supposedly scientific sheep from the pseudoscientific goats.

Rather than seeking special principles to draw a sharp line between science and pseudoscience, we will simply apply to these new cases the program we have already developed. The question for us is not whether a particular inquiry is genuinely scientific. The question is simply whether the data cited do or do not provide evidence for a proposed hypothesis. We will find that there are types of inquiries for which the data cited typically turn out to be **inconclusive.** Such inquiries, we will say, are instances of **marginal** science. This leaves open the possibility that similar inquiries might one day move into the scientific mainstream.

The approach we are taking presumes only that there is some sort of model being proposed and that some data are being cited in support of the hypothesis that the proposed model represents the real world. So, the only sorts of inquiries excluded from our approach would be those that either (1) deny using models to represent the world or (2) deny the relevance of an appeal to empirical data in support of the corresponding hypotheses. In the first case, I would say that we are not dealing with a scientific inquiry at all. Some studies of poetry could be examples of such nonscientific inquiries.

In the second case, if one makes no appeal to data about what has actually been experienced in the world, what could be the basis for claims that the proposed models do represent the world? In the past, many people have claimed to have ways of authenticating models as representing the world without appealing to empirical data. And some people still do. Claims regarding religious doctrines often take this form. So this dispute can be both interesting and important, but we do not pursue it in this text. Science has become so prominent in Western culture that even advocates of the most outlandish hypotheses typically cite empirical data in support of their claims. In all these cases, we can apply our standard program for evaluating the proposed hypotheses.

It is a curious fact about modern culture that subjects on the margins of established science go through phases ranging from widespread interest to relative obscurity. At any particular time, a few will be relatively popular, whereas others languish. What follows is a survey of some perennial favorites.

4.1 FREUDIAN PSYCHOLOGY

Our first case, Freudian psychology, is clearly a marginal science. A century after Freud's early work, the categories of his theory have become part of everyday language. Yet the scientific status of his theories continues to be a subject of much debate within the scientific community.

Sigmund Freud was born in 1856 and lived most of his life in Vienna. He studied medicine and then spent more than a decade conducting research in neurophysiology. Unable to continue making a living doing research, he began attempting to treat people who, because he knew something about the brain and nervous system, came to him seeking help for various psychological disorders. He spent the rest of his life developing a theory of the mind and a technique **(psychoanalysis)** for treating people with psychological problems. Freud's theory and the clinical technique developed side by side over several decades until his death in 1939. His evidence for the correctness of the theory came primarily from his clinical practice. What follows is a partial sketch of Freud's mature theory.

FREUD'S THEORY

In Freud's model, the mind has several different structures, each with distinct characteristics and functions. One structure consists of three parts, the **unconscious** mind, the **preconscious** mind, and the **conscious** mind. The difference is a matter of awareness. We are not aware of things in our unconscious mind but are aware of things in our conscious mind. Objects of the preconscious mind can, with special efforts, sometimes be brought to awareness.

Another structure also consists of three parts: the id, ego, and superego. The **id** consists of primitive, primarily biological, desires whose fulfillment produces pleasure. The **superego** contains the rules of proper behavior that are learned from one's parents and others. It corresponds to what we normally call our "conscience." The **ego** is the part of the mind that engages the world and attempts to balance the demands of the id with the requirements of the superego. The id is mostly unconscious whereas the superego is mostly conscious. These structures are pictured in Figure 4.1.

FIGURE 4.1

The elements of Freud's model of the human mind.

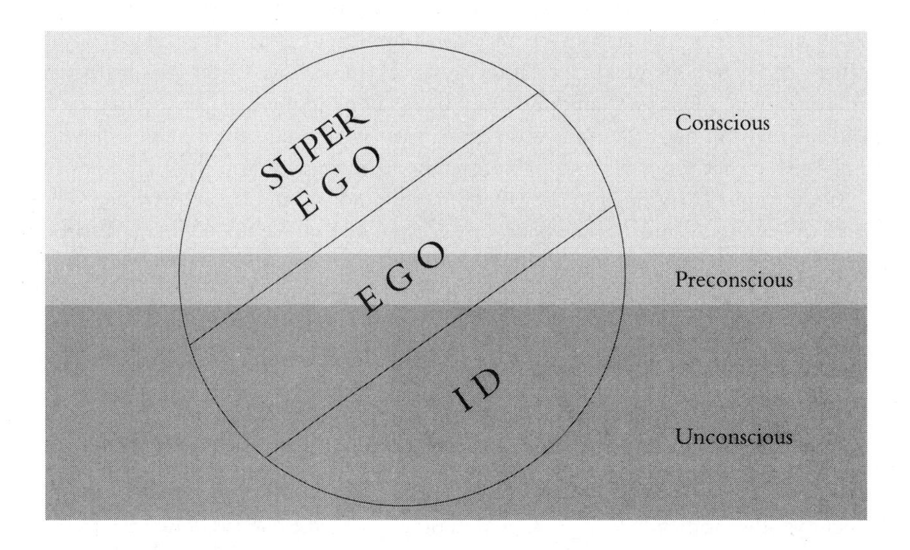

Freud also constructed a model of psychological **development** based on his model of the mind's structure. A young child, he said, is ruled primarily by its id. Early in childhood, boys and girls develop Oedipal, or Electra, complexes in which they form an emotional attachment to the parent of the opposite sex and reject the parent of the same sex. Thus, for example, Freud thought that little girls typically love their fathers and dislike their mothers. Successful ego development requires adapting to the demand of the superego that one identify with the parent of the same sex.

Caught between the conflicting demands of the id and the superego, the ego develops a number of **defense mechanisms** for coping with the stress. One is to **repress** the demands of the id by pushing them farther down into the unconscious. Another is to **project** thoughts or feelings from their real object onto another object. Operating defense mechanisms requires lots of psychic energy. In some cases, the ego may not be strong enough to cope successfully with the demands placed on it and loses touch with reality, directing the person to perform highly inappropriate, "psychotic," actions. Shakespeare's character, Lady Macbeth, always washing her hands, provides a classic example of such a psychosis.

Finally, Freud thought that psychological disorders could be cured if the patient could bring the source of the conflict into consciousness and come to understand its true causes. It is the job of the therapist, he thought, to help the patient perform this task.

THE CASE OF LITTLE HANS

Little Hans was the son of a Viennese physician who was also a friend of Freud's and a follower of his teachings. In the fall of 1907, 4-year-old Hans developed an extreme fear of horses, so much so that he refused to go outside, where there were many horses in the streets pulling carriages. He even expressed the fear that a horse might come into his bedroom and bite him. His parents were much perplexed, so the father took Little Hans to see Dr. Freud.

Freud learned that Hans had spent the previous summer in a resort some distance from Vienna. There he had many playmates and spent much time alone with his mother during periods when the father was back in Vienna tending to his patients. Sometimes, when Hans was anxious about being alone in the dark, his mother let him spend the night in her bed. Hans was also alarmed when he heard someone else being warned not to get too close to a horse because it might bite him.

On returning to Vienna in the fall, the family moved to a larger apartment where Hans had few friends and his own bedroom. Earlier, he had shared his parents' bedroom. Hans' father now objected to his coming into the parents' bedroom in the mornings. And Hans spend much less time with his mother, there now being a nursemaid who would take him for walks in the park. On one of these walks, Hans was very frightened by a horse falling down in the street. It was shortly after this episode that Hans developed his extreme fear of horses. He expressed particular fear of the things the horses wore around their eyes and mouth.

FREUD'S HYPOTHESIS

Freud hypothesized that Hans was undergoing an Oedipal crisis. His id missed his mother's companionship and attention. But his ego was unconsciously afraid his father would be angry with him for wanting to spend more time with his mother. However, because Hans' superego had been taught that one should love one's parents, his ego repressed his fear of his father and displaced it onto horses. Why horses? Well, he had learned to fear being bitten by horses. Freud also thought that Hans must be associating the blinders and muzzles of the horses with his father's glasses and beard.

Applying his own theories to the case, Freud asked the child if his father's glasses and beard did not remind him of the blinders and muzzles of the horses. He then suggested to the child that maybe he really was afraid his father would disapprove of his desire for more time with the mother. Freud also asked the father to reassure Hans that he was not really angry an him for wanting more of the mother's attentions. Little Hans engaged in some symbolic defiance of the father. Over the next few days it seemed to the father that the symptoms did lessen somewhat. It was several months later, however, before the symptoms disappeared.

Analysis

Step 1. Real World. The real-world object of study is Little Hans and his fear of horses.

Step 2. Model. The model is Freud's model of psychological development in which little boys typically develop emotional attachments to their mothers and fear of their fathers. Because children are taught to love both their parents and boys to identify with their fathers, a psychological conflict may arise. To cope with such conflicts, a boy's ego may project the fear of the father onto another object, leading to abnormal behavior. So Freud suggested that Hans might be projecting his fear of his father onto horses.

Step 3. Prediction. Freud's model of clinical practice implies that bringing the true conflicts to consciousness and resolving them will eliminate the abnormal behavior. So, the model predicts that by making Hans aware of the real source of his fear and reassuring him that nothing bad will happen if he admits his real feelings, his fear of horses will go away.

Step 4. Data. After treatment, Hans' fear of horses appeared to diminish and finally disappeared several months later.

Step 5. Negative Evidence? No. The data and the prediction do pretty much agree.

Step 6. Positive Evidence? Would the data have been likely to agree with the prediction even if Freud's model did not really fit the case? Are there other plausible models that would have yielded the same predictions?

Standard descriptions of this case do not mention other models, so we are left on our own to evaluate the question in Step 6. But it requires only a rudimentary knowledge of young children to come up with very plausible rival models.

Everyone knows that children desire attention and affection. By expressing fear of the dark, Hans gained the privilege of sleeping in his mother's bed. That tactic did not work with the father. Developing an extreme fear of horses, however, did gain Hans considerable attention, even from the father, who took him off to see his friend Freud. Having gained the attention he desired, Little Hans' symptoms gradually declined.

That the symptoms should go away in several months was, in any case, quite predictable, simply because children around the age of 4 are typically very changeable. They will outgrow most "phases" in a few months no matter what one does. Hans's fear of horses can be seen as a somewhat extreme phase but hardly that unusual for a 4-year-old.

The conclusion is that the results of this clinical case do not really provide much evidence for the correctness of Freud's theory (or for the efficacy of his method of treatment). Neither do they refute it. The data cited are inconclusive regarding Freud's hypotheses.

4.2 ASTROLOGY

Most scholars and scientists regard astrology as a marginal science at best. Yet, polls indicate that as many as one-third of all Americans believe that there is something to the practice of astrology. Millions read their horoscopes in the daily newspaper. Special monthly magazines with more detailed daily horoscopes are available at news stands. There are also roughly 10,000 "professional" astrologers who make at least part of their living casting horoscopes and giving advice based on astrological lore.

The practice of astrology goes back to the Babylonians (about 2000 BC), to whom we also owe the beginnings of astronomy. The versions of astrology practiced today derive mainly from classical Greece (400 BC to 200 AD). The fact that the familiar signs of the zodiac are divided into earth signs, air signs, fire signs, and water signs is based on the Greek theory that everything is made of four basic elements: earth, air, fire, and water. The major classical works on astrology were written by the second-century Greek astronomer, Ptolemy, the same person who developed the theory of the universe that Copernicus and Galileo challenged fourteen centuries later. Even some of the major figures in the scientific revolution of the seventeenth century, such as Johannes Kepler, combined the study of astrology with their work in astronomy.

At a time when the sun, moon, and planets were associated with gods (Jupiter, Mars, and so on) who were thought to influence human life, it was not unreasonable to suppose that the positions of the sun, moon, and planets at our birth might have some influence on our subsequent life. It also helps to believe that the earth is the center of the universe and not merely a middle-sized planet in orbit around a middle-sized star.

These beliefs have long since been given up. It is now well known that the gravitational force of the planets on the earth is minuscule. This book exerts a much greater gravitational force on you right now than the planet Mars ever could. Where you now sit, the radio waves picked up by your portable radio are many times stronger than radio waves from Jupiter, and the magnetic field of the magnet that drives the radio's speaker is many times stronger than the magnetic field originating in any astronomical body other than the earth itself. There is just no good scientific reason to believe that there are any forces of the type assumed by astrology. Yet people continue to believe in astrology. Why?

In interviews with people who put at least some stock in astrological descriptions and predictions, the most common answer to the question why they believe in astrology is simply "it works." In saying that it works, people seem to be claiming that the descriptions and predictions based on astrological theories are realized in practice. What sorts of descriptions and predictions are these? Do they provide evidence that the models of astrological theory do fit the real world?

Looking up my own sun sign (Sagittarius) in an astrological magazine, I find the following description:

> It represents the intended capture of unknown knowledge, wisdom, truth, and perfection in the philosophies. It represents all things dealing with higher thought, which bring people greater awareness of themselves and their place in the universe. Education, courts, religion, and literature are represented here.

The daily "prediction" for a typical day for my sign reads something like this:

> Your personality will glow; you'will attract much attention with charm and pleasing ways. Make work enthusiastic, especially if it is linked with younger people. Use ingenuity and skills that are at their height of performance. Be generous financially; contribute to a worthy cause. Health is excellent, and travel aspects are good. Carry out a plan you know is valuable in practical ways. Love breakups are possible, some dishonesty in another's attitude.

As a matter of fact, I find it fairly easy to interpret much of both the description and the prediction as being true of me in general and of my actions on a particular day. So let us analyze the relevance of this data for the hypothesis that astrological theories do fit the real world.

Analysis

Step 1. Real World. The subject matter includes the personality, attributes, and everyday actions of ordinary people, myself included.

Step 2. Models. The models are those provided by traditional astrological theory in which the positions of the sun, moon, planets, and stars at the time of peoples' births determine (or at least influence) their later personalities, attributes, and everyday actions in ways described in these models.

Step 3. Predictions. The predictions in this case are those given in the excerpts quoted above.

Step 4. Data. The data, in my own case, are my personality, attributes, and the actions I performed on the day in question.

Step 5. Negative Evidence? No. The data and the predictions do agree pretty well.

Step 6. Positive Evidence? Were the predictions likely to agree with the data even if the models of astrological theory do not provide a good fit to the real world? Yes. For reasons to be discussed below, these predictions were fairly likely to agree with the data whether or not the models in question fit the real world. So the agreement between the actual data and the predictions fails to provide any evidence in favor of the hypotheses that make up astrological theory.

There are two general reasons why the predictions based on astrological models were likely to agree with the data concerning my attitudes and activities even if these models exhibit little resemblance to the real world. These reasons deserve special attention because they highlight typical features of the predictions associated with many marginal sciences.

THE PREDICTIONS ARE VAGUE

The descriptions and predictions derived from astrological theory are stated in quite general terms. Anyone with a little imagination can easily see themselves in the descriptions. The description for Sagittarians, for example, seems to fit a university professor well. But read the description for Gemini:

> It is the symbol of the negative and affirmative mental aspects; the combination of different ideas that are joined in an earthly and idealistic decision; an adaptable memory for facts; communication and the search for knowledge.

That fits me as well as the description for my own sign.

Similarly, the daily predictions and advice are formulated in a vague way that makes it easy to interpret them as both relevant and true. "You will attract much attention with charm and pleasing ways." How much attention? From whom? What kind of charm? What sorts of "pleasing ways." Because answers to these questions are missing, this prediction is very likely to be classified as fulfilled for anyone on almost any given day.

Here we have an *alternative* explanation for the agreement between the predictions and the data. They agree because the predictions are framed in a vague form that can readily be interpreted as holding true for almost anyone. So a fairly good agreement between data and prediction is very likely quite apart from any fit between astrological models and the real world. There is, therefore, little basis for taking the agreement between data and predictions as providing evidence that the models of astrological theory fit the real world.

THERE ARE MULTIPLE PREDICTIONS

As exhibited in the above excerpts, astrological descriptions and predictions generally have several parts. The typical daily horoscope contains at least a half-dozen predictions or recommendations. This increases the chances that one or two will stand out both as particularly relevant and correct. In general, it is fairly likely that one or two of a half-dozen vague predictions should be easily interpreted as having come true—whether or not the models of astrological theory bear any relation to the real world.

A standard deck of cards provides a useful analog model. There is only 1 chance in 52 of getting the ace of spades in a single draw. The chances of getting the ace increase, however, if you are allowed to make several draws.

The fact that there are multiple predictions, in addition to each individual prediction being fairly vague, strengthens the *alternative* explanation of the agreement between the predictions and the data. If there are many predictions, that increases the chances of one or two appearing to be correct. If they are all fairly vague, that makes it difficult to argue that any particular prediction is clearly incorrect. The result is a strong impression that the predictions are, by and large, correct. This impression, however, may be mainly a response to the vagueness and multiplicity of the predictions and have little bearing on the actual fit between astrological models and the world.

ASTROLOGY AS AN INTERPRETATIVE FRAMEWORK

When people say that astrology works, they may mean much more than simply that the descriptions and predictions of astrological theory seem to come true. They may regularly use astrological categories to *interpret* both their own actions and the actions of other people and find these interpretations highly satisfying. "Why is Linda always so self-assured?" "Oh, she's an Aries, and Aries are like that." Nevertheless, the fact that astrological lore can be used in this way may have little to do with how well astrological models actually fit the real world. It may simply be due to the extreme flexibility of the framework and to the fact that people who use it in this way seldom have any interest in noting, or remembering, cases in which specific predictions fail. It is an interesting and distressing fact that many people can find an interpretative framework such as astrology to be highly satisfying even though the models that underlie it may actually bear little resemblance to the real world.

4.3 EXTRATERRESTRIAL VISITATION

It is a recurring theme in American popular culture that the earth has been or is now being visited by aliens from another world. There are many variations on this theme. Within the community of people familiar with these matters, this is known as the hypothesis of *extraterrestrial visitation* (ETV). Strictly speaking, ETV is a special version of the broader view that there are genuine *unidentified flying objects* (UFOs). Those who believe in ETV think they have an explanation for the existence of UFOs. One might think there are genuine UFOs, however, without believing that they have an extraterrestrial origin.

As an example of this genre of theory, let us look at Erich von Daniken's *Chariots of the Gods?* This book is reputed to have sold more than 30 million copies in 35 languages. Whatever its scientific success, it has certainly been a commercial success.

Von Daniken claims that the ETV hypothesis is true and, moreover, that the supposed visitations took place early in human history. He thus proposes to explain various happenings in the early history of the human race as being the direct result of actions by these early extraterrestrial visitors. In support of his claims, he produces many examples of archaeological or anthropological findings that otherwise seem difficult to explain.

Many different cultures have myths about gods who came from the heavens and performed great feats. Why is it that so many cultures, widely separated in place and time, have myths of this type?

In Egypt and in Peru, there are huge temples, pyramids, and other structures constructed out of cut stones weighing many tons. How could ordinary men have constructed such things with only the simple tools then available?

The plain of Nazca in Peru exhibits what resemble roads cut in patterns. It is difficult to imagine why or how these were constructed.

On Easter Island in the Pacific Ocean, there are hundreds of stone statues weighing up to 80 tons erected a fair distance from the source of the rock from which they were carved. Who could have carved them? How could they have been moved and set up on a remote island that could not support more than a few thousand people?

Von Daniken has an easy answer for all these questions. These things are all explainable as the direct result of the activities of ancient astronauts. Von Daniken assumes that any beings capable of reaching earth from somewhere else in the universe would have no difficulty performing feats such as building pyramids. Now let us subject von Daniken's claims to a standard analysis.

Analysis

It is already revealing of Von Daniken's reasoning that one finds it almost necessary to consider the data before the predictions. His model of the ancient astronauts themselves is not detailed enough to generate specific predictions about what they might have done while visiting the earth.

Step 1. Real World. The subject matter encompasses parts of human history on earth.

Step 2. Model. Von Daniken's model of human history includes visitations by ancient astronauts, extraterrestrial beings who performed various feats while on earth.

Step 4. Data. The data include (1) the existence of similar myths about gods from the sky among widely separated cultures, (2) the existence of pyramids in

Egypt and Peru, (3) the patterns cut on the plain of Nazca, (4) the statues on Easter Island, and other similar things.

Step 3. Predictions. The prediction is that we can now find all the unusual things noted above.

Step 5. Negative Evidence? No. The data and the prediction do agree. All the things von Daniken's model says we should find have indeed been found.

Step 6. Positive Evidence? Would our finding all the things von Daniken discussed be likely even if there had been no visitations by ancient astronauts? Are there other plausible explanations for the existence of the data as cited?

As usual, everything depends on how we answer these questions.

AN ALTERNATIVE MODEL

There is one obvious alternative explanation for the agreement between von Daniken's predictions and the data that is quite independent of any similarity between von Daniken's model and the real world. This is that von Daniken deliberately constructed his model to yield predictions agreeing with the known data. Such a process of model construction requires only imagination. Almost anyone can do it. Even you or I. Let me show you how.

Imagine a model in which there once was an advanced race of humanoids fairly similar to us who evolved on the earth several thousands of years before the earliest peoples now known to archaeologists and anthropologists. According to this model, these early humanoids developed a fairly advanced technology that made them superior to other evolving prehuman primates. Using their advanced technology, these humanoids moved out from their original home in the Middle East and established outposts in Asia, South America, Easter Island, and so on. We can imagine that they even developed large ships and airplanes. It was this race of early humanoids that was responsible for the statues, temples, and other unusual things that we now find in isolated parts of the world. Moreover, it is the memory of this race that is recorded in the myths of various peoples around the world. Unfortunately, when it came to social organization, these advanced humanoids were no wiser than present-day humans and began warring among themselves. Eventually, they destroyed themselves and most of their artifacts. All that remains are the few traces that present anthropologists and archaeologists cannot explain. My hypothesis makes all these things easily understandable.

My terrestrial model, which does not require ETV, predicts exactly the same data as von Daniken's model incorporating ETV. And my model is initially no less plausible than his. So the agreement between von Daniken's predictions and the data is *not* necessarily unlikely if his hypothesis is false. Thus, the agreement between the data and his predictions does not provide evidence that his model fits, no more than it provides evidence that my model fits. Here, it is useful to remember Halley's successful prediction of the return of a comet 76 years later. In this case, ensuring the agreement between prediction and data was beyond the power of anyone's imagination. The only alternative to Newton's model was the improbable supposition that another, very similar, comet just happened to come by at exactly the right time, 76 years later.

WHAT ABOUT THE DATA?

Writers such as von Daniken often have a good intuitive sense of how scientific data are evaluated. He devotes many pages trying to convince the reader of the fantastic nature of the artifacts he describes. This is to make it seem that the existence of such things would be highly unlikely unless something like his hypothesis is accepted. Average readers, however, have little detailed knowledge of the things he describes. They are dependent on the author to supply the data. In this situation, the author may be tempted to distort or withhold known facts to make his case appear better than it really is. It seems clear that von Daniken succumbed to this temptation.

In his discussion of the statues on Easter Island, von Daniken cites the work of the anthropologist-adventurer Thor Heyerdahl. In the book cited, Heyerdahl reports actually observing some modern-day inhabitants of Easter Island carving, moving, and setting up statues similar to those originally found on the island. Using only a crude wooden sled, it took fewer than 200 men to move a 12-ton statue. Using large poles as levers and stones to prop it up, it took 12 men only 18 days to set up a statue weighing about 25 tons. Heyerdahl's book even contains a picture showing the statue in the process of being set up. Thus, most of what von Daniken says about this case is just plain false. There is a relatively simple, perfectly natural explanation of how these statues could have come to be where they are.

The moral for our purposes is that it takes more than good reasoning not to be misled into thinking that there is evidence for a hypothesis when, in fact, there is none. You have to learn when to be suspicious of what is presented as data and when to check further on your own. And you have to take the time to do it. In general, you should maintain a healthy skepticism regarding things that seem to go against most of what you already think you know. Sometimes you even have to consider authors' motives. Are they interested in learning the truth, or are they primarily concerned with attracting attention and selling books?

4.4 REINCARNATION

Reincarnation is the very ancient belief, found in many Eastern religions, that the "spirits" of people who die move to inhabit the new bodies of people being born. The spirits are said to be "reincarnated" in a new body. This is still a widely held belief, even in the United States. It has recently been popularized, for example, by the movie actress Shirley MacLaine.

What sort of empirical evidence could there be for such a belief? In this century, appeal is often made to evidence that has been produced by hypnosis. It is a fact that people under hypnosis sometimes recount stories that seem to be from another life. Professional hypnotists interested in such phenomena sometimes speak of "regressing" a person to an earlier life. The idea is that, under hypnosis, the spirit remembers events from an earlier incarnation.

IN SEARCH OF BRIDEY MURPHY

In the United States, the most famous case of regression is described in a book first published in 1956 entitled *In Search of Bridey Murphy*. The author, Morey Bernstein, was a businessman who first learned hypnotism as a hobby. In the book, he reproduces transcripts of tape recordings made during a half-dozen sessions with a woman given the fictitious name of Ruth Simmons. All the sessions were witnessed by several other people. Although Ruth Simmons was said never even to have visited Ireland, much less lived there, under hypnosis she related many details about her supposed early nineteenth-century life in County Cork, Ireland, as a woman named Bridey Murphy.

The transcripts contain detailed answers to a variety of questions about the whole life of Bridey Murphy. There was the time in her childhood when she and her brother Duncan pulled the straw off the roof of the family's barn. There was her marriage to Brian MacCarthy, who she first met at the age of 17, officiated by Father John. And there was her death, childless, at the age of 66. There is even mention of small towns that do not appear on maps but do nevertheless exist. Moreover, she gave her answers in an Irish brogue quite different from her normal speaking voice. After one session, she does an Irish Morning Jig as part of a posthypnotic suggestion. Although Bernstein does not come right out and say so, the clearly implied conclusion of the book was that the woman called Ruth Simmons was, in fact, the reincarnation of an Irish woman named Bridey Murphy. So reincarnation is a reality.

Analysis

Step 1. Real World. The real world of this example is our ordinary world of people, places, and things. Ruth Simmons is a particular ordinary person.

Step 2. Model. According to the model, ordinary people are reincarnations of the spirits of other ordinary people who lived in other places at earlier times. In particular, Ruth Simmons is said to be the reincarnation of the spirit that earlier was incarnated in Bridey Murphy.

Step 3. Prediction. According to the model, people under hypnosis can sometimes recall details of their earlier incarnations. So maybe Ruth Simmons could recount details of her supposed earlier life as Bridey Murphy.

Step 4. Data. Under hypnosis, Ruth Simmons recounts, in an Irish brogue, details she says were from her earlier life as Bridey Murphy.

Step 5. Negative Evidence? No. The prediction and the data do agree.

Step 6. Positive Evidence? Would the data have been likely to agree with the prediction even if reincarnation does not occur? Are there other plausible models that could explain Ruth Simmons' ability under hypnosis to give details, in a brogue, regarding the life of a woman in Ireland nearly 200 years ago?

Surely there must be other, more ordinary ways that someone who had never been to Ireland could be able, under hypnosis, to recount details about nineteenth-century life in Ireland, even in a brogue. Near the end of his book, Bernstein does consider some such alternatives (e.g., that Ruth Simmons was recounting something she had heard or read). But such possibilities are quickly rejected as not compatible with the spontaneity of the answers given under hypnosis, her speaking with a brogue, and her being able to do an Irish jig. The book, however, does not provide the reader with enough information about Ruth Simmons' own early life even to suggest other alternative models for this case. So, readers are left to their own imaginations.

Might not Ruth Simmons have had a grandmother born in Ireland who could have told her granddaughter stories in a brogue about her earlier life in Ireland? This grandmother could even have taught Ruth the Morning Jig. To make this possibility more interesting, we could imagine that Ruth Simmons had a genuinely "split personality." One was her regular personality, and the other was an imaginary person she unconsciously constructed from her grandmother's stories. It is well known that multiple personalities can be uncovered through hypnosis and that the hidden personalities can speak quite spontaneously with different tones of voice. Nor should Bernstein himself have been unaware of this possibility. It was much discussed at the time he wrote his book. Indeed, one of the most famous cases of multiple personalities was described in the book *The Three Faces of Eve,* published just a year after Bernstein's own book on Bridey Murphy.

Even with only such possibilities to rely on, one should regard the data presented as being inconclusive regarding the existence of reincarnation in the real world. A nice thing about this case is that we need not rest content with our imaginations. After publication of Bernstein's book, a Chicago newspaper reporter took up the case and published his findings. He learned that Ruth Simmons was really a housewife from Colorado named Virginia Tighe. Digging into Mrs. Tighe's past, he learned she had an Irish aunt that had entertained her as a child with stories about Ireland. Moreover, in high school, Mrs. Tighe had been in a drama program in which she had learned to deliver lines in a heavy Irish brogue. Finally, a neighbor lady who had lived across from Mrs. Tighe's family for many years recounted how the young Virginia had been entranced by her stories of life in Ireland. The neighbor lady's maiden name was Bridey Murphy.

It does not matter for our purposes whether Virginia Tighe lied to Morley Bernstein or whether she really believed she had been regressed through hypnosis to an earlier life. Nor does it matter whether Bernstein himself was completely honest. Even taking his account at face value, we have a relatively ordinary alternative explanation of how, under hypnosis, Ruth Simmons could have come to relate the events she did and in the manner she did. She was remembering things that, as a child, she had learned from others and recounting them, under hypnosis, as her own experiences and in an accent she had practiced in high school.

4.5 EXTRASENSORY PERCEPTION

A 1990 Gallup Poll reported that nearly half of adult Americans believe in the existence of some form of **extrasensory perception** (ESP). In fact, the term *extrasensory perception* covers several different kinds of supposed phenomena. One is **clairvoyance,** the ability to "see" things not present (e.g., things far away). Another is **precognition,** the ability to "see" or "experience" things before they happen. A third is **telepathy,** the ability to "read" another person's mind. There is also a related idea, that of **psychokinesis,** the ability to change physical objects (e.g., bending spoons) just by thinking about them.

CLAIRVOYANCE

Let us focus on clairvoyance because it is a phenomenon that everyone can at least imagine thinking they have experienced. The typical "experience of clairvoyance" resembles the following scenario. Jack and Jill are best friends. One day, for no apparent reason, Jill experiences a sudden fright that convinces her that something terrible has happened to Jack. She tries to put the feeling out of her mind. Later that day, she learns that, in fact, Jack has been badly injured in an automobile accident. It turns out that the accident occurred right about the time she had the feeling that something terrible had happened. Jill finds herself seriously contemplating the possibility that clairvoyance is a reality. Does she indeed have evidence for this belief?

Analysis

Step 1. Real World. The real world of this example is our ordinary world of people, places, and things. Jill is a particular ordinary person.

Step 2. Model. According to the model, at least some ordinary people are clairvoyant on some occasions. In particular, Jill's feeling that something terrible had happened to Jack is said to be an example of clairvoyant perception.

Step 3. Prediction. According to the model, people can perceive events outside the range of their normal sense organs. So, maybe Jill could sense Jack's accident.

Step 4. Data. Jill did have a clear feeling that something terrible had happened to Jack at what turned out to be the time of his accident.

Step 5. Negative Evidence? No. The prediction and the data do agree.

Step 6. Positive Evidence? Would the data have been likely to agree with the prediction even if clairvoyance does not occur? Are there other plausible models that could explain the coincidence of Jill's experience with Jack's real accident?

What makes this sort of scenario convincing as evidence for clairvoyance is the apparently extreme improbability of Jill's experience of dread occurring at about the same time as the very thing she dreaded was, in fact, happening. How could she have known something bad was happening to Jack other than by some form of ESP?

Just how improbable is something such as the coincidence of Jill's feeling with Jack's accident? Not as improbable as we might think. In the first place, feelings such as Jill's are typically somewhat vague. She did not have the distinct impression that Jack was in an automobile accident at the corner of Fifth and Main streets. She only had a strong feeling that *something* terrible had happened to Jack. Lots of things could have produced a similar coincidence. Second, this was most likely not the only time Jill had ever had a similar feeling of disaster regarding Jack. As in our case, she tried to put those feelings out of her mind. And when, in fact, nothing bad had happened, she forgot about the earlier feeling of dread. This time differed only in that something terrible did happen. Moreover, Jack's being in a bad accident is something that itself had some probability of happening whether or not Jill had any feeling that something terrible had happened. So there is a plausible alternative model, namely, that Jill's feeling of dread and Jack's accident happening at roughly the same time was just an ordinary coincidence. It was not something very likely to happen, but not something fantastically improbable either.

Finally, Jack and Jill are not the only people in the world. There are millions of people like them. Every day some of these millions of people have unexpected feelings of dread regarding their loved ones. And every day something terrible happens to some of those millions of people who are those loved ones. So, it is practically certain that, on any given day, some people who are the object of feelings of dread turn out to be people to whom something terrible does indeed happen. Of course, to those particular people to whom this happens, it seems like an amazing coincidence, something requiring an extraordinary explanation, such as clairvoyance. So, every day people are being convinced that clairvoyance is a reality. In fact, there may be nothing special going on at all. It is all easily understandable as the normally expected result of lots of ordinary people doing perfectly ordinary things.

SPEAKING OF PROBABILITY

The above analysis of "clairvoyant experiences" required thinking about probabilities in somewhat sophisticated ways. It should come as no surprise that the most serious research on the possibility of ESP involves sophisticated statistical reasoning. Part Two of this book explores such reasoning in more detail.

4.6 THE BURDEN OF PROOF

By and large, the results of our evaluations in this chapter have been *inconclusive.* In most cases, we have concluded that the data cited do not provide evidence for thinking that the hypotheses put forward are true. It may seem to many people that this is unsatisfying. They would like to be able to conclude that the hypotheses in question are *mistaken*—the proposed models do not fit. Although understandable, this feeling is based on a misunderstanding both of our objectives and of the real power of the program that we have developed.

In debating, as in the law, there is a concept of **the burden of proof.** When a claim is disputed, the question is who has the responsibility for proving it true or false. That party carries the burden of proof. As a *consumer* of scientific information, one should always take the position that the burden of proof is on the *producers*, or purveyors, of that information. They have to convince you that they are right. That means they have to provide you with data that constitute good evidence for their claims. You, like a jury, need only evaluate what they provide. Thus, if you conclude that the data supplied do not provide good evidence for their claims, you have done your job. You have reached the useful conclusion that you need not, at least for the moment, pay any more attention to their claims.

Being able to conclude that the data presented are irrelevant to whether the proposed model is correct is, in fact, a very powerful conclusion. It means that we can safely ignore the hypothesis in question. Of course, this leaves open the possibility that the hypothesis might still be true and that other data might provide strong evidence to that effect. Until presented with such data, however, we may remain uncommitted.

In written presentations and conversations, advocates of a particular point of view will often attempt to *shift* the burden of proof onto you, the audience. They will challenge you to prove that they are wrong. You should not give in to the temptation to take up the challenge. They want you to think that unless you can prove they are wrong, you must agree that they are correct. But this is simply not so. Your not being able to show that they are wrong does not mean that they are right. That is, your inability to produce evidence *against* their claims does not constitute evidence *for* their claims. It may only indicate your general ignorance of something about which you have every right to be ignorant. So remember, it is not your job to prove that they are wrong. It is their job to show that they are right.

In debate and the law, as in warfare, the advantage always lies with the defense. If you allow the burden of proof to shift to you, that will put you on the offensive side of the debate. This requires that you be able to produce data disagreeing with the predictions of their models. Not being especially up on the subject, you are unlikely to have such data on the tip of your tongue. And even if you can come up with some relevant data, advocates of the position are likely to reveal still more details about their models that render your data irrelevant to, or maybe even supportive of, their position. Far better to stick with the defensive position. Keep the burden of proof where it belongs—on the other side.

• Exercises

Analyze these reports following the six-point program for evaluating theoretical hypotheses developed in the text. Number and label your steps. Be as clear and concise as you can, keeping in mind that you must say enough to demonstrate that you do know what you are talking about. A simple "yes" or "no" is never a sufficient answer.

Exercise 4.1

An Experiment with Time

Get yourself into a relaxed position and place a clock with a sweep second hand in your line of sight so that you gaze naturally on it without any effort. Gaze at the clock for a while, absorbing the rhythm of the second hand. Then close your eyes and imagine yourself in a relaxed position somewhere else, such as lying on a familiar, quiet beach. Imagine as many details as you can to make the imagined scene as realistic as possible. Pretend you are really there listening to the waves. Now, very slowly, open your eyes and just let them gaze straight ahead. Do not attempt to focus on the clock. Just let it be unfocused in your line of sight. If you do it right, you may have the experience that the second hand seems to skip a beat or even seems to stand still for a second or two. Do not think about it or focus your eyes on the clock. That will destroy the desired effect. Whether or not you succeed in reproducing this effect, the experience as described seems plausible enough that we may suppose that some people should sometimes have had this experience. Assuming, then, that the above phenomenon exists, consider the following explanation of why it happens.

A person's psyche, sometimes called the "observer," can, at least briefly, leave the body and travel at the speed of light to distant places. So, if you imagine the scene realistically enough, your psyche is thought actually to be there observing the scene at the beach. While it is gone, your body remains home functioning normally except that there is no "consciousness" receiving the signals from your senses. The reason the second hand seems to stand still, on this account, is that your consciousness has momentarily left your body, and when it returns, it picks up where it left off. Your body, meanwhile, continues to follow the physical rhythm of the second hand. This produces the anomalous experience of seeming to see the second hand stand still while feeling that it should have moved forward. If one accepts this account, it could also help to explain the possibility of such things as clairvoyance, out-of-body experiences, and reincarnation.

EXERCISE 4.2

TRANSACTIONAL ANALYSIS

Transactional analysis (TA) is a form of psychological therapy based on the theory that each person has a composite personality consisting of three parts: "child," "parent," and "adult." A person's "parent" personality is made up from that person's experiences with his or her own parents (or substitutes). It includes lots of "don't's" and some "do's." The "child" personality is made up of a person's earliest (mostly nonverbal) feelings, such as feelings of helplessness or curiosity. The "adult" personality develops as a person learns to control his or her own life. Associated with each component personality are particular ways of interacting with others. According to the theory, mismatches between people's various personalities lead to conflict and unhappiness.

Experience with patients is often cited as evidence for this theory. For example, a couple comes to a TA therapist. The therapist has them discuss some problem and observes how they interact. The therapist then formulates a hypothesis about their interaction. The husband, for example, might be seen as responding with his "child" personality, while the wife is seen as responding with her "parent" personality. Neither "adult" personality, the therapist reasons, is happy with the responses from the other person. The therapist infers that they will both be happier if the mismatch can be eliminated by both parties learning to respond directly each other's "adult" personality.

In several succeeding sessions, the therapist intervenes in discussions attempting to bring out the "adult" personality in both husband and wife. Typically, the couple benefits from the therapy in that, afterward, they are somewhat better able to communicate and are generally happier.

EXERCISE 4.3

DIANETICS

Dianetics is a theory of the mind, together with a method for treating mental disorders, first expounded by a former science fiction writer, L. Ron Hubbard in his 1950 book, *Dianetics: The Modern Science of Mental Healing*. According to Hubbard, the mind has two parts, an *analytical* mind and a *reactive* mind. The reactive mind cannot think or remember. All it can do is record sensory input when the analytical mind is unconscious, as in sleep. It is nevertheless a very good recorder of all sensory input: sights, sounds, smells, tastes, and textures. These recordings are called *engrams*. They are stored in a *reactive bank*. When, at some later time, the person experiences something similar to the stored engram, the engram may be "keyed into" the person's regular memory, so the person experiences something similar to what happened when the engram was originally recorded. For example, a person bumps his head and passes out. While unconscious, a nearby loud motor starts running. Later, if that person bumps his head in a similar circumstance but not so severely as to pass out, he may experience the sensation of hearing a loud motor-like noise, even if there is no motor around. One of the more interesting features of Hubbard's theory is that the reactive mind forms before birth, so that a person is born with engrams already in their reactive bank.

Dianetic therapy consists of having a person attempt consciously to key into engrams, the older the better, in a quiet setting with an "auditor" who gently asks leading questions. If an engram can be brought before the analytical mind in this fashion, it will be "erased" and no longer cause problems. A person for whom all debilitating engrams have been erased is said to be "clear."

In the half-dozen or so years after publication of Hubbard's book, hundreds of people trained as "auditors" and centers for dianetic therapy were set up in dozens of cities across the United States. Thousands of people claimed to be cured of a wide variety of mental symptoms after roughly 20 hours of treatment. Many were convinced of the soundness of Hubbard's theory.

EXERCISE 4.4

PREDICTING THE STOCK MARKET

When the stock market crashed in 1929, an economist with unorthodox views claimed that the crash proved his theory was right. He had predicted the crash a year before. It turned out that every year since 1921 he had been predicting a crash for the following year. But this did not prevent him from continuing to cite the 1929 crash as evidence for his views.

EXERCISE 4.5

AQUARIANS

According to astrological theory, Aquarians, those born between January 21 and February 18, are said to be generally scientific but eccentric (i.e., brilliant but unconventional). In support of this hypothesis, it is often noted that several famous scientists (e.g., Copernicus, Galileo, and Thomas Edison) were Aquarians.

EXERCISE 4.6

NEAR-DEATH EXPERIENCES

The term *near-death experience* (NDE) was popularized by Dr. Raymond Moody in his 1975 book, *Life after Life.* He reported results of extensive interviews with roughly fifty people who had come very close to death, some even revived after being pronounced "clinically dead." Although different in many details, he found their experiences remarkably similar. Many had the experience of appearing to be calmly looking down on their own bodies ("out-of-body experiences"), perhaps watching physicians working frantically to revive them. Many had a sense of moving down a dark tunnel toward a light and then entering a place of incredible brightness and beauty. Many of his subjects were convinced that they had glimpsed a world beyond this one and found their views of life and death profoundly changed by the experience. Moody concluded that his research provides strong evidence that there is indeed life after death.

Several later researchers have mostly confirmed Moody's original observations. One cardiologist, for example, studied some 2,000 patients, most having suffered a heart attack. More than half reported having had experiences similar to those described by Moody. A psychologist found similar results with a sample of more than 100 cases. Some researchers even claim to have found similar results with patients in India, where religious and cultural imagery is very different from that in the United States.

Explanations of these observations, however, differ. In his 1974 book, *Broca's Brain,* the astronomer Carl Sagan promoted the idea that NDEs are, in fact, recollections of the experience of being born! Others suggest they are produced by abnormal brain chemistry resulting from the obvious physical and psychological stress of the situation. More recently, Susan Blackmore, in her 1992 book, *Beyond the Body,* offered the explanation that people's minds construct a memory of the situation that, because normal sensory input had been disrupted, they mistakenly take to be the memory of a real situation.

EXERCISE 4.7

ALIEN ABDUCTIONS

In the late 1980s, claims of abductions by aliens regained notoriety through the publication of several books such as Budd Hopkins' *Intruders* and Whitley Strieber's *Communion.* In both cases, the authors discuss ordinary seeming people with apparently normal lives who nevertheless report, in all sincerity, being abducted by aliens, examined, and then released. In many cases, the abduction story was first revealed to the authors through hypnosis after the subjects had experienced memory gaps and abduction dreams. The subjects' stories exhibit similar scenarios. The aliens, for example, are typically small green or gray men. Their spacecraft are typically saucer-shaped. The fact that there have been no previous connections among most of the subjects is taken as evidence of the truth of their stories. How could they all tell roughly the same story if they did not know each other? Hopkins, Strieber, and apparently many others, are convinced that such abductions have actually taken place.

Others, of course, disagree. Psychologist Robert Baker argues that the agreement among the subjects is largely due to suggestions by the hypnotists themselves, both before and during hypnosis. The general culture, including movies and books, provides a quite standard reservoir of images on which to draw. Moreover, Baker argues, dreams and memories revealed under hypnosis tend to reinforce one another, so that the subjects cannot honestly tell the difference between the content of a dream and that of a genuine memory of something actually experienced.

EXERCISE 4.8

ELIJAH AND THE PROPHETS OF BAAL

Look up the story of Elijah and the Prophets of Baal in the Old Testament of the Bible, First Kings, Chapter 18. Assume that the events in question happened as reported. Treating Elijah's "two alters" proposal as a suggested crucial experiment, analyze the experiment in the standard fashion.

EXERCISE 4.9

WHEN PROPHECY FAILS

As part of a study of the dynamics of belief in groups, some social psychologists once infiltrated several small cults. Among the groups observed was one led by a woman who was given the fictitious name of Mrs. Marion Keech. The events described really took place. Mrs. Keech claimed to have made contact with extraterrestrial beings, and she regularly revealed to her followers what she claimed were messages from her contacts. One day, she said that her contacts had told her that they were going to destroy the world.

She even gave a specific day on which this was supposed to happen. These extraterrestrial beings also told her, she claimed, that they would rescue her, and anyone else who wished to be saved, if they would wait at a designated location. On the appointed day, Mrs. Keech and her followers were at the designated place. The day wore on, but the world did not end. Finally, Mrs. Keech informed her followers that she had received a telepathic message from her contacts informing her that they had decided to spare the world from destruction because she and her followers had been so strong in their faith that the rescue would indeed take place. The psychologist undercover observer reported that the assembled followers returned to their homes apparently *strengthened* in their belief that Mrs. Keech was indeed in contact with powerful extraterrestrial beings.

EXERCISE 4.10

PYRAMID POWER

The following case has been cited in support of the hypothesis that pyramids have special powers. A young woman who was having difficulty with her complexion was told to keep a pitcher of water under a pyramid and then wash her face in that water, with only the mildest soap, once in the morning and once in the evening. She was also told to put nothing else on her face, no creams or medications of any kind and no makeup. Although she has been in the habit of using quantities of makeup, she agreed to the experiment. Within 2 weeks there was a clearly noticeable improvement in her complexion.

EXERCISE 4.11

REINCARNATION

The headline of a recent issue of a national weekly newspaper states that there have been hundreds of cases of reincarnation in the United States. These cases, the headline proclaims, provide convincing evidence that there is "life after death." Turning to the inside pages, one finds accounts of patients who have been cured of various complaints by being hypnotized and then "regressed" to a "previous life." The following cases are typical of those presented.

A 50-year-old woman claimed to have suffered from severe headaches, several a week for more than 35 years. She claimed to have seen ten different physicians who had prescribed various pain killers and other drugs—none of which worked. Then, in a single 2-hour session under hypnosis, she "discovered" the true cause of her headaches. In an earlier life, she had been a young man in nineteenth-century New England. One day, while on the way to visit his fiancee, the young man fell into a gully, hit his head on a rock, and was killed. A year and a half after her session with the therapist, the woman claimed she had since suffered only one or two headaches.

A 25-year-old real estate dealer complained of several serious allergies, including a very strong reaction to corn. Under hypnosis, he was "regressed" back to an earlier life as a commander in a Mongolian army. In one campaign, the commander refused to order his men to kill innocent women and children. Because of this disobedience, his superiors had him tortured by being force-fed corn and water, which caused him to bloat up so much that he died. After "learning" of his earlier life, the realtor claimed to be rid of most of his allergies and to be able to eat corn with no ill effects.

Several of the psychologists engaged in this sort of therapy are quoted as being convinced that their work provides scientific evidence that reincarnation does occur and that there is indeed "life after death."

EXERCISE 4.12

PROJECT

Find an article or book on a popular scientific topic that interests you—not a topic that comes out of a formal science course. Evaluate the material following the standard program for evaluating theoretical hypotheses. You may turn this into a more extensive project by looking up other articles or books on the same subject. In particular, you may be able to find articles or books that explicitly set out to refute the views in the materials you read first. In this case, you can evaluate the opposing hypotheses as well.

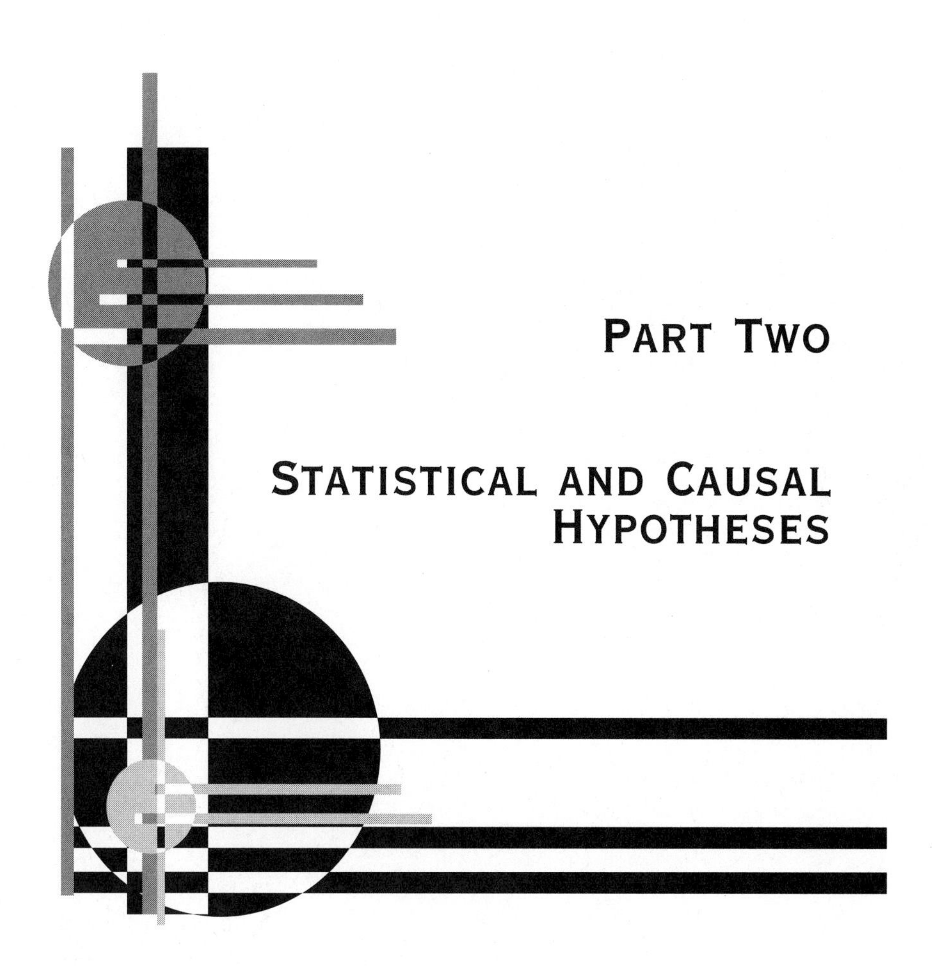

Part Two

Statistical and Causal Hypotheses

CHAPTER 5
STATISTICAL MODELS AND PROBABILITY

This chapter has two objectives: to acquaint you with a few basic types of *statistical models* and to provide you with some knowledge of the *probability models* necessary for understanding how statistical *data* may be used as evidence for statistical *hypotheses.*

5.1 WHY STATISTICAL AND PROBABILISTIC MODELS ARE IMPORTANT

There are many reasons why it is important to be able to understand and evaluate statistical models. The main general reason is that such models are widely used in science, particularly in the social, behavioral, and bio-medical sciences. These are the sciences whose results tend to be most relevant to the everyday concerns of almost everybody.

The reason these sciences use statistical and probabilistic models is that such models are appropriate for the kinds of questions scientists in these fields try to answer. One kind of question concerns the prevalence of various characteristics in large populations, such as the population of women in the United States. For example, what percentage of American women between the ages of 20 and 30 hold full-time jobs? The answer to that question, as we shall see, is a *statistical hypothesis*. It would be exceedingly difficult and very costly to determine the age and employment status of every woman in the United States. Indeed, that would be like performing a full-scale census, something that even the federal government attempts only once every 10 years. The way such questions are typically approached is by examining only a *sample* of the whole population. Information about the sample is then used as evidence for particular hypotheses about the population. But evaluating the data from the sample is not a simple matter. It requires the use of *probabilistic* models. So, we need to know about those as well.

A second kind of question typical of the behavioral and bio-medical sciences concerns the *causes* of characteristics exhibited by individuals. Does the dietary intake of cholesterol cause heart attacks in men? Not nearly enough is known about the biological and chemical mechanisms involved to answer that question for any particular person. By studying several large groups of men, however, we might be able to answer the question without knowing very much about the precise biological mechanisms involved. Here again, however, understanding causal claims and evaluating the evidence for them requires the use of *probabilistic* models. After learning about probabilistic models and how to evaluate statistical hypotheses, we can return again to causal models and causal hypotheses.

5.2 THE ELEMENTS OF A STATISTICAL STUDY

We begin by outlining the basic elements of any statistical study. The rest of this chapter is devoted to just two of these elements.

THE REAL-WORLD POPULATION

In any statistical study, there must be some **population** in the real world that is the object of the investigation. For example, American women between the ages of 20 and 30 are such a population. But "populations," in the scientific sense, do not have to be made up of individual people. They do not even have to be made up of biological individuals, such as penguins. The Census Bureau and the Internal Revenue Service study "households," which technically are not people but small groups of people. The FBI publishes statistics on homicides in the United States. For them, homicides form a "population." But homicides are not people; they are incidents involving people—a killer and a victim, for example.

Whatever the nature of the "individuals" making up a population under investigation, those individuals will have various characteristics, or **properties,** whose incidence in the population one seeks to determine. These properties can be almost anything: holding a full-time job, consisting of three unrelated people, or being committed with a gun. Just keep in mind that the properties of members of the population are also features of the real world.

THE SAMPLE

As already noted, most populations are too big for anyone to examine every member. The best that can be done is to examine some selected members of the population, called a **sample.** How the sample is selected turns out to be crucial. For the moment, it is only necessary to understand that a sample, like a population, is made up of real-world individuals with real properties. So, selecting a sample is a physical process that has to be carried out by someone, somewhere, at some time.

A MODEL OF THE POPULATION

As was emphasized in Part One of this text, thinking scientifically about anything requires constructing a model. In the present case, the model will be a **statistical model** of the real-world population under investigation. Whether the model is abstract, such as a set of numbers, or real, such as a jar full of marbles, the model is always something distinct from the population being studied.

FIGURE 5.1

The four elements of a statistical study.

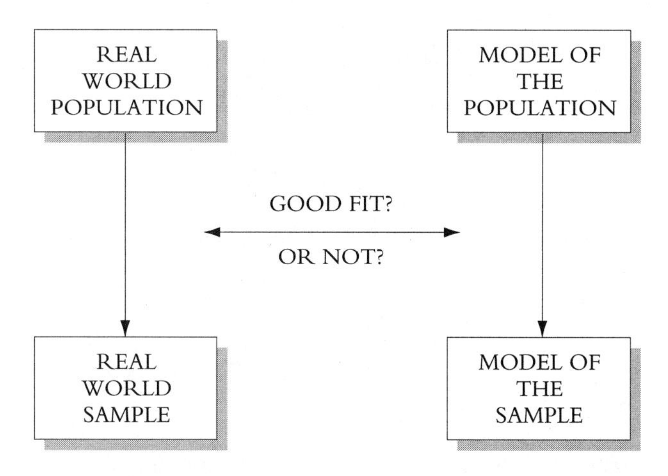

A MODEL OF THE SAMPLE

Finally, corresponding to the sample from the real population is a **model of the sample.** The model of the sample is to be thought of as a sample from the model of the population.

PUTTING THE ELEMENTS TOGETHER

Figure 5.1 pictures the four elements of a statistical study in their proper relationships with one another. Looking across the top, there is the real-world population, pictured on the left, with its corresponding model at the top right. Looking across the bottom, there is the real-world sample, pictured on the left, with its corresponding model at the bottom right. The arrow on the left going down from the real-world population to the sample represents the physical process by which the sample is selected from the population. The corresponding arrow on the right represents a model of that process, which may be a physical process but might also be purely conceptual. Overall, the whole right-hand side of the diagram represents a model of the real-world population and sample pictured on the left.

Here, you should recall the similar diagram (Figure 2.9) used to represent the elements of a study involving a *theoretical* hypothesis. The corresponding elements are similarly placed, but here they are used somewhat differently. In the case of theoretical hypotheses, agreement between the data and a prediction from the model was used to judge the fit between the real world and the model. Here, we will be using auxiliary information to judge the overall fit between the real world on the left-hand side of the diagram and the models on the right-hand side. Once that judgment is made, we will then use what we know about relationships between the models on the right-hand

FIGURE 5.2

Our standard model of a population.

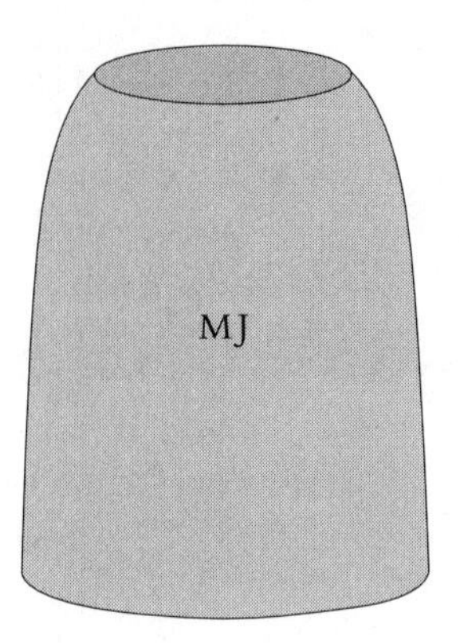

side to draw conclusions about the real-world population using data about the actual sample.

In the remainder of this chapter, we explore relationships on the right-hand side of Figure 5.1. That is, we explore various statistical models of populations and idealized relationships between models of populations and models of samples. In the following chapter, we begin using these models to understand the relationships in the real world pictured on the left-hand side of the diagram.

5.3 PROPORTIONS AND DISTRIBUTIONS

Current thinking about statistical models and probability originated in studies of various games of chance in the late seventeenth century. One of the models used in those earliest studies was that of a jar filled with marbles of various colors. We will take marbles in a jar as our standard model for thinking about populations and samples. In principle, this is a physical model, although we may do no more than talk about the model and never actually pick any marbles out of any jars. In this text, the closest we can come to a real jar of marbles is the picture in Figure 5.2.

PROPORTIONS

One of the simplest statistical models consists of a jar full of marbles, some of which are red and some of which are any other colors but red. The number of red marbles divided by the total number of marbles in the jar is the **proportion** of red marbles in the jar. For example, if there were 100 marbles in the jar and 60 of them were red, the proportion of red ones would be $^{60}/_{100}$, or $^{6}/_{10}$, or .60, or 60%.

In what follows, I will assume you know how to go back and forth between fractions, decimals, and percentages. If, for any reason, this makes you uneasy, now is the time for a quick review. We are going to be seeing many simple proportions in various guises. Figure 5.3 provides an example of how we shall represent a proportion.

FIGURE 5.3

A representation of a proportion.

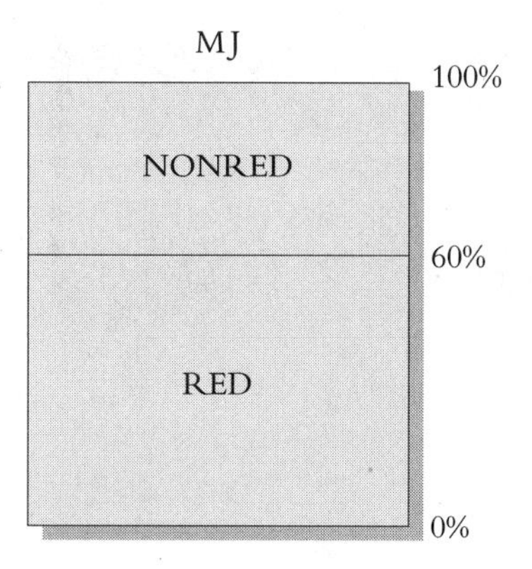

The letters "MJ" at the top describe the population, which is *m*arbles in the *j*ar. The red marbles are pictured as being in the bottom part of the box, and the nonred marbles are pictured in the top part. The proportion, in this case 60%, is written off to the right. Note that all the marbles are accounted for, because every marble in the jar is either red or nonred.

VARIABLES

Before we can proceed to examine more complex statistical models, we need to introduce some new technical ideas. These ideas are standard in the mathematical study of statistics and probability. They are more easily grasped, however, by means of examples than through formal definitions.

The first idea is that of a variable. A **variable** is a general property that may exhibit different specific forms. For example, *color* may be thought of as a variable. Among its specific forms are red, green, and blue. Similarly, *size* could be a variable. Its specific forms could be, for example, large and small. The specific forms of a variable are called the **values of the variable.** Thus, in the example just given, the variable, color, has three possible values: red, green, and blue.

There are two important restrictions on the set of possible values of a variable: they must be exclusive and exhaustive. That the set of possible values be **exclusive** means that a member of the population can exhibit only one value. Each value of the variable *excludes* all others. In our example, no marble could be both red and green. That the set of possible values be **exhaustive** means that every member of the population must exhibit some value. Thus, the set of possible values must *exhaust* the possibilities for values of the variable. In the example, if red, green, and blue are the possible values of the color variable, then there simply cannot be any yellow marbles in the jar.

The language of variables applies primarily to statistical *models,* which are idealized representations of real populations. Among ordinary real objects, one might have great

FIGURE 5.4

A representation of a distribution.

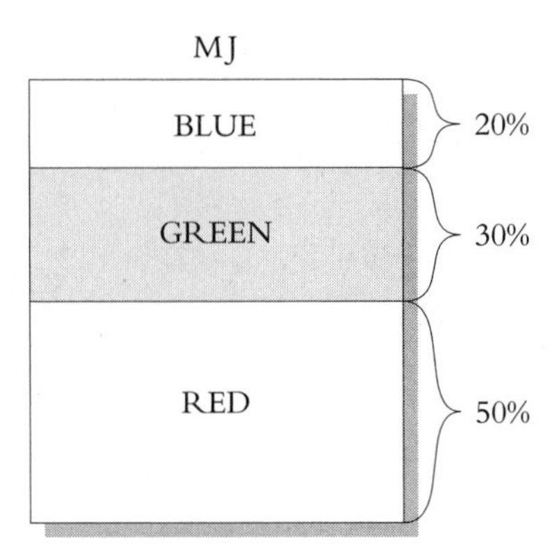

difficulty determining whether something should be classified as red or not. Maybe it should be called orange or purple. When talking about statistical models, all such ambiguities are explicitly eliminated. Among the marbles in our imaginary jar, there are, *by definition,* none for which the determination of red, green, or blue is the least bit uncertain.

DISTRIBUTIONS

A **statistical distribution** is defined by a single variable with any number of possible values. For each possible value of the variable, there will be a definite percentage of the population assigned that value. For example, suppose our jar of 100 marbles has 50 red marbles, 30 green ones, and 20 blue ones. Here, the variable is color, and the three possible values of the variable are red, green, and blue. The corresponding percentages are thus 50%, 30%, and 20%, respectively. Note that because the values of the variable are exclusive and exhaustive, the percentages given must add up to 100%. Each marble is counted once and only once. Figure 5.4 exhibits the kind of diagram we typically use to picture distributions. An equivalent representation would be a pie diagram, as shown in Figure 5.5. These should be familiar to users of electronic spreadsheets.

In our earlier example of a simple proportion, the variable was color, and it had only two possible values, red and nonred. Thus, proportions are really special cases of distributions in which the variable has only two possible values. In general, the variable in a distribution can have any number of possible values.

5.4 SIMPLE CORRELATIONS

Correlation is a relationship between *two variables,* each with various numbers of possible values. We will concentrate on the simple case in which each of the two

FIGURE 5.5

Representing a distribution with a pie diagram.

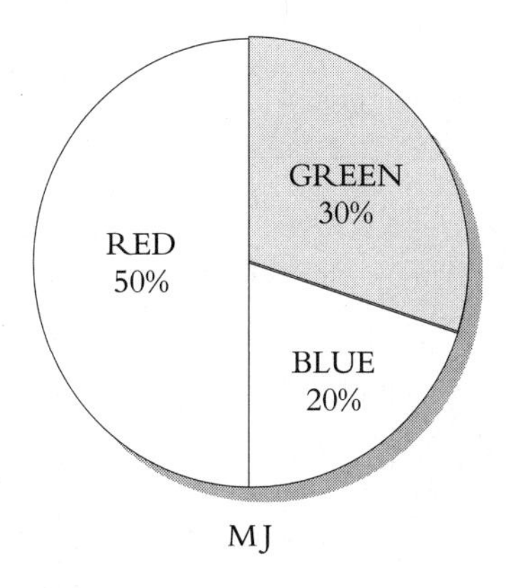

variables has only *two* possible values. As before, we will take color as one variable and suppose it has only two possible values, red and green. To deal with correlations, we shall have to expand our model to include a second variable. Let us suppose, therefore, that marbles come in two *sizes,* large and small. So, our second variable is size, and its two possible values are large and small. Figure 5.6 pictures our model for this case.

VARIABLES NOT CORRELATED

For our first case, imagine that our model population has 60 red and 40 green marbles. Among the red, we will suppose that there are 45 large and 15 small. Among the green, we will imagine 30 large and 10 small. Thus, among both the red and the green

FIGURE 5.6

A model of a population with a possible correlation.

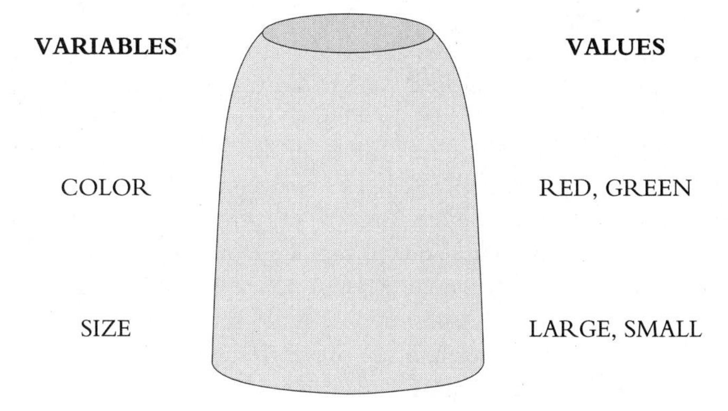

FIGURE 5.7

A model of a population in which size and color are not correlated.

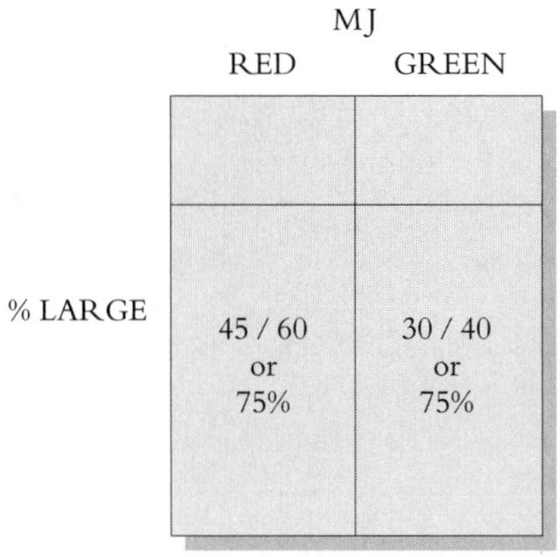

MJ	RED	GREEN
% LARGE	45 / 60 or 75%	30 / 40 or 75%

marbles, three-quarters, or 75%, are large. Figure 5.7 exhibits the form of the diagrams we will use to represent correlations.

Having the percentage of large marbles being the **same** among both the red and the green marbles represents the special case in which we say that, in the model population, the two *variables,* color and size, are **not correlated.** What this means, intuitively, is that, if we are interested in the proportion of large marbles, it does not matter whether we look among the red or the green. The proportion of large marbles is the same in both.

VARIABLES CORRELATED

If, in the model population, the percentage of large marbles among the red marbles is **different** from the percentage of large among the green, then we say that the two *variables,* color and size, **are correlated.** Here, there are two possibilities: the percentage of large marbles among the red can be either *greater* than or *less* than the percentage of large marbles among the green.

If the percentage of large marbles among the red is **greater** than the percentage of large among the green, we say that, for this population, being large is **positively correlated** with being red. For example, suppose that 45 of the 60 red marbles are large but that only 10 of the 40 green marbles are large. In that case, the percentage of large marbles among the red is 75%, but the percentage of large among the green is only 25%. In this particular population, the properties red and large tend to go together. The idea of positive correlation is one way of making precise the idea of two properties "going together" in a particular population. Figure 5.8 pictures this example in which being large is positively correlated with being red.

The other possibility, if color and size are correlated, is that there is a **smaller** percentage of large marbles among the red than among the green. For example, suppose

FIGURE 5.8

A model of a population in which large size is positively correlated with red color.

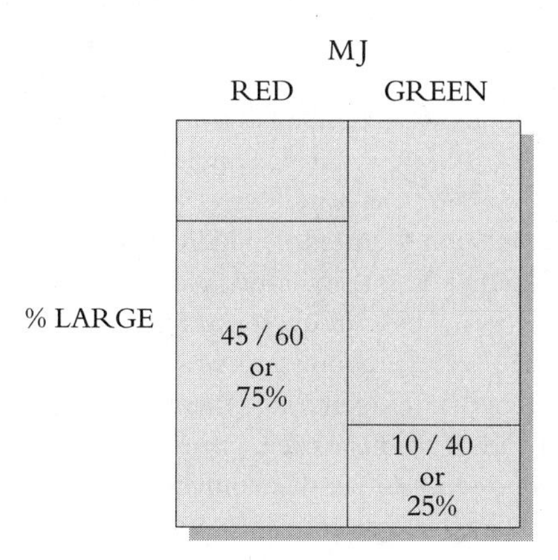

that only 15 of the 60 red marbles are large, but 20 of the 40 green marbles are large. In that case, the percentage of large marbles among the red is 25% and the percentage of large marbles among the green is 50%. In such a population, we would say that being large is **negatively correlated** with being red. The properties large and red tend *not* to go together. This case is pictured in Figure 5.9. Note that neither of these two percentages is greater than 50%. For the values of two variables to be correlated, it is not necessary that either percentage be greater than 50%. All that matters is that there is a *difference* in the two percentages.

FIGURE 5.9

A model of a population in which large size is negatively correlated with red color.

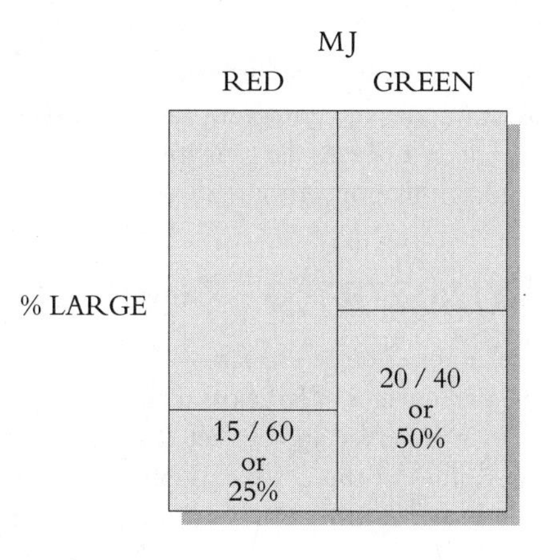

Once you understand what it is for there to be a positive or negative correlation between values of correlated variables, you should realize that there are many different ways to describe the same correlation among the variables. For example, Figure 5.8 pictures a model population in which there is a *positive* correlation between large and red marbles. That same correlation could be described as a *negative* correlation between large and green marbles. Or it could be described as a *positive* correlation between small and green marbles. Or it could be described as a *negative* correlation between small and red marbles. You should make sure that you understand why all these statements are just different ways of describing the same correlation among the variables color and size in the particular population pictured in Figure 5.8.

One other general point is that whether two variables are correlated depends entirely on the particular population in question. Figures 5.7, 5.8, and 5.9 all concern the variables color and size, but the populations are different because there are different numbers of marbles assigned to the values of these two variables. Thus, whether the variables are correlated and, if so, how their values are related differ from population to population. It makes no sense to say that somehow the properties of color and size are correlated, in general, with no reference to a particular population.

SUMMARY

The various correlation relationships for the model populations discussed above may be summarized as follows:

> If, for the population in question, the percentage of large marbles among the red marbles is the **same** as the percentage of large marbles among the green marbles, then the variables size and color **are not correlated** in this population.
>
> If, for the population in question, the percentage of large marbles among the red marbles is **different** from the percentage of large marbles among the green marbles, then the variables size and color **are correlated** in this population.
>
> If, for the population in question, the percentage of large marbles among the red marbles is **greater** than the percentage of large marbles among the green marbles, then the property of being large is **positively correlated** with the property of being red in this population.
>
> If, for the population in question, the percentage of large marbles among the red marbles is **less** than the percentage of large marbles among the green marbles, then the property of being large is **negatively correlated** with the property of being red in this population.

5.5 SYMMETRY OF CORRELATIONS

In all the models of correlations discussed so far, we have focused on the color variable and, then, considered the percentages of large or small marbles among those of different possible colors. This focus is reflected in the fact that all the diagrams of correlations exhibited thus far list the values of the color variable on top and represent the values of the size variable by a scale of zero to 100% on the side. But the association of two

FIGURE 5.10

Equivalent representations of the lack of correlation between size and color in the population pictured in Figure 5.7.

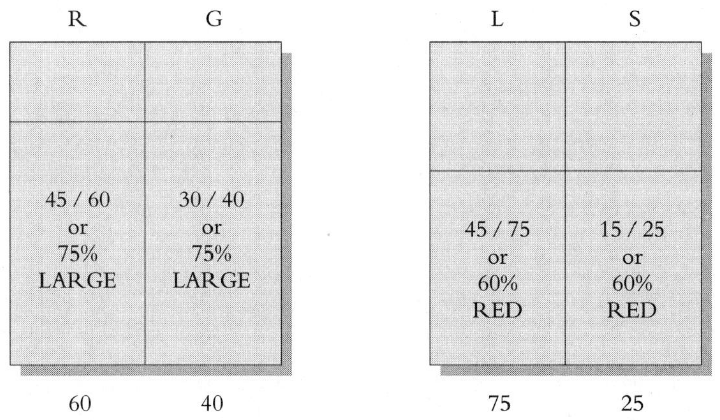

R	G
45 / 60 or 75% LARGE	30 / 40 or 75% LARGE
60	40

L	S
45 / 75 or 60% RED	15 / 25 or 60% RED
75	25

variables defined as correlation does not seem to favor one variable over another. So, we should be able to represent the same relationships if we focus first on the size variable. That means listing the values of the size variable on the top of our diagrams. Figure 5.10 provides two pictures of the model shown in Figure 5.7 in which there is no correlation between color and size. The picture on the left repeats Figure 5.7. The picture on the right shows the same population but with the values of the size variable listed on top.

It is easy to derive the right-hand picture from the left-hand picture. Because there are 45 large red marbles and 30 large green ones, the total number of large marbles must be 45 plus 30, or 75. Likewise, there must be 15 plus 10, or 25, small marbles. Now, among the 75 large marbles, 45 are red, for a proportion of $^{45}/_{75}$, or 60%, red. Similarly, among the small marbles, 15 are red, for a proportion of $^{15}/_{25}$, or 60%, red. Thus, the percentage of red marbles is the same among both the large and small marbles. So, the right-hand diagram tells us that there is no correlation between color and size in this population, which is just what the left-hand diagram told us. The corresponding percentages are different in the two diagrams, 75% and 60%, respectively, but what matters for the lack of correlation is the equality of the two percentages in each diagram.

We have worked out this equivalence only for one specific model, but the result is completely general. If representing a population using a diagram with the values of one variable on the top yields a result of no correlation between the variables, using a diagram with the values of the other variable on top will likewise yield a result of no correlation.

A similar result holds for positive and negative correlations among the various values of the two variables. For example, if the positive correlation between large and red marbles in Figure 5.8 is represented with the size variable at the top of the diagram, the result is a positive correlation between red and large marbles. This equivalence is

FIGURE 5.11

Equivalent representations of the positive correlation between large size and red color in the population pictured in Figure 5.8.

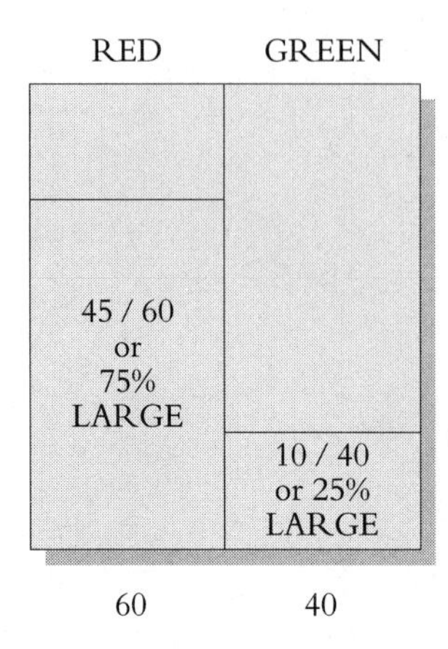

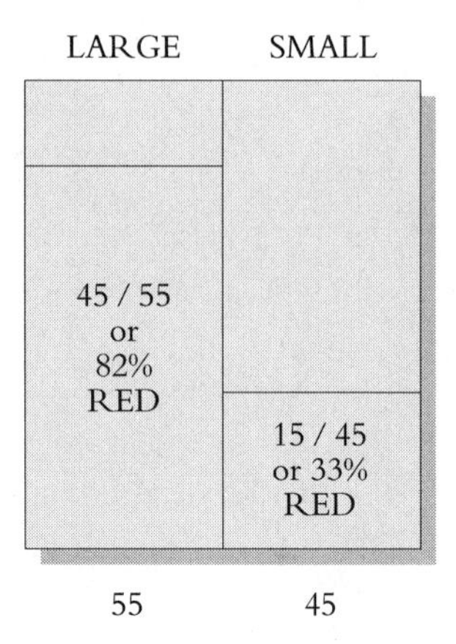

shown in Figure 5.11. In general, if being large is positively correlated with being red in a population, then being red is positively correlated with being large in that population. That is what is meant by saying that positive correlation is *symmetrical.* The same holds, of course, for negative correlation.

The general symmetry of positive correlation can be demonstrated by examining Figure 5.10. Suppose that we were to exchange one small red marble for a large red marble. That would raise the proportion of large marbles among the red marbles to $46/60$ in the left-hand diagram. That indicates a (small) positive correlation between large and red. At the same time, however, the proportion of red marbles among the large marbles in the right-hand diagram in Figure 5.10 goes up to $46/76$, or 61%, and the proportion of red among the small marbles goes down to $14/24$, or 58%. That yields a (small) positive correlation between being red and being large in this population. Thus, a change in the population that produces a positive correlation between large and red automatically produces a positive correlation between red and large. This shows that correlation must be a symmetrical relationship.

5.6 STRENGTH OF CORRELATIONS

Thus far, we have largely treated correlation as just a *qualitative* relationship. Either there is correlation between two variables or there is not. If there is a correlation between the variables, then some values of the variables are positively or negatively correlated with others. It seems intuitively clear, however, that correlation can also be a *quantitative* relationship. Some correlations seem to be "stronger" than others. For example, we just considered a model in which the difference in percentages of red marbles among the large and small was just the difference between 61% and 58%. Intuitively, that is a small difference, corresponding to a weak correlation. In other models we have considered, the difference was that between 75% and 25%, which intuitively seems a much bigger difference, corresponding to a much stronger correlation.

For our purposes, we will take the *difference* between the two proportions, expressed, however, as decimals rather than percentages, as a rough measure of the *strength of the correlation* between the values in question. More precisely stated, for our standard model,

> ***Strength of Correlations:***
> The strength of the correlation between the properties of being large and being red, in the population, is the *difference,* expressed as a decimal, between the proportion of large marbles that are red and the proportion that are green.

For example, in the population shown in Figure 5.8, the strength of the correlation between large and red is (.75 − .25) = .50. That, by this measure, is a fairly strong correlation. The strongest possible correlation would have the value 1.00, which would happen if all the red marbles were large and all the green ones were small. There would be a perfect association between large and red. Similarly, the smallest possible correlation would have the value −1.00, which would happen if none of the red marbles were large and all the green ones were large. If the variables are not correlated, the difference would, of course, be zero, yielding a strength of correlation of .00, which is just what we should expect.

Measuring the strength of a correlation by the simple difference in proportions has the great advantage that we can perform the calculation in our heads. Thus, without resorting to a calculator, we can get a good idea of how strong a correlation really is. This is not, however, the measure you would find in any textbook on statistics. For professional purposes, a difference in percentages is not a sufficiently good measure. One defect is that it is *not* symmetrical. That is, the difference in percentages may vary depending on which variable one represents on the top of the diagram. You can see this in Figure 5.11, where the strength of the correlation is .50 in the left-hand diagram and .49 in the right-hand diagram. Nevertheless, it is the same correlation.

The appendix to this chapter exhibits the kind of representation for the strength of correlations we find in standard statistics textbooks. This representation is symmetrical. As you will see, however, this measure is obviously too complex to compute in our heads. For our purposes, it will be better to have a measure that we can use easily and quickly, even if it is not quite up to the standards of professional statisticians.

5.7 PROBABILITY MODELS

Statistical models are models of *populations.* As indicated at the beginning of this chapter, we need also to understand the process of selecting a *sample* from a population. For that, an understanding of probability models is required. It turns out, however, that probability models have the same structure as statistical models. So, what we have just learned about statistical models will be useful in developing an understanding of probability models.

FIGURE 5.12

The distribution of marbles in the population Model 1.

COLOR		SIZE
Red	100	50 L, 50 S
Green	50	25 L, 25 S
Blue	30	15 L, 15 S
Yellow	20	10 L, 10 S

A PROBABILITY MODEL

We begin with a more complex version of our model of marbles in a jar. This time, we assume that our jar contains 200 marbles of four colors (Red, Green, Blue, and Yellow) and two sizes (Large and Small) distributed as shown in Figure 5.12. Call this Model 1. In the context of probability models, statisticians talk about **random variables** rather than just variables. So, here we have two random variables, Color and Size. As before, the possible values associated with any one variable must be both *exclusive* and *exhaustive*.

Probability is a measure associated with the **values** of random variables defined for a particular population. The measure associated with any particular value has a numerical value equal to the **proportion** of members of the population assigned to that value. For example, in our model population, the proportion of marbles that are red is $^{100}/_{200}$, or $\frac{1}{2}$. So, the probability of red in this population is .50.

Here, it is helpful to introduce the standard notation used in the study of probability and statistics. Let **C** and **Z** stand for the random variables, color and size, respectively. Let R, B, G, Y, L, and S stand for the values of these variables. Then, the expression **P**(**C** = R) = .50 is read as: the probability that the variable color has the value red is one-half. Often, explicit reference to the variable is left out, yielding the abbreviated expression **P**(R) = .50.

Probability models have a definite structure, which is just the structure of proportions. The details of this structure are given by some possible ways of forming combinations of proportions. In fact, there are only *two* basic ways of forming combinations that matter for probability models.

SIMPLE ADDITION RULE

One way of combining probabilities is to consider the probability of a member of the population exhibiting *either* one of two or more values of random variables. For example, we could ask about the probability that a marble is either red or green. Examining the population of marbles, we find that there are 100 red and 50 green, for a total of $^{150}/_{200}$ that are either red or green. Thus, **P**(R or G) = .75. Because **P**(R) = .50 and **P**(G) = .25, we might think that the probability of the combination red or green is just the **sum** of their respective individual probabilities. That suggestion is a bit hasty.

Consider the combination of marbles that are either red or large. What is the probability of that combination? That is, what is the probability, **P**(**C** = R or **Z** = L)?

FIGURE 5.13

The distribution of marbles in the population Model 2.

COLOR		SIZE
Red	100	80 L, 20 S
Green	50	10 L, 40 S
Blue	30	5 L, 25 S
Yellow	20	5 L, 15 S

Looking at the composition of the population, we see immediately that there are $^{100}/_{200}$ red marbles and $^{100}/_{200}$ large marbles. So, **P**(R) = .50 and **P**(L) = .50. The sum of these two probabilities is 1. But that cannot be right, because that would mean that *all* of the marbles are red or large, and we know that there are some that are neither (e.g., the 25 small green marbles). What has gone wrong?

The problem is that, in counting up the red marbles and then counting up the large marbles, we counted the large red marbles *twice*. There are, after all, fifty large red marbles in the population. Put in terms we have just learned, red and large are not *exclusive* values of random variables. The simple addition rule suggested above works only for exclusive values.

Letting A and B stand for any values of random variables, we can now state this simple rule as follows:

Simple Addition Rule for Probabilities:

If A and B are exclusive values of random variables,
P(A or B) = **P**(A) + **P**(B)

We will shortly learn how to deal with values of variables that are not exclusive.

SIMPLE MULTIPLICATION RULE

Another way of combining probabilities is to consider the probability of a member of the population exhibiting *both* of two values of random variables. For example, we could ask about the probability that a marble is both red and large. From the description of our model population, we see that there are $^{50}/_{200}$ marbles that are both large and red. So, **P**(R and L) = .25. As we have already determined that **P**(R) = .50 and **P**(L) = .50, it appears plausible that the probability of both red and large is just the **product** of the two individual probabilities. Again, this would be a somewhat hasty conclusion.

To see why the above simple rule is not quite right as it stands, consider the population with a composition as shown in Figure 5.13. The only difference between Model 2 and Model 1 is that the relative numbers of large and small marbles among the various colored marbles has been changed. The total numbers of colored marbles and of large and small marbles remain the same. Thus, for the population in Model 2, **P**(R) = .50 and **P**(L) = .50. But the proportion of large red marbles is $^{80}/_{200}$, which is .40 and not the product of .50 times .50, which is .25. What has gone wrong?

FIGURE 5.14

A demonstration that color and size are not correlated in Model 1 but are correlated in Model 2.

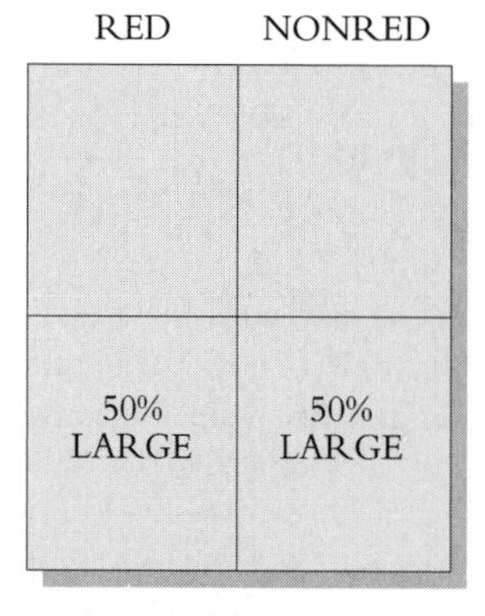

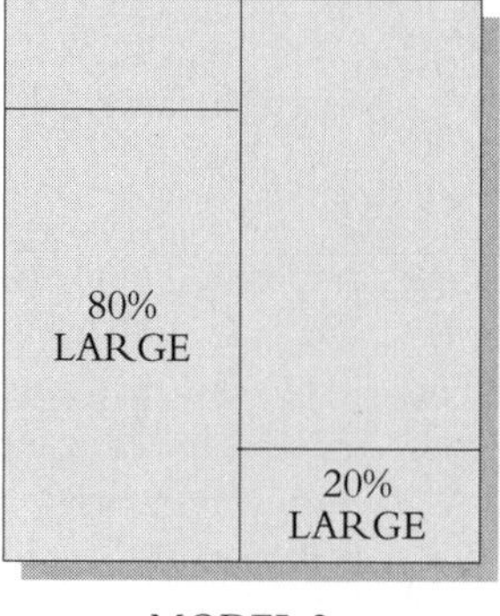

The problem is that, in Model 1, the variables color and size were *not correlated.* In Model 2, these variables *are correlated.* This difference is pictured in Figure 5.14. The simple product rule works only if the variables corresponding to the respective values are not correlated.

> ***Simple Multiplication Rule for Probabilities:***
> If A and B are values of random variables that are not correlated, then
> **P**(A and B) = **P**(A) × **P**(B).

We will now develop a rule that works even for values of correlated variables.

CONDITIONAL PROBABILITIES

Let us look in a slightly different way at the probability of marbles that are both red and large. Think of picking out a large red marble as a two-stage process in which you first select the color red and then look for large marbles only among the red ones. The probability of a marble being large, given that it is among the red ones, is known as a **conditional probability** and is symbolized as **P**(L/R). It can also be described as the probability of large *conditional on* red. Using this notation, we can generalize the multiplication rule as follows:

> ***General Multiplication Rule for Probabilities:***
> If A and B are values of two random variables, then
> **P**(A and B) = **P**(A) × **P**(B/A).

This rule applies whether or not the variables in question are correlated. If the variables are not correlated, then **P**(B/A) = **P**(B), and the general rule reduces to the simple rule.

Applying this general multiplication rule to our earlier example for large red marbles in Model 2,

$$\mathbf{P}(\text{R and L}) = \mathbf{P}(\text{R}) \times \mathbf{P}(\text{L/R}) = .50 \times .80 = .40$$

That, of course, is the correct answer, because in Model 2 there are $^{80}/_{200}$ marbles that are both red and large.

Now that we have a generalized version of the multiplication rule, we can produce a generalized version of the addition rule as well. This rule applies whether or not the values of the variables are exclusive.

General Addition Rule for Probabilities:
If A and B are two values of random variables, then
$\mathbf{P}(\text{A or B}) = \mathbf{P}(\text{A}) + \mathbf{P}(\text{B}) - \mathbf{P}(\text{A and B})$.

Applying this rule to determining the probability of large red marbles in Model 1,

$$\mathbf{P}(\text{L or R}) = \mathbf{P}(\text{L}) + \mathbf{P}(\text{R}) - \mathbf{P}(\text{L and R}) = .50 + .50 - .25 = .75$$

This is correct, because there are $^{150}/_{200}$ marbles that are either large or red (or both) in Model 1. Thus, the generalized addition rule takes care of double counting by subtracting (once) the members of the population for which the two values overlap. If the values of the variables *are* exclusive, then $\mathbf{P}(\text{A and B}) = 0$, and the general addition rule reduces to the simple addition rule given earlier.

5.8 THE FLIPPANT JUDGE

As an introduction to the study of sampling, we will now work through a simple problem whose solution requires the sort of calculations necessary to understand the sampling process. As you will see, all that is required are the simple addition and multiplication rules.

THE PROBLEM

Imagine a jury consisting of three judges. The first two judges, through long experience, have established that their probability of reaching a correct decision is ¾. That is, on the average, three-quarters of the times when they conclude that the defendant is guilty (or not guilty), the defendant is, in fact, guilty (or not guilty). The other one-quarter of the time they are mistaken one way or the other. The third judge is, unknown to anyone, irresponsible. For each case, he merely flips a coin. If the coin comes up heads, he says "guilty." If it comes up tails, he says "not guilty." The chances of this judge being correct are, of course, ½. The jury is pictured in Figure 5.15.

The final verdict is decided by a two-thirds majority. If any two of the three judges declare the defendant not guilty, that is the jury's verdict—and vice versa. Suppose that you have been brought before this jury. What is the probability that the *jury* reaches a correct verdict in your case? Before reading the solution, take a few minutes to see if you can solve the problem on your own. Nothing more is required than applications of the simple addition and multiplication rules.

FIGURE 5.15

The Jury.

First judge	Second judge	Third judge
		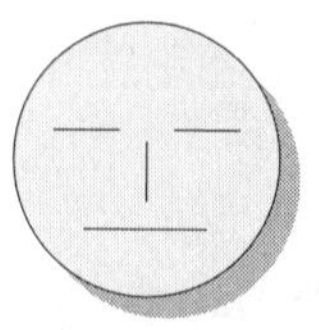
$P(C) = 3/4$	$P(C) = 3/4$	$P(C) = 1/2$

THE SOLUTION

The key to the solution is to figure out precisely what probabilities to calculate and in what order. The only complication is that there are several different combinations of correct and incorrect decisions by individual judges that leave the correctness of the jury's decision unchanged. So, we need first to determine which combinations of individual correct decisions constitute a correct verdict.

For each judge, there is a random variable indicating the status of his or her judgment. Let C stand for the value of the variable indicating that the corresponding judge is correct. Likewise, let M indicate that the corresponding judge is mistaken. Remembering that the *jury* reaches a correct verdict whenever two or more of the judges are correct, the combinations for which the jury reaches a correct verdict are all pictured in Figure 5.16.

The combinations that make the jury correct are clearly mutually exclusive. So, to determine the overall probability of a correct verdict, we need only apply the *addition rule* to the probabilities of these combinations. We want to know the probability that one or another of these combinations obtains. But first, we need to calculate the probabilities of each of these combinations themselves.

The first possibility for a correct verdict, for example, is the combination of the first judge being correct while the second and third judges are also correct. The second possibility is the combination in which the first and second judges are correct while

FIGURE 5.16

Combinations of correct decisions by individual judges that yield a correct verdict by the whole jury.

First judge	Second judge	Third judge
C	C	C
C	C	M
C	M	C
M	C	C

the third is incorrect. And so on. Moreover, because the judges operate independently, the variables corresponding to decisions by individual judges are *not correlated.* For example, the percentage of correct decisions by the second judge is the same whether we consider only cases in which the first judge is correct or only cases in which the first judge is incorrect. So, we can apply the *simple multiplication rule* to each combination. Thus, the probabilities corresponding to correct verdicts are

$$\mathbf{P}(1C, 2C, 3C) = \mathbf{P}(1C) \times \mathbf{P}(2C) \times \mathbf{P}(3C) = 3/4 \times 3/4 \times 1/2 = 9/32$$
$$\mathbf{P}(1C, 2C, 3M) = \mathbf{P}(1C) \times \mathbf{P}(2C) \times \mathbf{P}(3M) = 3/4 \times 3/4 \times 1/2 = 9/32$$
$$\mathbf{P}(1C, 2M, 3C) = \mathbf{P}(1C) \times \mathbf{P}(2M) \times \mathbf{P}(3C) = 3/4 \times 1/4 \times 1/2 = 3/32$$
$$\mathbf{P}(1M, 2C, 3C) = \mathbf{P}(1M) \times \mathbf{P}(2C) \times \mathbf{P}(3C) = 1/4 \times 3/4 \times 1/2 = 3/32$$

The probability that the jury's verdict is correct is simply the sum of these probabilities, which is $24/32$, or $3/4$. The effect of the irresponsible judge, therefore, is to cancel out the judgment of one of the good judges. The jury could do equally well with only one of the good judges.

You should now calculate the probabilities for the combinations leading to *incorrect* verdicts. Their sum, of course, should be $1/4$.

5.9 SAMPLING

Whether we are talking about sampling from a real population, such as all Americans older than 18, or a model population, such as our idealized jar of marbles, the process of sampling can be pictured as in Figure 5.17. The idea is to learn something about the whole population by examining a small selection of individuals from that population. What can be learned, however, depends crucially on *how* the selecting is done.

REPLACEMENT

There is one preliminary distinction to be made before we can proceed. This is the distinction between sampling **with replacement** and sampling **without replacement.**

FIGURE 5.17

A representation of a sampling process.

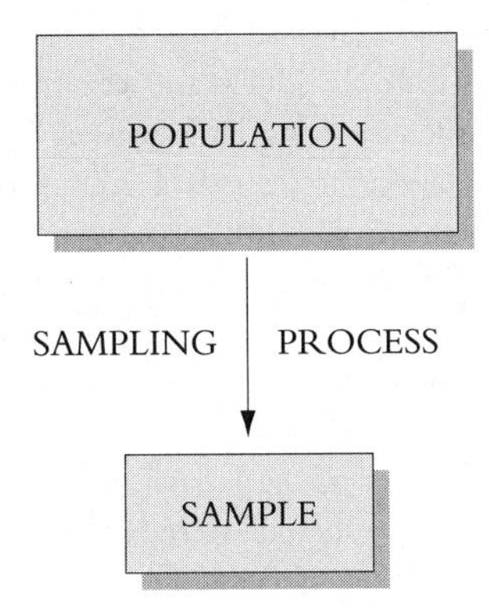

The difference is whether an individual already examined is eligible to be selected again later in the sampling process. Are the individuals already examined *replaced* (i.e., put back into the population) or are they not replaced?

This distinction is important only if the sample constitutes a sizable fraction of the whole population. Suppose we were to select, in sequence, *without* replacement, 50 marbles from among the 200 marbles of the population in Model 1. No matter whether the first marble selected turned out to be red or not, the proportion of red marbles in the population would be different when selecting the second marble than when selecting the first. That is to say, the population sampled when selecting the second marble would be a *different population* than that sampled when selecting the first. The same holds for the succeeding 48 selections. These shifting proportions make it very difficult to infer anything about the proportion of red marbles in the original population of 200 marbles. This problem is eliminated if we assume that individual marbles are replaced immediately after each selection, so that, for the next selection, the population is just the same as it was earlier. For this reason, we will always assume that sampling from our small model populations is done *with replacement*.

When we turn to applying our models to real-world populations, replacement is of little practical importance. Most real-world populations are much larger than any samples we might consider. For example, when sampling from a population of 100 million adult Americans, removing even a few thousand individuals from the population would make almost no difference in the proportions of individuals exhibiting properties of interest, such as being a smoker or a registered Democrat. Thus, for all practical purposes, sampling without replacement from a large population is like sampling with replacement from a small population.

What this all really means is that, from a theoretical point of view, *the size of the population is of no importance in understanding the process of sampling*. In practice, the size of the population makes a big difference. The actual process of sampling is typically much more difficult for a large population than for a small one. We explore some of these difficulties when we come to applying our simple models to real-world populations.

RANDOM SAMPLING: TWO TRIALS

In statistics texts, the selection of an individual from a population is often called a **trial.** As the smallest sample involving more than one trial is a sample with two, we consider this case first. A sample of two is too small to be of much use in evaluating claims about a population, but it is easy to understand the probabilities involved. To keep things as simple as possible, let us consider sampling (with replacement) from our original model population of 200 marbles (Model 1). We will focus on just the color variable and then only on two values of that variable, red (R) and nonred (N).

The easiest way to think about sampling is to imagine a **sequence of trials,** each consisting of the selection of one member from the population. We can then represent each trial by different random variables, which are conveniently labeled $\mathbf{X_1}$, $\mathbf{X_2}$, $\mathbf{X_3} \cdots \mathbf{X_n}$. Each of these random variables has two possible values, R and N. The case of just two trials would be represented by the sequence $(\mathbf{X_1}, \mathbf{X_2})$.

There are only four possible results of selecting two marbles from the population of Model 1. We might get a red marble on both trials, a red marble on the first and

FIGURE 5.18

A hypothetical population of pairs of selections of a marble from the population of Model 1.

1. (X_1, X_2) Trials actually performed.

2. (X_1, X_2)
3. (X_1, X_2)
4. (X_1, X_2)
⋮
n. (X_1, X_2)

} Large hypothetical set of pairs of trials

a nonred marble on the second, a nonred marble on the first and red marble on the second, and, finally, a nonred marble on both trials. These four possible results may be symbolized as

(R,R) (R,N) (N,R) (N,N)

A common way of thinking about sampling is to imagine not only the sequence of two trials actually carried out but a large hypothetical set of sequences of two trials each. If carried out, each member of this set would have one of the four possible results described above. This set is pictured in Figure 5.18. It is helpful to think of this set as itself a population, not of marbles but of sequences of two selections of marbles from the population of Model 1.

We can now characterize the crucial process known as **random sampling.** There are two things necessary for the sampling process to be *random.* (1) On each trial, the probability of red must equal the probability of red in the population, which in Model 1 is .50. This may be represented by the proportion of results of each trial in the large imaginary set of two trials being .50 (i.e., half of the first trials in the set of two trials would yield an R, and half of the second trials in the set of two trials would also yield an R). (2) There is *no correlation* between the outcomes of the two trials. For example, if we looked at members of the set of two imaginary trials in which the first trial yielded an R and then for that set counted up the proportion of results of the second trial that also showed an R, that proportion would again be .50.

It is important to realize that randomness is not a feature of a sample by itself. You cannot tell a random sample just by looking at the sample. Randomness is a feature of the *process* by which the sample is selected. We have followed tradition in characterizing that process in terms of the results that would be expected if the whole sampling process itself were repeated many times. Later, we learn something about the kinds of actual physical selection processes, operating on real populations, that could be expected to achieve the desired results in repeated applications.

We can now proceed to the calculation of probabilities for the various possible results of selecting two marbles, at random, from our model population. The assumption of random sampling, together with the fact that the population of Model 1 contains 50 percent red marbles, means that, in a large set of two trials each, the first trial would yield a red half of the time. That is, $\mathbf{P}(\mathbf{X}_1 = \mathrm{R}) = .50$. Similarly, $\mathbf{P}(\mathbf{X}_1 = \mathrm{N}) = .50$. By the same reasoning, $\mathbf{P}(\mathbf{X}_2 = \mathrm{R}) = .50$ and $\mathbf{P}(\mathbf{X}_2 = \mathrm{N}) = .50$.

The assumption of random sampling also tells us that the two random variables, $\mathbf{X}_1$ and $\mathbf{X}_2$, are not correlated. Thus, if we wish to compute the probability of getting a red marble on both the first and second trials, we can use the simple multiplication rule. That is,

$$\mathbf{P}(\mathbf{X}_1 = \mathrm{R} \text{ and } \mathbf{X}_2 = \mathrm{R}) = \mathbf{P}(\mathbf{X}_1 = \mathrm{R}) \times \mathbf{P}(\mathbf{X}_2 = \mathrm{R}) = .50 \times .50 = .25$$

By a similar calculation, $\mathbf{P}(\mathrm{R,N}) = \mathbf{P}(\mathrm{N,R}) = \mathbf{P}(\mathrm{N,N}) = .25$.

You should realize that the different possible results of multiple sampling do not have to have the same probability. They do in our example because half of the marbles in our model population are red. If we had considered the values green and nongreen instead, then the probabilities would not all be the same. For example, $\mathbf{P}(\mathrm{G,G}) = \frac{1}{4} \times \frac{1}{4} = \frac{1}{16}$, but $\mathbf{P}(\mathrm{G,N}) = \frac{1}{4} \times \frac{3}{4} = \frac{3}{16}$. It is a little easier to deal with the case in which the original population probabilities are 50-50, so we will continue to use that example.

In most applications of sampling, we are not interested in the *order* in which the results occur in a set of trials. It is the relative number, or **relative frequency,** of *types* of individuals that is important for the evaluation of statistical hypotheses. Thus, for example, it usually makes no difference whether a trial had the result (R,N) or (N,R). The important thing is that these two results both have one red and one nonred marble. That is, the relative frequency of red marbles is the same in both of these results, namely, one of two, or ½.

The result of selecting two marbles might be no R's, one R, or two R's. That is, the *relative frequency* of R's can have three different possible values: $\frac{0}{2}$ (0), $\frac{1}{2}$ (.50), and $\frac{2}{2}$ (1.00). Let us use the letter **Y** to represent the random variable with these three values. Now, what are the probabilities corresponding to **P(Y)?**

For no R's or two R's, the calculations are easy. $\mathbf{P}(0 \text{ R's}) = \mathbf{P}(\mathrm{N,N}) = \frac{1}{4}$. Similarly, $\mathbf{P}(2 \text{ R's}) = \mathbf{P}(\mathrm{R,R}) = \frac{1}{4}$. The probability of getting one R out of two trials is more difficult to calculate. It is the probability of getting either the result (R,N) or the result (N,R). But these two sequences represent exclusive possibilities. So, we can use the *simple addition rule:*

$$\mathbf{P}(1 \text{ R}) = \mathbf{P}[(\mathrm{R,N}) \text{ or } (\mathrm{N,R})] = \mathbf{P}(\mathrm{R,N}) + \mathbf{P}(\mathrm{N,R}) = \tfrac{1}{4} + \tfrac{1}{4} = \tfrac{1}{2}$$

These three probabilities form a probability distribution for the relative frequency of R's in two random selections from our model population. This distribution is shown in Figure 5.19, which is our first example of a **sampling distribution.** You should study it carefully because most of the probability distributions that are important in understanding statistical reasoning are sampling distributions. If, at a later stage, you find your understanding of sampling distributions getting fuzzy, come back to Figure 5.19. You should now be able to follow every step in the derivation of this distribution. Other sampling distributions are more complicated mainly because they involve larger numbers of trials. They are not *in principle* any more complex.

FIGURE 5.19

Sampling distribution for the relative frequency of Red in two trials from a population for which **P**(R) = ½.

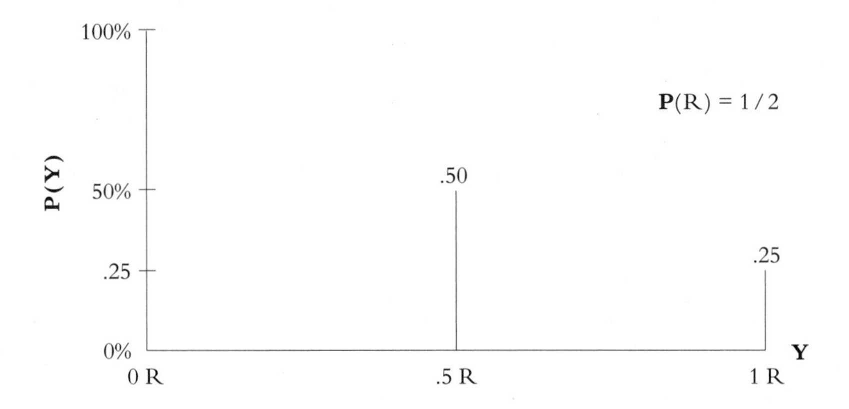

THREE, FOUR, AND FIVE TRIALS

Let us now consider *three* trials, with replacement, from our model population. Here, we must consider the sequence of random variables $(\mathbf{X}_1, \mathbf{X}_2, \mathbf{X}_3)$, where each random variable can take on the values R or N. In this case, there are *eight* different, mutually exclusive, possible arrangements of the results of the three trials. These are

(R,R,R) (R,R,N) (R,N,R) (N,R,R)
(R,N,N) (N,R,N) (N,N,R) (N,N,N)

As before, we imagine a large set of samplings consisting of three trials each. The assumption of *random sampling* implies that, in this set, half the triples would exhibit an R on the first trial, half would exhibit an R on the second trial, and half would exhibit an R on the third trial. So $\mathbf{P}(\mathbf{X}_1 = R) = \mathbf{P}(\mathbf{X}_2 = R) = \mathbf{P}(\mathbf{X}_3 = R) = .50$. Random sampling also implies that the results of different trials are *not correlated.* To compute the probability of the result (R, R, R), therefore, we can use the *simple multiplication rule.* That is,

$$\mathbf{P}(R,R,R) = \mathbf{P}(\mathbf{X}_1 = R) \times \mathbf{P}(\mathbf{X}_2 = R) \times \mathbf{P}(\mathbf{X}_3 = R) = \tfrac{1}{2} \times \tfrac{1}{2} \times \tfrac{1}{2} = \tfrac{1}{8} = .125$$

As **P**(R) = **P**(N) = ½, for each random variable, each of the other seven possible outcomes of three trials will have exactly the same probability.

For a sample consisting of three trials, the random variable **Y** has *four* different possible values. That is, the *relative frequency* of R's obtained in three trials could be none of three, one of three, two of three, or three of three. We have just determined that **P**(3 R's) = .125. The probability of no R's is the same.

FIGURE 5.20

Sampling distribution for the relative frequency of Red in three trials from a population for which **P**(R) = ½.

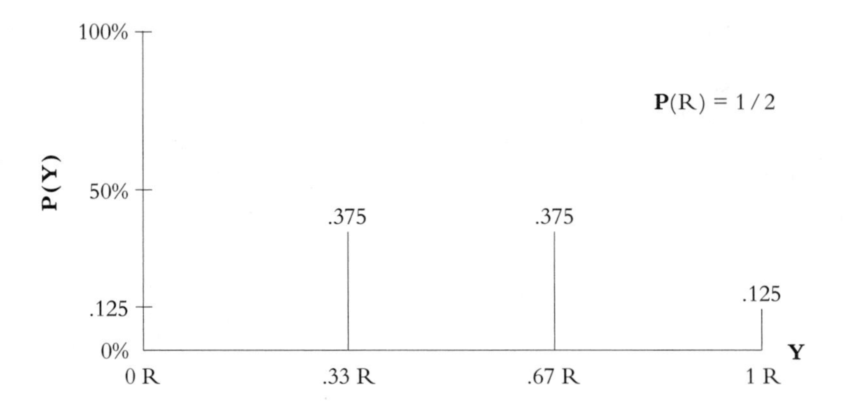

The probability of obtaining 1 R or 2 R's is determined, as before, by using the *addition rule.* This time, there are three mutually exclusive sequences that have only one R. These are (R,N,N), (N,R,N), and (N,N,R). The probability of getting one or another of these three is, by the addition rule, the sum of the three probabilities—that is, ⅜ (or .375). As you can easily verify for yourself, the probability of getting 2 R's is also ⅜. So, the *sampling distribution,* **P(Y),** for three trials is as shown in Figure 5.20.

To work out the distributions of **P(Y)** for *four* and for *five* trials would require looking at 16 and 32 different possible sequences, respectively. That is best left as an exercise for the student. The general procedure is exactly as above. Use the *multiplication rule* to calculate the probabilities of the individual sequences. Then, use the *addition rule* to calculate the probabilities for the various possible relative frequencies of R's. The end result of going through the calculations for both four and five trials is shown in Figure 5.21.

As you will soon learn, a sample of four or five is still much too small to evaluate any interesting statistical hypotheses. But you should look closely at the sampling distributions in Figures 5.19 through 5.21 and make sure that you understand where they come from. Sampling distributions for more trials are very tedious to calculate by hand. For only 10 trials, there are 1,024 different sequences of results to consider, and for 25 trials, more than 30 million. To work out these sampling distributions from first principles requires a good calculator or a small computer. In principle, however, nothing is involved except repeated applications of the simple multiplication and addition rules.

5.10 LARGE SAMPLES

Figure 5.22 exhibits the sampling distributions for the relative frequency of red marbles in 10, 20, and 50 trials on our model population. Figure 5.23 exhibits the sampling

FIGURE 5.21

Sampling distributions for the relative frequency of Red in four and five trials from a population for which **P**(R) = ½.

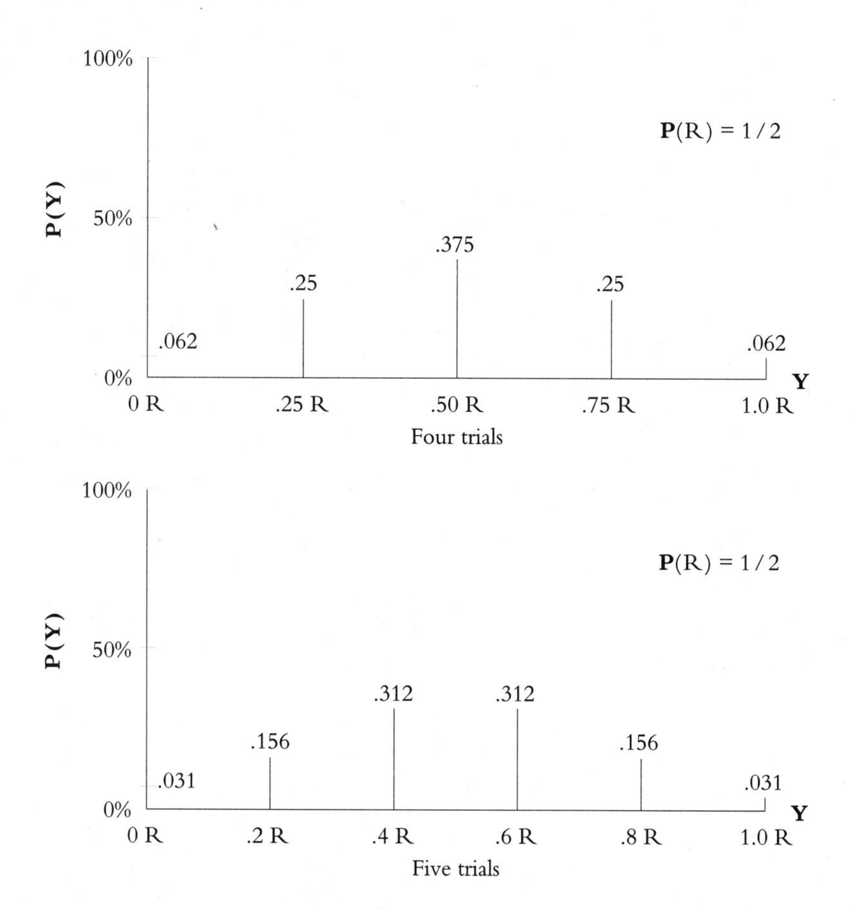

distributions for 100, 250, and 500 trials. Figure 5.24 is a "blow-up" of Figure 5.23. That is, it exhibits the same distributions but on an enlarged scale so that you can see the individual probabilities somewhat better.

Remember that these sampling distributions are not in principle any different from the sampling distributions for smaller numbers of trials. It is just that, for large numbers of trials, there are many more possible relative frequencies of red marbles in the sample to be considered. So the distribution has considerably more probability values to calculate (or look up in a table).

EXPECTED FREQUENCY

One obvious feature of all these sampling distributions is that the **most probable** sample frequency for red marbles agrees with the ratio of red marbles in the population.

FIGURE 5.22

Sampling distributions for the relative frequency of Red in 10, 25, and 50 trials from a population for which **P**(R) = ½.

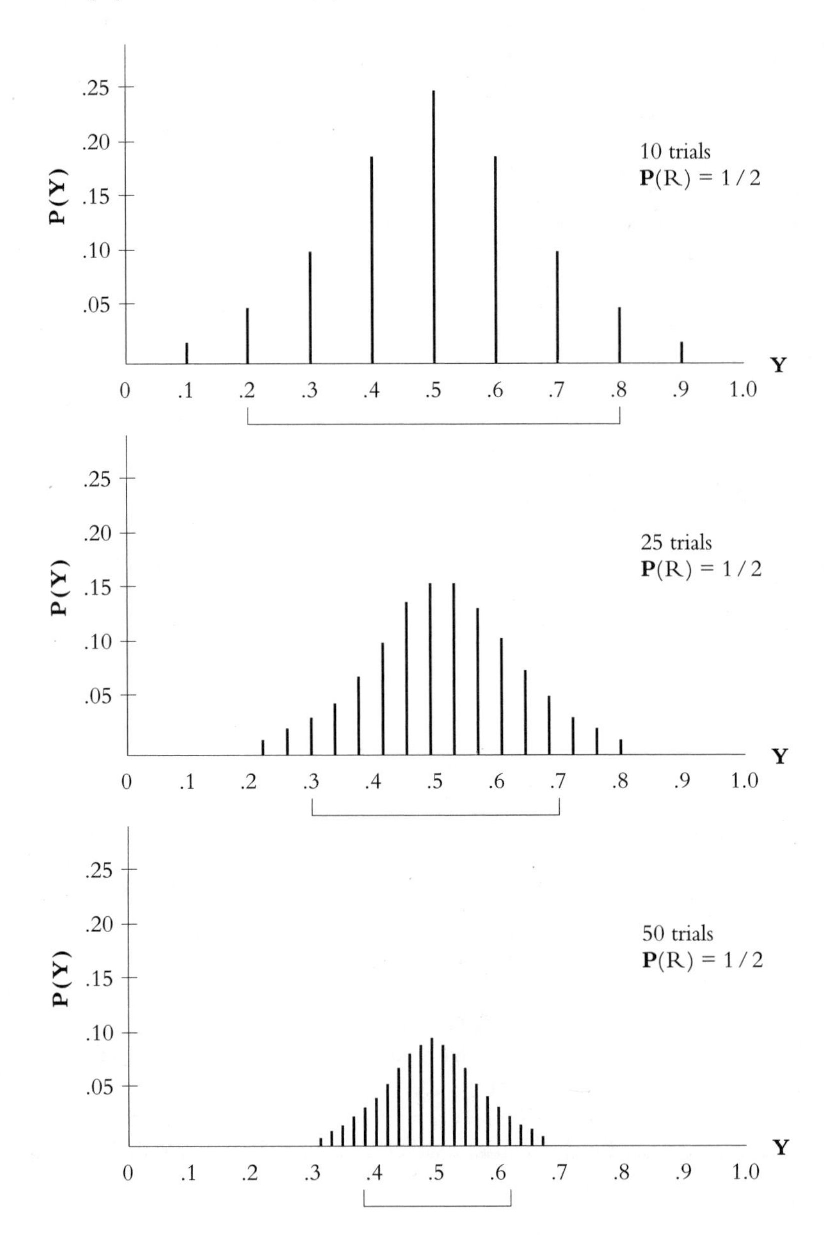

FIGURE 5.23

Sampling distributions for the relative frequency of Red in 100, 250, and 500 trials from a population for which **P**(R) = ½.

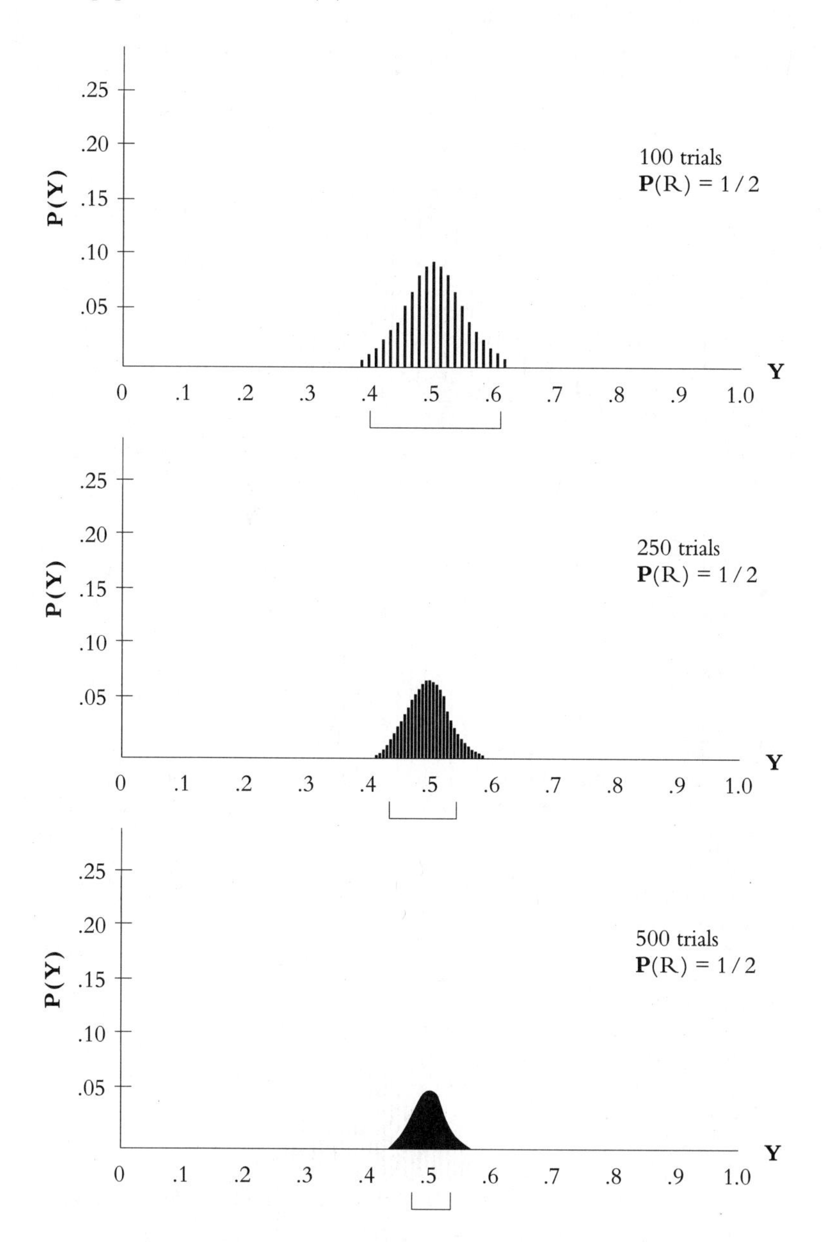

FIGURE 5.24

Enlarged sampling distributions for the relative frequency of Red in 100, 250, and 500 trials from a population for which **P**(R) = ½. Note that **P(Y)** extends only from 0 to .10 and **Y** only from .40 to .60.

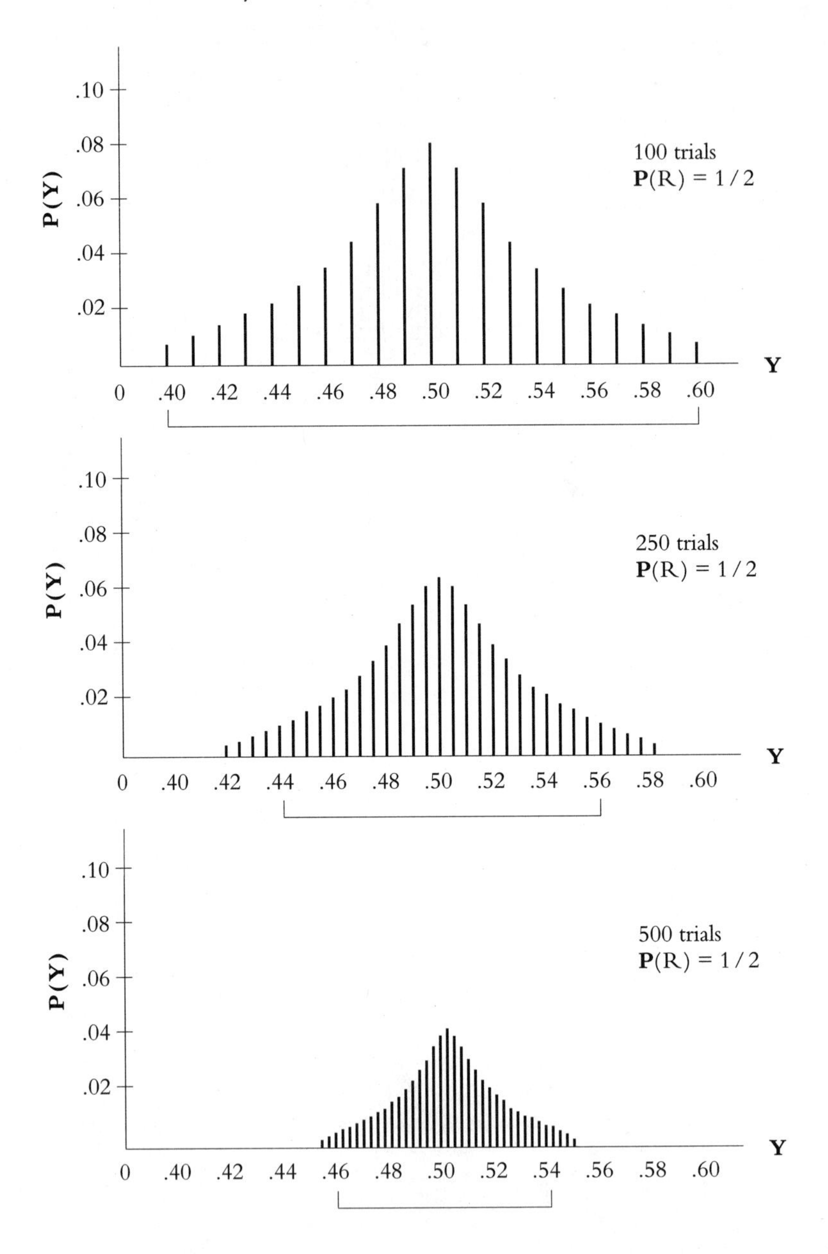

In our example, the ratio of red marbles in the population is .50 and the sample frequency with the greatest probability is always .50 (or as near to .50 as possible). For most of the sampling distributions we shall encounter, the most probable frequency coincides with what, in statistics textbooks, is variously called the **expected** frequency, **average** frequency, or **mean** frequency.

STANDARD DEVIATION

In looking at the distributions in Figures 5.19 through 5.24, you may have noticed that the probability of the most probable frequency is *lower* for large samples. The probability of getting half red marbles is 50% for a sample of 2, 25% for a sample of 10, 8% for a sample of 100, and only 5% for a sample of 250. Thus, the larger the sample, the less likely you are actually to get the expected frequency. This may strike you as strange, even contradictory. But it makes sense when you think about it.

If you make only a few trials, say, two or four, there is a pretty good chance that you will get half red marbles. In fact, the probability is .375 for four trials. However, if you do 100 trials, you would not really expect to get *exactly* fifty red marbles. You would, nevertheless, expect to get pretty *near* to fifty red marbles. The problem is to define "nearness" within probability distributions.

Deviation from the mean is fundamentally a matter of *differences* in relative frequencies. A relative frequency of .40, for example, differs by .10 from a mean relative frequency of .50. However, deviations from the mean of a sampling distribution are usually measured *indirectly* by way of *probabilities*. The unit of measure for deviation is known as the **standard deviation** (SD). Explaining the origin of this notion involves what, for us, are unnecessary complexities. The operational use of the notion, however, is quite simple.

To begin with a specific distribution, consider the sampling distribution for relative frequencies in 100 trials from a population with half its members exhibiting the property of interest. The expected number is 50, but the probability of getting exactly 50 of 100 is only .08. However, the probability of getting between 46 and 54 is roughly ⅔, or 67%. All sample frequencies from .46 to .54 would therefore be said to be *within one standard deviation of the mean*. Why 67% defines a standard deviation is, from our standpoint, arbitrary. The real reason is mainly of historical interest.

Similarly, all sample frequencies from .40 to .60 have a combined probability of roughly 95%. All frequencies in this range are said to be *within two standard deviations of the mean*. Again, the connection between 95% and two standard deviations is fairly arbitrary. A similar relation holds between *three* standard deviations and a probability of 99%. The combined probability of all frequencies within three standard deviations of the mean is about 99%. These relationships are shown in Figure 5.25.

The reason for defining deviation, or nearness, in terms of probability is that the resulting measure is *independent* of the number of trials. Two standard deviations means the same thing for any sampling distribution, regardless of the size of the sample. It refers to all the possible sample frequencies around the mean having a combined probability of 95%.

FIGURE 5.25

Standard deviations.

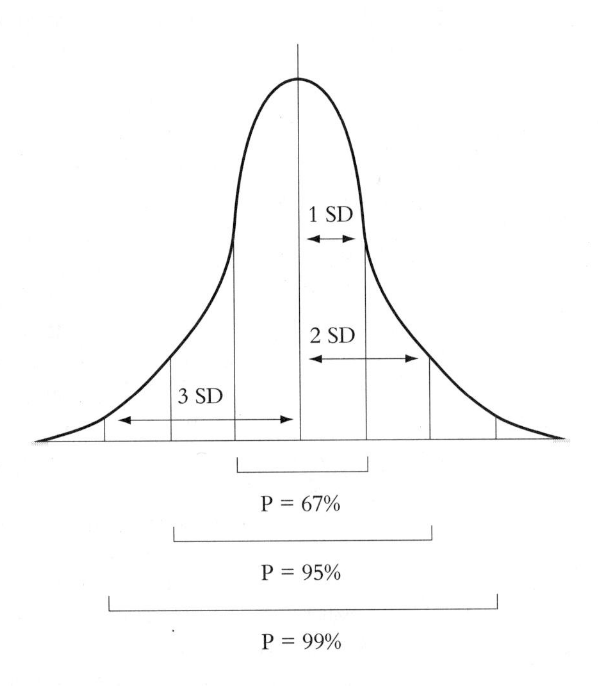

THE VALUE OF LARGE SAMPLES

Even considering only a few trials, you can begin to see why larger samples are desirable. For larger samples, the probability of observing a relative number of R's near the ratio of R's in the population (i.e., 50%) *increases.* In Figures 5.19 through 5.21, this is best seen by looking at the ends, or "tails," of the distributions. For larger samples, the probability of selecting a relative number of R's that is not near to half decreases. Obviously, selecting either no R's or all R's is as far from getting half R's as possible. With only two trials, there is a 50% probability that you will select either no R's or all R's. (Use the addition rule.) For three trials, the probability of selecting no R's or all R's drops to 25%. With four trials, it drops to about 12%, and with five, to about 6%. So, if selecting near to half R's means merely not selecting some number as far as possible from half, the probability of getting near to one-half R's increases from 50% to roughly 94% as the size of the sample increases from two to five. This trend becomes more pronounced as the number of trials is increased still further.

Now, look again at the sampling distributions in Figures 5.22 and 5.23. Below the axis in each graph, there is a bracket indicating all the sample frequencies corresponding to two standard deviations from the expected frequency. These frequencies have a combined probability of roughly 95%. In a sample of 50, for example, this set includes all possible sample frequencies from .36 to .64. As the size of the sample gets *larger,* the frequencies in this set get closer and closer to the expected frequency. This means that the *difference* between the mean and the frequencies within 2 SD's of the mean gets smaller and smaller. That is to say, the likely deviation of the sample frequency from the mean gets smaller and smaller.

We have just seen that if you pick a fixed high probability, say, 95%, then the set of possible sample frequencies with that high a probability gets closer to the mean value for larger samples. We might turn things around, however, by fixing the range of frequencies and letting the probability change. For example, let us say that any frequency in the interval .40 to .60 is "near" to .50. Then, for a sample of ten the probability that the sample frequency is "near" to .50 is only 65%. (By the addition rule, **P** (.4 or .5 or .6) = **P**(.4) + **P**(.5) + **P**(.6) = .20 + .25 + .20 = .65.) However, for a sample of 100, the probability that the sample frequency will be similarly "near" to .50 is 95%. Thus, the larger the sample, the more probable it is that the sample frequency will be "near" to the expected frequency.

It should now be fairly clear why scientists, in general, prefer large samples to small ones. The expected frequency of any property in a random sample is the same as the proportion of that property in the population. Thus, the larger the sample, the more probable it is that the frequency observed in the sample will be "close" to the actual proportion in the population. So, in general, larger samples should be better indicators of the actual proportions in populations—which are, of course, what we really want to know. We see how all this works in the next chapter.

5.11 SAMPLING WITH UNEQUAL PROBABILITIES

The examples we have used for most of this chapter involved sampling with *equal* probabilities. That is, the two possible results of any single selection, red or nonred, both had a probability of one-half. For most people, this case is easiest to grasp.

For you to see that there is no fundamental difference when sampling with *unequal probabilities,* Figure 5.26 shows two sampling distributions for the relative frequency of green marbles from our model population. In Model 1, **P**(G) = .25. In Figure 5.26, the number of trials is 25 and 50 respectively. You should compare these sampling distributions with those shown in Figure 5.22. The chief difference is that the distribution shifts "downward," so that its mean value is .25 rather than .50. It is also a little asymmetrical. The asymmetry, however, is less pronounced for larger samples. And, as before, the larger the sample, the greater the probability that the sample frequency will be near the population ratio, which in this case is .25.

FIGURE 5.26

Sampling distributions for the relative frequency of Green in 25 and 50 trials from a population for which **P**(G) = ¼.

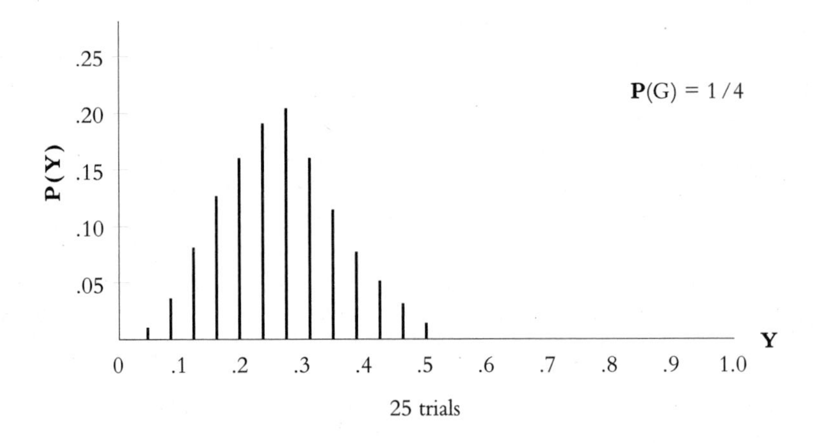

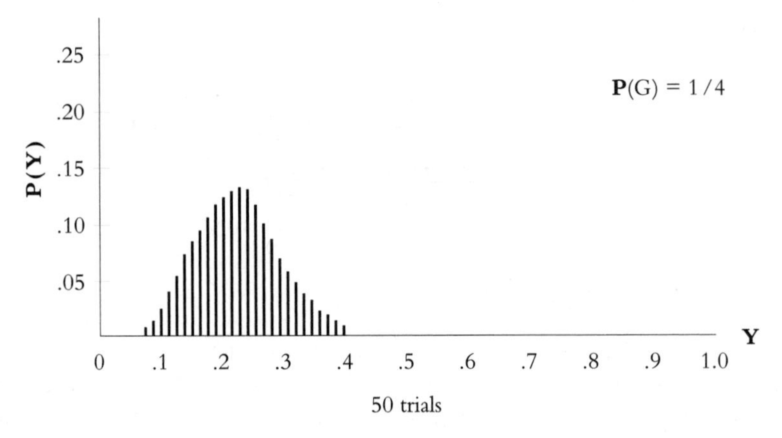

APPENDIX

A CORRELATION COEFFICIENT

Figure 5.27 exhibits the kind of representation of the strength of correlation on finds in standard textbooks of statistics. Here,

a = the number of marbles that are red and small
b = the number of marbles that are green and small
c = the number of marbles that are red and large
d = the number of marbles that are green and large

FIGURE 5.27

A representation of the strength of a correlation as found in typical statistics textbooks.

	RED	GREEN	
SMALL	a	b	a + b
LARGE	c	d	c + d
	a + c	b + d	

The **correlation coefficient,** r, is given by the following formula:

$$r = \frac{(bc - ad)}{[(a + b)\ (c + d)\ (a + c)\ (b + d)]^{1/2}}$$

As with the difference measure defined earlier, this measure varies from −1.0 to +1.0 and has value zero when the variables are not correlated. Unlike our difference measure, however, this measure is also symmetrical. Nevertheless, this measure is obviously too complex to compute in our heads.

• EXERCISES

EXERCISE 5.1

Consider a jar of marbles with the following composition:

Red: 40. 20 Large. 20 Small.
Green: 30. 20 Large. 10 Small.
Blue: 20. 15 Large. 5 Small.
Yellow: 10. 5 Large. 5 Small.

A. Diagram the statistical distribution for the color variable following the form of either Figure 5.4 or Figure 5.5.

B. Diagram the statistical distribution for the size variable following the form of either Figure 5.4 or Figure 5.5.

C. Diagram the four possible distinct correlations involving values of the color variable and the size variable.

EXERCISE 5.2

Use the *addition* rule to calculate the following probabilities for the population described in Exercise 5.1. You may check your answer by going directly to the ratios in the population.

A. **P**(R or G) B. **P**(R or B) C. **P**(R or Y)
D. **P**(G or B) E. **P**(G or Y) F. **P**(B or Y)

EXERCISE 5.3

Use the *multiplication* rule to calculate the following probabilities for the population described in Exercise 5.1. You may check your answer by going directly to the ratios in the population.

A. **P**(R and L) B. **P**(R and S) C. **P**(G and L)
D. **P**(G and S) E. **P**(Y and L) F. **P**(Y and S)

EXERCISE 5.4

Use the multiplication and addition rules, together with your answers to Exercises 5.2 and 5.3, to calculate the following probabilities for the population in Exercise 5.1. You may check your answers by going directly to the ratios in the populations.

A. **P**[(R or B) and L] B. **P**[(G or Y) and S] C. **P**[(G or B) and L]
D. **P**[(R and L) or G] E. **P**[(B and S) or Y] F. **P**[(G and S) or R]

EXERCISE 5.5

Rank the following events in order of increasing probability (i.e., number the least probable, 1, and the most probable, 3).

A. Jack and Jill went up the hill.

B. Jill went up the hill.

C. Jack or Jill went up the hill.

EXERCISE 5.6

In the example of the flippant judge, do all the calculations that show that the probability of the jury reaching an **incorrect** verdict is ¼. (If you are mathematically inclined, you might try showing that, if the good judges have a probability, **p**, of being correct, then the probability of the jury being correct is likewise **p**, no matter what **p** is. Thus, no matter what the reliability of the good judges, the flippant judge cancels out one of the good judges.)

EXERCISE 5.7

Following the method used to determine the sampling distributions in Figures 5.19 and 5.20

A. Work out the details leading to the sampling distribution for four trials, as shown in Figure 5.21. You will have to consider 16 different possible results of the four trials.

B. Work out the details leading to the sampling distribution for five trials, as shown in Figure 5.21. You will have to consider 32 different possible results of the four trials.

EXERCISE 5.8

Following the method used to determine the sampling distribution in Figure 5.20, work out the sampling distribution for the relative frequency of **green** marbles on three draws from the population of Model 1 as pictured in Figure 5.12. In this case, **P**(G) = ¼ and **P**(N) = ¾.

EXERCISE 5.9

The following are some probabilities for the relative frequency, **f,** of red marbles in ten draws from a jar of marbles when **P**(R) = .50. **P(f** = 0) = .001; **P(f** = .1) = .01; **P(f** = .2) = .04; **P(f** = .3) = .12; **P(f** = .4) = .20; **P(f** = .5) = .25. Using these values and the fact that the distribution is perfectly symmetrical [i.e., **P(f** = .6) = **P(f** = .4), and so on], determine the following probabilities:

A. **P[f** = (0 or 1.0)]

B. **P[f** = (0 or .1 or .2 or .3)]

C. **P[f** = (.3 or .4 or .5 or .6 or .7)]

EXERCISE 5.10

The following are some probabilities for the relative frequency, **f,** of red marbles in 100 draws from a jar of marbles when **P**(R) = .50. **P(f** = .35) =.001; **P(f** = .40) = .011; **P(f** = .45) = .049; **P(f** = .46) = .058; **P(f** = .47) = .067; **P(f** = .48) = .075; **P(f** = .49) = .078; **P(f** = .50) = .080. Using these probabilities and the fact that the distribution is perfectly symmetrical, determine the following probabilities:

A. **P[f** = (.35 or .40 or .60 or .65)]

B. **P[f** = (.48 or .49 or .50 or .51 or .52)]

C. **P[f** = (0 through .44 or .56 through 1.00)]

EXERCISE 5.11

Listed below are three possible sample frequencies. For which of the following six sampling distributions are these frequencies within two standard deviations of the mean? 10 trials? 25 trials? 50 trials? 100 trials? 250 trials?

500 trials? You will have to look at Figures 5.22, 5.23, and 5.24 to answer this question.

A. **f** = .7 B. **f** = .6 C. **f** = .55

EXERCISE 5.12

The game of squash may be played according to two different sets of rules, one of which has 9 points to a game and the other 15 points per game. Suppose you regularly play squash with a person whose overall squash skills are just slightly better than your own. Are your chances of winning (a) better, (b) worse, or (c) the same, with the shorter as opposed to the longer game? Explain.

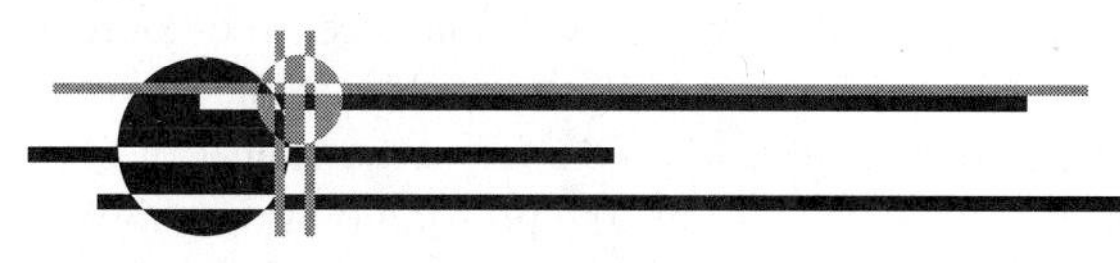

CHAPTER 6
EVALUATING STATISTICAL HYPOTHESES

The purpose of having learned about statistical and probabilistic models is to be able to *evaluate statistical hypotheses.* The relationship between models and hypotheses was exhibited in Figure 5.1. As we shall use the term, a **statistical hypothesis** is a claim about a real-world population. It is a claim that the real population has the structure of a specific statistical model. For example, the claim that a majority of smokers in the United States are men is a claim about the population of Americans who smoke. The claim has the form of a simple proportion. The relevant variable is sex. The two possible values of this variable are male and female. So, the statistical hypothesis claims that the real-world population of American smokers fits a simple proportion model, with the proportion of individuals exhibiting the value male being greater than 50%.

In principle, the truth of the above statistical hypothesis could be ascertained by determining the sex of every smoker in America. In practice, that is impossible. We can at most examine a sample from the population. So, evaluating a statistical hypothesis is typically a matter of determining whether a given sample from the population contains data that provide evidence for the truth of the hypothesis.

Sample data consist of observed **relative frequencies** of individuals exhibiting the properties of interest. For example, we might find that a sample of 100 smokers contained 55, or 55%, males. Is that good evidence that more than 50% of all American smokers are male? The answer to this question is given by the statistical theory of estimation.

6.1 ESTIMATION

For any property, or any value of a random variable, call it A, there is some *probability* of A in the population, **P**(A). A randomly selected sample from the population will exhibit some *relative frequency* of A's, **f**(A). In the typical case, the actual numerical value of **P**(A) is *unknown,* but the numerical value of **f**(A) is *known.* **Estimation** is a statistical technique for using the observed value of **f**(A) as evidence for claims about the unknown value of **P**(A). We wiii first develop our understanding of the process of estimation in the context of our standard model of marbles in a jar. That means that we will be concentrating on the right-hand side of Figure 5.1. Later in this chapter, we begin applying our models to real-world populations pictured on the left-hand side of Figure 5.1.

In our standard model, there are two variables, color, with values red and nonred; and size, with values large and small. We assumed that half the marbles in the jar were red, so **P**(R) = .50. We then determined *sampling probabilities* for various values of **f**(R) in samples of different sizes. With **n** = 100, for example, the probability is roughly 8% that exactly $^{50}/_{100}$ red marbles would be selected. That is, the sampling probability that **f**(R) would turn out to be exactly .50 is only 8%. Ordinarily, we would not regard 8% as a high enough probability to claim we had good evidence for thinking that the process of sampling 100 marbles would yield exactly 50 red ones. This leaves us with two questions. How high a probability is required to have good evidence for a claim? What claim about **f**(R) could we make that had a suitably high probability?

In answer to the first question, statisticians typically adopt the convention that a probability of 95% is sufficient for having good evidence. This is a reasonable convention. In typical circumstances, most people are willing to regard a 95% chance of being right as sufficient assurance. Unless otherwise indicated, that is the standard we will use from now on. What, then, can we say about **f**(R) which has a probability of 95% of being correct? Well, we know that for any randomly selected sample from a jar with **P**(R) = .50, the probability that **f**(R) will be within two *standard deviations* (SD) of .50 is 95%. That holds for any sample size. For a sample of 100, two standard deviations includes all possible values of **f**(R) from .40 through .60. So, we can say that there is good evidence that random selection of 100 marbles from a population with **P**(R) = .50 will produce a sample in which **f**(R) lies between .40 and .60.

We have just reviewed the situation in which the proportion of red marbles in the population, **P**(R), is *known*. We have considered what one could then say about the relative frequency of red marbles, **f**(R), in a randomly selected sample. The typical real situation, however, is roughly the *reverse* of this. We learn the relative frequency, **f**(A), of some property in a randomly selected sample and wish to infer something about the *unknown* proportion, **P**(A), of that property in the population.

Although beyond the technical level of this text, there is an elementary result in statistical theory that allows us to extend our analysis of the case in which **P**(R) is known to the case in which **P**(R) is unknown. Suppose, this time, that we randomly select **n** marbles from a jar in which the proportion of red marbles, **P**(R), is *unknown*. Our sample, of course, exhibits some definite relative frequency, **f**(R), of red marbles. We now construct an interval of values for the unknown value of **P**(R) by adding and subtracting two standard deviations from the observed value of **f**(R). That is, we construct the interval **P**(R) = **f**(R) ± 2SDs. Statistical theory tells us that there is a 95% probability that any interval, so constructed, will include the true value of **P**(R).

For example, with n = 100, two standard deviations amounts to a difference of about .10. If we observe 50 red marbles in a random sample of 100 marbles from a jar whose proportion of red marbles is unknown, we construct the interval, **P**(R) = .50 ± .10. That interval either will or will not include the unknown value of **P**(R). Statistical theory assures us, however, that 95% of all intervals constructed by this general method will, in the long run, include the true value of **P**(R).

In statistical terms, the interval, .40 to .60, is called the **95% Confidence Interval** for the numerical value of **P**(R). So, in general, whenever a randomly selected sample turns up a frequency **f**(A) of some property, there is good evidence that the confidence interval corresponding to the size of the sample includes the proportion, **P**(A), in the population. Estimation, then, turns out to be a matter of constructing the appropriate confidence interval.

MARGIN OF ERROR

In the context of deriving sampling probabilities from a population with a known proportion of red marbles, we introduced the notion of a standard deviation. For any sample size, the probability that the observed numerical value, **f**(R), would fall within two standard deviations of the numerical value of **P**(R) was 95%. The corresponding notion for estimation is **Margin of Error** (ME). For an observed relative frequency, **f**(R), the 95% confidence interval for the numerical value of **P**(R) can be constructed by taking the numerical value of **f**(R) plus or minus the margin of error. For example, on observing 50 red marbles in a sample of 100 randomly selected marbles, we construct the 95% confidence interval for **P**(R) as being equal to **f**(R) ± .10. That is, the estimated value of **P**(R) = **f**(R) ± **ME** = .50 ± .10.

It cannot be emphasized too strongly that every estimate of a population probability from a sample frequency must carry a margin of error. So, every estimate must be an interval. One of the greatest mistakes you can make in statistical reasoning is simply to equate the unknown population probability, **P**(A), with the observed sample frequency, **f**(A). If you did that as a regular policy, you would be wrong most of the time. As we noted above, if **P**(R) in our model population were in fact .50, the chance that a random sample of 100 would yield 50 red marbles is only about 8%. Thus, in general, if you went around equating **P**(A) with **f**(A) for samples of 100, you would be right only about 8% of the time. Adding the appropriate margin of error means that you would be right about 95% of the time.

SAMPLE SIZE AND MARGIN OF ERROR

The concept of a margin of error, like that of standard deviation, is defined to be independent of sample size. The particular proportions of **P**(A) included within the margin of error, however, depend crucially on the sample size. This should already be evident from Figures 5.22 to 5.24, which show the standard deviation encompassing an ever narrower range of sample frequencies as the sample size increases. The same is true for the margin of error. Table 6.1 shows the margin of error for a range of sample sizes from **n** = 10 to **n** = 10,000. As you will note, the corresponding margin of error ranges from .32 to .01.

Table 6.2 provides a shorter version of Table 6.1. Here, the margins of error are rounded off to make them easier to memorize. Thus, for example, Table 6.1 gives the correct margin of error for **n** = 500 as being close to .04. In Table 6.2, the margin of error for **n** = 500 is given as .05. This is much easier to remember. Think of Table 6.2 as providing convenient "rules of thumb" for margins of error. You should have these numbers on the tip of your tongue so that you can give a quick evaluation of statistical data as you come across it every day. For sample sizes intermediate to those covered by these rules of thumb, simply interpolate. For example, taking the margins of error for **n** = 500 to be .05 and for **n** = 2,000 to be .02, you can easily interpolate that the margin of error for **n** = 1,000 must be about .03.

TABLE 6.1
APPROXIMATE 95% CONFIDENCE INTERVALS FOR AN OBSERVED SAMPLE FREQUENCY OF .50 IN SAMPLES OF VARIOUS SIZES

SAMPLE SIZE	CONFIDENCE INTERVAL	MARGIN OF ERROR
10	.18 to .82	± .32
25	.30 to .70	± .20
50	.36 to .64	± .14
100	.40 to .60	± .10
250	.44 to .56	± .06
500	.46 to .54	± .04
1000	.47 to .53	± .03
2000	.48 to .52	± .02
10000	.49 to .51	± .01

Figure 6.1 summarizes the process of estimating proportions in a population on the basis of sample frequencies. First, note the sample frequency, **f**(A). Then, use the sample size, **n,** together with Table 6.1 or the rules of thumb given in Table 6.2, to determine the appropriate margin of error. Estimate **P**(A) to be in the interval **f**(A) ± **ME.**

Note that the *sample size* is an absolutely crucial piece of information in estimating proportions in populations. Without some knowledge of the sample size, knowledge of the sample frequency is not very useful. What if **n** were only 10? That would mean a margin of error of .32 and, thus, a confidence interval covering more than half the whole range from 0 to 1.

CONFIDENCE LEVEL AND MARGIN OF ERROR

We have adopted a 95% **confidence level** in constructing our margins of error. This means that the probability of the interval, **f**(A)± **ME,** including the true value of

TABLE 6.2
"RULE OF THUMB" MARGINS OF ERROR FOR SELECTED SAMPLE SIZES

SAMPLE SIZE	MARGIN OF ERROR
25	± .25
100	± .10
500	± .05
2000	± .02
10000	± .01

FIGURE 6.1

Estimating a proportion in a population using the observed relative frequency in a random sample.

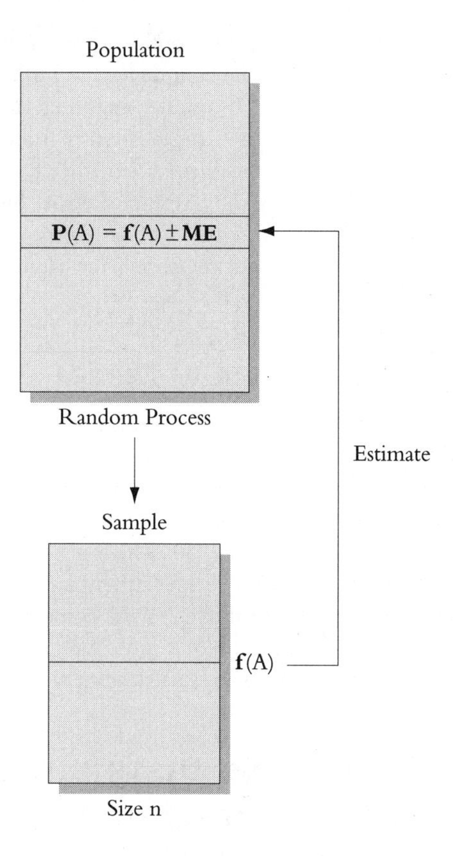

P(A), is 95%. Although we will generally follow the convention of using a 95% confidence level, it is instructive to consider the consequences of adopting a different convention.

Let us, for the moment, stick with a sample size of 100. Because margin of error is related to deviation in sample frequencies, let us look first at deviations. From Chapter 5, we know that the probability of getting exactly $^{50}/_{100}$ red marbles in a random sample of 100 from a population with ½ red marbles is about .08. Likewise, the probability of getting $^{49}/_{100}$ is .078. Because this sampling distribution is symmetrical, the probability of getting $^{51}/_{100}$ is likewise .078. So, the probability of getting either 49 or 51 of 100 is .156. Similarly, the probability of getting 48 or 52 of 100 is .150. Because these are all exclusive possibilities, the probability of getting between 48 and 52 (inclusive) of 100 is the sum, or .386. Continuing this process until the probability sums to .95, we have to include all possible sample frequencies out to $^{40}/_{100}$ and $^{60}/_{100}$, which individually have probabilities of only .011.

If we wish to *raise* the probability of including the actual sample frequency to 99%, it is clear what we have to do. We have to include some more possible sample frequencies until the sum of all their probabilities equals .99. In fact, we need only include four more: $^{39}/_{100}$, $^{61}/_{100}$, $^{38}/_{100}$, and $^{62}/_{100}$. So, raising the probability of inclusion *increases* the corresponding deviation.

Returning to *margins of error,* raising the confidence level increases the margin of error. Thus, for a sample of 100, *raising* the confidence level from 95% to 99% *increases* the margin of error from ±.10 to ±.12. By similar reasoning, *lowering* the confidence level from 95% to 90% would *decrease* the margin of error from ±.10 to ±.08.

In general, then, there is a trade-off between confidence level and margin of error. Raising the confidence level increases the margin of error. Similarly, lowering the confidence level decreases the margin of error. The only way to avoid these particular trade-offs is to *increase the sample size,* but increasing the sample size introduces new costs and new trade-offs.

SAMPLE FREQUENCY AND MARGIN OF ERROR

The margins of error given in Tables 6.1 and 6.2 are most accurate for sample frequencies of about .50. The farther from .50 the sample frequency is, the less accurate the given margins of error. In general, as **f**(A) moves toward 0 or 1, the margin of error becomes *smaller* and less symmetrical. It becomes shorter on the side toward 0 or 1, depending on whether **f**(A) is less than or greater than .50. These distortions are not too serious so long as **f**(A) is between .10 and .90. For smaller and larger values, the distortions can become substantial. Apart from the above general comments, however, there are no simple rules that can serve as useful rules of thumb. You simply must be aware that your rules of thumb are misleading for very small and very large values of **f**(A).

6.2 EVALUATING DISTRIBUTIONS AND CORRELATIONS

What we have just learned about estimating proportions from sample frequencies can be applied to the evaluation of both distributions and correlations. We continue considering only the model populations and samples pictured on the right-hand side of Figure 5.1.

EVALUATING DISTRIBUTIONS

Figure 6.2 shows how estimation works for a distribution in which there are more than two values of a single variable. The model shows a population of Red, Green, and Blue marbles in unknown proportions. A randomly selected sample with **n** = 250 yields **f**(R) = .56, **f**(G) = .24, and **f**(B) = .20. The margin of error is .06. So the estimates are **P**(R) = .56 ± .06; **P**(G) = .24 ± .06; and **P**(B) = .20 ± .06. The actual population probabilities are, of course, constrained by the fact that the proportions of red, green, and blue marbles must add up to 100%.

FIGURE 6.2

Estimating a distribution in a population using the observed relative frequencies in a random sample.

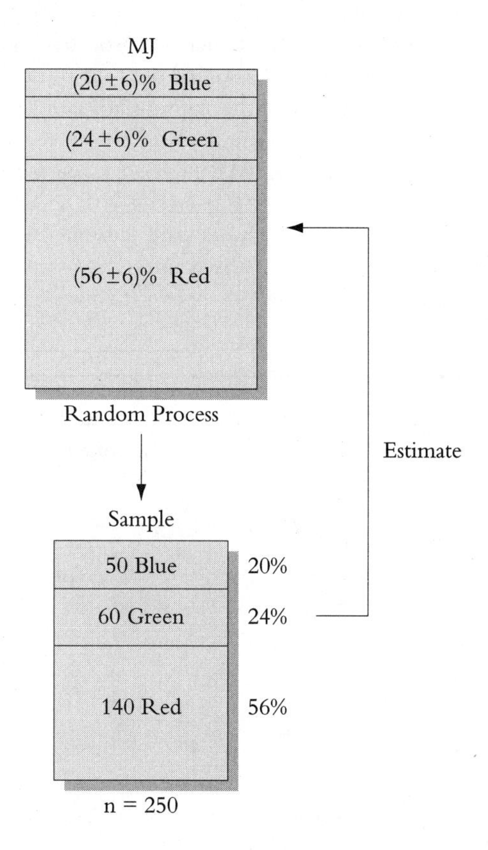

EVALUATING CORRELATIONS

When evaluating correlations, there are two kinds of situations. In one, the sample frequencies provide evidence for the existence of a correlation. In the other, the sample frequencies *fail* to provide evidence for the existence of a correlation. The sample frequencies can never provide evidence that there is no correlation at all, because estimates always include a margin of error. The most we can do is find evidence that a suspected correlation has little or no *strength*.

EVIDENCE FOR A CORRELATION

Return to the model of marbles in a jar with two variables, color and size, and values red or nonred and large or small, respectively. The proportions, however, are *unknown*.

Imagine a randomly selected sample with **n** = 600, of which 500 turn out to be red and 100 nonred. Among the red marbles in the sample, 325⁄500 turn out to be large. Thus, adopting the notation for conditional probabilities to sample frequencies, **f**(L/R) = 65%. Among the nonred marbles in the sample, 35⁄100 are large, so **f**(L/N) = 35%.

There is a clear difference in the *sample* between **f**(L/R) and **f**(L/N). The question is whether this difference in sample frequencies constitutes good evidence for the existence of a correlation in the *population*. To find out, one must construct the relevant interval estimates. To estimate **P**(L/R), the appropriate sample size is not the total number of marbles selected, but only those that turned out to be red, which, in our example, is 500. By our rules of thumb, **ME** = .05. So, we estimate **P**(L/R) = **f**(L/R) ± **ME** = (65 ± 5)%. Similarly, for **n** = 100, **ME** = .10. So, we estimate **P**(L/N) = **f**(L/N) ± **ME** = (35 ± 10)%. These conclusions are illustrated in Figure 6.3.

Inspecting Figure 6.3, we see that the two interval estimates *do not overlap*. That is, the interval estimate for **P**(L/R) is wholly above the interval estimate for **P**(L/N).

FIGURE 6.3

An example of evidence for the existence of a correlation.

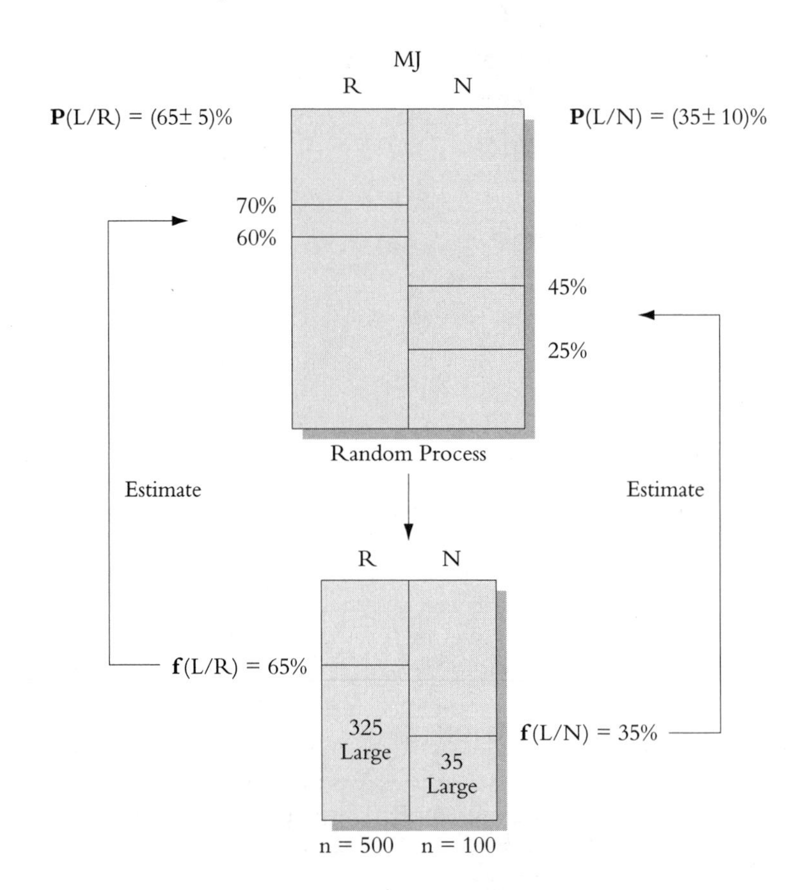

That is good evidence for concluding that **P**(L/R) really is larger than **P**(L/N) in the population. But this is just to say that color and size are correlated in the population and, indeed, that being large is *positively correlated* with being red.

LACK OF EVIDENCE FOR A CORRELATION

To illustrate this case, we need only make a small change in the above example. This time, suppose that the observed sample frequencies of large marbles among the red and nonred marbles are $^{325}/_{500}$ (65%) and $^{55}/_{100}$ (55%), respectively. As before, we estimate **P**(L/R) = **f**(L/R) ± **ME** = (65 ± 5)%. But this time we estimate that **P**(L/N) = **f**(L/N) ± **ME** = (55 ± 10)%. This new example is shown in Figure 6.4.

In this case, the two interval estimates *overlap*. This means that, as far as the evidence from the sample is concerned, the proportion of large marbles might be, for example, 62%, among both the red and nonred marbles. Thus, for all we can reliably infer from

FIGURE 6.4

An example of failure to have evidence for the existence of a correlation.

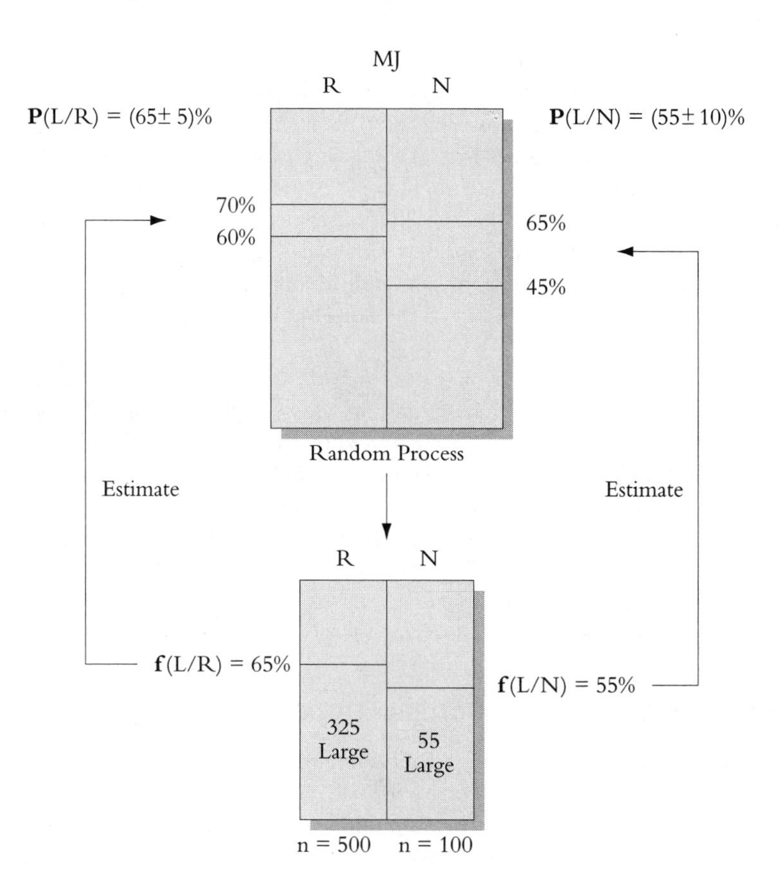

examining the sample, there might be no correlation at all between color and size in the population. However, we do not have good evidence that this is, in fact, the case. There might also be a correlation. For all we can tell, it could be the case that **P**(L/R) = 70% and **P**(L/N) = 45%. We also do not have good evidence that this is not the case. In general, then, whenever the respective interval estimates overlap, the appropriate conclusion is simply that there is no good evidence for there being a correlation between the variables in question. Remember that this conclusion is not to be confused with the mistaken conclusion that there is evidence that there is no correlation.

Note again that there is nothing of importance in the fact that both observed sample frequencies in this example are greater than 50%. All that matters here is whether the *difference* between the sample frequencies is small enough that the corresponding intervals overlap.

ESTIMATING THE STRENGTH OF A CORRELATION

Whether or not the sample frequencies provide good evidence for the existence of a correlation in the population, there is one more thing we can do by way of evaluation. We can estimate the **strength** of the correlation. In Chapter 5, we defined the strength of a correlation as the *difference* between two proportions in the population. Here, we do not know the exact proportions. We have only interval estimates of the proportions. How can one take the difference between two intervals?

The basic idea is simple. For each interval, we are 95% confident that the true value of the population ratio lies in that interval. But we know nothing more about where in the interval the true value might be. We know only the end points. We can, however, use the end points of the two intervals to determine both the maximum and the minimum difference allowed by the two intervals. The *maximum* allowed difference is between the top of the higher interval and the bottom of the lower interval. The *minimum* allowed difference is between the bottom of the higher interval and the top of the lower interval.

In our first example, shown in Figure 6.3, the maximum allowed difference in proportions is .70 – .25 = .45. The minimum allowed difference is .60 – .45 = .15. So, the estimated strength of the correlation is the interval (.15, .45). In the second example, shown in Figure 6.4, the maximum allowed difference in proportions is .70 – .45 = .25. The minimum allowed difference is .60 – .65 = –.05. So, the estimated strength of the correlation is the interval (.25, –.05). Note that when the initial intervals overlap, the minimum strength of the correlation must be a negative number. This indicates that the interval includes zero strength as a possibility, and thus, in the population, a correlation in either direction, or none at all, is not ruled out.

CONFIDENCE LEVELS FOR CORRELATIONS

We have devised a simple method for determining whether sample frequencies provide evidence for the existence of a correlation in the corresponding population. This simple method, however, contains an assumption that only someone very familiar with statistical methods would notice. The assumption is that the margin of error for a difference in two proportions is the sum of the margins of error for the individual proportions. This assumption is mistaken.

It is easier to get some idea of what is really going on by considering the original standard deviations from which our margins of error are derived. The examples shown in Figures 6.3 and 6.4 are each equivalent to sampling two populations independently, one consisting of red marbles and the other of nonred marbles. For every nonred marble sampled, five red ones are sampled. After each set of selections, one computes the difference in the relative frequencies of large marbles in the two samples. As one samples, each relative frequency will vary randomly. The *difference* in relative frequencies, however, will vary *less*. This is because the individual relative frequencies might both go up together or down together, leaving the difference relatively unchanged. Or one might go up and the other down in such a way as actually to decrease the difference. The net result is that the standard deviation of the difference is *less* than the sum of the standard deviations. And so also for our derived margins of error. How much less is again something too complex to compute in our heads. For further details, see the appendix to this chapter.

Our simple method for evaluating correlations thus uses larger margins of error than are appropriate. There is, fortunately, an easy way to compensate for this error. We know that, in general, increasing the margin of error is equivalent to raising the confidence level. In fact, what our simple method does is effectively increase the confidence level for the difference in estimates from 95% to 99%. So, all our conclusions about correlations carry a confidence level of 99% rather than the more standard 95%.

The practical effect of this choice is that, for some observed differences in sample frequencies, we will conclude that there is no evidence for a correlation when someone else, using a genuine 95% confidence level, would say there is evidence for a correlation. That is, we are being more conservative in declaring there to be evidence of a correlation than someone using a 95% confidence level for correlations. This conservative bias seems a reasonable price to pay to have a method we can use effectively without carrying out mathematical calculations.

6.3 STATISTICAL SIGNIFICANCE

Statisticians often talk about the "statistical significance" of data, and this terminology sometimes turns up in popular reports of statistical studies. It is important, therefore, to be able to interpret correctly claims about statistical significance, or the lack thereof.

STATISTICALLY SIGNIFICANT DIFFERENCES

The notion of statistical significance applies primarily to *sample frequencies*. Mostly, it applies to *differences* between sample frequencies. There are fundamentally two factors that contribute to differences between sample frequencies. First, there may be a real difference between the corresponding proportions in the population from which the sample has been drawn. Second, the sampling process itself introduces random variations in sample frequencies, which exist whether or not there is a real difference in population proportions. Statistically significant differences are differences in sample frequencies that are unlikely to have been produced by the sampling process alone. They are, therefore, differences that are likely to indicate real differences among proportions in the population.

We have already learned enough to make rough determinations of when differences in sample frequencies are statistically significant. In brief, differences in sample frequencies are *statistically significant* whenever the corresponding interval estimates *do not overlap.* If the corresponding interval estimates *do overlap,* then the differences in sample frequencies are *not statistically significant.* For example, the sample differences shown in Figure 6.3 are statistically significant. Those shown in Figure 6.4 are not statistically significant. That is basically all there is to it.

Now and then a popular report will contain the claim, "The reported difference in sample frequencies is statistically significant at the .05 level." This means that the difference in question is statistically significant using a 95% confidence level. The convention is that the significance level equals 1 minus the confidence level. Our simple method for evaluating correlations, which effectively uses a 99% confidence level, tells us when observed sample differences are "statistically significant at the .01 level."

STATISTICAL SIGNIFICANCE AND STRENGTH OF CORRELATIONS

All too often we come across reports of statistical studies in which all that is reported is whether differences in sample frequencies are statistically significant. In this case, we have much less information to go on than if the actual sample frequencies are given. Some evaluation, however, is still possible, depending on whether differences are reported as statistically significant or not statistically significant.

DIFFERENCES REPORTED AS STATISTICALLY SIGNIFICANT. Imagine a report about a sample from a jar of marbles that are either red or nonred and either large or small. Apart from the sample sizes, all that is reported is that the difference between the sample frequencies of large marbles among the red and among the nonred is statistically significant, with a greater percentage of large among the red. What can you say about the strength of the correlation between large and red marbles in the population?

In fact, all you know is that there is a positive correlation between large and red in the population. So the strength of the correlation between large and red must be greater than zero. How much greater might it be? You have no way of knowing. The gap between the intervals might be small or large. For all you know, the strength of the correlation might be close to 1! Thus, you have good evidence for concluding that there is a positive correlation between large and red but no evidence at all regarding the strength of the correlation.

Note that knowing the size of the sample is of little help. Small samples yield wide intervals, and large samples yield narrow intervals. However, not knowing by how much the intervals are separated, you are left in the dark about the strength of the correlation. All you can say is that it is greater than zero.

DIFFERENCES REPORTED AS NOT STATISTICALLY SIGNIFICANT. Now imagine another sample from the same model population. This time, it is reported that the difference between the sample frequencies of large marbles among the red and among the nonred marbles is *not* statistically significant. Here, our evaluation of the situation does depend on what we know about the sample size. Of course, if no information about sample size is given, then all we can say is that there is no evidence for the existence of any correlation between large and red marbles.

If the sample size is known to be relatively small, then a simple report of no statistically significant difference in the frequency of large marbles is quite uninformative. You know that the relevant intervals overlap, but you do not know by how much. You do know that the intervals are quite wide. If they in fact overlap only slightly, then the appropriate estimate of the strength of the correlation would be an interval from zero to the sum of twice the individual margins of error. For example, if there were 100 red and 25 nonred marbles, a report of no statistically significant difference would still be compatible with a strength of correlation as great as $(2 \times .10) + (2 \times .25) = .70$, which is considerable.

The only case in which a simple report concerning statistical significance without sample frequencies is really informative is if it claims no statistically significant difference with very large samples. Very narrow intervals, even if only slightly overlapping, still yield a low estimate for the strength of correlation. For example, with 2,000 each of red and nonred marbles sampled, the maximum estimated strength of correlation compatible with overlapping intervals is .08, which is still quite small.

These possibilities are summarized in Table 6.3. The general lesson is that it is better to be told the actual sample frequencies than simply that their difference is or is not statistically significant.

EVALUATING CORRELATIONS: A QUICK AND DIRTY METHOD

There is a quick and dirty method for evaluating sample data indicating the possibility of a correlation. It can be applied without even drawing diagrams such as those of Figures 6.3 and 6.4.

First, note the sizes of the two relevant partial samples. Then, use the rules of thumb to determine the two margins of error. Add the margins of error. Then, look

TABLE 6.3
SUMMARY OF RELATIONSHIPS AMONG SAMPLE SIZE, REPORTED STATISTICALLY SIGNIFICANT DIFFERENCES, AND ESTIMATES OF STRENGTH

SAMPLE SIZE	SSD	ESTIMATE OF STRENGTH
Large	No	Low Strength
Large	Yes	Can't Tell
Small	No	Can't Tell
Small	Yes	Can't Tell

to see if the observed difference in sample frequencies is greater or less than the sum of the margins of error. If the observed difference in sample frequencies is greater, it is statistically significant, and you have evidence of a correlation in the population. If the observed difference in sample frequencies is smaller, you do not have evidence of a correlation in the population. Finally, if the difference in sample frequencies is statistically significant, subtracting the sum of the margins of error from the difference in the sample frequencies yields an estimate of the minimum strength of the correlation. With a little practice, you can learn to do all this in your head while simply looking at the reported data.

Turning, for the last time, to the example shown in Figure 6.3, we see that the two partial sample sizes are 500 and 100. The margins of error are thus .05 and .10, respectively. Their sum is .15. The difference in observed frequencies is .65 − .35 = .30. So, this difference in sample frequencies is statistically significant (at the .01 level), and we have evidence of a correlation. Its minimum estimated strength is .30 − .15 = .15. Similarly, the observed difference in sample frequencies in the example shown in Figure 6.4 is only .10 (.65 − .55). That is less than the sum of the margins of error (.15). So, this difference is not statistically significant (at the .01 level), and we fail to have evidence of a correlation.

6.4 SURVEY SAMPLING

One of the most prominent uses of statistical methods is in **survey sampling.** In the United States, for example, there is a whole industry, including such well-known companies as the Gallup Organization, devoted to ascertaining the characteristics, attitudes, and opinions of various segments of the American population. Opinion polling has become so influential a part of American life that almost any national political campaign now employs its own team of "pollsters." In this section, we examine one recent prominent survey. It will function as our primary example as we learn how probability and statistical models are *applied* to populations in the real world.

THE NATIONAL HEALTH AND SOCIAL LIFE SURVEY

In 1987, health officials around the country faced the specter of a national epidemic of Acquired ImmunoDeficiency Syndrome (AIDS). At that time, there were no prospects of finding a cure or vaccine for what seemed a universally fatal disease. It was known, however, that the disease can be transmitted from person to person through sexual contacts. To assess the possibility of an epidemic, particularly in the majority, heterosexual population, it became urgent to know about the sexual practices of the population at large. Unfortunately, there had been little reliable research on this subject since the Kinsey Reports in about 1950. Indeed, part of the reason there had been so little serious research was the negative public reaction to Kinsey's findings. Whatever the validity of Kinsey's results, however, they were clearly of marginal relevance to the social practices of the late 1980s. New research was needed.

In July 1987, the National Institutes of Health (NIH) invited proposals for research on "Social and Behavioral Aspects of Fertility-Related Behavior." A group based at the University of Chicago, working through a related research firm, the National

Opinion Research Center, was awarded a contract to design the study, called the National Health and Social Life Survey (NHSLS). Nevertheless, despite its bureaucratic title, word of the proposed study reached a conservative senator who introduced a budget amendment in the U.S. Senate forbidding the NIH from funding any such study. Eventually, several private foundations provided enough money for a smaller study, which was conducted in 1992. The results were published in 1994 in two books issued simultaneously. The first, 300 pages long and written for the general public by a professional science writer, was titled *Sex in America: A Definitive Survey.* The second, titled *The Social Organization of Sexuality: Sexual Practices in the United States,* contains 700 pages written for professionals. Publication of the study received wide coverage in newspapers and magazines throughout the country.

HOW THE SURVEY WAS CARRIED OUT

The NHSLS was restricted to American adults, aged 18 to 59, whose understanding of English was sufficient to respond meaningfully to questions posed by an interviewer. The sexual behavior of those younger or older raises too many special issues to be covered in a general survey of behavior and attitudes. There are also special problems in obtaining informed consent to participate from anyone younger than 18 years of age.

The individuals interviewed were selected at random from the whole population of the United States by the following procedure. First, the country was divided into many geographic areas. Several areas were then selected by an appropriate random method. Within the chosen areas, cities, towns, and rural areas were also selected at random. Neighborhoods in these areas were again selected at random. Finally, within the chosen neighborhoods, individual dwelling units were randomly chosen. This process yielded roughly 9,000 households identified by address only. Of these, roughly 4,400 were discovered to contain at least one person meeting the basic restrictions of age and proficiency in English. If a household contained more than one eligible person, one was chosen at random to be interviewed. For all sorts of reasons, including simple refusal to be interviewed, the study finally produced 3,159 usable interviews at a total cost of about $450 per interview. The actual process of interviewing all the subjects took 7 months and involved 220 specially trained interviewers. The individual interviews were designed to last about 90 minutes.

SELECTED DATA

The interviews covered a wide range of issues, from simple social information (e.g., marital status, age, education, race/ethnicity, and religion) to more sensitive material (e.g., number of partners and frequency of sexual relations) to highly sensitive issues (e.g., infidelity, masturbation, and homosexuality). Here, we examine data concerning only a few of the less sensitive topics covered. Those wishing to know more may consult the published reports.

Among all 3,159 subjects, 54% reported their marital status as married. The other 46% reported themselves as unmarried. The unmarried category was further divided into never married (28%), divorced/separated (16%), and widowed (2%). The unmarried, however, were also divided into those currently cohabiting, which amounted to 7%

of the total sample, and the noncohabiting, comprising the remaining 39% of the total sample.

As for age, 16% were in the 18- to 24-year-old bracket, 14% in the 25 to 29 bracket, 32% in the 30 to 39 bracket, 23% in the 40 to 49 bracket, and 15% in the 50 to 59 bracket.

Regarding education, 14% reported having less than a high school education; 29% reported completing high school or an equivalent; 33% reported only some college education; 17% said they were college graduates; and 7% reported having advanced degrees.

In the category of race/ethnicity, 76% were recorded as white, 13% as black, 8% as Hispanic, and 3% as other. The above basic social information about the sample is pictured in Figure 6.5.

Turning to more complex relationships, the survey data included information on the social characteristics of both individuals and their sexual partners. Focusing exclusively, for a moment, on unmarried heterosexual participants, the survey found that 97% of black women had black men as partners, but only 6% of white women had black men as partners. Similarly, 82% of black men had black women as partners, but less than 1% of white men had black women as partners.

One might expect there to be a strong tendency for people to select partners from their own racial groups. Less expected were similar data for other social variables. For example, among Catholic men, 68% had Catholic women as partners, but only 20% of conservative Protestant men had Catholic partners. Similar data were found for age and levels of educational attainment. Not one woman with a postgraduate degree, for example, reported having had sexual relations with a man who had not finished high school!

Among aspects of the NHSLS featured in the popular press were the data on numbers of sex partners and frequency of sex. Table 6.4 provides an abbreviated version of the published data on numbers of sex partners in the 12 months before being interviewed. Table 6.5 provides a similarly abbreviated version of the published data on frequency of sex. After developing a program for evaluating statistical hypotheses, we will return for a closer look at some aspects of all these data.

6.5 EVALUATING STATISTICAL HYPOTHESES

We will now develop a "program" for evaluating statistical hypotheses similar to that developed in Chapter 2 for evaluating theoretical hypotheses. We first develop the program informally, using an example from the NHSLS. Then, we set it out in a form that can be easily remembered for future use. Before proceeding, it would be helpful to refer back to Figure 5.1, which exhibits basic relationships among the main elements of any statistical study.

THE REAL-WORLD POPULATION

Every statistical study is done with the intent of learning something about a specific **real-world population.** The first task in evaluating any statistical hypothesis is to identify that population. This is not as easy as it might seem. There are at least two

FIGURE 6.5

The distribution of characteristics in the sample from the NHSL Survey for six social variables.

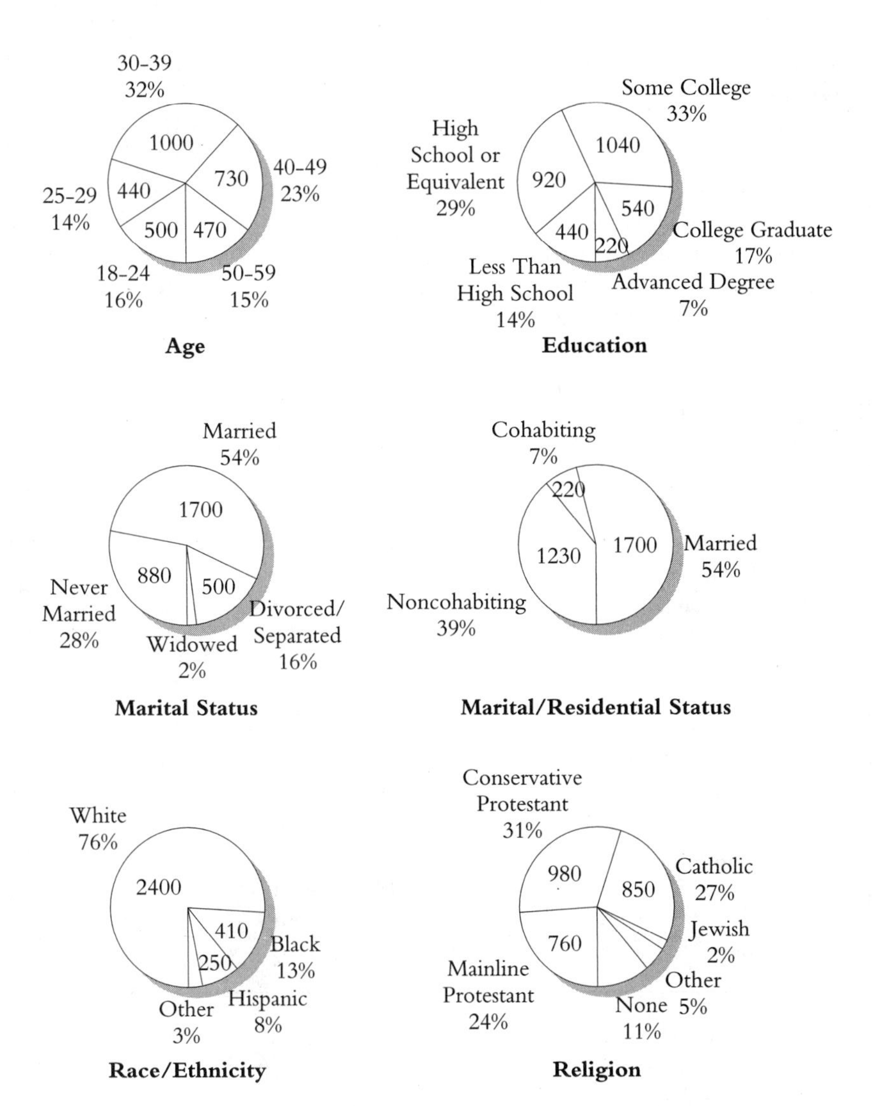

different ways of identifying the population in question. One way is to identify the *population of interest.* This is the population the investigators wished to study and about which they wished to draw conclusions. In the NHSLS, for example, the population of interest was clearly American adults aged 18 through 59.

Our techniques for estimating percentages in populations, however, only apply to the *population actually sampled.* All the calculations we have considered assume random

TABLE 6.4
SEX PARTNERS PAST TWELVE MONTHS

	0	1	2 TO 4	5+
Total	12%	71%	14%	3%
Gender				
Men	10	67	18	5
Women	14	74	10	2
Marital status				
Never married, noncohabiting	25	38	28	9
Never married, cohabiting	1	74	20	5
Married	1	94	4	1
Divorced, separated, widowed, noncohabiting	31	40	26	3
Divorced, separated, widowed, cohabiting	1	81	15	3
Education				
Less than high school	16	66	15	3
High school graduate or equivalent	11	73	13	3
Some college/vocational	11	71	14	4
Finished college	12	69	15	4
Advanced degree	13	74	10	3
Current Religion				
None	11	69	13	7
Mainline Protestant	11	74	13	2
Conservative Protestant	13	70	14	3
Catholic	12	72	13	3
Jewish	3	76	18	3
Race/Ethnicity				
White	12	73	12	3
Black	13	60	21	6
Hispanic	11	70	17	2

Row percentages total 100 percent

sampling from the population about which conclusions are to be drawn. And random sampling requires that every member of the population have an equal chance of being selected when the sample is chosen. So, the population actually sampled might be different from the population of interest. Strictly speaking, our conclusions apply only to the population actually sampled. Other sorts of considerations would have to be invoked to extend these conclusions to a broader population of interest.

In the NHSLS, the population actually sampled included only individuals living in dwelling units, where a dwelling unit might consist of a single person. And only

TABLE 6.5 FREQUENCY OF SEX
PANEL A: BY AGE, MARITAL STATUS, AND GENDER

SOCIAL CHARACTERISTICS	NOT AT ALL	A FEW TIMES PER YEAR	A FEW TIMES PER MONTH	2 OR 3 TIMES A WEEK	4 OR MORE TIMES A WEEK
Gender					
Men	14%	16%	37%	26%	7%
Women	10	18	36	30	6
Age					
Men					
18–24	15	21	24	28	12
25–29	7	15	31	36	11
30–39	8	15	38	33	6
40–49	9	18	40	27	6
50–59	11	22	44	20	3
Women					
18–24	11	16	32	29	12
25–29	5	10	38	37	10
30–39	9	16	36	33	6
40–49	15	16	44	20	5
50–59	30	22	35	12	2
Marital status					
Men					
Noncohabiting	23	25	26	19	7
Cohabiting	0	8	36	40	16
Married	1	13	43	36	7
Women					
Noncohabiting	33	23	24	15	5
Cohabiting	1	8	35	42	14
Married	3	12	46	32	7

Row percentages total 100 percent

those competent in English were considered as possible subjects. This means that college and university students living in dormitories, military personnel living in a barracks, and the homeless were not part of the population actually sampled. No such person had any chance at all of being selected as part of the sample for this study. So, strictly speaking, any conclusions reached cannot be applied to these people. Of course, one might have other than statistical grounds for thinking that the people excluded by the sampling process are little different in the relevant respects from those included. If so, it is helpful if those reasons can be made explicit.

When evaluating a statistical hypothesis, then, it is important to identify the

TABLE 6.5 FREQUENCY OF SEX
PANEL B: BY EDUCATION, RELIGION, AND RACE/ETHNICITY

SOCIAL CHARACTERISTICS	NOT AT ALL	A FEW TIMES PER YEAR	A FEW TIMES PER MONTH	2 OR 3 TIMES A WEEK	4 OR MORE TIMES A WEEK
Education					
Men					
Less than high school	15	20	28	30	7
High school graduate or equivalent	10	15	34	32	9
Any college	9	18	38	28	7
Women					
Less than high school	19	15	35	23	8
High school graduate or equivalent	11	16	37	30	6
Any college	14	17	36	26	7
Current Religion					
Men					
None	13	25	25	26	11
Mainline Protestant	8	19	38	27	8
Conservative Protestant	11	15	35	32	7
Catholic	8	17	36	31	8
Women					
None	10	19	36	26	9
Mainline Protestant	13	17	40	25	5
Conservative Protestant	15	14	36	26	9
Catholic	14	16	37	28	5
Race/Ethnicity					
Men					
White	10	17	35	30	8
Black	8	16	39	30	7
Hispanic	9	15	33	29	14
Women					
White	13	16	37	27	7
Black	17	18	33	25	7
Hispanic	11	10	36	33	10

Row percentages total 100 percent

population actually sampled. That is the population to which our conclusions apply. If there is a broader population of interest, we must look for separate reasons for thinking that the conclusions can indeed be extended to this broader population.

SAMPLE DATA

Like the above report on the NHSLS, many reports of statistical studies provide lots of information about the **sample.** It is generally impossible to evaluate it all at once. You have to pick out some particular piece of data on which to focus your evaluation. When you have finished evaluating that bit of data, you can go on to another. With experience, you can learn to go through lots of data relatively quickly. But you will still have to take it one bit at a time.

The first bit of data presented above from the NHSLS was that 54% of the subjects reported their marital status as married rather than unmarried. Because "married" and "unmarried" are exclusive and exhaustive categories, we need not have been told that the other 46% reported themselves as unmarried. We can figure that out for ourselves.

A STATISTICAL MODEL

Formulating a **statistical hypothesis** about the real-world population requires constructing a **statistical model.** What statistical model? That is best determined by looking at the data at hand and deciding for what sort of statistical model the data might be relevant. This is not as difficult as it might seem because we have only *three* possible statistical models from which to choose: proportions, distributions, and correlations.

The most efficient way to proceed is to determine what **variables** and what **values** of these variables might be introduced to represent the data. Recall that a proportion has one variable with two values; a distribution has one variable with three or more values; a correlation has two variables with two values each. The data we are considering suggest an obvious variable—*marital status,* which has the two values married and unmarried. This bit of data, therefore, is relevant to the evaluation of a *proportion* in the population.

RANDOM SAMPLING

Before we can evaluate the relevance of the data for the hypothesis, we must first determine whether our model for **random sampling** fits the actual process by which the sample was selected from the real-world population. That is, does the model pictured on the right-hand side of Figure 5.1 fit the real-world situation pictured on the left? All our calculations involving sample sizes and confidence intervals were developed in the context of a random sampling model. If that model does not fit the real-world situation, none of our rules about overlapping or nonoverlapping intervals have any relevance.

Recall from Chapter 5 that a randomly selected sample is one in which (1) all members of the population who might exhibit a property of interest have an equal chance of being selected and (2) there is no correlation between the outcome of one selection and any other. The NHSLS was exceptional in that strenuous efforts were taken to ensure randomness in sampling. But other surveys, such as those conducted regularly by *The New York Times*/CBS news organization, are also very carefully done to ensure randomness in sampling.

The only major failing of the sampling procedure used in the NHSLS was its restriction to people living in dwelling units. Based on data from other studies, however, the research team estimated that fewer than 3% of all Americans aged 18 through 59 were excluded from the population actually sampled. Thus, even if all these people had somehow been included, there is little chance that the actual data would have been importantly different from what it, in fact, turned out to be.

EVALUATING THE HYPOTHESIS

Assuming, then, that the actual sampling process can be represented by a model of randomly selecting marbles from a jar, what does the data tell us about the population? In particular, what can we conclude about the proportion of married people in the population sampled?

FIGURE 6.6

Analysis of the NHSL Survey data yielding the estimate that between 52% and 56% of all Americans aged 18 to 59 are married.

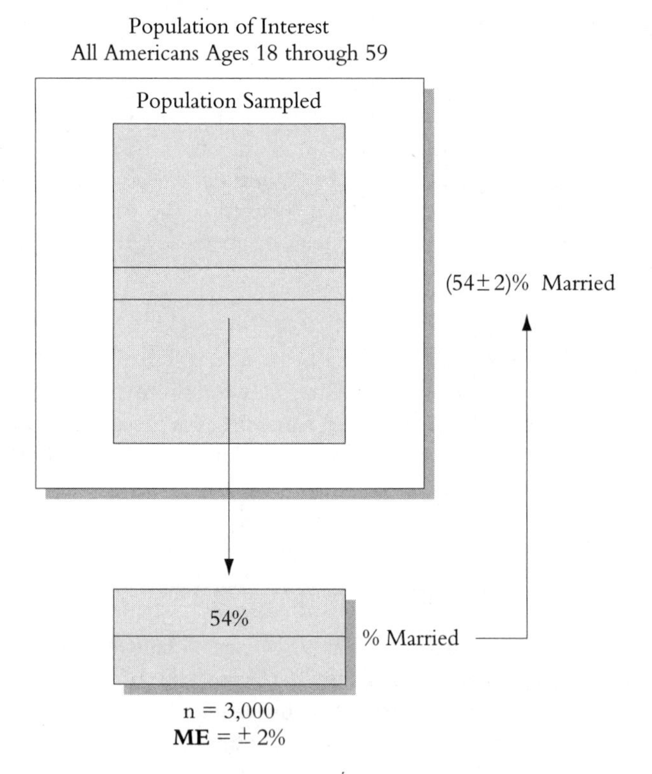

Because the data under consideration reflect the whole sample of more than 3,000 people, the margin of error can be taken as 2%. So, we estimate that the proportion of married people in the population sampled is between 52% and 56%. Qualitatively, we have good evidence that more than half of Americans between 18 and 59 are married.

SUMMING UP

At this point in the evaluation of any statistical hypothesis, one should review what has been learned to extract the "take home lesson" from the information presented. Two points are particularly important to review.

One is how well the actual sampling process can be modeled by a random sampling model. Here, you can make only rough qualitative judgments. Except for the fact that it excluded roughly 3% of the population of interest, the NHSLS scores high in this regard.

Second is the actual conclusion you are to draw. Given the good fit of a random sampling model to this case, we can, indeed, be highly confident (95%!) that the interval between 52% and 56% includes the true value of the proportion of married people (in the stated categories) both in the population sampled and in the population of interest. This analysis is pictured in Figure 6.6.

6.6 A PROGRAM FOR EVALUATING STATISTICAL HYPOTHESES

We now set out our program for evaluating statistical hypotheses and apply it to some of the other data from the NHSLS.

The Program

Step 1. The Real-World Population. Identify the real-world population actually sampled in carrying out the study. Note any important differences between the population sampled and the population of interest.

Step 2. The Sample Data. Identify the real-world sample and the particular data from that sample whose relevance for hypotheses about the population you wish to evaluate. Be sure to include sample sizes when available.

Step 3. The Statistical Model. Identify the relevant *variables* and the *values* of these variables. Then identify the statistical model of the population that is appropriate for evaluation in the light of the data already identified. If the data have the form of a correlation, give a clear statement of the statistical hypothesis asserting the existence of the corresponding correlation in the real-world population.

Step 4. Random Sampling. How well does a random sampling model represent the actual process by which the sample was selected from the population? Possible answers: (a) very well, (b) moderately well, (c) somewhat well, or (d) not very well. Explain the factors relevant to your answer.

Step 5. Evaluating the Hypothesis. Assuming a random sampling model is applicable, what can you reasonably conclude about the real-world population? If a correlation is possible, is there good evidence for the hypothesis stated in Step 3? Estimate the strength of the correlation.

Step 6. Summary. In the light of your answers in all previous steps, give a summary statement of how well the statistical data support your evaluation in Step 5. Possible answers: (a) very well, (b) moderately well, (c) somewhat well, or (d) not very well. Note the major factors supporting your answer.

While working through the program, it is useful simultaneously to **diagram the study** following the examples of Figures 6.1, 6.2, 6.3, or 6.4. This might even be done on a separate sheet of paper. When doing Step 1, draw a box representing the population sampled. If relevant, surround this box with a larger box representing the population of interest. Label your boxes. When doing Step 2, add a smaller box below the first one to represent the sample. Label this box with relevant parts of the data such as sample sizes and observed frequencies. For Step 3, add the details to your picture of the population necessary to represent the appropriate statistical hypothesis. At Step 5, draw in the appropriate intervals representing estimates of population ratios. When appropriate, indicate statistically significant differences. At the end of your analysis, you should have a complete diagram of the study as it applies to the specific data you are considering.

Race and Choice of Partners

Now let us use the above program to evaluate another statistical hypotheses suggested by the NHSLS. In particular, let us look at the data on race and the choice of sexual partners. Among that data was the fact that among unmarried heterosexual participants, 97% of black women had black men as partners, but only 6% of white women had black men as partners.

Step 1. The Real-World Population. The population sampled consisted of English-speaking black and white unmarried American women, aged 18 through 59, who were sampled for the NHSLS. There should be little difference between the population actually sampled and the population of all American women in the indicated groups.

Step 2. The Sample Data. Among the women sampled, 97% of black women had black men as partners, but only 6% of white women had black men as partners. From the indicated social makeup of the total sample of a little more than 3,000, we know that roughly half, or 1,500, were women, and roughly half of these, or 750, were unmarried. Of these, 13%, or roughly 100, were black, and 76%, or roughly 600, were white.

Step 3. The Statistical Model. The data can be understood as treating two variables. The first variable is the race of the women sampled, with values black and white. The second variable is having black men as partners, with values yes and no. The data suggest a strong positive correlation between being a black woman and having black men as partners.

Step 4. Random Sampling. The NHSLS used an elaborate geographic method for ensuring randomness in the selection of its subjects. It was quite exceptional in this regard.

Step 5. Evaluating the Hypothesis. The rule of thumb margin of error for the sample of 100 black women is about .10 and that for the sample of 600 white women about .05. Given that the two observed sample frequencies are close to 1 and 0, respectively, the true margins of error must be even smaller. So, the observed difference is obviously statistically significant. The strength of the correlation can be estimated as greater than .76 [(.97 − .10) − (.06 + .05)], which is a very strong correlation.

Step 6. Summary. Given the extraordinary fit between the design of the NHSLS and a random sampling model and given the large difference between the two observed sample frequencies, we can be very confident that the population sampled exhibits a strong positive correlation between being a black woman and having black men as partners. The same applies to the population of interest, with perhaps only slightly less confidence in how strong the correlation might be.

Figure 6.7 exhibits a diagram corresponding to the above analysis.

In reviewing the above analysis, you should note especially that the sample size associated with any subgroup in the sample is the size of that subgroup, not that of the whole sample. This means that the relevant margins of error may differ for the two parts of the sample used in evaluating a correlation. Both margins of error will be larger than the margin of error associated with the sample as a whole.

NUMBERS OF SEX PARTNERS

Now let us take a look at the data in Table 6.4 showing reported numbers of partners in the past year for subjects in the NHSLS. Having just been through a detailed analysis of one bit of data from this survey, we need not do detailed analyses here. We will simply take a quick and dirty look for interesting proportions, distributions, and correlations (or lack thereof). This is the kind of analysis you can do in discussion or for yourself. It is not appropriate for homework exercises or examinations.

The distribution of the variable, number of partners, shown in the very first line, is already quite interesting. Because these percentages represent the whole sample of more than 3,000, the margin of error is at most 2%. So, we can pretty much just read the population ratios right off the sample frequencies. The remarkable fact is that more than 80% [(12 + 71) ± 2]% of American adults have had at most one (i.e., 0 or 1) partners in the previous year. In other words, fewer than 20% (one-fifth) have had more than one partner! That hardly seems a symptom of extreme moral decay.

Moving down to differences by gender, because men and women each make up roughly half the total sample, our margin of error here is about 3%. Double that, 6%, is the difference required for statistical significance (at the .01 level). So, the difference in percentages between men and women who have had no partners in the last year, (14 − 10 = 4)%, is not statistically significant (at the .01 level). However, the difference

FIGURE 6.7

Analysis of the NHSL Survey data indicating a strong correlation between the race of American women and the race of their partners.

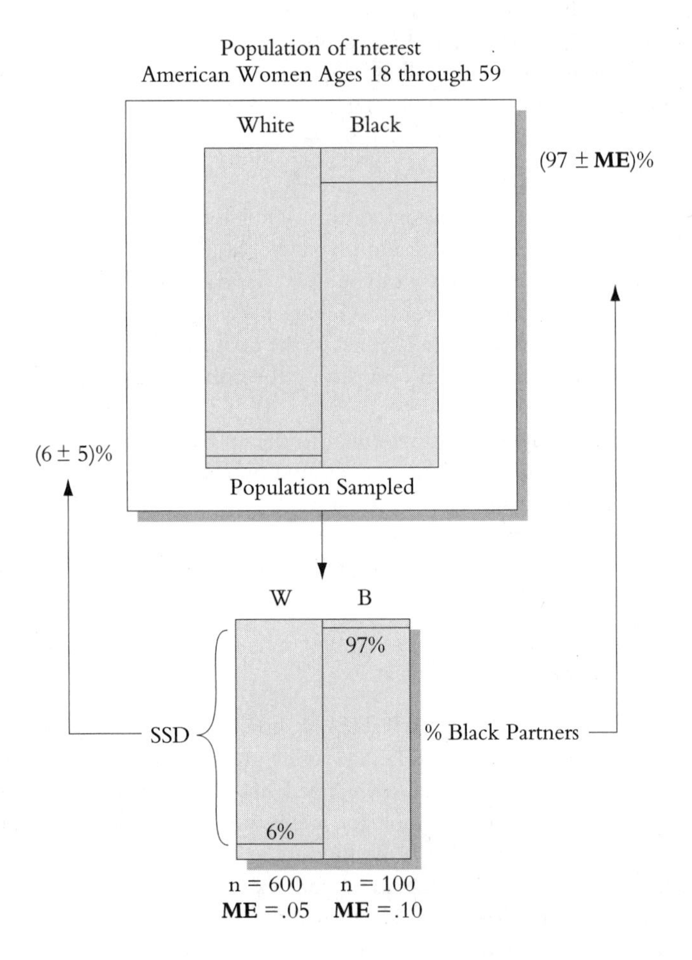

in percentages of men and women who have had more than one partner, (18 + 5 = 23)% – (10 + 2 = 12)% = (23 – 12)% = 11%, is statistically significant. The minimum estimated strength of this correlation, however, (.11 – .06 = .05), is not great. So, men appear to be somewhat more promiscuous than women, but not much more.

Looking at marital status, we find the remarkable figure that 95%, (1 + 94)% , of married subjects reported at most one partner in the past year. The number of married subjects in the study was about 1,700 (54% of 3,159), yielding a margin of error of about 2%. So, we can conclude, with more than 95% confidence, that at least 93% of married persons in the population sampled would report having been faithful to their spouses during the past year.

The data are similar for those never married but cohabiting. Among subjects in this category, 75% reported at most one partner in the past year. Here, we have to think hard about the sample size. We know that the never-married group comprised 28% of the total sample, or roughly 900 subjects. We also know that 7% of the total sample were cohabiting. By the definition for "cohabiting" used in the study, all these were among the 46% of the sample reported as unmarried. So, roughly 15% of the unmarried were cohabiting. Assuming the rate of cohabiting is roughly the same among the never-married and the divorced/separated subjects, there must have been about 135 (15% of 900) who were both never married and cohabiting. That makes the margin of error for this group a little less than .10. Because the margin of error for the married group is 2%, differences between the married and the never-married but cohabiting groups that are greater than 12% will be statistically significant. So, there is a positive correlation between being married (rather than simply cohabiting) and having at most one partner in the past year. Its minimum estimated strength, however, is only .08 (.20 − .12).

The most interesting differences are between those married or cohabiting and those neither married nor cohabiting. Look, for example, at the difference in frequencies for no partners among the never-married noncohabiting subjects (25% of 765) as opposed to the never-married cohabiting subjects (1% of 135). The margins of error for the noncohabiting subjects is about .04. Because the frequency of no partners among the cohabiting subjects is so low, the margin of error must be less than the rule of thumb margin of .10. The reported difference (25% − 1% = 24%) is, therefore, clearly statistically significant. So, among the never-married subjects, there is a positive correlation between not cohabiting and having no partners at all. Nor does this disadvantage seem to be made up in terms of higher percentages with more partners. The frequencies for two or more partners in these two groups are (28% + 9% = 37%) and (20% + 5% = 25%), respectively. This difference (12%) might be statistically significant, but the correlation would be very weak.

Turning, finally, to religion, we find the again remarkable fact that there are no statistically significant differences in the frequencies of those who had at most one partner during the previous year. The largest group, conservative Protestants, comprise 31% of the sample, or roughly 980 subjects. That yields a margin of error of about .03. So, we need at least a 6% difference for statistical significance. The sums of the first two columns in the rows for the three largest religious groups, however, vary only from 83% to 85%—clearly not statistically significant differences. The lowest sum is 79%, but that is for a much smaller group, which means an even larger margin of error. So, again, we can be quite sure there are no statistically significant differences here.

FREQUENCY OF SEX

Turning to Table 6.5, we find immediately that there seem to be no statistically significant differences between men and women for any of the values of the variable, frequency of sex in the past 12 months. Because men and women each constitute about half the total sample, there are roughly 1,500 each, for a margin of error between .02 and .03. Double that is a difference of 4% to 6%. Yet, none of the reported differences are more than 4%.

The various age categories for men and women range in size from 200 to 500. Differences in frequency of sex by age categories, therefore, have to be about 8% to be statistically significant. Not many are. One dramatic difference, clearly statistically significant, shows up between men and women in the oldest age group, 50 to 59. There is a clear positive correlation between being a woman in this age group and having no sex at all. The minimal strength of this correlation is at least .10.

Turning to marital/residential status, from the statistics given, we can easily calculate that, for both men and women, there are roughly 100 cohabiting unmarried, 600 noncohabiting unmarried, and 850 married subjects. The most striking difference, which holds for both men and women, is between those cohabiting or married and those noncohabiting. There are 950 of the former and 600 of the latter. So, a difference of 7% or 8% would be statistically significant. Taking no sex at all and some sex as two values of the frequency of sex variable, we see a strong positive correlation between noncohabiting and having no sex at all. For women, and noting the very low frequency for the married or cohabiting, the minimum strength of this correlation is about .21, which is pretty strong. The difference between noncohabiting men and women (600 each) for the same values of the frequency of sex variable (33% – 23% = 10%) is also statistically significant but only barely so. Clearly, being married or cohabiting is good for at least the quantity of one's sexual relations, and a little more so for women than men.

The main feature of the data on education, religion, and race/ethnicity is its general uniformity. We would have to look hard through all these data to find any statistically significant differences. Sometimes, a lack of statistically significant differences can be as informative as their presence.

6.7 PROBLEMS WITH SURVEY SAMPLING

Interval estimation is a procedure that can be used whenever a randomly selected sample is found to exhibit some property with a definite relative frequency. Survey sampling falls into this category, but it presents special problems because it is used to assess the attitudes of people in large and diverse populations. These special problems can be grouped into two general categories: problems concerning the *randomness of the selection process,* and problems with the *reliability of the responses.* You should learn to identify both of these problems in reports of surveys.

NONRANDOM SAMPLING

In survey sampling, especially public opinion polling, the population of interest is usually a fairly large subgroup of all Americans—for example, all adults of voting age, all registered voters, all women. It would be very difficult and costly to set up a system of sampling that gave every person in the whole population an equal chance of being selected, which is what a truly random sampling system would have to do. Thus, the population of people actually sampled (i.e., those who do have an equal chance of being selected) is usually only a subpopulation of the original population of interest. So, there is always the danger that the subgroup actually sampled is not sufficiently representative of the population of interest. If it is not, then, no matter how large the sample, the conclusion may not be correct for the original population of interest. Moreover, there may be no way of knowing how the population actually sampled might differ from the original population of interest.

The NHSLS, as we have seen, was particularly strong in its efforts to achieve a genuinely random sample of a very large percentage of all American adults. In this, the NHSLS represented a major advance on earlier research into the sexual habits of the general population. This earlier research illustrates well the unreliability of nonrandom sampling.

The first large-scale systematic study of sexual behavior in America, published by Kinsey shortly after World War II, did not use random sampling. He used what statisticians call "a sample of convenience," which is to say that he interviewed almost anyone he could convince to participate. The main qualification for getting into Kinsey's sample, therefore, was willingness to participate. Of course, one also had to be a member of some group that Kinsey contacted, fraternities and sororities, people in rooming houses or prisons, even hitchhikers. He also let it be widely known that he was seeking subjects for his survey. So, many of his subjects were volunteers who came to him. Over the years, Kinsey and several associates interviewed nearly 18,000 people.

The problem is that there is no way of knowing what connection there is between this sample and the population of interest. Without random sampling, none of our knowledge about probability or sampling applies. We are left guessing what the numbers might mean for the population at large. The fact that many subjects were volunteers itself suggests that they were not representative of the population as a whole. People who would actively volunteer for an interview about their sexual history very likely have a greater-than-average interest in that history and are, therefore, unlikely to represent average behavior. For example, 10% of the men in Kinsey's study reported exclusively homosexual behavior for at least 3 years. In the random sample of the NHSLS, by contrast, only 2.6% of the men reported exclusively homosexual relationships during the previous one year.

For all their faults, the Kinsey reports were superior to most of what followed. These included *The Playboy Report, The Redbook Report,* and *The Hite Report.* In these reports, questionnaires were distributed to potential subjects, the first and second to readers of *Playboy* and *Redbook*, respectively and the third through several different magazines and other groups. Right from the start, we know that the population sampled is different from the population of interest. Readers of *Playboy* are mostly younger men who have a higher than normal interest in sex. *Redbook*'s readers are mostly middle-class white women. To make matters worse, in such surveys, all the subjects are volunteers (i.e., people who voluntarily return the questionnaire). These turn out to be a very small fraction of potential subjects. Of roughly 5 million readers each of *Playboy* and *Redbook,* only about 2% returned the questionnaires. This is what statisticians call the "return rate." Even this low return rate, however, produces a sample of 100,000 responses, which seems impressive. There is, however, no reason to think that those 2% constituted a random sample of even just subscribers of the respective publications. Indeed, one would expect that the respondents came from among those most interested in the subject, which automatically makes their responses unrepresentative of the population as a whole. One simply cannot make up for a biased sampling method by getting a large sample.

Even a relatively high return rate, however, is no guarantee of unbiased sampling. The 1993 *Janus Report,* for example, was based on 2,800 questionnaires from 4,500 initially distributed to selected groups, for a return rate of 62%. The problem is which groups were selected in the first place. For example, to get enough people older than 65 so that the proportion in their sample would roughly match the proportion of people older than 65 in the whole population, they sought out subjects in sex therapy clinics. These subjects were obviously not likely to exhibit sexual behavior representative of their age group. Suppose you wanted to know the percentage of people 18 to 24 years old who had taken some college or university courses. You would not expect to get a reliable answer by sampling people in the student union of a large state university. Among subjects in the *Janus Report,* 70% of those older than 65 reported having sex once a week. Another study, which did use random sampling, found only 7% in this category.

UNRELIABILITY OF INFORMATION

The second major source of unreliable information in survey sampling is simply that people do not always give correct answers. There are many reasons why this may be so. Sometimes people are honestly mistaken. They may misremember things that happened 6 months ago. They may be victims of wishful thinking. Or they may not want to admit the truth to an interviewer because they are afraid of disapproval. So, they skew their answers in what they think are more acceptable directions.

There are few subjects more subject to worries about reliable answers than sexual practices. In fact, one of the main reasons Kinsey gave for not using random sampling in his research was his belief that one could not get randomly selected people honestly to disclose to a stranger the facts about their sexual practices.

In the NHSLS, special efforts were made to encourage people to give honest responses, and several methods were used to check that they had done so. To get people to participate, the interviewers tried to convince participants of the importance of the research for national health policy making. They also ensured potential participants of the confidentiality of their answers. They promised that, in processing the data, all connections between particular answers and particular people would be eliminated. There would be no way to trace who gave what answers. Then, in the course of the interview, several questions were asked several times in different ways at different times. These were later checked for consistency. Answers to some questions were written down privately by the respondents and put in a sealed envelope so they were not seen by the interviewer. Some of these questions turned up in another form later in the interview. Little difference was found between the sealed and unsealed answers. In addition, the NHSLS included eleven questions on sexual practices taken from an earlier survey on general social practices. These questions comprised only a very small part of that earlier survey, making misleading answers less likely. The response frequencies were very similar for the two surveys, suggesting a high degree of truthfulness in the NHSLS as well. Finally, the interviewers themselves were very confident that the participants were trying to be truthful.

Obviously, not all surveys can be so meticulous in trying to ensure truthful answers. Some, however, are much better than others, and one must learn to recognize indications of which are better. Here again, questionnaires clipped from a magazine and returned are particularly suspect. What is to prevent anyone from simply making up answers just for the fun of it?

APPENDIX

FORMULA FOR MARGIN OF ERROR

For those who can appreciate the mathematics, there is a fairly simple formula for calculating an approximate value for the margin of error, **ME,** as a function of both the sample size, **n,** and the observed sample frequency, **f.** The formula, which gives the value of one standard deviation, is

$$1 \text{ SD} = [(\mathbf{f})\ (1 - \mathbf{f})\ /\ \mathbf{n}]^{1/2}$$

To obtain our standard margin of error, which produces a 95% confidence interval, simply multiply the result by 2. For a 99% confidence interval, multiply by 3. An hour spent with a hand calculator will give you a good idea of how the margin of error varies when **f** has values near 1 or zero. However, because this formula is too complex to compute in our heads, we shall not use it in our evaluations.

FORMULA FOR STATISTICALLY SIGNIFICANT DIFFERENCES

There is also a relatively simple formula for determining whether a difference in observed sample frequencies is or is not statistically significant. Here, we designate the two observed sample frequencies as $\mathbf{f}_1$ and $\mathbf{f}_2$, respectively. The corresponding sample sizes we designate as $\mathbf{n}_1$ and $\mathbf{n}_2$. The formula, which yields the value of one standard deviation in the *difference* between the two sample frequencies, is as follows:

$$1 \text{ SD} = [\mathbf{f}_1\ (1 - \mathbf{f}_1)/\mathbf{n}_1 + \mathbf{f}_2\ (1 - \mathbf{f}_2)/\mathbf{n}_2]^{1/2}$$

Differences in sample frequencies greater than twice this amount are statistically significant at the .05 level. Differences in sample frequencies greater than three times this amount are statistically significant at the .01 level.

FORMULA FOR CORRECTLY ADDING MARGINS OF ERROR

There is also a simple formula for converting the sum of individual margins of error at the 95% confidence level to the margin of error for the difference, while keeping the confidence level at .95. The correct 95% margin of error for the difference is the square root of the sum of the squares of the two individual margins of error. That is,

$$\mathbf{ME}\ (\text{difference}) = [\mathbf{ME}_1^{\ 2} + \mathbf{ME}_2^{\ 2}]^{1/2}$$

In the examples of Figures 6.3 and 6.4, the 95% margin of error for the difference works out to be .11, not .15.

• EXERCISES

Analyze these reports following the six-point program for evaluating statistical hypotheses developed in the text. Number and label your steps. Be as clear and concise as you can, keeping in mind that you must say enough to demonstrate that you do know what you are talking about. A simple "yes" or "no" is never a sufficient answer. Some of these reports are taken directly from recent magazine or newspaper articles and are presented here with only minor editing.

EXERCISE 6.1

PEOPLE TELL LIES TO HAVE SEX

Asking about a sexual partner's health or sexual history is not a reliable means of avoiding AIDS, because many people lie to have sex, a researcher says. One-third of sexually experienced male college students and 10% of women admitted in a study that they had lied to get someone to have sex with them, the researcher said.

"Asking partners about risk factors is probably not a very good strategy for reducing the risk of AIDS," said Susan Cochran, associate professor in the Psychology Department of California State University at Northridge. She described results of her survey Saturday at the annual meeting of the American Psychological Association.

Cochran said she began the study after noticing that many women were reassuring themselves about having sex by asking sex partners about past behavior that carries a risk of AIDS infection. The virus that causes AIDS is spread by having sex with an infected person or using an infected needle or contaminated blood products. Questioning partners about their drug use and sexual history is not an effective substitute for taking precautions such as using condoms, she said.

The study focused on 422 unmarried, sexually experienced students at two colleges in southern California. Ages ranged from 18 to 25, with an average of 19. Forty-six percent were men.

Thirty-five percent of men admitted they had lied to have sex. In addition, 47% of men and 60% of women reported that somebody had lied to them to have sex. The study did not specify what the respondents had lied about.

"If you ask somebody if they have risk factors and they say yes, you can be reasonably assured they're not lying," Cochran said. "But if they say no, you're not really any further along than not asking."

EXERCISE 6.2

POLL FINDS DIVERSITY OF VIEWS WITHIN RELIGIOUS RIGHT

Ever since the presidential election of 1992, there has been a growing interest in the political role of conservative Christians identified as the "religious right." As part of an ongoing investigation into the phenomenon of the religious right in America, several major news organizations conducted a nationwide telephone poll of 1,339 adults in July 1994. Among all respondents, 37% identified themselves as Republicans, and 9% identified themselves as part of the "religious right."

Conservative Christians are much more likely to identify with the Republican than the Democratic party. But on some issues, such as abortion, those identifying with the "religious right" expressed views differing from those of most other Republicans. Among conservative Christians in the poll, 65% said abortion should not be permitted at all. Only 28% of all those contacted identifying themselves as Republicans expressed that view.

On other volatile issues, such as school prayer, there was closer agreement. Sixty-nine percent of all respondents favored a constitutional amendment allowing organized prayer in public schools. Among Republicans, seven in ten favored such an amendment, but among conservative Christians, the fraction in favor was eight in ten.

EXERCISE 6.3

POLL SHOWS MEN SINKING IN THE OPINION OF WOMEN

An increasing number of American women believe that most men are mean, manipulative, oversexed, self-centered, and lazy, according to a survey released Wednesday. And they are getting annoyed.

A poll by the Roper Organization found growing numbers of women expressing sensitivity to sexism and unhappiness with men on many issues. It compared data from identical questions asked 20 years ago.

Some of the changes were sizable. In 1970, two-thirds of women agreed that "most men are basically kind, gentle, and thoughtful." In the new poll, only half of the 3,000 women who were surveyed agreed.

The reason? "Women's growing dissatisfaction with men is undoubtedly derived from their own rising expectations," the survey's authors said. "The more independent women of today expect more from men." Those expectations apparently are going unfulfilled. Most women rated men negatively on their egos, libidos, and domesticity. Sizable minorities went further: 42% called men "basically selfish and self-centered."

Prurience took a particular pounding. Fifty-four percent of the women who were surveyed agreed that "most men look at a woman and immediately think how it would be to go to bed with her." In 1970, 41% had agreed.

The survey was conducted July 22 through August 12 by in-person interviews with a random sample of women across the country. It had a margin of error of ±2 percentage points.

Respondents overwhelmingly said women have made progress in obtaining job opportunities, equitable salaries, and acceptance as political leaders. But they also expressed greater awareness of continuing discrimination.

Moreover, six in 10 working women said juggling jobs and families put them under "a lot of stress," and nearly as many felt guilty about time they spend at work and away from their families.

The second greatest cause of resentment in survey respondents' lives was their mates' failure to help with household chores, cited by 52%. Only money was a greater cause of problems.

"As women contribute more to family income, they expect a more equitable division of the household responsibilities in return," the survey said. Although many men acknowledge responsibility for household work, it added, "Women indicate that men are failing to live up to this ideal and that their failure is a major source of irritation."

But diapers and dishes are by no means the sole problem: many women in the survey expressed negative views of men's attitudes, as well as their behavior. Among the findings,

- Fifty-eight percent of women agreed that "most men think only their own opinions about the world are important." That was up from 50% in 1970.
- Given the statement "most men find it necessary for their egos to keep women down," 55% agreed, up from 49% 20 years ago.
- Fifty-three percent agreed that "most men are interested in their work and life outside the home and don't pay much attention to things going on at home." That was up from 39% in 1970.

EXERCISE 6.4

CENSUS BUREAU REPORTS DIFFERENCES AMONG THE ELDERLY

As required by the Constitution, the U.S. government attempts to record information on every person in the whole country once every 10 years. It takes years to process the information collected. In 1992, the Census Bureau issued a special report on the elderly based on its data from the 1990 census.

According to this report, in 1990, about 12% of the nation's population, or 31 million people, were 65 or older. About 7%, or 18 million people, were 65 to 75; 4%, or 10 million, were 75 to 85; and slightly more than 1%, or 3 million, were 85 or older.

Among the many findings were that elderly women are more likely than elderly men to live alone. About 42% of women older than 65 were living alone. That was true of only 18% of men older than 65. Among those 85 or older, one-third of the men but two-thirds of the women were living alone. The report suggested several causes for this difference. One is the difference in life expectancy, which is 72 years for men and 78 for women. Another is the fact that widowers are much more likely to remarry than widows.

Despite the difference in life expectancy, men who survive past the age of 75 tend to be more healthy than women in that age group. Of men aged 75 and older, only 17% needed help with basic functions such as eating, dressing, and bathing. Thirty percent of women older than 75 required such help.

EXERCISE 6.5

HOW JURIES TREAT ACCUSED SPOUSE KILLERS

In June 1994, shortly after O. J. Simpson was charged with the murder of his former wife Nicole Brown, the U.S. Justice Department's Bureau of Justice Statistics received many requests for information about the disposition of cases in which the defendant was accused of killing a spouse. Having not previously gathered the relevant information, the bureau began a study that was published only after Simpson had been acquitted.

Their study was based on 540 cases resolved in 1988. In 318 cases, the accused was male, and in 222 cases, the accused was female. Eighty-seven percent of the men but only 70% of the women were declared guilty.

Among the male defendants, 11% were not prosecuted, 46% pleaded guilty, 41% were convicted in a trial, and only 2% were acquitted. None of the acquittals involved jury trials but were resolved by judges.

Among female defendants, 16% were not prosecuted, 39% pleaded guilty, 31% were convicted in a trial, and 14% were acquitted. The most common reason for acquittal was self-defense, a ground rarely available to male defendants.

Interestingly, the race of the victim seems to play little role. When the victim was white, 81% of the cases resulted in convictions. The rate of conviction was 79% when the victim was black.

EXERCISE 6.6

POLL FINDS MORE LIBERAL BELIEFS ON MARRIAGE AND SEX ROLES

Americans are more likely to believe that marriages in which the partners share the tasks of breadwinner and homemaker are a more "satisfying way of life" than they are to prefer the traditional marriage in which the husband is exclusively a provider and the wife exclusively a homemaker and mother.

Of those interviewed, 53% said they preferred the idea of shared marriage roles and 47% said they preferred the "traditional" marriage. But among those younger than 40 years of age, 61% preferred shared marriage roles, and 59% of those older than 40 preferred the traditional marriage.

The survey also detected sharp differences of opinion as to whether working women make better mothers than women who do not work. Of women who work, 43% said working women make better mothers, whereas only 14% of women who do not work shared this opinion.

The survey was conducted by telephone interviews with 1,603 adult Americans from all parts of the nation and representing different races, religions, ages, and occupations.

EXERCISE 6.7

HOMICIDE IS TOP CAUSE OF DEATH FROM ON-JOB INJURY FOR WOMEN

The leading killer of American women in the workplace is homicide. The Centers for Disease Control reported today that 42% of the deaths of American women resulting from on-the-job injury from 1980 to 1985 were homicides.

The second most frequent cause of death was vehicle accidents, at about 39%, said Catherine Bell, an epidemiologist with the centers' National Institute for Occupational Safety and Health. "If a woman's going to die from an injury at work, she's probably going to be murdered," Ms. Bell said.

Nationwide, for both sexes, about 13% of on-the-job injury deaths in the 6 years studied were homicides, the centers reported. Homicides accounted for 12% of men's occupational fatalities, as against the 42% for women. Findings regarding killings of men in the workplace are not complete. But most on-the-job deaths involve male workers, who traditionally dominate more-dangerous occupations, and most of those deaths are accidental.

Investigators for the safety institute identified 950 such killings over the 6 years of the study. Of that number, 389 of the women—or 41%—worked in the retail field. Researchers are not certain, but it appears that strangers in the store—not co-workers—are responsible for most workplace killings of women, Ms. Bell said. "They appear to be robbery-associated crimes in the retail trade," she said. "It quite likely is stranger violence."

The killings peaked in the winter. Sixty-four percent of the killings were shootings; 19% were stabbings.

The workplace homicide rate for black women was nearly double that for white women, but that was not necessarily unexpected. Nationwide, black women are nearly four times as likely to be murdered as are white women, the centers said, citing a 1986 study.

EXERCISE 6.8

WHAT MEN ARE REALLY LIKE

The typical American man believes that a faithful marriage is the ideal relationship. He wants sincerity, affection, and companionship in women above everything else. That is the conclusion of the recently published book *Beyond the Male Myth.*

The book is based on the results of a 40-item multiple-choice questionnaire designed to answer the questions women most wanted to know about men. The questionnaire was distributed by a public opinion polling organization to men in communities around the country. The men, who were approached in such places as shopping malls and office buildings, were asked to fill out the questionnaire and to deposit it into a sealed box. A total of 4,066 men responded.

More than half of the men surveyed regarded a faithful marriage as their ideal. And almost three-quarters of the men said that, besides love, their primary reason for getting married is the desire for companionship and a home life.

EXERCISE 6.9

AGGRESSION IN MEN: HORMONE LEVELS ARE A KEY

When men are domineering and intensely competitive, it may be just another case of raging hormones, specifically the male sex hormone testosterone, researchers say.

Scientists have long linked abnormally high levels of testosterone to an unusually early involvement with sex and drug use and to certain violent crimes such as particularly vicious rapes. But now a series of new findings shows that high testosterone levels play a role in the normal urge for the upper hand. Those men who are most likely to try to dominate in a social situation, be it in a prison yard or a board room, are likely to have higher testosterone levels than their peers, new data show.

The newest and strongest evidence about the effect of testosterone comes from a study of 1,706 men in the Boston area, aged 39 to 70. The men were selected at random as part of a larger study on aging. Those who agreed to participate were interviewed in their homes and given psychological tests, and blood samples were taken.

Those who had higher levels of testosterone and related hormones had a personality profile that researchers described as "dominant with some aggressive behavior."

"The picture we get is of a man who attempts to influence and control other people, who expresses his opinions forcefully and his anger freely, and who dominates social interactions," said John B. McKinlay, a psychologist at the New England Research Institute in Watertown, Mass., who was on the research team.

The study, which will be published in *Psychosomatic Medicine,* is considered significant because it is the first to examine so many randomly chosen men. Most studies of testosterone in humans have been on small numbers in select populations, such as prison inmates.

Scientists caution against placing too much stock in the importance of hormones such as testosterone in human affairs, because so many other factors, from childhood experiences to social status, shape the expression of a given behavior such as dominance or competitiveness.

"This doesn't mean that people can't be dominant or aggressive without high testosterone," said Dr. Robert Rose, a psychiatrist at the University of Minnesota medical school. "A woman, of course, can be as competitive as a man, even though her testosterone levels are much lower."

EXERCISE 6.10

EXERCISE AND THE TEEN-AGE GIRL

Many Americans are very health conscious and exercise regularly. But health officials around the country are worried about the relatively low levels of exercise found among today's teen-age girls. In a 1994 follow-up to a 1990 study, the Federal Center for Disease Control and Prevention in Atlanta interviewed 10,000 high school students around the country. For ninth-grade girls, they found that 35% engaged in 20 minutes of vigorous exercise at least three times a week. The comparable figure for ninth-grade boys was 53%. For seniors, by contrast, the corresponding figures were 25% for girls and 50% for boys.

Another study of 3,000 high school students in five metropolitan areas found a difference in exercise levels in private schools as opposed to inner-city public schools. Girls in private schools tended to be much more involved in competitive athletic activities than those in urban public schools.

In interviews, girls gave many reasons for their relative lack of involvement in athletic activities, including the traditional one of not wanting to mess up their clothes or hair. But the demands of helping around the home also figured prominently in their explanations. Health officials fear the lack of exercise will lead to excessive weight gain and related health problems in later years.

EXERCISE 6.11

AIDS PLAGUE HITS TEEN HETEROSEXUALS

The AIDS epidemic clearly has reached teen-age heterosexuals, growing evidence shows. The most ominous signs are in New York City, where the epidemic is most advanced, says Dr. Karen Hein, director of a program that serves and studies teens with AIDS.

"The very heterosexual epidemic everyone says has not occurred in the adult population has occurred among teen-age girls in New York City," says Hein, who pointed to danger signs picked up by several recent New York state and city studies:

> 1 in 100 19-year-old women giving birth statewide is infected with the AIDS virus, as is 1 in 1,000 15-year-olds.
>
> Half of the city's teen-age girls with AIDS say they got infected by having sex with males.
>
> State researchers found about 6 percent of homeless boys and girls at one city shelter were infected.

But teen-age mothers, runaways and clinic patients are not representative of all teens, says Lloyd Novick, of the New York State Health Department, Albany. Also, he says, studies of new mothers show teens are less likely to be infected than older mothers—meaning there is "substantial room for prevention," especially among young teens.

Hein adds that teens who do not have sex or share needles may worry too much about AIDS. But, she says, studies show more than half of all teens do have sex by age 19. And teens who are considering sex "need to learn you can't look into the eyes of someone you love and tell if they have the virus."

EXERCISE 6.12

SCIENTISTS SEEK SECRETS OF HAPPINESS

Happiness, a favored subject of philosophers, writers, and poets since the beginning of history, has only recently come under scientific scrutiny. The results so far suggest that many traditional beliefs about happiness are incorrect.

The results of many recent studies are contained in the book *Happy People,* by Jonathon Freedman, professor of psychology at Columbia University. In one study, Professor Freedman and associates published questionnaires in *Psychology Today* and *Good Housekeeping*. The questionnaires were returned by more than 100,000 people around the country. Among the conclusions were

1. Sixty-five percent of all Americans are either moderately or very happy.
2. The percentage of happy people is greater among those who are married than those who are single.
3. The percentage of happy people does not differ among those with strong religious feelings from those without such feelings.
4. Considering just those people with high incomes, there are fewer happy people among the college graduates than among those who did not go to college.

In the book, Professor Freedman suggests that some people may have a genetic disposition toward being happy—a disposition that may be connected with the presence of certain recently discovered chemicals in the brain.

EXERCISE 6.13

SIXTY-FOUR PERCENT OF AMERICANS ARE REGULAR DRINKERS

Sixty-four percent of Americans acknowledge some level of alcoholic consumption. That is the overall conclusion of a recent survey involving 500 in-home interviews in twenty cities around the country. Asked to characterize their own drinking habits, 35% said they were nondrinkers, 46% light drinkers, 17% moderate drinkers, and only 1% heavy drinkers. One percent refused to answer the question.

Among those with a college education, 75% classified themselves as either light or moderate drinkers, and only 49% of those with a high school education gave these responses. Fifty-seven percent of blue-collar workers gave the light or moderate response. The corresponding percentage for white-collar workers was 71%.

There were also variations by age and income. Sixty-two percent of those younger than 35 admitted to being light or moderate drinkers, compared with 69% for those 35 to 54 and 54% of those 55 and older.

Variation by income was similar, with 59% of those earning less than $15,000 a year classifying themselves as light or moderate drinkers. In the $15,000 to $25,000 category the percentage was 64% and rose to 76% for those earning more than $25,000.

EXERCISE 6.14

MAJORITY OF WOMEN PERCEIVE JOB BIAS

Fifty-four percent of women responding to a recent Gallup Poll said they do not think that women have equal employment opportunities with men. Forty-one percent thought they did have equal opportunities, and 5% had no opinion.

Perception of bias depends strongly on whether one has actually been in the labor force or not. Among those women who have been working, 65% thought women's opportunities were not equal to men, but this opinion was shared by only 32% of women who had never been formally employed.

Education is also a factor. Among college-educated women, 68% think there is bias against women, whereas only 49% of those with a high school education or less agreed with this view.

When asked if a woman of equal ability has an equal chance of becoming chief executive officer of a company, 71% of the college graduates said she did not. That opinion was shared by 50% of women with less education and by 56% of all women in the survey.

The survey, conducted by interview, has a margin for error of ±5 percent.

EXERCISE 6.15

WORKING WOMEN SPEAK OUT

In 1994, the Woman's Bureau of the Department of Labor conducted a large survey of the attitudes and problems of working women. Questionnaires were distributed through more than 1,000 businesses, through labor unions, and through newspapers and magazines. More than 250,000 of the questionnaires were returned.

Nearly 80% of those responding recorded being pleased or very pleased with their jobs. Only 4% reported their jobs as being disagreeable or awful. However, roughly half of all respondents claimed they were paid less than men performing comparable tasks.

The most frequently mentioned general problem with being a working woman was stress caused by the dual demands of work and family. Apart from more pay, the most frequently mentioned priority for specific improvement was health insurance.

Labor Department figures show that, on the average, a working women in 1993 earned 71 cents for every dollar earned by a man.

EXERCISE 6.16

EIGHT PERCENT SAY THEY WERE ABUSED IN CHILDHOOD

Fifteen percent of American adults claim to know children they suspect have been physically or sexually abused, and 8% say they themselves were abused as children.

Knowledge of victims is no higher now than it was in 1981, but awareness of the scope of the problem recently has been enhanced by highly publicized cases, such as the beating death of 6-year-old Lisa Steinberg by her adoptive father in New York City. The weight of public opinion, in fact, attributes the larger number of reported child abuse cases to greater public awareness of the problem than to an increase in actual victimization.

The National Committee for Prevention of Child Abuse said in its annual report last week that child abuse deaths in the 50 states rose 5% in 1988 from the year before. It estimated, based on data from 41 states and the District of Columbia, that there were 3% more child abuse reports filed last year than in 1987.

More women than men claim to have been abused as children. Reported victimization also is higher among 30- to 49-year-olds than among younger or older adults.

Social and economic factors such as education and income apparently have little bearing on child abuse, with adults from widely varying walks of life reporting about the same incidence of childhood maltreatment.

Knowledge of child abuse cases and personal victimization are strongly interrelated. Four in 10 of those who say they were child abuse victims claim to know children who have been abused. In sharp contrast, only one in 10 of those who were not abused are aware of children they suspect are victims.

These findings are based on nationwide telephone interviews with 1,000 adults, 18 and older conducted by the Gallup Organization. In addition to sampling error, question wording and practical difficulties in conducting surveys can introduce error or bias into the findings of opinion polls.

EXERCISE 6.17.

PROJECT

Find a report of a statistical study. You may find an example in a newspaper or news magazine. The Sunday supplement to your local newspaper is a good bet. When you have found something that you find interesting and substantial enough to work on, analyze the report following the standard program for evaluating statistical hypotheses.

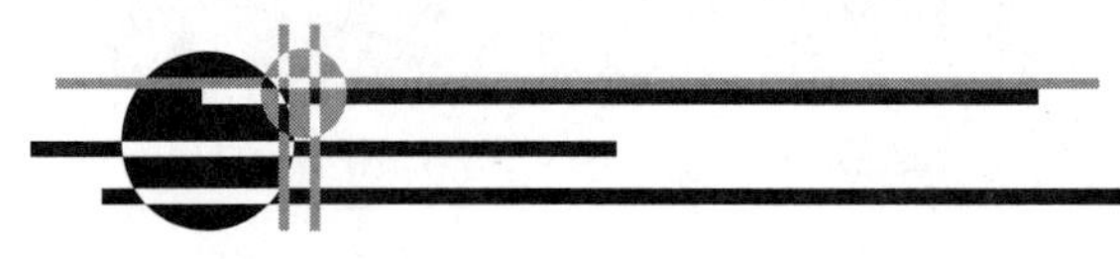

CHAPTER 7
CAUSAL MODELS

Many interesting and useful scientific findings concern *causal* relationships. Does a high level of cholesterol cause heart attacks? Does taking vitamin C prevent colds? We begin our study of causal relationships by distinguishing *causation* from *correlation*. Then, we develop several models of causation that will help us to understand and evaluate *causal hypotheses*.

7.1 CORRELATION AND CAUSATION

One of the most common mistakes in statistical reasoning is inferring the existence of a causal connection directly from a known correlation. This mistake continues to be made despite the fact that standard textbooks are full of examples illustrating the dangers of such reasoning. A few of these examples are worth repeating.

CORRELATION WITHOUT CAUSATION

Comparing lung cancer patients with people without lung cancer, we find that a history of using ashtrays is positively correlated with having lung cancer. That is, there is a much higher percentage of former or current ashtray users among the lung cancer patients than among others. But using ashtrays, obviously, does not cause lung cancer. Rather, cigarette smoking causes lung cancer, most lung cancer patients are former cigarette smokers, and most people who smoke use ashtrays.

Again, among small children there is a positive correlation between exhibiting red spots associated with measles and having a fever. But the spots do not cause the fever. Nor does the fever cause the spots. Both are produced independently by the measles virus.

More interestingly, anthropologists studying a tribe in the South Seas found the natives believing that having body lice promotes good health. It turns out that this was not just superstition. Almost every healthy person had some body lice, but many sick people did not. So the incidence of body lice among healthy people was clearly greater than the incidence of lice among sick people. Thus, there was a clear positive correlation between having body lice and being healthy.

The reason for the correlation, however, is not that having lice makes you healthy. It is that being sick causes you not to have lice. Lice are not stupid. They prefer healthy bodies to sick ones, particularly to feverish ones. When a person's temperature gets much higher than normal, the lice start looking for cooler surroundings.

In a more serious vein, researchers at a hospital connected with a major state university began comparing the recovery rates of patients. They discovered that, among all patients treated in the university hospital, those patients living within 50 miles of the university hospital had a higher recovery rate than patients from farther away. That is, among the university hospital's patients, there was a positive correlation between recovering and living within 50 miles of the hospital. Many different hypotheses were suggested in an attempt to explain why living near the university hospital causally promoted recovery.

In fact, there was no such causal relationship to be explained. The source of the correlation involved the simple fact that the university hospital had the best facilities in the state. Thus, seriously ill patients from all over the state were brought to this hospital. Less seriously ill patients, of course, were not. They were treated at their local hospitals, as were all those for whom the university hospital was their local hospital. So, of course, the recovery rate at the university hospital for patients living farther away was lower. These patients were, on the average, already much more seriously ill when they were admitted to the hospital.

CAUSATION IS NOT SYMMETRIC

These examples are instructive, but they fail to reveal the underlying nature of the difference between correlations and causal connections. A more enlightening difference is revealed by recalling that correlation is a *symmetrical* relationship. If A is positively correlated with B, then B will be positively correlated with A, and vice versa.

Now, whatever else may be true of causation, it is certainly *not* a symmetrical relationship. Speeding causes accidents, but obviously, accidents do not cause speeding. Taking poison may cause death, but death certainly cannot cause the taking of poison. In general, if being an A causes you to be a B, it does not follow that being a B would cause you to be an A. So, causation and positive correlation are fundamentally different kinds of relationships.

What is the source of the asymmetry of most causal relationships? Here, philosophers and statisticians disagree. Some emphasize *temporal* order. Causes, it is widely believed, operate only forward in time. You cannot cause something to happen in the past. Temporal order, however, cannot be the sole source of the asymmetry of causation. After all, using ashtrays typically precedes the onset of lung cancer.

Could one generate the required asymmetry using temporal order plus a more complex pattern of correlations involving other variables besides the two in the initial simple correlation? Some philosophers and statisticians think so, but we shall not pursue this idea here.

CAUSAL PRODUCTION

In our discussion of causal hypotheses, we use a primitive notion of **causal production.** Causes, we shall say, *produce* their effects or at least contribute to their production. The asymmetry of causation is part of the asymmetry of production. Exercise produces fatigue, but fatigue does not produce exercise. And production operates forward in time.

Talk about causal production does not go very far toward explaining what causation is, but it does at least give us a convenient way of talking about causal relationships. In the end, the *evaluation* of causal hypotheses will not depend very much on deep metaphysical issues about the nature of causation. So, we may as well use a simple intuitive notion of causal production, even if some find it metaphysically suspect.

7.2 CAUSAL MODELS FOR INDIVIDUALS

We begin by developing several simple models for causal connections in individuals such as humans or laboratory rats. These models are only a few of many similar models we could develop. Nevertheless, they are applicable to a wide variety of actual cases we find reported in the popular media.

A DETERMINISTIC MODEL

For purposes of the model, an individual is characterized by a **set of variables.** For the most part, we will consider only simple *qualitative* variables such as "is red" or "is not red," which we will use to represent such characteristics as "smokes cigarettes" or "does not smoke cigarettes." Among the variables characterizing an individual, we will pick out one that will represent a single characteristic that is under consideration as being a possible **causal factor** related to another single characteristic, a possible **effect.** We will designate the causal variable by the bold-faced letter **C,** which has possible values C and Not-C. Similarly, we will designate the possible effect by the bold-faced letter **E,** which has possible values E and Not-E. The rest of the variables ($\mathbf{S_1}$, $\mathbf{S_2}$, $\mathbf{S_3}$, ..., $\mathbf{S_N}$) characterize the **residual state** of the system. We will use the bold-faced letter **S** to designate the variable representing the 2^N possible residual states, including such particular states as (S_1, Not-S_2, S_3, ..., Not-S_N), which we will call, simply, S. Figure 7.1 pictures this model of an individual causal system.

Using this simple model, we can now give a more precise characterization of the notion of a **causal factor.**

> C is a *positive causal factor* (deterministic) for E in an individual, I, characterized by residual state, S, if in I, C produces E and Not-C produces Not-E.

> C is a *negative causal factor* (deterministic) for E in an individual, I, characterized by residual state, S, if in I, C produces Not-E and Not-C produces E.

FIGURE 7.1

A model for causation in an individual.

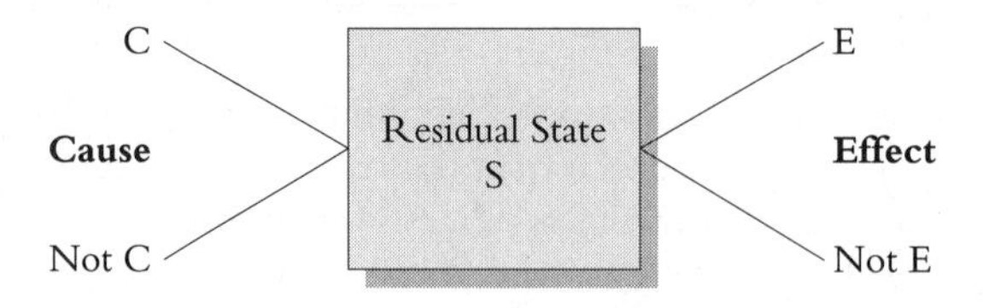

If C is either a positive or a negative causal factor for E in I, with S, then we say that the variable **C** is **causally relevant** for **E** in I. If C is neither a positive nor a negative causal factor for E in I, given S, then we say that the variable **C** is **causally irrelevant** for **E** in I, given S.

The reason this is called a **deterministic** model is that, given the residual state, S, the presence or absence of C *determines* the presence or absence of E in the individual, I. Or to put it the other way around, the presence of absence of E is *determined by* the presence or absence of C.

Several implicit features of this model are worth making explicit. First, to say that C is a positive causal factor for E in I is to say a lot more than both C and E are present in I. Being a positive causal factor implies that if C were not present, then E would also not be present. But the hypothetical situation in which C is not present in I may never exist. Once C is present, it may remain for the whole time I exists.

Second, the specification of the *residual state* is crucial. Another individual characterized by the same total set of variables might exhibit a different specific residual state. For example, its residual state might include Not-S_1 rather than S_1. For such an individual, C might not be a positive causal factor for E. It could be causally irrelevant or even negative. This implies that some of the variables making up the residual state of I may themselves be causally relevant for E.

To relieve the sense of abstraction involved in building up a causal model, let us apply the model to a real case that is discussed in the following chapter. There, it is claimed that ingesting saccharin is a positive causal factor for bladder cancer in laboratory mice. Consider an individual laboratory mouse, Izzy. Among the residual states of Izzy are that he is male, is white, is healthy, and so on. To say that saccharin is a positive causal factor for bladder cancer in Izzy, given his residual state, is to say that if he is given saccharin, he will get bladder cancer and that if he is not given saccharin, he will not get bladder cancer. As far as bladder cancer is concerned, for Izzy, given his residual state, saccharin makes all the difference.

COULD HUMANS BE DETERMINISTIC SYSTEMS?

There are many people who would question whether such a simple deterministic model could possibly be used to represent such a complex system as a human body. Before proceeding, we should pause to consider this point of view. The fact is that most people intuitively apply such a model, and much of modern medical research presumes that such a model is applicable.

Imagine two people as much alike as possible—say, identical twins. Suppose that both come down with the same fairly serious disease. Not having any other good options, the physician in charge decides to try treating the disease with a new drug. Both twins get the same dose. However, one twin recovers almost immediately but the second remains ill for a long time. Now, if you were the physician, would you not wonder why the drug worked on the one twin and not on the other? And would you not immediately assume that there must be *some difference* in the two cases that explains this difference in results? If this is your reaction, then you are assuming a deterministic model. That is, you are assuming that there is some combination of treatment and residual state that leads deterministically to recovery and some other combination that leads to failure to recover.The alternative is to say, "No, there is no difference whatsoever in the two cases, except in the result. Although the internal makeup and residual states were identical, the final states differed." Most people find this response almost incomprehensible. So, most people assume a deterministic model, perhaps despite themselves. Certainly, most physicians and medical researchers proceed as if deterministic models do apply. It is difficult to imagine a medical researcher saying, "Too bad. Some people get cancer and others don't. There is no other difference. There is nothing to research. That's just the way it is." Few, if any, medical researchers would give such a response. Moreover, any medical researcher who thought this way would probably not be very successful.

A PROBABILISTIC MODEL

There is, however, another approach. This is to assume that human bodies and other complex systems are to be represented not by deterministic but by **probabilistic** models. Despite much intuitive resistance to such an assumption, it is sometimes very useful and thus worth developing in further detail.

Let us continue thinking about the model pictured in Figure 7.1. This time, however, there is no longer a unique connection between the value of the causal variable and the value of the effect variable. For each value of the causal variable, either value of the effect variable might be realized. What the value of the causal variable does is change the *probability* of the value of the effect variable. More precisely,

> C is a *positive causal factor* (probabilistic) for E in an individual, I, characterized by residual state, S, if in I, the probability of E given C is *greater than* the probability of E given Not-C.
>
> C is a *negative causal factor* (probabilistic) for E in an individual, I, characterized by residual state, S, if in I, the probability of E given C is *less than* the probability of E given Not-C.

If the probability of E is the *same* for both values of the causal variable, we would say that **C** is *causally irrelevant* for **E** in I, given residual state S. As in the case of a deterministic model, specification of the residual state is crucial. For a different residual state, the probabilities could be different.

There is some difficulty with the understanding of probability in the above characterization of a probabilistic model. With a single individual, there is no obvious population to consider. What can we be talking about when we refer to the probability of E given C in I?

The suggestion most in keeping with our previous understanding of probability is to imagine the same individual, with the same residual state, being subjected time after time to alternating values of the causal variable. The relative frequency of E's when the causal variable has value C would then be the probability of E given C. Similarly, the relative frequency of E's when the causal variable has value Not-C would be the probability of E given Not-C. In actual applications, however, these probabilities are often purely *hypothetical.* There may never be more than one trial for a given individual.

Another suggestion is to suppose that causal productivity can vary in strength. That is, both C and Not-C can produce E, but the causal tendency of C to produce E may be stronger than the causal tendency of Not-C to produce E. Probability, on this account, is a measure of the strength of these causal tendencies.

These are all difficult notions. In what follows, we use both deterministic and probabilistic models for talking about individual systems. Most of the time, it will not make much difference which sort of model of individuals is assumed. The methods used for *evaluating* causal hypotheses in *populations* are essentially the same no matter which model of *individuals* is used.

7.3 CAUSAL MODELS FOR POPULATIONS

For many characteristics, particularly those studied in the bio-medical sciences and those of interest to public health officials, it is impossible to investigate possible causal relationships by studying just a few individuals. Not enough is known about the chemistry and physiology of individuals to distinguish those with relevantly different residual states. The only way to get at causal relationships is to study large groups of individuals, thereby implicitly averaging over differences in residual states. So, we need a model of causality that can be applied to populations. It must also be a model that will help us with the task of *evaluating* simple causal hypotheses.

To develop such a model, we begin with a *deterministic* model for individuals and then extend it to populations of such individuals. Later, we briefly consider how the model would differ if we started with a probabilistic model for individuals.

A COMPARATIVE MODEL FOR CAUSATION IN POPULATIONS

Our model for causation in a *population* will consist of a set of N individuals, each of which is modeled by a deterministic model of causation in individuals. The basic idea is this: we will say that **C** is causally relevant for **E** *in the population,* U, if there are any *individuals* in U for whom **C** is causally relevant for **E.** This basic idea, however, needs to be further developed. For our model to be useful, we need to be able to determine whether the causal relationship holds in the population even though there is no way to pick out individuals for whom **C** is causally relevant for **E.**

The key to a more useful model is to remember that whether **C** is causally relevant for **E** in an individual is independent of which values of each variable that individual, in fact, happens to exhibit at the moment. The important question for causation is whether a particular value of **C** *produces* a particular value of **E.** So, what we want to know is whether there are any individuals in the population for which C produces E and Not-C produces Not-E, or C produces Not-E and Not-C produces E.

One way to get at this question is to consider what would happen in the population if every individual exhibited the value C of the variable **C.** In particular, would any individuals now exhibiting values Not-C and Not-E exhibit value E for the effect variable if the value of their cause variable were changed from Not-C to C? Similarly, would any individuals now exhibiting values C and E exhibit value Not-E for their effect variable if the value of their cause variable were changed from C to Not-C? If there are any such individuals, then by the above account, **C** is causally relevant for **E** *in the population.*

In the original population, U, there will be some percentage of members exhibiting the effect, E. This percentage is the *probability* of E in the population, U, which we will symbolize as $\mathbf{P}_U$(E). Now imagine that every member of U that exhibits the value Not-C of the variable **C** is changed to exhibit the value C. This change results in a new population, which we will call X. X is just like U except that every individual member of X exhibits the value C of the causal variable, **C.** In the hypothetical population, X, there will be some percentage of members exhibiting the effect, E. This percentage is the *probability* of E in X, which we will symbolize as $\mathbf{P}_X$(E). It follows that, if there are any individuals in U for which C is a positive causal factor for E, but which in U exhibit Not-C and Not-E, then changing those individuals from Not-C to C will change them from Not-E to E in X. Thus, $\mathbf{P}_X$(E) will be *greater than* $\mathbf{P}_U$(E).

Similarly, imagine that every member of U that exhibits the value C of the variable **C** is changed to exhibit the value Not-C. This change results in a new population, which we will call K. K is just like U except that every individual member of K exhibits the value Not-C of the causal variable, **C.** In the hypothetical population, K, there will be some percentage of members exhibiting the effect, E. This percentage is the *probability* of E in K, which we will symbolize as $\mathbf{P}_K$(E). It follows that if there are any individuals in U for which C is a positive causal factor for E and that in U exhibit C and E, then changing those individuals from C to Not-C will change them from E to Not-E in K. Thus, $\mathbf{P}_K$(E) will be *less than* $\mathbf{P}_U$(E).

Putting these two results together, if there are any individuals in U for which C is a positive causal factor for E, no matter whether these individuals exhibit C and E or Not-C and Not-E in U, it must turn out that $\mathbf{P}_X$(E) is *greater than* $\mathbf{P}_K$(E). Thus,

> C is a *positive causal factor* for E in the population U whenever $\mathbf{P}_X$(E) *is greater than* $\mathbf{P}_K$(E).

A parallel chain of reasoning applies for the case in which C is a negative causal factor for E in some *individuals* in the initial population. In that case, it will turn out that $\mathbf{P}_X$(E) *is less than* $\mathbf{P}_K$(E). Thus,

> C is a *negative causal factor* for E in the population U whenever $\mathbf{P}_X$(E) *is less than* $\mathbf{P}_K$(E).

Finally,

> **C** is *causally irrelevant* for **E** in the population U whenever $\mathbf{P}_X$(E) *is equal to* $\mathbf{P}_K$(E).

A set of populations that might exhibit these relationships is pictured in Figure 7.2.

One interesting fact about these models is that it could turn out that **C** is causally irrelevant for **E** in the *population* U even though **C** is *not* causally irrelevant for **E** in all *individuals* in U. This could happen if there were some individuals in U for which C is a *positive* causal factor for E, and an equal number for which C is a *negative* causal factor for E. This is possible so long as different individuals in U have different *residual states*. In this case, $\mathbf{P}_X$(E) would turn out to be equal to $\mathbf{P}_K$(E). So long as we deal with individuals that differ in causally relevant ways, there will always be this sort of theoretical gap between models for individuals and models for populations. Population models

FIGURE 7.2

A comparative model for causation in populations.

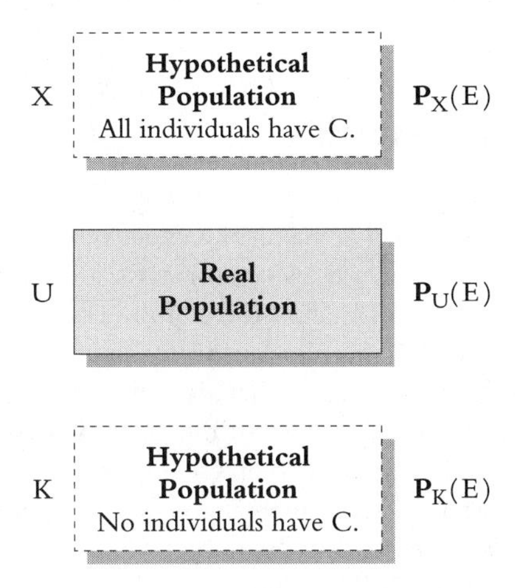

always average over individuals and, therefore, ignore what might be important differences among individuals.

WHAT IF THE INDIVIDUALS ARE PROBABILISTIC?

The above model of causal factors in populations assumed that the *individuals* making up the population fit a simple deterministic model for causal factors in individuals. What if the individuals are probabilistic? The only difference is that $\mathbf{P}_X(E)$ and $\mathbf{P}_K(E)$ are no longer definite numbers but only averages over probabilities. Suppose, for example, that there is exactly one individual in U for which C is a positive causal factor for E, but which, in fact, exhibits Not-C and Not-E. On a deterministic model of that one individual, the number of cases of E in X will definitely be greater by one than the number in U. On a probabilistic model of that one individual, all we can say is that the *probability* of an additional case of E in X will be greater than in U. Here, it is perhaps easier to understand probabilities as causal tendencies than as hypothetical relative frequencies. In any case, it turns out that the *evaluation process* for causal hypotheses is pretty much the same whether we assume a deterministic or a probabilistic model for individuals. In most of our further work, therefore, we will assume the simpler deterministic model.

7.4 EFFECTIVENESS OF CAUSAL FACTORS

For some purposes, such as making a decision, it is often less important to know that something *is* a causal factor than to know *how much* of a factor it is. In the case of medical treatments, for example, it is more important to know *how many* people a given treatment is likely to help than simply to know that there would be some. In the case of treatments, the term we would use to talk about relative numbers would be *effectiveness*. We want to know how *effective* a given treatment would be if it were applied to a given population. Let us generalize this notion and use the word *effectiveness* to talk about any causal factor, whether it is good such as vaccinations or bad such as air pollution.

EFFECTIVENESS IN INDIVIDUALS

On a *deterministic* model of individuals, there are only three grades of effectiveness. A *positive causal factor* in an individual is maximally effective in bringing about the effect. C produces E and Not-C prevents E. A *negative causal factor* is maximally effective in the negative direction. C prevents E and Not-C produces E. The intermediate case is *causal irrelevance*. The presence of C is irrelevant to the presence or absence of E.

On a *probabilistic* model of individuals, there is a full range of degrees of effectiveness. Here, C being a *positive causal factor* for E means that E is *more probable* given C than given Not-C. In the extreme case, **P**(E/Not-C) = 0 and **P**(E/C) = 1. This coincides with C being a deterministic positive causal factor for E. C being a *negative causal factor* means that E is *less probable* given C than given Not-C. Here, the extreme case is when **P**(E/Not-C) = 1 and **P**(E/C) = 0. This coincides with C being a deterministic negative causal factor for E. The simplest definition of the effectiveness of C in producing E, **Ef**(C,E), in an individual, I, is the simple difference, in I, between **P**(E/C) and **P**(E/Not-C):

$$\mathbf{Ef}(C,E) = \mathbf{P}(E/C) - \mathbf{P}(E/\text{Not-}C)$$

This measure has maximum value +1 and minimum value −1, with zero effectiveness corresponding to *causal irrelevance* between the variables **C** and **E.** That is, causal irrelevance means that **P**(E/C) = **P**(E/Not-C).

EFFECTIVENESS IN POPULATIONS

For a population model, assuming a deterministic model for individuals, the simplest measure of the effectiveness of a causal factor in a population, U, is the difference between $\mathbf{P}_X(E)$ and $\mathbf{P}_K(E)$. That is,

$$\mathbf{Ef}(C,E) = \mathbf{P}_X(E) - \mathbf{P}_K(E)$$

This measure again ranges from −1 to +1, with zero effectiveness corresponding to causal irrelevance. This measure applies not to individuals but to populations. However, just as a given causal agent might be quite effective for one individual and not for others, a causal agent might be quite effective in one population and completely ineffective in another.

If we assume *probabilistic* individuals, the corresponding measure of the effectiveness of a causal agent in a population would be the difference in the *expected* values of $\mathbf{P}_X(E)$ and $\mathbf{P}_K(E)$ in the two hypothetical populations.

7.5 SUMMARY: HOW CAUSATION DIFFERS FROM CORRELATION

There is an obvious parallel between our models of positive *correlation* and of positive *causal factors*. Similarly, there is a parallel between our definitions of the *strength* of a correlation and of the *effectiveness* of a causal factor. But causation is not the same as correlation, and now we can see more clearly why this is so.

To make this summary more concrete, let us apply our models to the example of smoking (C) and lung cancer (E). No one questions whether there exists a *positive correlation* between smoking and lung cancer. There are clearly more cases of lung cancer among smokers than among nonsmokers. Yet, it is still regularly questioned whether there is good evidence for the *causal hypothesis* that smoking is a *positive causal factor* for lung cancer. There is a basis for this difference in opinion in the great difference between the two sorts of hypotheses.

A *correlation* is a relationship between properties that exist in some *actual* population. Thus, the correlation between smoking and lung cancer is defined by the relative numbers of lung cancer patients among smokers and nonsmokers in the population of adult Americans as it now exists.

Causal factors, on our model, are defined by relationships between two *hypothetical* versions of the real population. To say that smoking is a positive causal factor for lung cancer is not to say merely that there are, in fact, more cases of lung cancer among smokers than among nonsmokers in the existing population. That is only a correlation. It is to say there *would be* (or probably would be) more cases of lung cancer if everyone smoked than if no one smoked—everything else being the same. That is a very different claim. These differences between correlations and causal relationships are pictured in Figure 7.3.

You should make sure you have a good grasp of the difference between correlations and causal relationships in populations. This difference will be crucial when we come to consider *evaluating* causal hypotheses. It requires a lot more information to have good evidence for a causal hypothesis than for a claim of correlation.

- **EXERCISES**

EXERCISE 7.1

Diagram the following hypotheses discussed in Section 7.1 of the text:

(A) Among the islanders, having lice is positively correlated with being healthy.

(B) Among the islanders, having lice promotes good health.

(C) Among the islanders, being healthy is positively correlated with having lice.

(D) Among the islanders, good health causes one to have lice.

FIGURE 7.3

The difference between a correlation and a causal hypothesis.

X: Hypothetical population if everyone smokes.

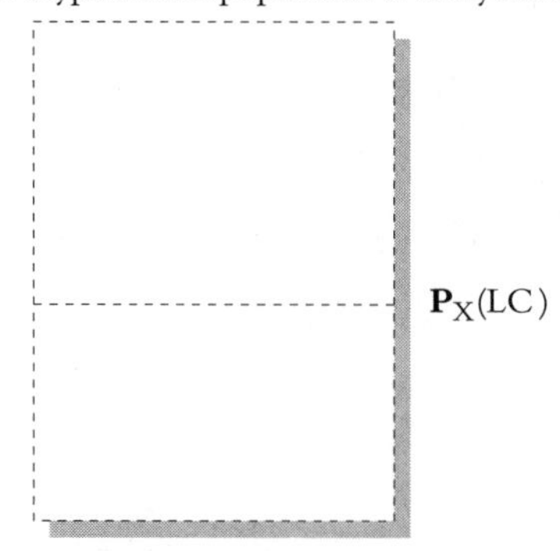

Smoking is a *positive causal factor* for lung cancer in the real population if $\mathbf{P}_X$(LC) is greater than $\mathbf{P}_K$(LC).

U: Real population

Smokers Nonsmokers

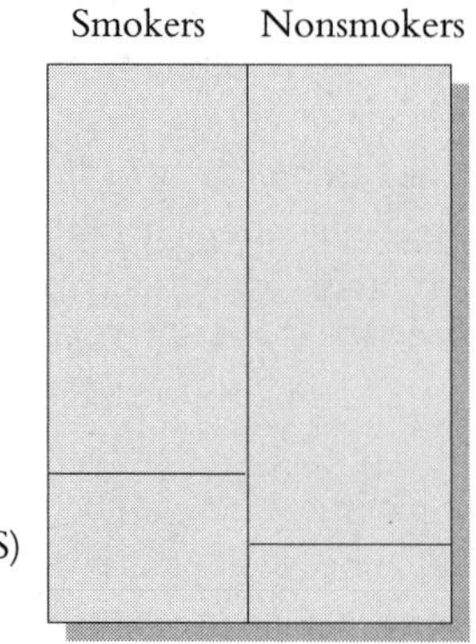

Lung cancer is *positivly correlated* with smoking in the real population if $\mathbf{P}_U$(LC/S) is greater than $\mathbf{P}_U$(LC/N).

K: Hypothetical population if no one smokes.

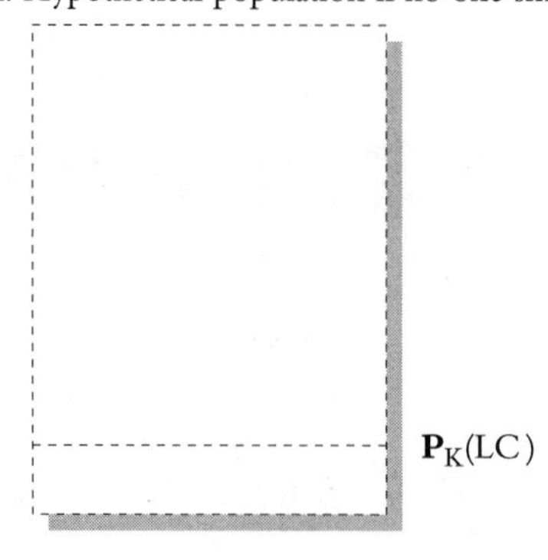

EXERCISE 7.2

It is well established that the death rate from heart attacks among widows is greater than the rate among married women in general. This fact has been cited as evidence for the hypothesis that being married prevents heart attacks. Diagram the established correlation between being married and suffering a heart attack. Then, diagram the suggested causal hypothesis. Explain in general terms why the established correlation by itself provides no evidence for the causal hypothesis. Can you think of an alternative explanation for the correlation?

EXERCISE 7.3

During World War I, the U.S. Navy argued in its recruiting literature that being in the Navy during the Spanish-American War was safer than living in New York City. The death rate in New York City during that war, they pointed out, was higher than that among sailors in the Navy. Diagram the correlation appealed to in the Navy's literature. Then, diagram the suggested causal hypothesis. Explain in general terms why the established correlation by itself provides no evidence for the causal hypothesis. Can you think of an alternative explanation for the correlation?

EXERCISE 7.4

A careful study of college students came up with the conclusion that there is a positive correlation between having a low grade point average and smoking cigarettes. Opponents of cigarette smoking concluded that smoking causes students to get lower grades. Others concluded that getting low grades causes people to smoke. Diagram the correlation revealed by the study. Then, diagram both of the suggested causal hypotheses. Is there any reason to think that the correlation provides better evidence for one causal hypothesis than for the other? Explain briefly.

EXERCISE 7.5

Imagine three individuals designated by their respective internal states as I_1, I_2, and I_3. Suppose that, given their differing internal states, C is a positive causal factor for E in I_1, a negative causal factor for E in I_2, and causally irrelevant for E in I_3. In the actual world, I_1 exhibits C and E, I_2 exhibits Not-C and E, and I_3 exhibits C and Not-E. Now, consider the *population* consisting of just these three individuals. In this population, is C a positive causal factor for E, a negative causal factor for E, or causally irrelevant for E?

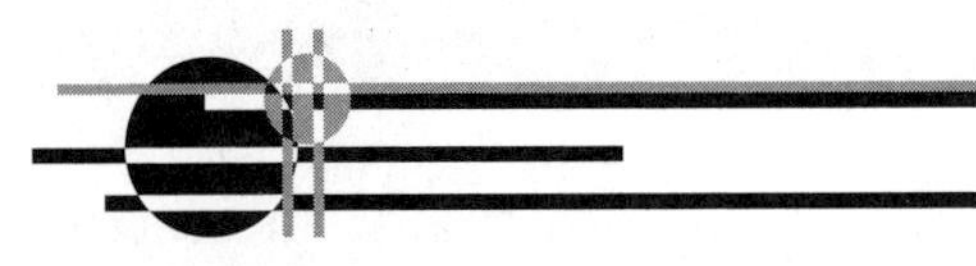

CHAPTER 8
EVALUATING CAUSAL HYPOTHESES

Does saccharin cause bladder cancer? Does smoking cause heart attacks? Does long-term use of oral contraceptives cause breast cancer in young women? In this chapter, we examine these three questions to illustrate three basic methods that may provide evidence for **causal hypotheses.** The first method provides the best evidence, and we shall use it as the standard by which to judge the shortcomings of the other two methods. The reason for taking the other methods seriously is that there are many questions that, for scientific, practical, or moral reasons, cannot be investigated using the scientifically best method.

The three studies we examine are interesting in themselves. You should be careful, however, not to get so involved in the specifics of a particular example that you fail to grasp the basic features of the method the example illustrates. Your main goal is to learn to recognize the type of study at issue. So, treat these cases as *analog models* to be used as guides when you face new cases to evaluate. Popular reports of scientific studies often do not tell you what type of study was involved. You have to figure that out for yourself. Because the quality of the evidence provided by these three methods is quite different, it is important to learn to recognize the differences.

8.1 SACCHARIN AND CANCER

In March 1977, officials of the U.S. Food and Drug Administration (FDA) learned of a Canadian study that showed that saccharin, a then popular artificial sweetener, causes cancer in laboratory rats. Two days after learning of this study, the FDA issued a preliminary ban on the sale of substances containing saccharin. The legal basis for the ban was a rule (the Delaney Clause) in a 1958 amendment to the Food, Drug and Cosmetic Act stating that any additive found to induce cancer in humans, *or animals,* shall be deemed unsafe. The proposed ban was strongly opposed by the soft drink and diet food industries and by large segments of the general public. Bills to revoke the Delaney Clause were introduced in Congress. Hearings were held and the congressional Office of Technology Assessment (OTA) was requested to review the evidence. The final OTA report upholding the Canadian findings was issued in October. In November, a bill was passed by the U.S. Congress temporarily suspending the FDA ban in favor of a warning label on foods containing saccharin.

Our concern at the moment is not with the public-policy or decision-making aspects of this episode, but with the *scientific* question of whether saccharin does indeed cause cancer in laboratory rats. As a matter of fact, few people questioned this scientific conclusion. Why, then, did the Canadian study provide such good evidence for this causal hypothesis?

The following are excerpts from the 1977 OTA report, *Cancer Testing Technology and Saccharin,* which reviewed and evaluated the Canadian study. You should study this report carefully because it describes an outstanding example of a **randomized experimental design.**

Saccharin Risks

The best evidence to date for concluding that saccharin is a potential human carcinogen comes from two-generation rat feeding experiments. These tests demonstrated that, over a long period, diets high in saccharin produced bladder tumors in rats. Evidence for carcinogenicity by other routes of administration and in other species of laboratory animals, while not convincing by itself, supports the conclusions from the two-generation rat experiments.

Animal Studies

The route of administration in animal tests is crucial. Accepted experimental protocols require that if human exposure is by ingestion, then the experimental animals must be fed the substance being tested. Forced feeding, although it allows a more precise dose, is not accepted. The induction of cancer in test animals following ingestion of saccharin shows that saccharin can potentially cause cancer when ingested by humans.

A situation that as nearly as possible duplicates human exposure to saccharin would be desirable. But for reasons mentioned earlier, using small animals is a necessary compromise. These practical modifications lead to other problems in relating the results of animal experiments back to human experience. Nonetheless, the weight of scientific evidence shows that these methods are valid for predicting carcinogenic effects in humans.

The positive feeding experiments were conducted over two generations. Rats of the first generation were placed on diets containing saccharin at the time of weaning. These animals were bred while on this diet, and the resulting offspring were fed saccharin throughout their lives. Members of the second generation were thus exposed to saccharin from the moment of conception until the termination of the experiment. Each animal of the second generation was examined for cancers at its death or at its sacrifice after 2 years on the experiment.

Each experiment had appropriate control groups that did not ingest saccharin. Compared to control animals, the saccharin-fed animals showed an excess of bladder tumors. These differences were sufficiently convincing to lead to the conclusion that saccharin caused cancer in rats.

A statistical analysis of the results of the two-generation rat-feeding experiment is shown in Table 8.1. Cancers were observed only at the highest dose levels of saccharin, 5 percent of the diet. Results are presented as a fraction; the numerator is the number of bladder cancers, and the denominator

TABLE 8.1
RESULTS AND STATISTICAL ANALYSIS OF RAT-FEEDING EXPERIMENTS

GENERATION	DOSE	CANCERS (M)	CANCERS (F)	TOTAL	SIGNIFICANCE
Parental	0%	1/36	0/38	1/74	p = .075
	5%	7/38	0/40	7/78	
Offspring	0%	0/42	0/47	0/89	p = .003
	5%	12/45	2/49	14/94	

is the number of animals (at least 18 months old) examined. The number of cancers found in the saccharin-fed animals exceeded the number found in the controls in each experiment.

Statistical methods are available to calculate the significance of the differences in cancer incidence observed between the experimental and control animals. Such a calculation was made by a standard procedure at the National Cancer Institute. The value "p" when multiplied by 100 gives the percent probability that the observed differences would arise by chance alone, if there actually was no difference between the experimental and control animals. In the first experiment in the table, "p" is equal to .075. Multiplying by 100 gives 7.5 percent. Thus, in that experiment, 7.5 percent is the probability that chance alone would produce at least this large a difference in cancer incidence even though there was no difference between the experimental and control groups. Any "p" value equal to or less than .05 is considered statistically significant. The results for the offspring generation in the experiments were significant by this criterion.

Bladder cancers were more frequent in male animals than in females. The explanation for this difference is unknown. In human populations, bladder cancers occur about twice as frequently among males, but that observation is ascribed to differences in exposure to carcinogens in the workplace and to smoking.

To conclude, the two-generation experiment showed that saccharin caused an increase in bladder cancer in second-generation animals, especially among males. In the experiment in which the first generation was examined, the increase fell just short of the standard test of significance. No cancer of any other site has been convincingly associated with saccharin.

We will now develop a standard model for evaluating studies such as these Canadian experiments.

8.2 RANDOMIZED EXPERIMENTAL DESIGNS

The Canadian study provides a clear example of a **randomized experimental design** (RED). We first examine the structure of such designs to understand how they can, in appropriate circumstances, produce good evidence in favor of a causal hypotheses. At the end of this section, we briefly take up some of the broader issues concerning the use of animal experiments to study human diseases.

REAL-WORLD POPULATION AND CAUSAL HYPOTHESIS

It seems obvious that the real-world *population of interest* in the Canadian study is human beings. After all, who really cares whether laboratory rats get cancer from ingesting too much saccharin? The *population actually sampled,* however, consisted entirely of laboratory rats. Statistical methods, therefore, only permit conclusions about rats. Any possible relationship between what happens to rats and what might happen to humans is a separate issue and must be evaluated using other sorts of evidence.

The **cause variable** in this study is the ingestion of saccharin. The **effect variable** is the occurrence of bladder cancer. The **causal hypothesis** of interest is that ingesting saccharin is a *positive causal factor* for the development of bladder cancer in laboratory rats.

According to the model developed in the previous chapter, the causal hypothesis asserts that there would be more cases of bladder cancer in the population of laboratory rats if all members of this population were exposed to saccharin than if none were. Figure 8.1 shows the populations, both real and hypothetical, used to model this hypothesis.

SAMPLE DATA

The sample data for the experiment are presented in Table 8.1. Actually, there are several sets of data. For the moment, we focus on the *totals* (male and female) in the *parental* generation. Here, the data are that among 74 rats given no saccharin, only 1

FIGURE 8.1

A model of the hypothesis that ingesting saccharin is causally related to developing bladder cancer.

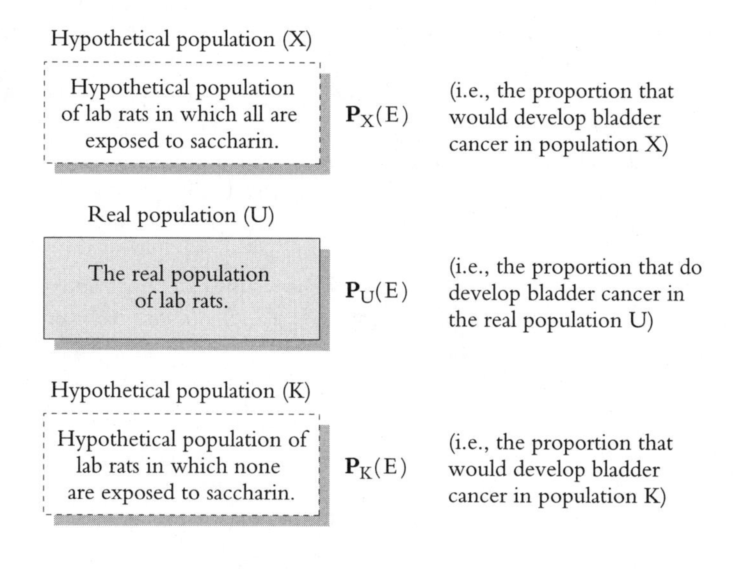

developed bladder cancer, while among 78 ingesting a diet of 5% saccharin, 7 developed bladder cancer.

EXPERIMENTAL DESIGN

As we already know, it is rarely feasible to examine the whole of any population. Scientists usually settle for a sample and then infer from the sample back to the population. But it is obviously impossible to sample a *hypothetical* population, let alone two hypothetical populations with incompatible characteristics. So, how does one test the causal hypothesis?

The answer is that scientists create real samples to play the role of samples from the two hypothetical populations. This is done by randomly selecting a sample from the *real* population and then randomly dividing it into two groups. All the individuals in one group are experimentally manipulated so that they have the condition that defines the hypothetical population we have called X (for "experimental"). The individuals in the other group are manipulated so that they have the condition that defines the hypothetical population that we call K (for "kontrol"). These two groups, then, are just as if they had been sampled from the two hypothetical populations. These groups are called the *experimental group* (x group) and the *control group* (k group), respectively.

To convince yourself that this procedure really is a satisfactory substitute for sampling the *hypothetical* populations, consider a single rat in the *real* population. Now, consider the following two procedures. (1) Depending on the flip of a coin, *every* rat in the real population either is or is not put on the saccharin diet. A rat is then selected at random. (2) A rat is randomly selected from the *real* population and then given a saccharin diet or not, depending on the toss of a coin. The probability of our chosen rat ending up in the experimental group is the *same* either way (i.e., 1/2N). This would also be true for any other rat. Thus, because our conclusion is to be based on what happens to rats in the experimental and control groups, we would reach the same conclusion either way. The second procedure has the advantage that it can actually be carried out in normal circumstances.

In the saccharin experiment, the researchers began with a group of laboratory rats, which, given the careful conditions under which these rats are bred, may be regarded as a random sample of all such rats. We can safely assume that designation of individual rats as experimentals or controls was done by some random process. The rats in the one group (the x group) were fed a 5% saccharin diet. The rats in the other group (the k group) received the same diet, minus the saccharin.

In the end, of course, there was an observed relative frequency of rats in each group that developed bladder cancer. We shall designate these two frequencies as $\mathbf{f}_{\mathbf{x}}(E)$ and $\mathbf{f}_{\mathbf{k}}(E)$, respectively. A model of the experiment concerning the parental generation is pictured in Figure 8.2. The two hypothetical populations are represented by broken lines indicating that they do not really exist. We would not normally include these two hypothetical populations in diagrams representing experimental studies. The first time through, however, it is convenient to have them handy for easy reference.

RANDOM SAMPLING

In randomized experimental designs, random sampling occurs in two places. First, the sample of subjects (in this case, laboratory rats) should be randomly selected from the

FIGURE 8.2

A model of the rat feeding experiment for the parental generation.

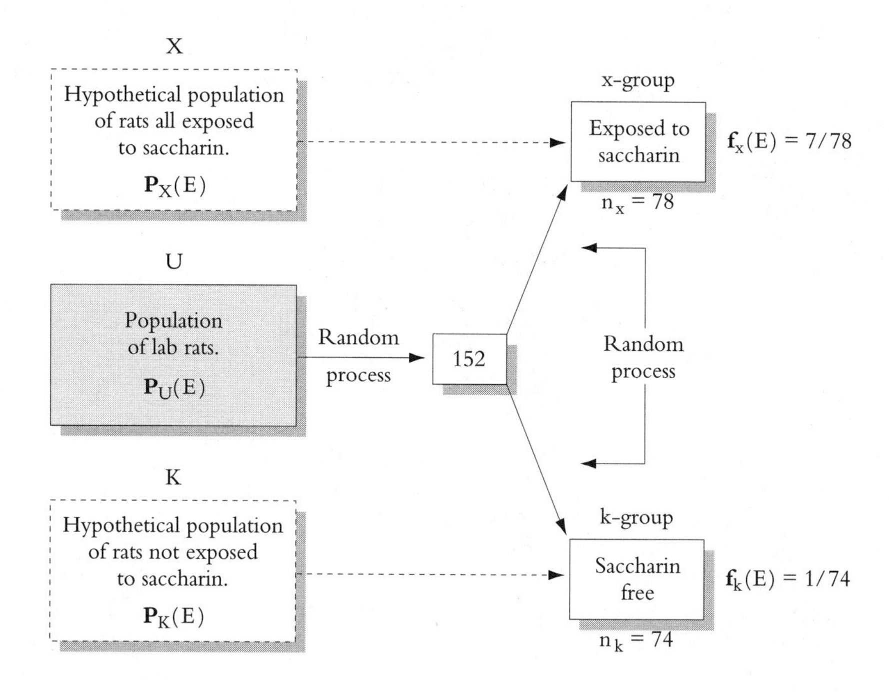

whole population. For example, we would not want a batch of rats that had accidentally been exposed to a rare chemical that sensitized them to saccharin. In such circumstances, the results of the experiment could be totally misleading regarding the population as a whole.

Second, the division of the initial sample into experimental and control groups must be performed randomly. For example, we would not want the control group to contain an excess of sickly rats who were already prone to bladder cancer. In that case, we might not get a statistically significant difference in the number of bladder cancers in the experimental and control groups, even if saccharin did cause bladder cancer in some members of the experimental group.

There is little explicit mention of random sampling in the OTA report on the Canadian saccharin studies. That must be because it is taken for granted in highly professional studies of this sort. If there had been even the slightest suspicion that the Canadian researchers had not followed the most careful procedures to ensure random sampling, you can be sure that the OTA would never have come out with such a politically unpopular review of their work.

EVALUATING THE CAUSAL HYPOTHESIS

Figure 8.3 shows a diagram of the data from the first part of the saccharin experiment. You will notice that this looks very much like a diagram of data that would be used

FIGURE 8.3

A diagram of the data from the parental generation in the rat feeding experiment.

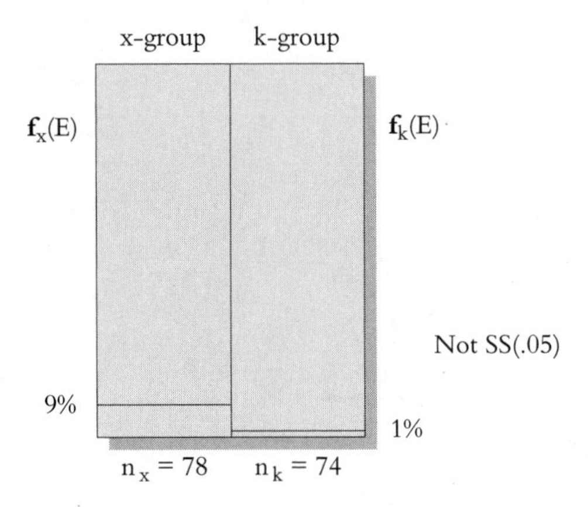

to evaluate the existence of a *correlation* between two variables. In this case, one variable is the *cause* variable, the presence or absence of saccharin in the diet, which characterizes the x group and the k group, respectively. The second variable is the *effect* variable, the occurrence (or not) of bladder cancer. The quantity $\mathbf{f_x}$(E) represents the relative frequency of bladder cancer in the x group, whereas $\mathbf{f_k}$(E) represents the relative frequency of bladder cancer in the k group. Evaluating the claim of a causal relationship between the cause and effect variables in the real population is thus similar to evaluating whether there is a correlation in the real population.

The relevant question is whether there is a *statistically significant difference* between $\mathbf{f_x}$(E) and $\mathbf{f_k}$(E). This is ascertained by using the values of $\mathbf{f_x}$(E) and $\mathbf{f_k}$(E) to estimate the values of $\mathbf{P_X}$(E) and $\mathbf{P_K}$(E). As before, we construct the relevant intervals, $\mathbf{P_X}(E) = \mathbf{f_x}(E) \pm \mathbf{ME}$ and $\mathbf{P_K}(E) = \mathbf{f_k}(E) \pm \mathbf{ME}$.

If the intervals do *not* overlap, the difference between $\mathbf{f_x}$(E) and $\mathbf{f_k}$(E) *is* statistically significant. That means that there is good evidence for a real difference between $\mathbf{P_X}$(E) and $\mathbf{P_K}$(E), which, in turn, means that there is good evidence for the existence of a causal relationship between the cause and effect variables.

If the intervals *do* overlap, the difference between $\mathbf{f_x}$(E) and $\mathbf{f_k}$(E) is *not* statistically significant. That means that there fails to be good evidence for a real difference between $\mathbf{P_X}$(E) and $\mathbf{P_K}$(E), which in turn means that there fails to be good evidence for the existence of a causal relationship between the cause and effect variables.

Note that in this latter case, there is no basis for claiming good evidence for a complete lack of any causal connection between the cause and effect variables. Only if there were an overlap of intervals with very large numbers of subjects in both the x group and the k group would we have good evidence for a very low level of *effectiveness* of the cause.

Estimating the *effectiveness of the causal factor* is similar to estimating the *strength of a correlation*. One simply calculates the difference between the two nearest and two farthest ends of the estimated intervals for $\mathbf{P}_X(E)$ and $\mathbf{P}_K(E)$. The resulting interval is the estimate of the effectiveness of the causal factor in the population. We need not repeat the details here.

In the OTA report, the difference in the incidence of bladder cancer in the experimental and control groups for the parental generation was reported as *not* statistically significant. That means that the first part of the experiment failed to produce good evidence in favor of the causal hypothesis that ingesting saccharin is a positive causal factor for bladder cancer in laboratory rats.

Actually, this particular report provides more information than is usual in more popular reports of statistical studies. From the information provided, we can easily infer that the difference between $\mathbf{f}_x(E)$ and $\mathbf{f}_k(E)$ for the parental generation would have been statistically significant if we used a confidence level of 92.5% rather than the standard 95%. That is, with a confidence level of 92.5% the intervals representing the estimates of the values of $\mathbf{P}_X(E)$ and $\mathbf{P}_K(E)$ would be narrow enough that they would just fail to overlap. So, the data from the first part of the experiment actually comes pretty close to providing good evidence for the causal hypothesis.

PROGRAM FOR EVALUATING CAUSAL HYPOTHESES

Before evaluating the evidence from the second generation of the Canadian saccharin study, we will develop a general program for evaluating causal hypotheses.

The Program

Step 1. Real-World Population and Causal Hypothesis. Identify the real-world population actually sampled in carrying out the study. Note any important differences between the population actually sampled and populations of interest. Identify the cause variable and the effect variable. State the causal hypothesis to be evaluated.

Step 2. Sample Data. Identify the real-world samples and the particular data from those samples whose relevance for the causal hypothesis you wish to evaluate. Be sure to include sample sizes when available.

Step 3. Design of the Experiment. Identify the model that best represents the design of the experiment. Explain briefly the reasons for your choice.

Step 4. Random Sampling. How well does a random sampling model represent the actual process by which the sample was selected from the population? Answer: (a) very well, (b) moderately well, (c) somewhat well, or (d) not very well. Explain the factors relevant to your answer.

Step 5. Evaluating the Hypothesis. Assuming a random sampling model is applicable, is there or is there not evidence for the causal hypothesis stated in Step 1? If possible, estimate the effectiveness of the causal factor.

Step 6. Summary. In the light of your answers in all previous steps, give a summary statement of how strongly the data support the causal hypothesis mentioned in Step 5. Possible answers: (a) very strong, (b) moderately strong, (c) somewhat strong, or (d) not very strong. Note the major factors supporting your answer.

As with the earlier program for evaluating statistical hypotheses, it is useful simultaneously to **diagram the study** following the examples of Figures 8.4, 8.12, or 8.14. This might be done on a separate sheet of paper. When doing Step 1, draw a box representing the population sampled. If relevant, surround this box with a larger box representing the population of interest. Label your boxes. When doing Step 2, add smaller boxes off to the right representing the samples. Label these boxes with relevant parts of the data such as sample sizes and observed frequencies. For Step 3, connect the boxes in the way appropriate for the type of design used in the study. In Step 5, indicate statistically significant differences or the lack thereof. At the end of your analysis, you should have a complete diagram of the study.

The Second-Generation Saccharin Experiment

Now, let us evaluate the Canadian saccharin experiment focusing on the data from the *second* generation of rats in the experiment. These rats, recall, were conceived by parents who were members of the original experiment. Rats in this experimental group were thus exposed to saccharin from conception until death.

Step 1. Real-World Population and Causal Hypothesis. The population sampled consisted of rats bred for laboratory experiments. The cause variable is ingestion of saccharin, and the effect variable is bladder cancer. The hypothesis at issue is that ingestion of saccharin is a positive causal factor for bladder cancer in a population of laboratory rats. By itself, this study says nothing about humans, which is undoubtedly the ultimate population of interest.

Step 2. Sample Data. The overall data, including both male and female offspring, shows 14/94 cases (15%) of bladder cancer in the experimental group exposed to saccharin, and 0/89 cases (0%) of bladder cancer in the control group not exposed to saccharin.

Step 3. Design of the Experiment. The experiment fits the model for randomized experimental design. The sample from the population was randomly divided into two groups, one of which was administered the causal factor by the experimenters.

Step 4. Random Sampling. The fact that this was a professional study reviewed by the OTA suggests that standard scientific measures were taken to ensure a random selection processes. It should fit a random sampling model very well.

Step 5. Evaluating the Hypothesis. The difference between $\mathbf{f_x}$(E) and $\mathbf{f_k}$(E) is reported as being statistically significant at the .05 level. And $\mathbf{f_x}$(E) is obviously greater. So, there is good evidence that ingestion to saccharin from conception is a positive causal factor for bladder cancer in rats. Because of the low values of **f**(E), the margins of error are smaller than stated in our usual rules of thumb. We can be confident that the effectiveness of the causal factor is greater than zero.

Step 6. Summary. This is clearly a careful study in line with random sampling models. The report indicates that we could raise the confidence level to 99.7%

before the confidence intervals would become so large as to overlap, thus rendering the observed difference between $\mathbf{f_x}$(E) and $\mathbf{f_k}$(E) statistically insignificant at the .003 level. That is very strong evidence in favor of the causal hypothesis for rats. Applying this result to humans is another matter.

The study, as it applies to the second generation of rats, is diagramed in Figure 8.4.

OF RATS AND HUMANS

In all the furor over the proposed ban on saccharin, no responsible critics questioned whether the Canadian study proved that saccharin causes cancer *in laboratory rats.* Most of the controversy centered on the Delaney Clause. Many questioned whether it is wise to base *public policy* on such a cautious rule. Others questioned the *scientific* basis of the Delaney Clause, which is that animal studies are relevant to questions about human diseases.

The relevance of animal studies was questioned for two reasons. First, humans are different from rats. Or to put it in our language, the population sampled was not the human population. Second, the amount of saccharin used (5% of the rats' diet) was quite large. Some critics calculated that 5% of a human diet corresponds to the amount of saccharin in 800 bottles of diet soda. Who drinks 800 bottles of diet soda a day? There is something to these criticisms, but not nearly so much as many critics thought.

FIGURE 8.4

A model of the rat feeding experiment for the offspring generation.

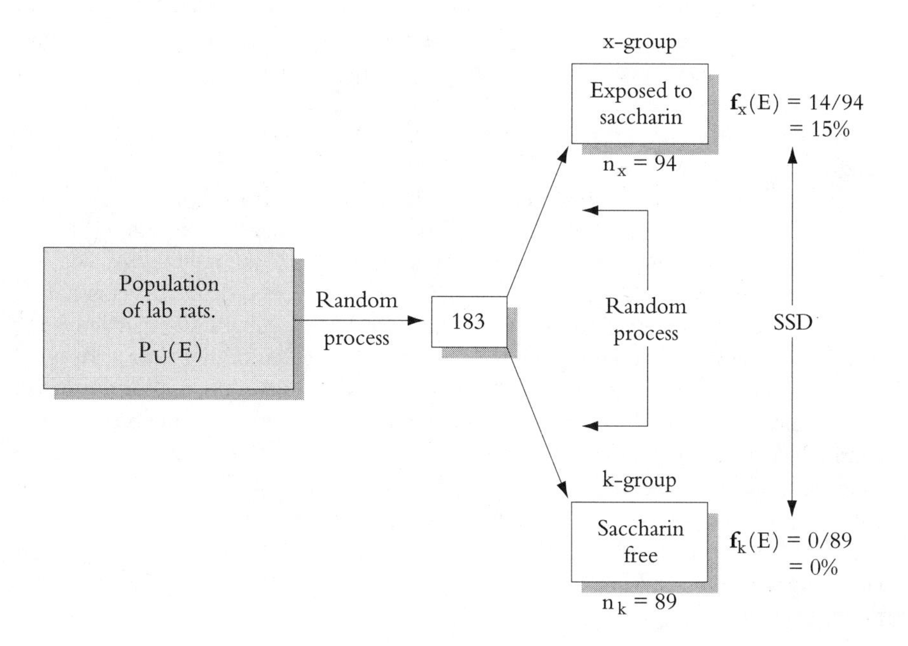

Most environmental hazards are not highly effective. If they were, lots more of us would be dead—or would never have been born. The typical cancer-producing agent strikes only one person in thousands, but that can be a large number. In a population of 200 million people, for example, 1 in 1,000 is 200,000 people. Even only 1 in 50,000 is 4,000 people.

We would not expect saccharin, or most substances, in *normal* doses to cause more than one cancer in 1,000 cases. To detect so low a degree of effectiveness using normal doses, however, would require an experiment using many thousands of rats. To breed and maintain so many experimental animals over a period of several years is almost impossible. So, instead, typical animal studies use many fewer animals and larger doses.

The assumption behind this strategy is that the number of cases of the effect is roughly proportional to the dose. Double the dose and you double the number of cancers. Therefore, knowing what large doses do, one extrapolates back to what normal doses would do. Now, the assumption that the effectiveness is proportional to the dose can be legitimately questioned. In particular, there could be a *threshold* for the effect. That is, below a certain dose there might be no effect at all in anyone. The number of cases would increase with increasing dose only *after* the threshold has been reached.

The problem is that almost no biological agent has been shown, in fact, to have a threshold. Saccharin, of course, might be an exception, but there is no positive justification for believing that it is. Nor, as we will see in Part Three, would it be a wise strategy to base decisions on the assumption that saccharin is an exception when there is no specific knowledge one way or the other.

It is often said by people who know little about medical research that any substance will cause cancer if given in big enough doses. That simply is not true. Many chemical substances have been tested on animals using large doses, and only a relatively few have been found to cause cancer. It may be true that large doses of anything will kill you, but few substances give you cancer in the process.

As for the statement that humans are not rats, that is obviously true. But of the roughly thirty agents known definitely to cause cancer in humans, all of them cause cancer in laboratory rats—in high doses. From this fact, it does not necessarily follow that anything causing cancer in rats will also do so in humans. But here again, it is difficult to justify basing practical decisions on the unsupported assumption that saccharin is an exception. And taking account of differences in dose and body weight, those fourteen cancers in ninety-four rats translate into roughly 1,200 cases of bladder cancer in a population of 200 million people drinking only one can of diet soda a day.

You can easily calculate that 1,200 cases of bladder cancer in a population of 200 million means that, on the average, any individual is facing a 6 in 1 million chance of getting bladder cancer. So, it may be argued, the risk is small, and people ought to be allowed to decide for themselves whether to take this risk. That, however, is an entirely different sort of question than the *scientific* question of whether there is any risk at all and, if so, how much. The answer to the scientific question seems to be that there is some risk, with 6 in 1 million being an informed guess as to how great the risk might be.

8.3 DOUBLE-BLIND STUDIES

Although randomized experimental studies are more easily performed with nonhuman subjects, special care must always be taken to ensure that the experiment itself does not introduce complicating factors that might affect the result. Thus, for example, in animal studies requiring surgical operations, the control subjects are typically given sham operations to ensure that the effect is not produced by the overall surgical procedure itself, rather than by the particular cause under investigation.

Experiments involving human subjects require even more subtle precautions. Consider, for example, the following experiment as described in Linus Pauling's famous book, *Vitamin C and the Common Cold.*

> A Swiss investigator, Dr. G. Ritzel, reported the results of a double-blind study. He studied 279 skiers, half of whom received 1 g of ascorbic acid [vitamin C] per day and the other half an identical inert placebo. He reported a reduction of 61 percent in the number of days of illness from upper respiratory infections in the vitamin C group as compared with the placebo group. These results have high statistical significance (probability in two samples of a uniform population only 0.1 percent).

To understand what "double blind" means, we must first consider what it means to do a study "blind." By definition, a study is **blind** if the *subjects* cannot tell whether they are in the experimental or control group. Because informed consent requires that the subjects know the overall purpose of the experiment, the control subjects must be given something that they cannot detect as not being vitamin C. Otherwise, all subjects would know immediately to which group they belonged. In the case Pauling cites, control subjects were given pills made of a known inactive substance that they could not distinguish from vitamin C. Any such inactive substance that is given to control subjects as a substitute for the suspected cause is known as a **placebo.**

The reason for going through all this trouble is to avoid a **placebo effect.** That is, it can happen that merely knowing that you are in the experimental group, and believing that the causal agent being studied does some real work, is enough to produce an apparent effect. For example, it has been well documented that patients suffering from headaches or other minor pains often report a lessening of the pain when given pills that they believe to be pain killers but that, in fact, contain no pain-relieving drugs at all. So, we can produce apparent effects with a placebo. In the present example, experimenters must worry that people might be able psychologically to suppress a mild incipient cold or that they might describe incorrectly how they feel, simply because they believe they are taking something that prevents colds. That could lead to a finding of fewer colds in the experimental group even if there were, in fact, no difference between the two groups. There are corresponding worries about subjects in the control group.

A study is called **double-blind** if the *experimenters* making the diagnoses are also kept in the dark about which subjects are in which group. The reason for this is that an experimenter may diagnose borderline cases in the direction that favors personal bias if it is known to which group a particular subject belongs. For example, there may be a question whether to diagnose a particular slight cough as a cold symptom. If the experimenter wants the experiment to show that vitamin C does prevent colds and knows this particular subject is taking vitamin C, there may be a bias in favor of not calling it a cold. Such biases, even if completely unconscious, might produce an apparent difference when none really exists. Of course, someone in charge of the overall experiment must have a list of which subjects are in which group so that the data can be compiled at the end of the experiment. That person, however, should not be performing diagnoses on subjects.

The clever use of placebos makes it possible sometimes to use the *same* subjects both as experimental and control subjects. For example, in one of the few experimental tests of the effects of marijuana on humans, nine marijuana-naive volunteers were tested for various psychomotor and psychological abilities, including hand-eye coordination and ability to concentrate. In this experiment, the same subjects served in both the experimental and control groups. That is, they were given either a measured amount of marijuana or a placebo in a series of sessions. Which subjects got the marijuana and which got the placebo in any particular session was determined randomly by an experimenter other than those actually conducting the tests. The test scores achieved by the subjects when they, in fact, had the marijuana were regarded as the experimental data. The scores achieved by the same subjects when they, in fact, had the placebo were regarded as the control data. In this experiment, the average score of the subjects was significantly lower when they received the drug than when they received the placebo. The advantage of this sort of design is that the subjects in the experimental and control groups are automatically matched for every possible additional characteristic. They are, after all, the same people in both phases of the experiment.

A similar experiment was carried out with nine experienced marijuana users as subjects. These latter tests, however, could not be done blind because it proved impossible to devise a placebo that could fool the subjects into thinking that they might be getting marijuana when they were not. The average scores achieved by these subjects were not significantly different when given the drug and when not. The small size of the sample, however, made it unlikely that any but a very effective cause would produce a statistically significant difference.

8.4 SMOKING AND HEART DISEASE

Ever since Columbus took tobacco from the New World back to the Old, people have been saying that it is an evil weed that causes all manner of illness and disease. Others claimed it to be a blessing and cure for diverse ailments. It was not until after World War II that anyone undertook deliberate, well-planned studies of possible causal relationships between smoking and serious illnesses such as cancer and heart disease.

You can easily appreciate the difficulties in studying these questions. Laboratory experiments of the type used to study the effects of saccharin (and many other drugs) are out of the question. It is practically impossible to subject enough animals (e.g., laboratory rats) to high enough doses of tobacco smoke to produce statistically significant differences. At normal doses, you could not expect more than a few cases in a thousand of any disease over the lifetime of the subjects. At above-normal doses of tobacco smoke, however, experimental animals suffer from smoke inhalation.

Direct experiments on humans are, of course, out of the question. One would have to select randomly several thousand nonsmokers, say, at age 12, and randomly divide them into two groups. Everyone in the experimental group would be forced to smoke a pack of cigarettes a day, and everyone in the control group would be prevented from smoking at all. In 20 to 40 years, there might be enough data to conclude either that smoking is a causal factor for some diseases or that its effectiveness in producing these diseases, if any, is very low.

Such experiments cannot be performed on humans. It would be immoral if not actually illegal. Nor is it even very practical. The effort and expense of maintaining such a regime for 30 years would be too great. The studies undertaken in the 1950s, therefore, were not experimental studies. They were **prospective** studies. As you read the following description of these studies, try for yourself to pick out the basic differences between prospective and randomized experimental designs. That will prepare you for the discussion of prospective designs in the following section.

THE FRAMINGHAM STUDY

In 1950, the National Institutes of Health (NIH) sponsored a projected 20-year study of the causes of several diseases, particularly coronary heart disease (CHD). The study was carried out in Framingham, Massachusetts, a town of about 30,000 people, 18 miles west of Boston. Among the disadvantages of Framingham for such a study was the fact that its population was rather more homogeneous than the population of all Americans, let alone the population of humans in general. For example, there were relatively few Afro-Americans in Framingham. A homogeneous population, however, has its own advantages, and Framingham, in particular, had other advantages as well. Among these were a cooperative and very competent group of local physicians and a published list of the names, addresses, ages, and occupations of all residents older than 18 years of age.

From these lists, 6,507 individuals aged 30 through 59 (3,074 men and 3,433 women) were selected at random and invited to come into a clinic for a physical examination. All were informed of the long-term nature of the study, including physical examinations every 2 years for the next 20 years. With the help of the local physicians, 4,469 of the initial sample agreed to participate, and of these, 4,393 were found on examination to be free of any symptoms of CHD. In addition, another 734 disease-free volunteers were added to the sample for a final total of 5,127 (2,282 men and 2,845 women). Figure 8.5 shows the statistical distribution of ages at entry into the study for both men and women.

The study was officially concluded 24 years later, in 1974, although some aspects were continued for more than a decade. Among the findings was that CHD appeared to be predominantly a male disease. The 24-year incidence of CHD for men and women in the middle-age group (40 to 49) is shown in Figure 8.6. The difference between the percentage of men and the percentage of women who eventually exhibited CHD is clearly statistically significant.

FIGURE 8.5

The statistical distribution by age for both men and women at the beginning of the Framingham study.

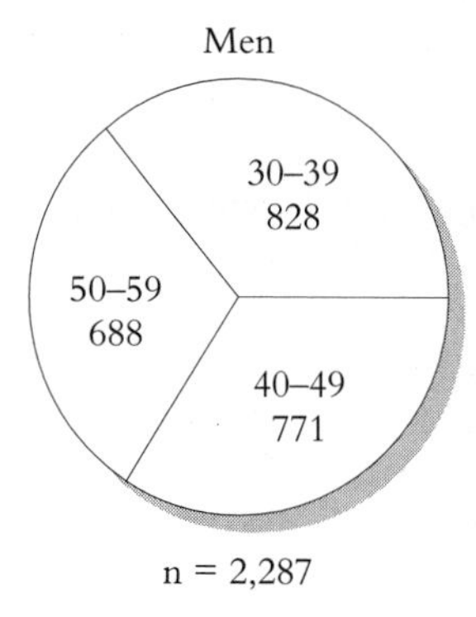

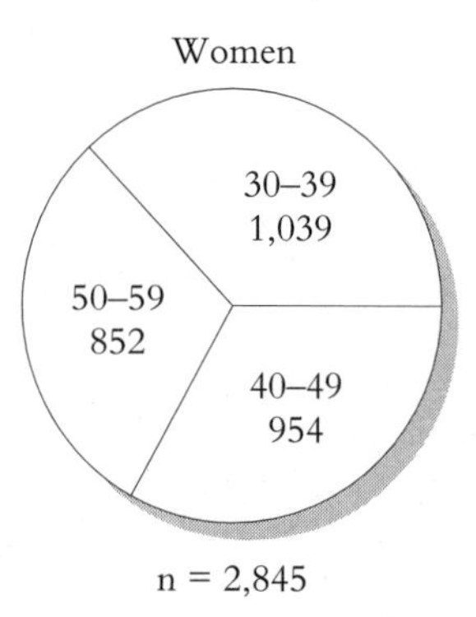

Some of the things that make men more prone to CHD are documented in the Framingham study. One of them appeared to be smoking. About half the men in the study were smokers. In the youngest age group at entry, there were, thus, roughly 400 each of smokers and nonsmokers. The data on CHD for these two groups are shown in Figure 8.7. This difference in incidence of CHD is statistically significant. By contrast, only about 20 percent of women in the same age group were smokers. The data for women are also shown in Figure 8.7. The reported difference in incidence of CHD is clearly not statistically significant.

FIGURE 8.6

The incidence after 24 years of coronary heart disease for men and women in the middle age group (40–49).

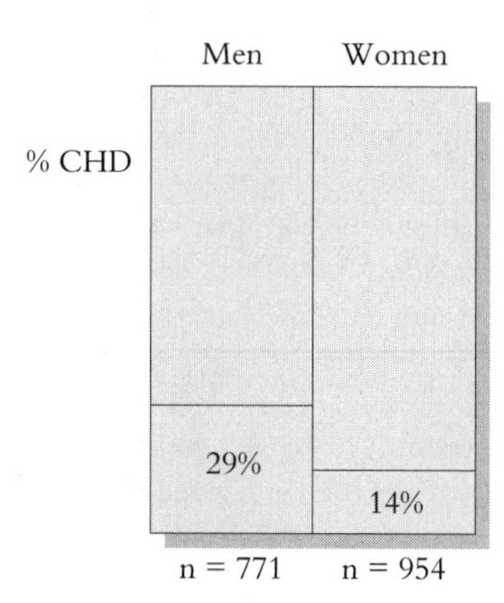

FIGURE 8.7

The data on coronary heart disease for smokers and nonsmokers among both men and women.

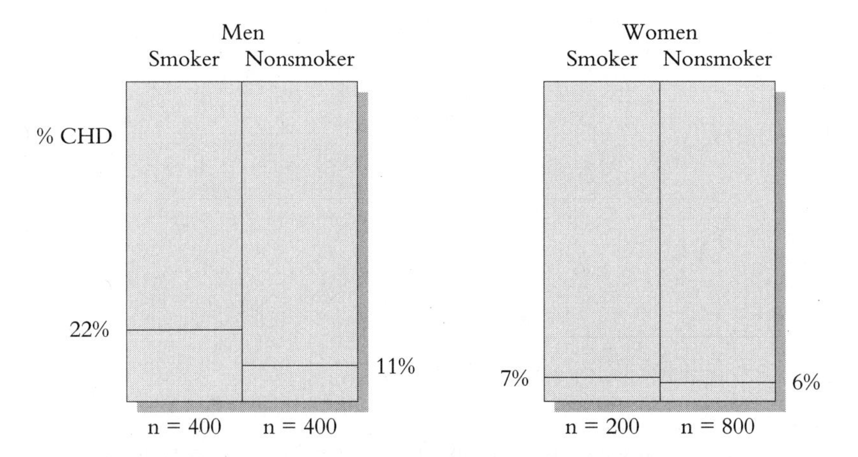

8.5 PROSPECTIVE DESIGNS

The Framingham study used a **prospective** design. The distinguishing feature of such a design is that it begins with two groups of subjects, one exhibiting the suspected causal factor (e.g., smoking) and the other not. Unlike experimental studies, however, the subjects are not assigned to the two groups by the investigators. The members of the population have already *selected themselves* into one of these two categories. The investigators merely sample from the two subpopulations (e.g., smokers and nonsmokers) as they already exist. The prospective feature of these studies is that any occurrences of the *effect,* in either group, would be in the *future* relative to the time the sample was selected. At the beginning of the study, no subject in either group exhibits the effect under investigation. People who already exhibited symptoms of CHD, for example, were excluded from the Framingham study.

The overall strategy in prospective studies is to get two groups that are, on the average, similar in every feature *except* the suspected causal factor. If there is then a statistically significant difference in the frequency of the effect, that provides evidence for the causal hypothesis. This type of design is pictured schematically in Figure 8.8. The sample of people having the suspected cause is still called the experimental group, even though there is no actual experimentation involved. The investigators do nothing to the subjects. They merely collect information about them and then wait to see what happens.

Comparing Figure 8.8 with Figure 8.2 makes it clear why prospective studies do not provide as direct a test of causal hypotheses as do randomized experimental studies. In a *randomized experimental study,* the two groups can be regarded as samples from the hypothetical populations in our model of a causal hypothesis. These samples are created through the process of random selection and direct experimental manipulation.

FIGURE 8.8

A model of a prospective study.

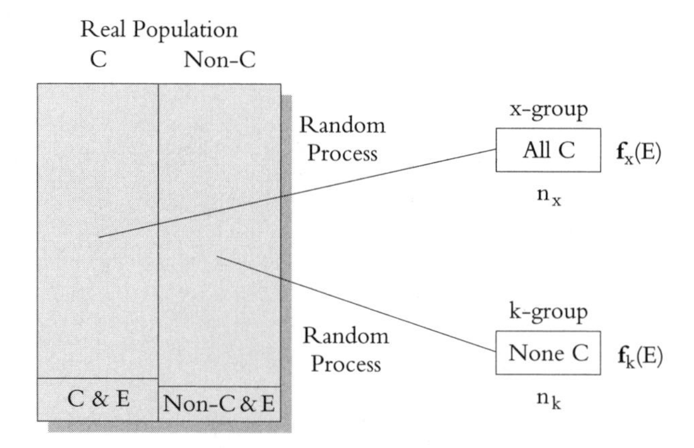

Prospective studies, however, are more like tests of *correlations* in that they are based on samples from the *actual* population as it exists. Prospective studies, however, differ from tests of correlations in that one is not merely looking at coexisting properties. The two groups are selected from among members of the population who do not yet have the effect. The effect shows up later, if at all.

In reading reports based on statistical studies, you must sometimes read very carefully to discover whether the data are based on a one-shot survey or on a genuine prospective study in which subjects initially without the effect are followed through time to see how many in each group later develop the effect. In a one-shot survey, you can ask people whether they had some condition earlier. But the reliability of the information you get about the prior condition may be influenced by whether the effect occurred or not. If you ask people with lung cancer about their previous smoking habits, for example, you are likely to get an exaggerated report, although the exaggeration might go either way. The subjects might think, "Why me? I didn't smoke that much," or they might think, "That's what did it. I smoked too much." Either way, you are not getting reliable information. That is one of the main virtues of genuine prospective studies over mere surveys.

CONTROLLING FOR OTHER VARIABLES

Step 4 in our program for evaluating causal studies requires us to consider how well the design of the study fits a random sampling model. It is here that prospective studies exhibit a distinct disadvantage relative to randomized experimental studies. This difference is illustrated by some results from the Framingham study.

One of the causal hypotheses investigated in the Framingham study is that the consumption of *coffee* might be a positive causal factor for CHD. Subjects enrolled in the study were, therefore, originally questioned about their coffee-drinking habits. A first look at the data after 24 years suggested that there might indeed be a causal connection between coffee consumption and CHD. Dividing all the subjects into those

FIGURE 8.9

A schematic picture of the overall Framingham data on coffee consumption and coronary heart disease.

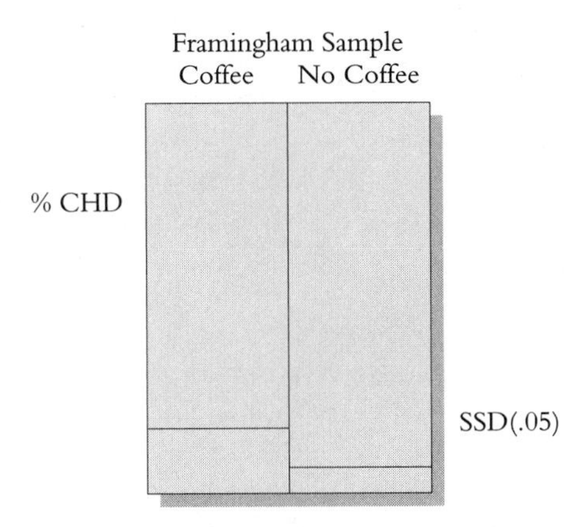

who drank coffee and those who did not yields a statistically significant higher rate of CHD among coffee drinkers than among all others. Figure 8.9 provides a schematic picture of these data.

A more careful examination of all the data, however, reveals that this causal hypothesis is not warranted. The reason is that there is a *correlation* in the population between coffee consumption and cigarette smoking. In particular, smoking is *positively correlated* with drinking coffee. That is, the percentage of smokers among coffee drinkers is greater than the percentage of smokers among those who do not drink coffee. So, the stereotype of the person holding a cup of coffee in one hand and a cigarette in the other has some basis in fact. This correlation is pictured in Figure 8.10.

A randomly selected sample of coffee drinkers, therefore, is very likely to contain a higher percentage of smokers than a randomly selected sample of those who do not drink coffee. If smoking does cause CHD, then there may be a statistically significant difference between the percentage of cases of CHD in these two groups, even if drinking coffee is causally irrelevant to CHD. The extra cases of CHD among the coffee drinkers may be caused by smoking, not by drinking coffee.

The standard remedy for this difficulty is to **control** for the other variable, which in this case is smoking—coffee drinking and CHD being the original two variables mentioned in the causal hypothesis we are considering. There are several ways to control for a third variable.

One way of controlling for a third variable is to restrict *both* groups to individuals *not* exhibiting the third factor. If there is still a statistically significant difference, it would have to be ascribed either to the originally suspected causal factor or to yet another factor correlated with it. If there is no statistically significant difference between the samples in which the suspected third factor has been eliminated, that is evidence that any effectiveness of the original causal factor in producing the effect by itself is not detectable by the experiment in question.

FIGURE 8.10

The correlation between coffee consumption and smoking in the general population of American adults.

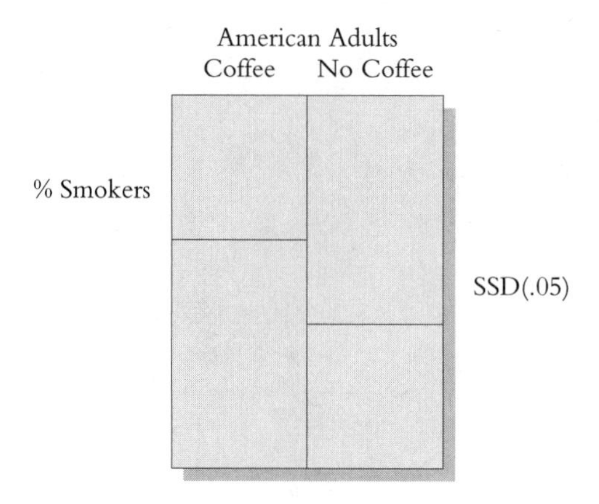

Investigators in the Framingham study looked at data remaining when all the *smokers* were eliminated from their sample. They then compared those remaining nonsmokers who drank coffee with those who did not. There was no longer a statistically significant difference in the rate of CHD between these two groups. These data are pictured schematically in Figure 8.11.

An alternative way of controlling for smoking would be to consider *only smokers.* Once again, a statistically significant difference in the rate of CHD would be evidence

FIGURE 8.11

A schematic picture of the Framingham data on coffee consumption and coronary heart disease when controlled for smoking.

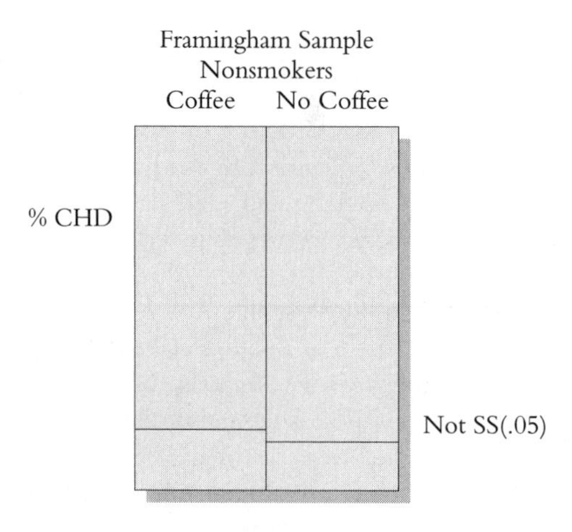

that coffee is a positive causal factor. Lack of a statistically significant difference would mean there is no evidence that coffee is a positive causal factor.

The disadvantage in this second way of controlling for smoking is that there might be some *interaction* between drinking coffee and smoking that contributes to CHD, even though neither by itself is a positive causal factor. That is, coffee drinking and smoking might be like binary chemical weapons consisting of two relatively harmless chemicals that, when combined, form a highly toxic gas. It is to avoid this sort of possibility that scientists prefer to control by eliminating the suspected third factor altogether.

Controlling for other variables has a cost. It reduces the size of the samples. There were fewer subjects in the Framingham study who drank coffee but did not smoke than there were who drank coffee, period. A reduced sample size makes it less likely that there will be a statistically significant difference, even if the original causal factor is somewhat effective.

To achieve adequate sample sizes, careful designers of prospective studies often proceed by **matching** the incidence of the suspected third factor in the control group with that in the experimental group. Thus, having obtained randomly selected samples of coffee drinkers and those not drinking coffee, the Framingham investigators could have examined both samples for smokers. Then, by randomly eliminating some smokers from the sample of coffee drinkers, they could have ensured that there would be the same number of smokers in both groups. Thus, the effect, if any, of smoking would be equalized in the two groups. Persistence of a statistically significant difference in the rate of CHD between the two matched groups would be evidence that coffee drinking was indeed a positive causal factor for coronary heart disease.

A drawback to matching samples for suspected third factors is that this strategy does not protect against interactive effects. If drinking coffee contributes to CHD only for smokers and not at all for nonsmokers, then the experimental group would tend to exhibit more cases of CHD than the control group with an equal number of smokers. Investigators could be misled into thinking that coffee, by itself, is a positive causal factor when it is really a factor only in interaction with smoking.

PROSPECTIVE VERSUS RANDOMIZED EXPERIMENTAL DESIGNS

We can now see why randomized experimental designs provide much better evidence for causal hypotheses than prospective designs. In a randomized experimental design, every characteristic possessed by members of the population is, on the average, matched in the experimental and control groups. This is true even for factors that are totally unknown to anyone. If half the population possessed a Q factor, roughly half of both the experimental group and the control group would possess Q.

Of course, because we are dealing with a random process, there is some small probability that the experimental group could end up with a very high percentage of Qs, whereas the control group could end up with a very low percentage of Qs. If there are many different potentially relevant Q factors, then it may even be quite probable that some one of these ends up with very different percentages in the two groups. That this particular Q factor should turn out to be highly relevant to the effect, however, would be an unlikely accident. So, even randomized experimental designs are not perfect, but the chances of their being terribly misleading are small. Not so with prospective designs, as illustrated by the example of coffee drinking and smoking.

In evaluating a study based on a prospective design, we must always look for indications that other potentially relevant variables have been controlled. If there are no such indications, we must use whatever general knowledge we have to decide whether lack of control for specific known factors (e.g., smoking) could render the data very misleading. If so, our conclusion regarding the quality of the evidence for the causal hypothesis must be tempered appropriately.

Evaluating the Framingham Study

Now, let us apply our program for evaluating causal studies to the Framingham data on smoking and CHD. We begin by focusing on the data for men.

Step 1. Real-World Population and Causal Hypothesis. The population of interest is human males or, more particularly, adult American men. The population actually sampled, however, consisted entirely of residents of Framingham, Massachusetts, in 1950. The causal variable is smoking, and the effect variable is CHD. The particular causal hypothesis to be evaluated is whether smoking is a positive causal factor for CHD among men in the population sampled.

Step 2. Sample Data. The sample consisted of randomly selected residents of Framingham. Included in the sample were about 400 each of male smokers and male nonsmokers, all aged 30 to 39. Among male smokers at the end of the study (24 years later), 22% had experienced some form of CHD. Among male nonsmokers, the percentage was 11%

Step 3. Design of the Experiment. The design fits a prospective model. It is not experimental because there was no random division into experimental and control groups. The subjects selected themselves into the categories of smoker or nonsmoker. All subjects were originally free of the effect, CHD.

Step 4. Random Sampling. Framingham is not a random sample of all American adults. Within Framingham, however, the sampling was randomly done, except for the 734 volunteers. There was no mention of any other variables controlled for in the data presented. So, the demands of a random sampling model were at least moderately well met.

Step 5. Evaluating the Hypothesis. In the observed range of sample frequencies, the margin of error for samples of 400 should be no greater than 5%. The observed difference in the rate of CHD between smokers and nonsmokers is, therefore, statistically significant, although not by a large margin. So, there is good evidence that smoking is a positive causal factor for CHD among men in the population sampled. Its effectiveness in this population is estimated to be in the range from .01 to .21.

Step 6. Summary. This study is about as well done as any prospective study can be. The main worry is that there were no controls for other possible causal factors

FIGURE 8.12

A diagram of the Framingham study for the hypothesis that smoking is a causal factor for coronary heart disease in American males.

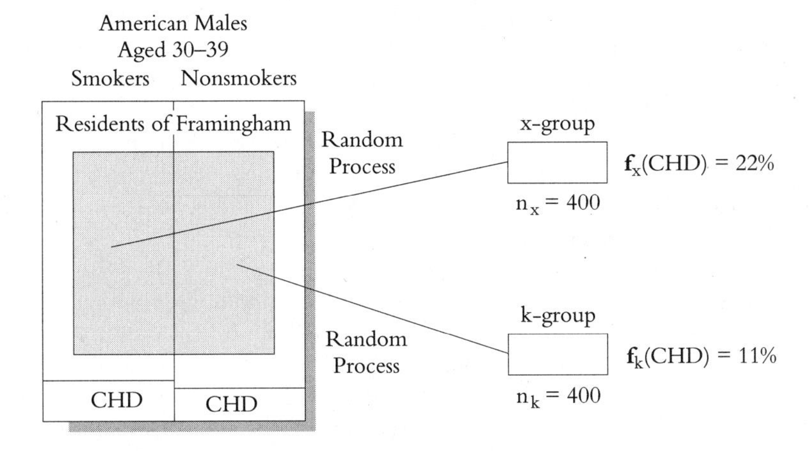

in the data presented. Nevertheless, assuming that coffee has been ruled out as an important causal factor, there are no other obvious candidates. So, unless there are other causal factors correlated with smoking, the evidence for the hypothesis that smoking is a positive causal factor for coronary heart disease among men in the population sampled is quite strong.

This analysis is diagramed in Figure 8.12.

We need not go through the whole analysis for the corresponding data on women. In the observed range of sample frequencies, the margin of error for n = 200 would be about .05 and for n = 800 about .02. Given that the recorded frequency of CHD among smokers and nonsmokers is 7% and 6%, respectively, the interval estimates would clearly overlap. Effectiveness would be estimated in the range from −.06 to +.09, which is comfortably around zero. There is, therefore, no evidence that smoking is a positive causal factor for CHD in this population of women. The evidence is that the effectiveness of smoking at producing CHD in this population of women is, at most, quite low. Unfortunately, this happy conclusion no longer holds for American women. As the rate of smoking among women has increased since the 1950s, so has the incidence of heart disease.

8.6 ORAL CONTRACEPTIVES AND BREAST CANCER

Since the introduction of oral contraceptives in the early 1960s, researchers have been on the lookout for evidence of negative side effects. Among the most obvious and serious possible side effects is breast cancer. Yet, 25 years after the use of oral contraceptives became widespread, there still was no consensus among researchers whether such use increases, decreases, or is irrelevant to the risk of breast cancer.

One reason for continuing uncertainty is the impossibility of conducting a clinical trial using a randomized experimental design. The decision whether to use oral contraceptives, and for how long, is left up to the users and cannot be randomly assigned by physicians or researchers. Prospective studies, however, are feasible. Because cancer typically takes many years to develop, however, useful prospective studies would have to have begun 20 years ago. Unfortunately, what prospective studies have been done did not involve enough subjects to have much chance of detecting moderate degrees of effectiveness for producing breast cancer. As we know, lack of a statistically significant difference with small samples provides little evidence for low effectiveness. We could, of course, have begun a large prospective study in the mid-1980s, but the results would not be known until well after the year 2000.

In the mid-1980s, researchers in Britain, members of the U.K. National Case-Control Study Group, attempted to investigate the question using a method that does not require waiting 20 years for an answer. A description of their study and its results was published under the title "Oral Contraceptive Use and Breast Cancer in Young Women" in *The Lancet,* a British medical journal, on May 6, 1989.

This study used a type of *retrospective* design. As you read on, try to figure out why the investigation should be called "retrospective." That will start you thinking about the main clue to recognizing the differences between retrospective and both experimental and prospective designs. We explore these differences in greater detail in the following section.

The U.K. researchers focused on eleven different areas in England, Scotland, and Wales, with a total population of 23 million people. Within this region, they identified all women who had been diagnosed as having breast cancer between January 1, 1982, and December 31, 1985, and who were younger than 36 years of age at the time of diagnosis. The restriction to younger women was necessary so that all had come of age after oral contraceptives were readily available. There were, therefore, no external restrictions on the age at which a woman in the study could have begun using oral contraceptives. The sample was further limited to white women with no prior malignancy, mental retardation, or psychiatric conditions. There were initially 1,049 women meeting these conditions. Of these, 166 had died before interviews could be conducted between January 1984 and February 1988. Another 128 had either moved out of the area or, for other reasons, would not take part. That left 755 women, or 72% of the initial sample, available for interviews regarding their previous use of oral contraceptives.

For each case in the sample of 755, the researchers selected, at random, one woman as a control from among the list of patients of the same physician as the corresponding case. The control subjects also had to meet the same conditions as the case subjects, except, of course, they had to be free of any symptoms of breast cancer. They also had to be no more 6 six months younger or older than the corresponding case. If a selected control could not be interviewed, another was chosen by the same random method. This process produced a control group of 755 women without any symptoms of breast cancer.

All subjects in both groups were interviewed for roughly an hour by professional interviewers. The most important part of the interview was filling in a calendar of events from age 14 until diagnosis of breast cancer. For control subjects, the calendar ended when the subject was the same age as her counterpart when she was diagnosed as having breast cancer. With this method, use of oral contraceptives could be coordinated with significant events such as marriage and births of children. There were also questions on a variety of relevant personal factors such as age, marital status (or cohabiting), education, weight, alcohol consumption, age at first period, diagnosed breast cancer in either mother or a sister, number of children, age at first full-term pregnancy, and breast feeding.

Both groups exhibited a high percentage of those who had used oral contraceptives at some time or other, 91% of the cases and 89% of the controls. There was, however, a difference in length of use. Among those with breast cancer, 470 of 755, or 62%, had used oral contraceptives for more than 4 years. Among the controls, 390 of 755, or 52%, had used oral contraceptives for more than 4 years. These percentages were similar for those with and without children. Among the subjects with breast cancer, 365 of the 595 with children, or 61%, had used oral contraceptives for more than 4 years. Among the controls with children, 319 of 616, or 52%, had used oral contraceptives for more than 4 years. Similarly, among subjects with breast cancer, 105 of the 160 with no children, or 66%, had used oral contraceptives for more than 4 years. Among the controls without children, 71 of 139, or 51%, had used oral contraceptives for more than 4 years.

How early one started using oral contraceptives seemed to make little difference. Looking only at those in both groups who had used oral contraceptives at some time, 468 of 688, or 68%, of the breast cancer patients had started using oral contraceptives earlier than age 22. Among the controls, 464 of 675, or 69%, started before age 22. The above data are summarized in Table 8.2.

The U.K. researchers devoted much of their report to discussing possible sources of bias in the study. The personal data for both groups revealed only four statistically significant differences: age at first period, breast cancer in mother or sister, a prior biopsy for benign breast disease, and breast feeding. Of these categories, however, only age at first period revealed a statistically significant correlation with long-time use of oral contraceptives. As you would expect, those with earlier first periods were more likely to be long-term users of oral contraceptives.

TABLE 8.2
WOMEN USING ORAL CONTRACEPTIVES MORE THAN 4 YEARS

	CASES	CONTROLS
All women	470/755 (62%)	390/755 (52%)
Women with children	365/595 (61%)	319/616 (52%)
Women without children	105/160 (65%)	71/139 (51%)
Women using oral contraceptives before age 22	468/688 (68%)	464/675 (69%)

More serious was the possibility of **nonresponse bias** either among patients or controls. Recall that 28% of the initial sample of 1,049 cases could not be interviewed. If these individuals tended toward fewer than the average number of years of using oral contraceptives, that would exaggerate the average duration of use among the remaining breast cancer patients. In addition, half of these nonrespondents had died, thus shortening the time they might have used oral contraceptives. Correspondingly, 80, or 11%, of the original 755 randomly selected controls did not participate. Of these, 68 were replaced by a second choice and 12 by subsequent choices. If potential controls with more years of use tended not to participate, that would diminish the apparent average duration of use among the controls. Fortunately, the U.K. group had access to physicians' records for most of the nonresponders. These records revealed no substantial biases.

Another worry addressed was **surveillance bias.** That is, women taking oral contraceptives typically have more regular examinations by medical personnel than those not taking oral contraceptives. So, women taking oral contraceptives are more likely to have breast cancers detected at an earlier stage. This implies that the sample of breast cancer patients would be likely to exhibit a higher rate of oral contraceptive use even if there were no causal connection between use of oral contraceptives and breast cancer. The difference in level of surveillance could be sufficient to produce a statistically significant difference in use of oral contraceptives in the two groups. After much analysis of the data, the U.K. researchers concluded that differences in surveillance were sufficient to reduce the average time until diagnosis of breast cancer by about 2 months. This difference, however, would account for only 4% of the difference in long-term use of oral contraceptives between cases and controls.

The U.K. researchers also worried about **recall bias.** That is, perhaps women diagnosed for breast cancer would tend unconsciously to report having taken oral contraceptives for longer than they, in fact, had. Women in the control group might have a lesser tendency to bias their recall in this way. Indeed, comparison of interview data with physicians' records revealed that, on the average, breast cancer patients reported about twice as long a time using oral contraceptives as was indicated by the physicians' records. The same, however, was true for the control group. So, *differences* between the two groups in reported length of time using oral contraceptives could not be attributed to recall bias.

Finally, there was the possibility of **interviewer bias**. It was impossible for the interviewers not to know which subjects were breast cancer patients and which were controls. So, the interviewers might unconsciously have caused the subjects to bias their responses in the suspected direction. Or the interviewers might unconsciously have biased how they themselves recorded the responses. The interviewers, however, were professionally trained, and the form of the interview was highly standardized both in terms of questions asked and possible answers that might be recorded. So, interviewer bias was ruled out as the source of the observed differences in the two groups.

8.7 RETROSPECTIVE DESIGNS

As noted above, the study just described used a **retrospective** design. The name comes from the fact that the study begins with a sample of subjects that already have the *effect* (breast cancer) and looks *back* in time to isolate a suspected *causal factor* (use of oral contraceptives). Such studies are, therefore, *backward looking*—unlike both experimental and prospective designs, which are *forward looking*. The backward-looking feature of retrospective designs is connected with most of the important differences between retrospective and other designs for testing causal hypotheses.

NONRANDOM SELECTION OF THE EXPERIMENTAL GROUP

Even though no actual experimentation is involved, the group exhibiting the effect being studied is still called the *experimental group*. This group is clearly not even randomly selected from the population actually sampled, let alone the broader population of interest. The U.K. breast cancer study, for example, was restricted to women in designated regions of the United Kingdom. Within these regions, the researchers initially identified every breast cancer patient younger than age 36 at diagnosis who also met several other minimal criteria. A random selection of 1,000 women in the designated population would be extremely unlikely to turn up 1,000 women with diagnosed breast cancer.

The British study was somewhat unusual in that it did initially include every woman exhibiting the effect in the population sampled. That was possible because of the British system of nationalized health care, which requires that everyone be registered with a general practitioner. So, in this study, there could be no sampling biases in the initial selection of the experimental group from the population actually sampled. There was, however, a possibility of nonresponse bias. Because not everyone initially identified as a potential member of the experimental group actually participated in the study, there was a possibility that those who did not participate differed in relevant ways from those who did. As noted above, the U.K. researchers made special efforts to ascertain that there was, in fact, little response bias.

Most retrospective studies do not begin with all cases of the effect in so large a population as the U.K. study. Studies in the United States, for example, typically survey only patients in a few designated research hospitals or members of a particular health plan. So, the population actually sampled is rather small and pretty obviously not representative of the general population. Patients in research hospitals or health plans are typically at a higher than average socio-economic level. They do not, for example, include many of the roughly 15% of Americans who do not have health insurance. For all such studies, there is a special problem of generalizing conclusions from the relatively narrow population actually sampled to a more general population of interest.

CONSTRUCTING THE CONTROL GROUP

Like prospective studies, retrospective studies suffer from the possibility that the **self-selection** of subjects into subpopulations with the effect and without the effect may be biased in a way relevant to the percentage of subjects exhibiting the suspected causal factor. It is for this reason that attempts are made to match the control subjects with the experimental subjects.

The control subjects in the British study, for example, were matched one for one with experimental subjects as having the same general practitioner and close to the same birth date. When there was more than one person meeting these conditions, one was selected at random. This was the only place random sampling entered into the study.

CONTROLLING FOR OTHER VARIABLES

In addition to the variables matched in constructing the control group, information about other variables may be obtained that permits control for these variables when analyzing the data. In the British study, for example, all subjects were asked whether they had any children. This made it possible later to determine whether having experienced a full-term pregnancy is relevant to any observed association between use of oral contraceptives and breast cancer. In all, there were a dozen other variables that could be controlled when examining the data. Each controlled variable, of course, reduces the effective sample size, thus diminishing the chances of detecting a causally relevant variable of low-to-moderate effectiveness.

As in the case of prospective studies, in retrospective studies it is impossible to control for every variable that might be correlated with a potential causal factor such as the use of oral contraceptives. The assumption that there are no relevant correlations among uncontrolled variables is always somewhat questionable. If the control group was matched with the experimental group for most variables that, on the basis of previous experience, might be relevant, that is the most we can do.

Figure 8.13 pictures the essentials of a retrospective design. You should note, in particular, that the frequencies observed in the two groups are not frequencies of the effect, but frequencies of the *cause*. Similarly, the subpopulations from which the samples come are not those that do or do not have the suspected cause but those that do or do not have the *effect*. In retrospective studies, the roles of the cause and effect variables are, roughly speaking, reversed. Thus, you can almost always tell when a reported study is retrospective because the frequencies given will be the frequencies of subjects with the *cause* in groups of subjects that either all have or all do not have the *effect*.

FIGURE 8.13

A model of a retrospective study.

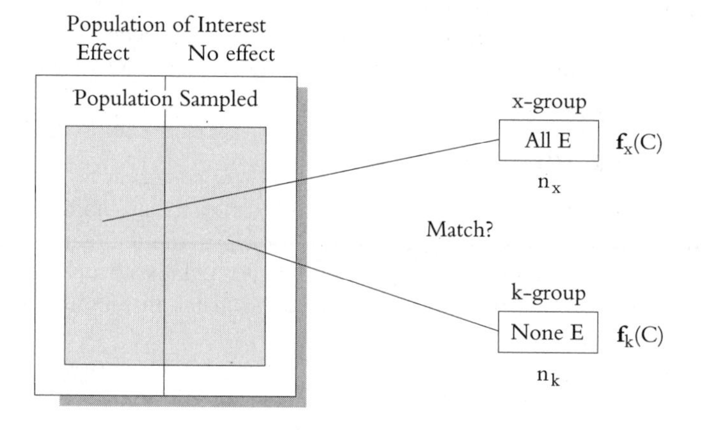

Reports of experimental and prospective studies always report the frequencies of the *effect* in the two different groups that do or do not exhibit the suspected *cause*.

RETROSPECTIVE STUDIES AND SURVEY SAMPLING

It should be obvious that using retrospective designs to study human populations is similar to using techniques of survey sampling. Indeed, some of the techniques (e.g., interviewing) are exactly the same. Our understanding of both retrospective studies and survey sampling may, therefore, be deepened by considering in more detail the similarities and differences in these two forms of investigation.

In principle, all the information obtained in a retrospective study could be obtained by survey sampling. Indeed, we could dispense with the difficult problem of creating a control group matching the given experimental group. A random sample of the population and information on relevant variables, including such things as previous use of drugs of any kind, could do the trick. We could easily compare the percentages of reported prior long-term use of oral contraceptives among breast cancer patients with the percentage among others. So, why does anyone bother with retrospective studies?

The problem is numbers. If the overall rate of breast cancer among young women is only 1 in 500, we would need a sample of 50,000 to expect 100 cases of breast cancer. Even with 100 cases, the margin of error is 10%. So, to get margins of error comparable with those in the U.K. breast cancer study, we would need a sample of more like 500,000. Obtaining such a large sample is just too difficult and too expensive for anyone to undertake. And many effects of great medical interest are much more rare than breast cancer in young women. It is to overcome the naturally low rate of most effects that researchers begin with all the cases of the effect they can find and then go through the trouble of trying to construct a control group that might be as reliable as one obtainable with good survey sampling techniques.

EFFECTIVENESS AND RETROSPECTIVE STUDIES

There is an additional disadvantage to retrospective studies. The data they yield allow no estimate of the *effectiveness* of a causal factor. Effectiveness is defined in terms of the percentage of the population that would experience the *effect* depending on whether all or none had the *cause*. The frequencies of the effect in two samples, as in a prospective study, may thus be used directly to estimate the effectiveness of the causal factor in the population. Retrospective studies, however, give you the frequency of the *cause* in groups with and without the *effect*. There is no way to use these frequencies to estimate the effectiveness of the causal factor. Knowing that 62% of women younger than 36 diagnosed for breast cancer had used oral contraceptives for more than 4 years tells you nothing about the percentage of women using oral contraceptives for more than 4 years who would get breast cancer. But this is the percentage you need to estimate effectiveness.

This feature of retrospective studies is especially serious because the effectiveness of the causal factor is the most useful information when it comes to making *decisions*. Just knowing that something is a positive causal factor, without knowing how effective it might be, is of limited usefulness in decision making. But that is the most you can get from a retrospective study all by itself. However, it is sometimes possible to combine information from a retrospective study with other information to reach an estimate of effectiveness.

In the case of the U.K. study, researchers were able to combine the results of this study with other information on the occurrence of breast cancer and the use of oral contraceptives to determine a rough estimate of the probability of breast cancer among young women who had used oral contraceptives for more than 4 years. This probability turned out to be less than 1 in 300. That is 70% higher than the probability of breast cancer among young women not using oral contraceptives, which is about 1 in 500. But 1 in 300 is still a relatively low probability. Moreover, this estimate does not take account of the protective effect of taking oral contraceptives against other conditions such as heart disease later in life. Thus, even assuming the stated conclusions of the U.K. study are correct, it is not at all clear that the increase in risk of breast cancer is large enough for sexually active women to forgo the obvious benefits of using oral contraceptives. We return to this issue in Part Three.

EVALUATING RETROSPECTIVE STUDIES

The basic strategy for evaluating retrospective studies is the same as that for evaluating experimental and prospective studies. We look for a statistically significant difference between the frequency of the cause in the experimental and control groups. If there is such a difference, that is evidence that there is a causal connection between the cause variable and the effect variable in the population. If there were no connection at all in the population and all selections of subjects were performed randomly, any differences in frequency of the cause in the two groups could only be due to the chance effects of sampling. By definition, statistically significant differences are unlikely to be due to chance alone.

The main trouble with retrospective studies is that the processes by which the samples are generated are at best only partially random. Any observed statistically significant difference between the two sample groups may all too easily be merely a reflection of biases in the selection process that produced the samples. There is also the possibility of correlations existing in the population that, even with random sampling, could lead to a statistically significant difference in the sample groups even if there were no causal connection between the variables being studied.

As a rule of thumb, it is probably best always to regard conclusions based on *retrospective* studies as, at most, moderately well supported by the data. A causal hypothesis supported by data from a good retrospective study is not to be ignored, and a positive result should be taken seriously by scientists and responsible agencies. Retrospective studies may provide a good reason to undertake other studies, either experimental or prospective. Nevertheless, evidence for causal hypotheses based on retrospective data alone cannot be regarded as being as good as evidence based on equally well-executed experimental or prospective studies.

Evaluating the British Study

As a summary of our discussion of retrospective studies, let us apply our standard program for evaluating causal hypotheses to some of the data in the U.K. study.

Step 1. Real-World Population and Causal Hypothesis. The population actually sampled consisted of women younger than 36 years of age in various regions of Great Britain. This population should be quite representative of young women in Britain but perhaps a little less so of similar women in western Europe and the United States, who seem to be included in the ultimate population of interest. The cause variable is use of oral contraceptives, and the effect variable is breast cancer. The primary causal hypothesis under consideration is that long-term use of oral contraceptives is a positive causal factor for breast cancer in young women.

Step 2. Sample Data. Of 755 subjects with breast cancer, 62% had used oral contraceptives for more than 4 years; of 755 control subjects free of breast cancer, 52% had used oral contraceptives for more than 4 years. Among 595 experimental subjects with children, 61% had used oral contraceptives for more than 4 years. Among 616 control subjects with children, 52% had used oral contraceptives for more than 4 years. Overall, the study controlled for a dozen other variables.

Step 3. Design of the Experiment. The design is retrospective. This is indicated by the fact that the study began with a sample of women, all of whom had been diagnosed for the effect, breast cancer. The control group of women free of breast cancer was constructed by matching for other characteristics of members of the experimental group.

Step 4. Random Sampling. Random sampling was used only in the selection of control subjects who shared a general practitioner with experimental subjects. However, the possible influence of many other potentially relevant variables was considered. Possible sources of bias were identified and investigated by comparing physicians' records with the data from interviews. In short, everything possible was done to compensate for the lack of random sampling throughout the design. There should, therefore, be a moderately good fit to a random sampling model.

Step 5. Evaluating the Hypothesis. Assuming a random sampling model, there is clearly a statistically significant difference between the frequency of long-term use of oral contraceptives between the experimental and control groups. The margin of error for samples of 755 is in the range of 3% or 4%. The difference in frequencies is 10% (62% − 52%), which is more than twice the margin of error. On a random sampling model, there is, therefore, good evidence that long-term use of oral contraceptives is a positive causal factor for breast cancer in young women. Controlling for having had children did not eliminate the statistically significant difference in observed frequencies of long-term use of oral contraceptives. Retrospective data do not permit estimates of effectiveness.

Step 6. Summary. This is a retrospective study, but an exemplary one. Random sampling was used when possible, and serious efforts were made to compensate for the general lack of random sampling elsewhere in the design. There is, therefore, moderately strong evidence that the causal hypothesis is correct.

This study is diagramed in Figure 8.14.

FIGURE 8.14

A diagram of the British study for the hypothesis that use of oral contraceptives is a causal factor for breast cancer in young women.

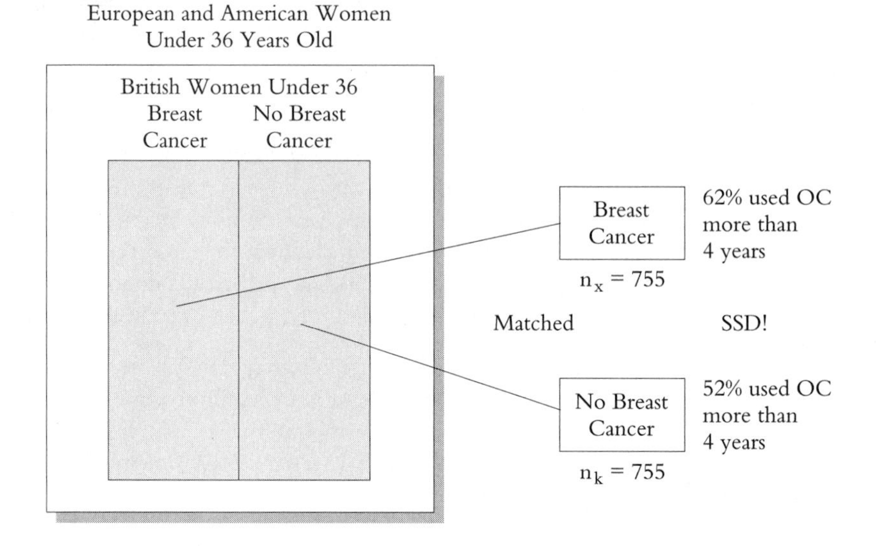

8.8 STATISTICAL EVIDENCE FOR CAUSAL HYPOTHESES

Although the use of statistical studies to investigate causal hypotheses is widespread, there are recurrent controversies about this practice. The objections cut both ways. The tobacco industry provides a classic example of one sort of objection. For 25 years, spokesmen for the industry have publicly disputed whether statistical studies can possibly prove the existence of a causal connection between smoking and any diseases. In many cases, this dispute centers on the crucial difference between experimental and prospective designs. There are, of course, no experimental studies of the effect of smoking on humans. And prospective studies always leave open the possibility that there is an unknown factor correlated with smoking that is the real culprit, and smoking itself is innocent. Thus, according to this suggestion, people who choose to smoke are already different from those who do not so choose, and it is this unknown difference, not smoking, that causes heart disease, lung cancer, and other diseases.

On the other side, advocates of unorthodox treatments for new and deadly diseases such as AIDS often argue that retrospective studies based on a few cases provide sufficient evidence to license new treatments. Experimental or prospective studies, which may take considerable time, are said to be unnecessary and unjustifiably to deny the new treatment to members of the control group and to the affected population at large.

We briefly examine both sorts of objections. Both are dangerously misleading, although for different reasons.

CAN PROSPECTIVE STUDIES PROVE A CAUSAL CONNECTION?

In *prospective* studies, scientists can control only for factors with which they are already familiar. Moreover, the *number* of variables that can be controlled in a single study is not very large. The more variables controlled, the more difficult it is to maintain a large enough sample for a sensitive and reliable test. This means that, in practice, a prospective study cannot eliminate more than a moderate number of ways that an observed statistically significant difference could have been produced by biased self-selection rather than by the proposed cause. In theory, things are even worse. In principle, there are innumerable ways that the self-selection process might be biased. So, no matter how many variables might be matched, the *theoretical possibility* of biased self-selection still remains. Because of this possibility, no prospective study can ever provide as good evidence for a causal hypothesis as a randomized experimental study. A question mark always hangs over even the best prospective studies.

In some cases, however, this question mark can be reduced to the barest theoretical possibility. In the mid-1960s, the National Cancer Institute sponsored a prospective study that enrolled more than 400,000 men between the ages of 40 and 80. Using a computer, the investigators matched almost 37,000 smokers with an equal number of nonsmokers for the following remarkably large number of other variables: age; race (white, black, Mexican, Indian, Oriental); height; nativity (native born or foreign born); residence (rural or urban); occupational exposure to dust, fumes, vapors, chemicals, radioactivity, etc.; religion (Protestant, Catholic, Jewish, or none); education; marital state; consumption of alcoholic beverages; amount of sleep per night; usual amount of exercise; nervous tension; use of tranquilizers; current state of health; history of cancer other than skin cancer; and history of heart disease, stroke, or high blood pressure. Every pair of men exhibited the same values of all these different variables, but in each case, one was a smoker and one a nonsmoker.

After nearly 3 years and more than 2,000 deaths, the rate of death from all causes was twice as great for the smokers as for the nonsmokers. Nearly half of all the deaths were due to heart disease, with the rate for smokers being double that for nonsmokers. Even more dramatically, the death rate from lung cancer for smokers was nine times that for nonsmokers.

In addition, the larger study from which the matched pairs were selected provided evidence for *correlations* that are very difficult to reconcile with any factor other than smoking. Death rates for smokers increase with years smoked, amount smoked, and with amount of inhalation. For former smokers, death rates decrease with the length of time since quitting. It is difficult even to imagine what other factor or factors might produce these correlations. The tobacco industry continues to claim that smokers are "a different kind of people" who smoke because they are "different" and also get lung cancer, heart attacks, and so on, because they are "different." But this is just a theoretical possibility for which there is no positive evidence whatsoever.

So, even though it is technically true that statistical data from a prospective study cannot "prove" the existence of a causal relationship, the overall evidence can be so strong that there is no basis for questioning the conclusion. There is only the bare theoretical possibility that there might be an unknown factor, correlated with smoking, that is the real causal factor.

THE ETHICS OF EXPERIMENTAL DESIGN

You should now have a clear idea why, of all statistical studies, randomized experimental designs provide the best evidence for the existence of a genuine causal factor. It should also be clear why, in some cases, insisting on a randomized experimental design can create severe ethical conflicts.

An example of such conflicts occurs in the testing of new treatments for life-threatening diseases such as AIDS. Use of a randomized experimental design requires that subjects run a fifty-fifty chance of ending up in the control group. If that happens, then, necessarily unknown to them, these subjects would not be receiving the new treatment, but another, possibly less effective, treatment. The situation is further complicated by the fact that the new treatment may not be approved for general use until the results of experimental studies are known. So, victims not part of the experiment have no legal means of getting even a chance to try the new treatment. Is that politically or morally justified? Should not anyone have the right to any treatment they want, regardless of the evidence available?

However, making approval of a new treatment dependent on favorable results in a randomized experimental trial makes it very likely that only treatments known to be effective are, in fact, used. Allowing approval with lesser evidence would mean that more people would end up using treatments that not only are not the most effective available but might be worse than no treatment at all. That could result in even greater suffering and greater expenditures of public funds.

Which is the best course of action cannot be settled by scientific investigation. That is a problem for the political process. It is a matter of public policy, not scientific method, under what conditions a new treatment should be available to the public. Statistical theory can only assure us that using randomized experimental trials is the most reliable way to determine the actual effectiveness of a new treatment. It provides no basis for insisting that the most reliable method must always be followed. There may be strong moral or political reasons to settle for less.

8.9 SUMMARY

Figure 8.15 provides a scheme for beginning an analysis of most studies appealing to statistical data. The first decision is whether the study is merely statistical or an investigation of a causal hypothesis. If just statistical, then you must determine whether you have data for a distribution or a correlation. A distribution has only one variable; a correlation has two. Here, you apply the program for evaluating statistical hypotheses developed in Section 6.6. If the study is not just statistical but causal, then you must determine the type of design employed.

Table 8.3 summarizes important characteristics of all three sorts of designs for investigating causal hypotheses. Familiarity with differences among the three types will

FIGURE 8.15

A classification schema for studies using statistical data.

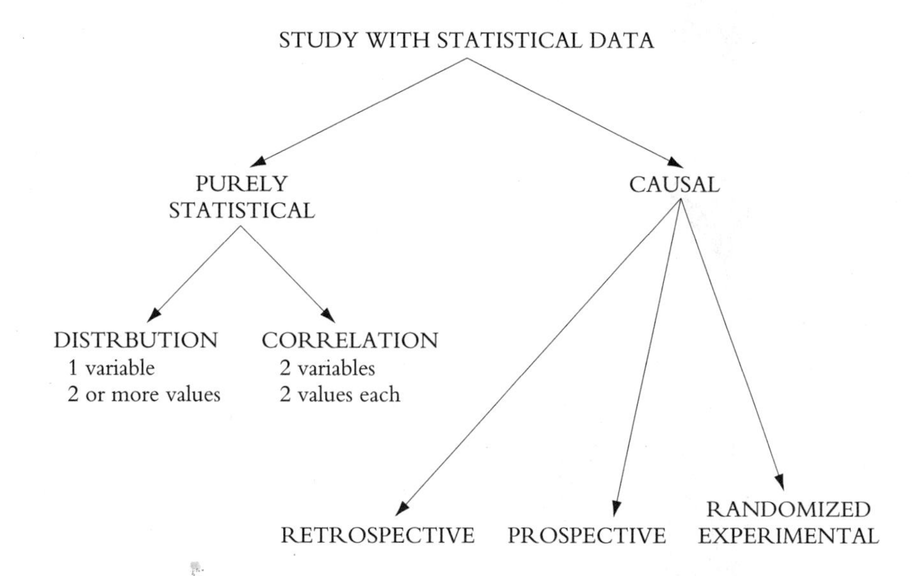

help you in identifying the type of design in reports of studies as you encounter them. Retrospective studies are easily distinguished from the other two types because of the nature of the experimental and control groups and the fact that the reported percentages are percentages of subjects who had the cause, not percentages of those who developed the effect. If by this indicator the study is clearly not retrospective, then your best strategy is to look for indications of random assignment, perhaps with use of a placebo. That would indicate a randomized experimental design rather than a prospective design. You must learn to make these determinations because your best indication of the reliability of the conclusion may be simply the type of design employed. Here, you use the program for evaluating causal hypotheses developed in Section 8.2.

TABLE 8.3
CHARACTERISTICS OF DESIGNS FOR EVALUATING CAUSAL HYPOTHESES

	Random Assignment	Random Sampling	Other Control Variables	Description of Groups	Description of Percentage Data	Estimate of Effectiveness
Randomized Experimental	Yes	Maybe	Not Necessary	X = All C K = All NON-C	%E	Possible
Prospective	No	Maybe, Sometimes Not	Possible	X = All C K = All NON-C	%E	Possible
Retrospective	No	Maybe, Usually Not	Possible	X = All E K = All NON-E	%C	Not Possible

• **EXERCISES**

Analyze these reports following the six-point program for evaluating causal hypotheses developed in the text. Number and label your steps. Be as clear and concise as you can, keeping in mind that you must say enough to demonstrate that you do know what you are talking about. A simple "yes" or "no" is never a sufficient answer. Some of these reports are taken directly from recent magazine or newspaper articles and are presented here with only minor editing. References to professional journals such as The New England Journal of Medicine *are genuine. You may find it instructive occasionally to go back to the original public source of the information you are analyzing.*

EXERCISE 8.1

BLOOD CLOTS AND THE PILL: EARLY EVIDENCE

In the 1960s, physicians in Great Britain and the United States discovered a surprising number of fatal blood clots in otherwise healthy young women whose medical histories made such a condition extremely unlikely. Even though they had only a relative handful of such cases, that was many more than they had experienced in the past in such seemingly healthy young women. Looking at the medical histories of these few women, they discovered that most of the victims had begun taking oral contraceptives less than 1 year before the fatal clot appeared. Because the use of such contraceptives had only recently become widespread, the physicians immediately suspected that the pill was responsible for the sudden increase in fatal clots among young women.

To test the suggested causal hypothesis, physicians in Britain began a search of records in nineteen different hospitals for the previous 2 years (1964 to 1966). They looked for women who had been treated for nonfatal clots of the legs or lungs (clots in the heart or brain tend to be fatal). They needed nonfatal cases so that they could locate the women in question and find out if they had indeed taken birth control pills before developing the clot. Such information was not generally available in regular hospital records. Their search turned up 58 cases of clots suffered by young, married women with no prior disposition for developing blood clots. Of these 58 women, 26 (45%) were discovered to have been taking oral contraceptives the month preceding their admission to the hospital for treatment.

The British researchers also studied 116 married women admitted to one of the participating hospitals for some serious surgical or medical condition other than blood clotting. Members of this group were carefully chosen to match members of the original group in age, number of children, and several other possibly relevant factors. Of these 116 subjects, only 10 (9%) were found to have been taking oral contraceptives.

EXERCISE 8.2

VITAMIN C AND THE COMMON COLD: THE SALISBURY STUDY

The following report on a study done at the Common Cold Research Unit in Salisbury, England, is adapted from Linus Pauling's book *Vitamin C and the Common Cold.*

> These investigators reported observations on human volunteers and concluded that "there is no evidence that the administration of ascorbic acid has any value in the prevention or treatment of colds produced by five known viruses." Of the 91 human volunteers, 47 received 3 g of ascorbic acid per day for 9 days and 44 received a placebo. They were all inoculated with cold viruses on the third day. In each of the two groups, 18 developed colds. The incidence of colds observed in the subjects receiving ascorbic acid (18/47) was 6 percent less than that in the control group (18/44). This difference is not statistically significant.
>
> The number of subjects, 91 in the two groups, was not great enough to permit a statistically significant test of a difference as large as 30 percent in the incidence of colds in the two groups to be made, although a difference of 40 percent, if it had been observed, would have been reported as statistically significant (probability of observation in a uniform population equal to 5 percent).

EXERCISE 8.3

STUDY FINDS DECAF COFFEE MAY RAISE CHOLESTEROL LEVELS

Drinking decaffeinated coffee appears to raise levels of harmful cholesterol in the blood and might play a role in heart disease, according to a study presented Monday.

Drinking decaffeinated coffee boosts low-density lipoprotein (LDL)—the so-called bad cholesterol—an average of 7 percent, the research found. That could translate into about a 12 percent increase in the risk of heart disease, said Dr. H. Robert Superko, director of the Lipid Research Clinic at Stanford University, who directed the research.

"Does coffee cause heart disease?" Superko said. "I don't know. We can only say that coffee causes cholesterol changes. It's not like going out and eating cheesecake, but the overall impact could be great," considering decaffeinated coffee's popularity.

In the latest study, presented at the American Heart Association's annual meeting, coffee-drinking volunteers were randomly assigned to one of three groups—regular coffee, brewed decaffeinated, or no coffee. Cholesterol levels remained steady in those who stayed on caffeinated coffee or gave up coffee entirely. But in the decaf drinkers, LDL levels rose nine milligrams per deciliter, or 7 percent.

EXERCISE 8.4

PREVENTION OF BIRTH DEFECT TIED TO VITAMINS IN PREGNANCY

Women who take over-the-counter multivitamin pills early in pregnancy sharply reduce the risk of having a baby with a type of serious neurological defect, a new study has found. These neural tube defects are among the most common and most devastating, causing effects varying from death to paralysis. They affect 4,000 babies a year, or 1 to 2 in 1,000.

In the study of nearly 23,000 pregnant women, about half said they had taken multivitamin pills containing folic acid in the first 6 weeks of pregnancy. The incidence of neural tube defects in babies born to those who took the pills was about one-fourth that of women who did not take them. The study, the largest on the subject so far, was published November 24, 1989, in *The Journal of the American Medical Association.*

The chief author of the study, Dr. Aubrey Milunsky, director of Boston University's Center for Human Genetics, said he felt that all women should take over-the-counter multivitamin pills containing folic acid while trying to become pregnant and during the first 6 weeks of pregnancy. "Our data are impeccable," Dr. Milunsky said. . . .

The idea that vitamin deficiencies might have something to do with neural tube defects originated after World War II, Dr. Milunsky said, when women in England, Holland, and Germany who had been malnourished gave birth to unexpectedly large numbers of babies with neural tube defects. Since then, researchers have been trying to see if vitamin supplements can prevent the birth defects. . . .

In the new study, Dr. Milunsky's group questioned about 23,000 women who were about 16 weeks pregnant and were having prenatal tests for birth defects, including neural tube defects. The women were questioned for about half an hour in an interview that produced twelve pages of information on all aspects of health practices. About half the women said they had taken multivitamin tablets containing folic acid in the first 6 weeks of pregnancy.

The researchers then determined which women had fetuses with neural tube defects. They found that the incidence of neural tube defects was 0.9 per 1,000 in the women who took vitamins in the first 6 weeks of pregnancy but was 3.5 per 1,000 in the women who did not.

Dr. Milunsky said he deliberately tried to avoid a methodological problem that had plagued previous studies. In those studies, including one by the Child Health Institute and one by the Federal Centers for Disease Control, that found that vitamins protected against neural tube defects, women were asked after they had had their babies whether they had taken vitamins. Such studies can suffer from a recall bias because women can selectively remember, or forget, what they took if they have an abnormal baby.

But the new study does not meet what researchers consider the highest standard, a randomized controlled study. In such a study, women would take either a multivitamin pill or an inactive dummy pill in the first few weeks of pregnancy, and the incidence of neural tube defects in the two groups would be compared. It remains possible that women who took vitamins on their own and not because they were randomly assigned to take them differed in some other way from women who did not. This difference, rather than the vitamins, could have accounted for the lowered incidence of neural tube defects. . . .

EXERCISE 8.5

STUDY FINDS NO LINK BETWEEN BREAST IMPLANTS AND DISEASE

In the early 1990s, there were many highly publicized cases of women who had silicon breast implants and later developed various diseases involving connective tissue, such as rheumatoid arthritis. In 1992, the U.S. Food and Drug Administration declared a moratorium on breast implants. The number of law suits eventually became so great that the major manufacturers of implants agreed to settle a class action suit involving thousands of women for $4.2 billion. It was argued at the time that the implants sometimes leaked silicon and that silicon had been shown adversely to affect connective tissue in experimental animals. And juries were sympathetic to women obviously suffering from serious diseases.

Now, several years later, the first epidemiological studies are being completed, and they show no evidence of any link between having breast implants and the diseases in question. One study, published June 16, 1994, in *The New England Journal of Medicine,* looked at 749 women in Olmsted County, Minnesota, who had implants between 1964 and 1991. These women were all part of the Rochester Epidemiology Project, which has computer records of virtually every visit to a physician or hospital by everyone in the county. The project is run by the famed Mayo Clinic, which is located in Rochester, Minnesota.

The 749 women were matched with 1,498 comparable women. As of 1994, five women with implants and ten without implants had developed one of a dozen different connective tissue diseases. In an editorial accompanying the report, Dr. Marcia Angell said that the study does not necessarily mean that implants are completely safe but that it is unlikely that any woman will develop connective tissue disease as a consequence of having had a silicone breast implant.

EXERCISE 8.6

FLU SHOTS EFFECTIVE AMONG HEALTHY ADULTS

Influenza is one of the nation's major public health problems. It is responsible for between 10,000 and 40,000 deaths and more than 150,000 hospitalizations annually. It is estimated that the total cost to the economy attributable to influenza is at least $12 billion a year. Effective influenza vaccines have been available for 50 years. It is well established that these vaccines are effective for persons at particular risk from influenza, especially the elderly and those with chronic health problems that are magnified by influenza. However, whether it is cost-effective to vaccinate otherwise healthy persons younger than 64 years of age has been a matter of controversy for many years. A new study, reported in the October 5, 1995, issue of *The New England Journal of Medicine,* suggests a positive answer to this question.

Between October 10 and November 30, 1994, 849 subjects in the Twin Cities of Minneapolis and St. Paul were enrolled through local advertisements. To be eligible, participants had to be between 18 and 64 years old and have no conditions that would place them at high risk for complications of influenza. At the time of enrollment, subjects completed a questionnaire covering basic demographic and health-related characteristics. Follow-up telephone interviews were conducted within 2 weeks and then monthly through April 1995. These interviews were used to determine episodes of upper respiratory illness, days of work lost due to respiratory illness, and visits to a physician for respiratory illness.

Participants were randomly assigned either to a group given a flu vaccination or a group given a placebo. Neither subjects nor attending physicians were informed of the assignments until the study was finished. Complete follow-up data were obtained for 416 of the placebo recipients and 409 vaccine recipients. The placebo group reported 582 (116%) episodes of upper respiratory illness, the vaccine group 429 (105%). The placebo group reported 508 (122%) days of sick leave due to upper respiratory illness, the vaccine group 286 (70%). The placebo group reported 229 (55%) visits to a physician's office for upper respiratory illness, the vaccine group 127 (31%).

Using average costs for vaccinations and wages for a day's work, the researchers estimated that vaccinations saved an average of nearly $47 per person vaccinated.

In an editorial accompanying this report, it was noted that the interviews could not distinguish upper respiratory illness due to flu from that due to other causes such as common colds, which should have been equally distributed between the two groups. This may account for the relatively small difference in reported episodes of upper respiratory illness. It was also noted that the effects of flu vary widely from year to year and from region to region. These results, therefore, may not be applicable to other regions of the country or to other years in the same region.

EXERCISE 8.7

DIET AND CANCER

The risk of fatal colon cancer is lower for men and women consuming larger amounts of vegetables and high-fiber grains. That is the conclusion of a study by American Cancer Society researchers reported October 7, 1992, in the *Journal of the National Cancer Institute.*

This study draws on data from the Cancer Prevention Study II (CPS-II), a study begun in 1982 by the American Cancer Society. Roughly 77,000 cancer society volunteers in all fifty states enrolled 1,185,124 men and women, mostly friends, neighbors, and acquaintances. Participants had to be at least 30 years of age; the average age was 57. Participants completed a four-page questionnaire, supplying information on things such as diet, smoking, alcohol intake, physical activity, weight, use of medications, and family history of cancer. The volunteers reported on the status of participants at 2-year intervals after enrollment. By the end of 1988, 79,820 (6.7%) of the participants had died and 21,704 (1.8%) had dropped out of the study.

The ACS researchers eliminated from consideration participants who might bias their results, such as people with a history of cancer at the time of enrollment. This left a sample of 764,343, of whom 1,150 (611 men and 539 women) had died of colon cancer by the end of 1988. Reports on cause of death were obtained for all these cancer victims. Each of these victims was matched by age, race, and sex with up to five other participants, for a total of 5,746 people in the comparison group.

The percentage of colon cancer victims ranking in the highest category for consumption of vegetables and high-fiber grains was significantly lower than the percentage for the comparison group. The same was true for aspirin use. Curiously, the data yielded no statistically significant differences for total fat intake, exercise level, or body mass. These characteristics have been implicated as causal factors for cancer in earlier studies.

EXERCISE 8.8

STUDY SHOWS EXERCISE CUTS HEART ATTACK RISK

A study of nearly 17,000 Harvard alumni has found that there were fewer heart attacks among those who participated regularly in strenuous exercise than among those who were less active.

The study was begun in 1968 by determining the health and exercise patterns of men who had entered Harvard as freshmen between 1920 and 1950. Of these, 16,936 were found to be free of heart disease. Each man was classified as having a "high" or "low" exercise level, depending on whether he expended more or less than 2,000 calories a week on exercise. By 1976, 572 of the men had experienced a serious heart attack. But the rate of heart attacks was 64 percent higher in the low-exercise group.

It was suggested that perhaps the high exercisers were simply those people who were more healthy and athletic all along. They exercised more because they were more healthy, not vice versa. But this suggestion was ruled out because a check of men who had participated in varsity sports as undergraduates showed the same pattern of heart attacks depending on their level of activity in later life.

EXERCISE 8.9

DRINKING IN PREGNANCY RISKY, STUDY SAYS

Even moderate drinking by women in the first month or two of pregnancy, often before they realize they are pregnant, can impair the child's intellectual ability on reaching school age, a new study indicates. The researchers found significant effects for women who consume a daily average of one to three drinks, each containing half an ounce of pure alcohol. That is equivalent to one to three daily cocktails, bottles of beer, or glasses of wine.

The scientists interviewed 491 Seattle women in the fifth month of pregnancy and followed up with assessments of their children, measuring intelligence, reaction time, and attentiveness. The study took into account factors such as parents' incomes and educations, which are known to affect a child's intelligence, and found that drinking had an effect apart from these influences. The impairment was noticed even when the pregnant woman cut back her drinking in the first or second month of pregnancy.

The most recently published finding from the research involved 53 mothers who had on average three drinks or more a day in the first month or so of pregnancy. Their children were found at age 4 to score substantially lower on intelligence tests than the children of mothers who did not drink at all. Specifically, the average score on IQ tests for these children was 105, 5 points below the average for all children in the study.

Separately, the researchers have reported that children born to mothers who had as little as one to two drinks a day in the first months of pregnancy were found by their early school years to have a slower reaction time and to have difficulty paying attention. These conclusions also were based on the 491 women and their children. Although previous studies have indicated that very heavy drinking by a pregnant woman can cause mental retardation in her children, the Seattle research is the first to show effects on the intellectual capacities of children at school age whose mothers drank at moderate levels while pregnant.

"We recommend that women who are trying to become pregnant or might become so do not drink alcohol at all," said Dr. Ann Streissguth, a psychologist in the psychiatry and behavioral sciences department at the University of Washington school of medicine, who directed the Seattle study. "The effects on children occur even at the social drinking level. The women in our study did not see themselves as having alcohol problems."

Not all children whose mothers drank had problems. The study found that although there is a strong relationship on average between a mother's drinking while pregnant and deleterious effects on a child's intellectual development, there is no certainty that a given child will show the effects. "The effects vary greatly in individual cases," Streissguth said. "There are many children who were exposed to alcohol who were not affected at all."

Experts in the field see the two reports from the Seattle study as particularly significant. "This is the first good study of the relationship between normal drinking levels in pregnant women and intellectual effects in their children," said Dr. Claire Coles, a psychologist at the Human Behavior Genetic Research Laboratory at the Emory University medical school in Atlanta. Coles is conducting similar research but is not involved in the Seattle study.

The findings were reported in the February 1989 issue of *Developmental Psychology.*

EXERCISE 8.10

ANTIOXIDANT VITAMINS FAIL TO PREVENT CANCER

Many studies have shown that a diet high in fruits and vegetables offers some protection from various cancers, particularly cancer of the colon. What is not known is why this is so. One theory points to the high-fiber content of fruits and vegetables and another to a lower intake of meat and fats by people who eat more fruits and vegetables. A recently popular theory is that substances plentiful in fruits and vegetables, particularly antioxidant vitamins such as beta-carotene, vitamin C, and vitamin E, protect against cancer. This popular theory is now challenged by a scientific study published in *The New England Journal of Medicine* for July 21, 1994.

Researchers in six clinical centers reviewed records of patients who had a precancerous polyp removed from their large intestines between December 1984 and June 1988. All invasive cancers begin as such polyps, although only a few polyps develop into invasive cancers. They initially selected more than 2,000 such patients who were younger than 80 years old, in good health, and free of further polyps as shown by a recent colonoscopy (a visual examination of the lower intestine using fiberoptics). Of these, 981 agreed to partake in a multiyear study. After a 3-month trial period, 864 subjects who proved sufficiently diligent in taking their medications were allowed to continue.

These remaining subjects were randomly assigned to one of four groups to be given daily (1) a placebo, (2) 25 mg of beta-carotene, (3) 1 g of vitamin C and 400 mg of vitamin E, and (4) the same doses of beta-carotene, vitamin C, and vitamin E. After 1 year, all subjects were given a full colonoscopy and then again after another 3 years. The number and size of precancerous polyps that developed between these two examinations were used to measure the effect, if any, of taking antioxidant vitamins. Neither the patients nor the examining physicians were informed which patients were in which group until the end of the study.

Due to death (forty-four cases) and other circumstances, 751 subjects completed the study. Those who dropped out were fairly evenly distributed among the four initial groups. The main result was that there were no statistically significant differences in the number or size of precancerous polyps that developed among subjects in the four different groups during the 3-year period between examinations.

Advocates of the antioxidant theory and makers of supplemental vitamins argue that 3 years is too short a time for the beneficial effects of antioxidant vitamins to show up. The benefits, they claim, are longer term.

EXERCISE 8.11

SCIENTISTS STUDY ASPIRIN, HEART ATTACKS

Aspirin, a drug that is taken for everything from arthritis to removing warts, may have still another use: preventing heart attacks. The most convincing evidence comes from two studies conducted by researchers at Boston

University, who since 1966 have been compiling data relating drug exposure to the diagnosis of patients admitted to hospitals.

The first study involved 325 heart attack patients and 3,807 other patients. It revealed that only 0.9% of the heart attack patients had been taking aspirin regularly before their attack (e.g., for arthritis). Aspirin taking was much higher—4.9%—among those patients who had not had heart attacks.

A second follow-up study of 451 heart attack and 10,091 other patients at 24 Boston hospitals showed the same kind of results: 3.5% of the heart attack patients said they had been taking aspirin regularly compared with 7% of those with other diagnoses.

EXERCISE 8.12

FINDINGS ON ASPIRIN CONFIRMED IN REPORT

Healthy men over 50 years of age who take one aspirin every other day cut the risk of having a heart attack nearly in half, a nationwide study has found, confirming preliminary reports announced last year.

The final report of the study's findings, which was published in *The New England Journal of Medicine* for July 20, 1989, went beyond the preliminary one, however, by asserting that the benefit of aspirin was evident only for men over the age of 50. The study included men 40 years old and older. . . .

"We have found a clear-cut, conclusive benefit from taking aspirin in preventing the first heart attack," said the study's leader, Dr. Charles H. Hennekens of Harvard Medical School and Brigham and Women's Hospital in Boston. . . .

In an editorial accompanying the study, doctors from Mount Sinai Medical Center in New York said the study indicated that it was reasonable to advocate aspirin for patients with a high risk of heart disease but that it should be used "cautiously, if at all," in others. . . .

The research, known as the Physicians' Health Study, examined 22,071 healthy male doctors who were 40 to 84 years old at the time the study began in 1982. Of those, 11,037 took 325 milligrams of aspirin every other day and the remainder took placebos, harmless and ineffective substitutes.

The men who took aspirin had 44 percent fewer heart attacks than those taking placebos. Among those who received aspirin, there were 10 fatal heart attacks and 129 non-fatal heart attacks. Among the non-aspirin group, 26 died of heart attacks and 213 had non-fatal ones. . . .

EXERCISE 8.13

TREATMENTS AND COSTS FOR ACUTE LOW BACK PAIN

Back pain is one of the most common reasons people seek medical help and is the second most common reason given for taking time off from work. Estimates of the annual cost of back pain in the economy of the United States range as high as $25 billion. There is, therefore, ample justification for studying the costs and effectiveness of various modes of treatment for back pain. One recent study appeared as a special article in *The New England Journal of Medicine* for October 5, 1995.

Using state licensing files, researchers at the University of North Carolina randomly selected practitioners in six categories: (1) urban primary care physicians, (2) rural primary care physicians, (3) urban chiropractors, (4) rural chiropractors, (5) orthopedic surgeons, and (6) physicians in a health maintenance organization (HMO). They secured cooperation from 208 practitioners, roughly equally divided among the six categories.

The practitioners enrolled patients who came to them for treatment of back pain. To be in the study, patients had to have had back pain for less than 10 weeks, not sought other help, not previously had surgery for back pain, and not be pregnant. In addition, patients had to speak English and have a telephone. Only 8% of eligible patients refused to take part in the study.

A total of 1,633 patients were enrolled between June 1992 and March 1993. The numbers were similar for each of the six categories of provider. Patients were interviewed within 1 week of enrollment by telephone by staff members at the University of North Carolina Survey Research Unit. They were then re-interviewed at 2, 4, 8, 12, and 24 weeks, or until they pronounced themselves completely recovered. Complete data were obtained for 1,555 of the patients initially enrolled.

There was no statistically significant difference in the average time to functional recovery among patients treated by the different categories of provider. Patients seeing different categories of providers all recovered in an average of 2 weeks.

There were, however, significant differences in the total cost of treatment. The average fees for urban chiropractors ($800) and orthopedic surgeons ($750) were significantly higher than those for urban primary care physicians ($500) or HMO providers ($450). There were also differences in the number of visits by patients to the different categories of provider. Patients of urban chiropractors made an average of 15 visits, whereas those of orthopedists made an average of 5.5 visits and those of urban primary care physicians made an average of 4.5 visits.

Finally, at the end of their treatment, patients were asked questions about their level of satisfaction with the treatment they received. Of the 606 patients treated by chiropractors, 42 percent reported the overall results as "excellent." Among the other 1,027 patients, regardless of type of provider, only 26.5 percent rated the overall results of treatment as "excellent."

EXERCISE 8.14

BENZPYRENE AND LUNG CANCER

It has been known for some time that prolonged contact with the chemical benzpyrene can cause skin cancer. It has also been discovered that small amounts of this chemical are contained in cigarette smoke and in polluted urban air. This suggests that benzpyrene may be the agent that causes lung cancer in smokers and in inhabitants of large cities.

To test this hypothesis, a specialist in environmental medicine studied the health of 5,900 roofing workers. These workers breathe large amounts of benzpyrene, which is an ingredient in coal tar pitch and asphalt—both common roofing materials. The amount of exposure to benzpyrene for these workers was estimated to be equivalent to that from smoking thirty-five packs of cigarettes a day! At the beginning of the study, all the workers had been members of the Roofers Union for at least 9 years. Six years later, the frequency of lung cancer deaths recorded among these workers (43/5,900) was reported to be not significantly different from the frequency expected in the general population.

EXERCISE 8.15

LUNG CANCER IN NONSMOKING WOMEN

One of the most contentious issues in debates over the dangers of smoking is the possibility of disease caused by "secondary smoke" (i.e., smoke produced by others). Studies cited as showing such effects have often been criticized as being based on too small a sample or subject to recall bias. Partly as an attempt to answer these criticisms, some researchers have conducted a large study reported in the November–December (1991) issue of *Cancer Epidemiology, Biomarkers, and Prevention.*

The study involved 420 women diagnosed for lung cancer between December 1985 and December 1988 in five metropolitan areas of the United States: Atlanta, Houston, Los Angeles, New Orleans, and San Francisco. These women were all determined to have smoked fewer than 100 cigarettes in their entire lives and were classified as "nonsmokers." This determination was based on interviews either with the women themselves or a close relative and, where possible, by urine analysis.

For comparison, 780 nonsmoking women free of lung cancer were selected at random from the general population in the same regions. These women all agreed to be interviewed and have a urine analysis to verify their status as nonsmokers. They were matched by age with the lung cancer victims. A second comparison was made with 351 nonsmoking women diagnosed for cancer of the colon during the same years. It was thought that this group would be subject to the same sorts of recall biases as lung cancer patients. There has never been any evidence of a connection between smoking and cancer of the colon. These women were also tested for smoking and matched by age with the lung cancer victims.

Of the 420 lung cancer victims, 294 (70%) had spouses who smoked (cigarettes, cigars, or pipes). Most of these (281) exhibited a particular form of lung cancer called adenocarcinoma. Among these 281 subjects, 203 (72%) had spouses who smoked. By contrast, among the colon cancer subjects, 231 of 351 (66 %) had spouses who smoked. Among nonsmoking women in the general population, 492 of 780 (66%) had spouses who smoked. Combining the two comparison groups, 723 of 1,131 (64%) had spouses who smoked.

For all subjects, an attempt was made to determine levels of exposure to tobacco smoke in occupational or social settings outside the home. There were no significant differences among the three groups in this regard. Nor were there any significant differences among the three groups at the five study sites or by age, race, income, education, or residence (rural or urban).

Finally, there were no significant differences among the three groups in amount of childhood exposure to tobacco smoke generated by parents or other family members.

EXERCISE 8.16

PROZAC EFFECTIVE IN REDUCING SYMPTOMS OF PMS

Because the symptoms of premenstrual syndrome (PMS) are similar to those of depression, it has long been suspected that drugs effective in treating depression (e.g., Prozac) might also be effective in treating PMS. This suspicion seems to be confirmed by a study published June 8, 1995, in *The New England Journal of Medicine.*

Women with a history of PMS were recruited in seven university-based women's health clinics in Canada. To be in the study, women had to meet a number of criteria such as not being under treatment for any other psychiatric symptom and not currently taking oral contraceptives. Of the 405 women initially selected, 92 dropped out during an initial "washout" trial in which all women were given a placebo. The remaining 313 women were randomly assigned to one of three groups given, respectively, a placebo, 20 mg of Prozac per day, or 60 mg of Prozac per day.

All the subjects were initially given a psychiatric test that has been proven to be a reliable indicator of mood disturbances. A 50% improvement in score at later times was taken to indicate improvement in the severity of PMS symptoms. Of the 313 women in the randomized trial, 277 completed the first menstrual cycle of the trial. Of these, 52% of those receiving either dose of Prozac showed improvement compared with only 22% of those receiving a placebo. By the end of the trial, consisting of six menstrual cycles for each subject, 53% of all cycles involving Prozac (437 of 832) but only 28% of cycles involving a placebo (113 of 410) showed improvement.

The difference in improvement between the two Prozac groups was not significant. However, incidence of reported negative side effects was significantly greater for those taking the higher dose. Largely because of these negative side effects, only 71 of 104 women assigned 60 mg of Prozac per day completed the full six cycles. Similarly, only 78 of 105 in the placebo group completed the full six cycles, mainly because of lack of perceived improvement.

The researchers concluded that 20 mg of Prozac a day is a safe and effective treatment for PMS. Whether the same effect could be achieved by taking the drug for only part of a cycle could not be determined from this study.

EXERCISE 8.17

STUDY CASTS DOUBT ON LINK BETWEEN MEDIA, TEEN SUICIDE

The notion that teen-agers who read or hear about teen suicides will be more likely to kill themselves appears to be false, according to a study by the U.S. Centers for Disease Control. No evidence exists that media reports of suicide prompt others to take their own lives, said the study, published November 22, 1989, in *The Journal of the American Medical Association.*

The study examined two clusters of teen suicides in Texas that occurred from February 1983 to October 1984. Researchers based their conclusions on interviews with the parents of eight teen-agers from one cluster and six from the second cluster.

Teen-agers who committed suicide were found to have had lives disrupted by frequent changes in schools, residences and parental figures. The youngsters also had been prone to emotional illness or substance abuse requiring hospitalization, the study found.

Such youngsters also had been more likely to injure themselves or others and to have threatened or attempted suicide. They were more likely to have lost either a girlfriend or boyfriend shortly before their deaths, the study found.

Information gathered from the victims' families was compared with that from 42 living teen-agers in a "control" group matched by school districts, grade, race, and sex. Those who committed suicide had been less likely than the control subjects to have talked about death or suicide as well as less likely to have seen television shows about suicide, the study found.

Dr. David Clark, director of the Center for Suicide Research at Rush-Presbyterian-St. Luke's Medical Center in Chicago, disagreed with the study's findings and said it was conducted using research standards that have changed in the 5 years since it was done. He said that current standards require interviewing not only the parents but also brothers and sisters of the suicide victim and friends, because friends often know things about the victim that the parent does not.

EXERCISE 8.18

HIGH-FAT DIETS IN PREGNANCY MAY LEAD TO FUTURE TUMORS FOR FETUS

Women who eat high-fat diets while pregnant may be disposing their fetuses to cancers of the reproductive system later in life, a researcher said Wednesday. Such a connection would be particularly worrisome because physicians routinely advise pregnant women to increase their consumption of red meat, whole milk, eggs, and cheese. These foods are loaded with the vitamins and minerals needed for fetal development, and with fat.

Prenatal exposure to fats dramatically increased tumors of the ovary, uterus, and pituitary gland in female mice, said Dr. Bruce Walker, a professor of anatomy at Michigan State University. He reported his findings at a meeting of the American Association for Cancer Research in San Francisco.

Studying 261 female mice over their 2- to3-year life spans, Walker found that among the daughters of mice who had received a high-fat diet during their pregnancy—equivalent to the fat consumed by the typical American—54% developed reproductive-system tumors. Among daughters of mice who consumed a low-fat diet—equivalent to the diet of a typical Japanese woman—only 21% developed such tumors.

Walker said there are enough critical similarities between mice and humans to justify concerns about cancers of the breast, ovary, and uterus in women and testicular and prostate cancer in men.

A link between exposure to fats in the womb and later reproductive system cancers could clarify the continuing mystery over the role of dietary fat in the United States' high rate of breast cancer, Walker said. Breast cancer occurs far more frequently among U.S. women, who obtain an average of 37% of daily calories in fat, than in Japanese women, who get about 20% from fat.

Researchers have not been able to confirm that dietary fat promotes breast cancer. Among Japanese-American women who eat typical U.S. diets, for example, some have breast cancer rates approaching that of the United States, others approaching that of Japan.

Further examination of studies of these women demonstrates, Walker said, that Japanese-American women born in Japan have the lower breast cancer rates, whereas those born in the United States have the higher rates. The difference can be explained, he said, by the fat contents of food these women's mothers consumed while pregnant.

EXERCISE 8.19

LIMB AMPUTATION AND HEART DISEASE

A new study that says limb amputation can significantly increase the risk of death from heart disease may mean increased benefits for some military veterans. A National Academy of Sciences study, commissioned by the Veterans Administration (VA), is the first hard evidence of a long-suspected link between amputation and heart disease.

Earlier studies on civilians have shown increased rates of heart disease for amputees as compared with the rest of the population. However, these studies are questionable because many amputations are performed due to vascular problems in the limbs, and such problems are common among people who already have a prior history of heart disease.

Similarly, a 1969 study of 5,000 Finnish Army amputees of World War II showed higher rates of heart disease than among the civilian population. But this study was also questionable because veterans, having originally been drafted partly because of good health, tend to live longer than civilians, and the incidence of heart disease increases with age.

In the new VA study, medical records of about 12,000 wounded World War II veterans were examined. Among these, approximately 3,900 had lost one or more limbs and approximately 5,000 others had suffered serious wounds not requiring amputation. On tracking the records down to the present time, the amputees were found to have a 150% higher death rate from cardiovascular disease than the other wounded veterans.

In addition, about 3,000 veterans who had lost just a hand or a foot were found not to have a significantly higher rate of heart disease than wounded veterans without amputations. The VA is planning to extend benefits for those who lost an arm or leg but not for those who lost hands or feet.

EXERCISE 8.20

NEW SURGERIES FOR BREAST CANCER

Until very recently, the standard treatment for breast cancer in the United States was the Halsted radical mastectomy, a procedure developed in the 1890s by Dr. William S. Halsted. This operation removes the affected breast, the underlying pectoral muscles, all related lymph nodes, and some additional skin and fat. The radical nature of this surgery has led many women to fear the treatment as much as the disease itself, often prolonging the time until diagnosis, thus tragically increasing the need for the operation while decreasing its chances of success.

Recently, women's groups and some physicians have argued that, although this procedure may have been justified in Halsted's day, when most cancers were diagnosed only in later stages and other treatments did not exist, it is not justified today. Our understanding of cancer, the means for diagnosis, and methods of treatment are all much improved since that time. Some physicians have thus experimented with less radical procedures, including a "simple" mastectomy, which removes only the breast, and various forms of "partial" mastectomy, the most "conservative" of which removes only the tumor itself. All surgical treatments are now often combined with both radiation and chemical therapies.

From a patient's standpoint, the less radical procedures are clearly preferable, but are they effective? An early study in Finland compared 527 cases of radical mastectomy with 339 cases of partial mastectomy, all treated between 1948 and 1961. By 1971, there was no significant difference in the 10-year survival rates for the two groups. This study, however, was criticized on the grounds that the patients selected for the less radical treatment might have been those who, for other reasons, were more likely to survive anyway. Similar criticisms were directed at a French study of 514 patients treated by partial mastectomy between 1960 and 1970. The latter group showed no significant difference in 10-year survival rates when compared with a similar group of 304 American patients treated by radical surgery.

In 1971, the National Cancer Institute began a study involving 1,700 patients at 34 Canadian and American institutions. The women in the study agreed to be assigned at random to different treatment groups, including radical surgery and simple mastectomy. Six years after the last patient joined the study, there was no significant difference in survival rates among the several treatment groups.

EXERCISE 8.21

PROJECT

Find a report of a causal study. You may find an example in a newspaper or news magazine. The Sunday supplement to your local newspaper is a good bet. When you have found something that you find interesting and substantial enough to work on, analyze the report following the standard program for evaluating causal hypotheses. If the article contains a reference to the original scientific report, you may find it instructive to look up that reference in a library.

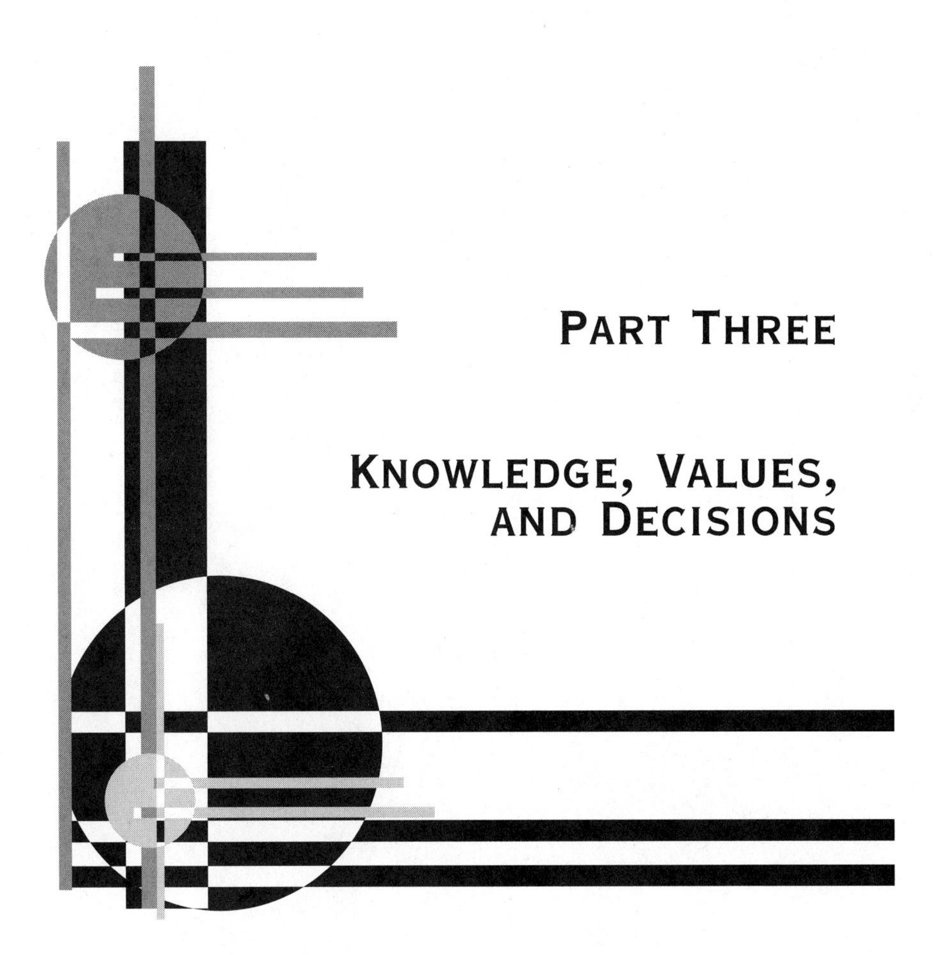

Part Three

Knowledge, Values, and Decisions

CHAPTER 9
MODELS OF DECISION MAKING

The results of scientific investigations often have implications for individual or public policy decisions. This is particularly true of causal investigations such as studies of possible causal connections between saccharin and bladder cancer or between smoking and heart attacks. To conclude this text, we explore some relationships between scientific knowledge, values, and decisions, both for individuals and for society.

We begin, as usual, by constructing some appropriate *models,* in this case models of decision making. Following a long tradition in which the study of probability and decision making focused on games of chance, we will take a simple game as our model of decision making. We will assume that the player is you, the reader. In the following chapter, we apply these models to some cases of real-life decision making.

9.1 OPTIONS

The game that serves as our model for decision making involves the familiar jar of marbles, which here may contain either red, green, or blue marbles. A single marble is to be selected at random. You are to bet on the color of the marble that will be selected. Thus, you can bet on either red, green, or blue. In the language of decision theory, you have three **options,** assuming, of course, that you have already agreed to play the game.

According to our model, a decision is always a decision to do something. Making a decision, therefore, is choosing a course of action. On this understanding, there is no decision to be made unless there is more than one thing that you might do. You must be facing a choice involving two or more different possible courses of action. These are your options.

Standard models of decision making require that the options in any decision be specified so that one option, and only one option, can be chosen. In terms already familiar from our study of probability models, the options must be both *mutually exclusive* and *exhaustive.* We could not, therefore, count betting on red and betting on red or green as two different options. These two options are *not mutually exclusive* because betting on the combination, red or green, is automatically to bet on red. The options must be specified in such a way that you could not choose more than one simultaneously.

However, you must be committed to choosing at least one option. If you are not, then the set of options is *not exhaustive.* The set of options in any decision must exhaust the actions regarded as possible in the circumstances. As we have described the particular decision in question, for example, betting on yellow is not an option. The options specified above (bet on red, bet on green, bet on blue) are both mutually exclusive and exhaustive.

9.2 STATES OF THE WORLD

In addition to the set of options, any model of a decision must include reference to the relevant possible **states of the world.** Specifying this set is not always easy. For example, you might think that, in our game, there are two relevant possible states of the world, winning and loosing. Those two states, however, will not do for our model of decision making. For our model, the possible states of the world must be specifiable *independently* of the options. This is not so for winning or loosing. Winning, for example, is a complex event consisting of an option and the result of the draw. Thus, one of the three possible ways of winning is betting on red when it turns out that the marble selected is red. In our example, the way to specify the possible states of the world without involving any reference to the options is simply to list the three possible results of the draw: red is drawn, green is drawn, or blue is drawn.

Like the options, the possible states of the world must be specified in a way that makes them *mutually exclusive* and *exhaustive.* Thus, as far as any particular decision problem is concerned, the actual state of the world will end up being one, and only one, of the initially specified possibilities. If that turns out not to be so, the decision problem itself must be reformulated.

9.3 OUTCOMES

Figure 9.1 combines our options and the relevant states of the world into a **decision matrix.** The form of the matrix is standard in decision theory. The options are listed in rows off to the left, and the possible states appear across the top. The resulting boxes, or cells, define what decision theorists call **outcomes.** Thus, the possible outcomes corresponding to a particular decision problem may be described as **option-state pairs.** The fact that each option-state pair determines an outcome means that the number of outcomes to consider will always be the *product* of the number of options and the number of states.

FIGURE 9.1

A decision matrix for a model decision problem.

	Red is drawn	Green is drawn	Blue is drawn
Bet on red			
Bet on green			
Bet on blue			

In this model, winning corresponds to a set of outcomes. Indeed, we see immediately that, among the nine possible *outcomes* of the decision, there are three outcomes associated with winning and six outcomes associated with losing. One of the outcomes corresponding to winning consists of betting on red when red turns out to be the color of the marble selected.

9.4 VALUES

Our model of your decision now lacks only one important component. How much is the bet? In particular, is the amount you stand to win or lose the same for each option? In general terms, these are questions of **value.** Of what value to you is winning or losing? How much is it worth? Your values attach not to options alone nor to states alone but to option-state pairs (i.e., *outcomes*). It is time we looked at the role of values in decision making.

Once we have determined the available options and set out the relevant possible states of the world, the next most important component in any decision is the relative values assigned to the possible outcomes. Determining the best option, in any model of decision making, is largely a matter of weighing the relative values of the various outcomes.

It is important to realize that assigning values to outcomes in a decision matrix does not require any kind of general or absolute measure of value. It is enough just to be able to compare the *relative value* of any outcome with any other outcome in the particular matrix at issue.

RANKING VALUES

There are two fundamentally different ways of assigning values to outcomes. One way is simply to **rank** the outcomes in order of increasing value. Because all we need is to be able to compare one outcome with another, how we label the outcomes is quite arbitrary. For example, we could assign the least valued of all outcomes the value 1. The next most-valued outcome could get the value 2; the next the value 3, and so on. In our example, the most-favored outcome would get the value 9, because there are in all nine possible outcomes. But we could equally well go up by twos, with the lowest-ranked outcome being assigned 2, the next lowest assigned 4, and so on. This assignment of values would not change the relative ranking of the outcomes.

When we have only a ranking, there can be no presumption, for example, that the outcome ranked 3 would be one-third as valuable as that ranked 9. Because any numbers that maintain the same ordering will do for a value ranking, the concept of an outcome being three times as valuable as another simply does not make sense in this context. The most we can say is that the higher ranked of any two outcomes is more valued. How much more is not defined.

MEASURING VALUES

For a more fine-grained model, we would like an actual **measure** on the outcomes. Then, we could say that one outcome was worth twice as much as another. In our

FIGURE 9.2

The decision matrix complete with value assignments for all outcomes.

	Red is drawn	Green is drawn	Blue is drawn
Bet on red	+10	−10	−10
Bet on green	−10	+10	−10
Bet on blue	−10	−10	+10

example, this is indeed possible. The standard way of assigning values to bets is in terms of money, which is generally regarded as a measure of value. Thus, an outcome that nets you $10 is twice as good as one that nets you only $5. There are, however, many real-life situations for which we might want to develop a decision model but for which we would be hard pressed to assign dollar amounts to outcomes—even though we could easily judge which were more valued than others.

Because all that matters is the *relative* measure of one outcome compared with other possible outcomes in a particular decision matrix, the *scale* for the measurement is arbitrary. A convenient general strategy for measuring values is to begin by identifying the least-valued and most-valued outcomes. Assign the least valued the measure 0 and the most valued the measure 100. Completing the matrix is then a matter of fitting in all the other outcomes according to their relative value on a scale of 0 to 100.

To complete our model decision problem, let us suppose for the moment that the game has the following simple value structure. If you win, by any of the three possible ways of winning, you get $10. If you lose, by any of the six possible ways of losing, you must pay $10. With these value assignments, the completed decision matrix is that shown in Figure 9.2.

9.5 SCIENTIFIC KNOWLEDGE AND DECISION STRATEGIES

It takes a lot of knowledge to construct a decision matrix. We have to know the available options, the relevant possible states of the world, and the relative values of all the resulting outcomes. Yet, none of this is the kind of knowledge that results from typical scientific studies. What well-defined scientific studies provide is evidence regarding the occurrence of one or another of the possible states of the world.

For purposes of decision making, there are three grades of knowledge we might have. Given the kinds of evidence that might actually result from a real-life scientific study, each of these cases represents an idealized state of knowledge, but that is true of all models. The important point is that, for each of these idealized states of knowledge, there are definite strategies for identifying the most desirable options. Understanding these strategies and why they lead to desirable options provides a basis for *evaluating* decisions, whether in the making or after a choice has already been made.

9.6 DECISION MAKING WITH CERTAINTY

One of the most important lessons of this text has been that we can never be absolutely certain of the truth of any scientific conclusion. No matter how good the evidence for any hypothesis, it is always possible that it is wide of the truth. So, the idea that we might be absolutely certain which state of nature will occur is an idealization. What is called **decision making with certainty** is simply a situation in which the evidence for the occurrence of one particular state of the world is so good that we ignore the small chance that we are wrong. If you are unwilling to ignore such small chances, then all your decision problems will involve what we will shortly identify as either "risk" or "uncertainty."

HIGHEST-VALUE STRATEGY

Decision making with certainty, then, includes any decision problem in which you act as if you know for sure which of the possible states of nature is or will be the real state. In our model, for example, you might be told by a completely reliable source that all the marbles in the jar are red. In that case, you know that the marble to be drawn will certainly be red. Your course of action is clear. Bet on red. Let us consider this situation a little more systematically.

Look back at Figure 9.2 and examine the outcomes included in the state that a red marble is drawn. These appear under the heading "Red is drawn." Of these outcomes, the one corresponding to the option of betting on red has the value +$10. Those outcomes corresponding to the options of betting on green or on blue have the value –$10. So, of the three outcomes compatible with the state of red being drawn, the one associated with the option of betting on red has the highest value.

This analysis suggests the following general strategy for decision making when we presume certain knowledge of the actual state of nature.

> ***Highest-Value Strategy:***
> Presuming certain knowledge of the actual state of nature, choose the option associated with the highest-valued outcome compatible with the known state.

If all decisions were made presuming certain knowledge of the state of the world, there would be little need ever to consider a full decision matrix. We did so in this example because we assumed we had the decision problem set up and then got the knowledge that made it a decision problem with certainty. This sort of thing might happen in real life, but usually we get the information when considering the options. We would not, then, need to consider more than one state of the world. Apart from determining the available options, evaluating the decision problem is mainly a matter of assigning relative values to the outcomes. If you can manage even just to rank the outcomes by increasing value, it will be obvious what option to take.

Unfortunately, there are few decisions for which this simple model applies. We often have to act in situations in which all the available information still leaves open several possible states of nature. We now turn to these more interesting cases.

9.7 DECISION MAKING WITH COMPLETE UNCERTAINTY

In real life, we are hardly ever *completely* uncertain which of the states will occur. So, any model of decision making with complete uncertainty, like that of certainty, is an idealization. It can be a useful idealization, however, in cases in which there really is very little relevant information available and perhaps no clear way to use what little there is.

To evaluate a decision assuming complete uncertainty about the state of nature is really to consider the decision on the basis of the decision matrix all by itself. That does not seem to be an easy thing to do, and indeed, it is not. There are some systematic ways to go about it, however, and these are worth knowing.

BETTER AND WORSE OPTIONS

There is a way in which one option can be clearly better than another, quite apart from any information about the states. Figure 9.3 exhibits a set of values for our model decision that illustrates this possibility. Look at the values associated with the outcomes for betting on green and betting on blue. If red is drawn, the payoff for either option is −\$5; if blue is drawn, the payoff is +\$5. Thus, if either red or blue is drawn, then having bet on green has the same payoff as having bet on blue. However, if green is drawn, having bet on green yields +\$10 but having bet on blue yields only +\$5. Thus, you are guaranteed to do as well betting on green as betting on blue, and there is at least one possible state for which having bet on green has a higher payoff. So, overall, green is clearly the better bet.

Let us generalize this idea by formulating it explicitly.

FIGURE 9.3

A value assignment illustrating the existence of one option that is better than another, but no option that is best overall.

	Red is drawn	Green is drawn	Blue is drawn
Bet on red	+10	+5	0
Bet on green	−5	+10	+5
Bet on blue	−5	+5	+5

Better Options:
For any two options, A_1 and A_2, if there is at least one state for which A_1 has a higher-valued outcome than A_2, and there is no state for which A_2 has a higher-valued outcome than A_1, then option A_1 *is better than* option A_2.

Note that this characterization of better options can be used even if your value matrix contains only a value ranking of the outcomes.

If A_1 is better than A_2, we will say that A_2 *is worse than* A_1. Note that, in the matrix of Figure 9.3, betting on red is neither better nor worse than betting on green. That is, on the above understanding of what makes one option better than another, neither of these options is better than the other.

It would be silly to take a worse option if a better one is available. Thus, if a value matrix for any problem exhibits an option that is worse than some other option, you can simply forget about the worse of the two. Under no circumstances would you decide to take the worse option. Here, we have a general rule for use when approaching a decision problem with complete uncertainty regarding which state obtains.

Eliminate Worse Options:
If there are any options that are worse than some others, eliminate the worse options from further consideration.

BEST OPTIONS

If it is possible for one option to be better than another, then it is possible for one option to be the best option available. It merely needs to be better than all the others. More formally,

Best Option:
If one option in a decision problem is better than every other option, that option is the *best option* available for the problem.

Quite clearly, if your value matrix for a decision problem exhibits a best option, you should take it. We can state this simple idea as a general strategy for decision making with uncertainty.

Best-Option Strategy:
If a decision problem contains a best option, choose it.

In real life, best options are a rare commodity. Indeed, neither of the two matrices we have so far considered contains a best option.

SATISFACTORY OPTIONS

You might well wonder whether there is not some way to specify options that, although not best, are, nevertheless, good enough. What would it mean for an option to be "good enough"? The general idea seems to be something like this. In any decision problem, the person making the decision has some idea of the lowest value that would be regarded as a *satisfactory* payoff of the problem. If there were an option that would *guarantee* at least this minimum value and no option guaranteeing any higher value, we might well choose the option with the guaranteed minimum satisfactory value.

To make this general idea a little more precise, let us define the **satisfaction level** of a decision maker in a particular decision problem as follows:

> ***Satisfaction Level:***
> The minimum value (or value rank) that the decision maker regards as a satisfactory payoff for a given decision problem is the *satisfaction level* of that decision maker for the problem in question.

Using the idea of a decision-maker's satisfaction level, we can characterize a **satisfactory option:**

> ***Satisfactory Option:***
> If every outcome associated with an option has a value at least as great as the decision-maker's satisfaction level for the decision problem, that option is a *satisfactory option* for the decision maker in the given problem.

We can now formulate another strategy for decision making with complete uncertainty.

> ***Satisfactory-Option Strategy:***
> If a decision problem with no best option contains a satisfactory option, choose it.

For the decision problem shown in Figure 9.3, betting on red is a satisfactory option if your satisfaction level extends as low as zero.

This formulation of the satisfactory option strategy leads to a preferred option only so long as there is just *one* option that is satisfactory. If there happens to be more than one, you have a further decision problem. You must apply some other strategy to the remaining set of satisfactory options. Presuming that any option worse than any other has already been eliminated, none of the remaining satisfactory options would be technically better than any other. However, if one option allowed the decision maker to have a *higher* satisfaction level than the others, that would clearly be the better choice. If two options have the same satisfaction level, you might simply flip a coin.

PLAYING IT SAFE

Figure 9.4 provides yet another version of our model decision problem. This version has no best option, as you should quickly verify for yourself. Indeed, no option is, by our earlier characterization, better than any other. Moreover, if you set your satisfaction level at any positive amount, then there is also no satisfactory option either.

However, if you are willing to *lower* your satisfaction level to zero, then betting on blue would be a satisfactory option. This option guarantees you a payoff of no less than zero. No other option has so positive a guarantee. This is a completely general feature of decision matrices. By lowering your satisfaction level sufficiently, you are bound eventually to find an option with the highest possible satisfaction level.

There is another, more standard way of characterizing the option with the highest attainable satisfaction level. For every option, there is a least-valuable outcome. In the

FIGURE 9.4

Another version of the model decision problem.

	Red is drawn	Green is drawn	Blue is drawn
Bet on red	+10	0	−5
Bet on green	+5	+10	−5
Bet on blue	0	+5	+5

context of decision theory, the value of this outcome is called the **security level** of the corresponding option. In other words,

Security Level of an Option:
The lowest-valued (or lowest-ranked) outcome associated with an option is the *security level* of that option.

Informally, the security level of an option is the value of the worst outcome you might get if you choose that course of action.

The option with the *greatest* security level is the same as the option with the highest attainable satisfaction level. There is, therefore, a simple strategy for finding this option. Just list the security levels for all options, and look for the option with the highest security level. This suggests the following play-it-safe strategy.

Play-It-Safe Strategy:
Choose the option with the greatest security level.

The reason I call this a play-it-safe strategy is that it seeks to minimize losses and pays no attention to possible gains. If you care more about potential gains than potential losses, there is another strategy you might consider.

GAMBLING

Every value matrix has at least one *highest-valued* outcome. Most have only one. Let us assume only one for the moment. One way of characterizing a gambler is as a person who "goes for all the marbles" regardless of the risk. This means, in the present context, choosing the option that is associated with the highest-valued outcome. If you do this, you may not get that outcome, of course, but you could not get it at all if you chose some other option. Formulating this idea as an explicit strategy,

Gambler's Strategy:
Choose the option associated with the highest-valued outcome.

In case there is more than one outcome with the same highest value, a consistent strategy would be to look at the second-highest values and take the option corresponding to the highest second-high value as well as the highest value overall. If there is more than one of these options, go to the highest of the third values, and so on. This strategy must, in the end, yield a unique decision. The overriding question, of course, is, Should you gamble?

GAMBLING VERSUS PLAYING IT SAFE

Look again at Figure 9.4. The gambler's strategy recommends betting on green because it has the possibility of yielding payoffs of $5 and $10. The play-it-safe strategy recommends betting on blue because, for this option, the security level is $0 as opposed to −$5 for the other two options.

In general, the gambler's strategy looks at the high values for each option and takes the option with the highest high value ("maximax"). The play-it-safe strategy looks at the low value for each option and takes the option with the highest low value ("maximin"). Is there some reason to think that one of these strategies is inherently better than the other in cases of decision making with complete uncertainty?

The accepted answer among philosophers and decision theorists alike is, no. Taking a best option does seem clearly to be the correct thing to do. And taking a satisfactory option seems at least a good strategy. If neither of those two strategies applies, however, there seems no obviously correct strategy to follow.

The main reason for taking the time to formulate the strategies for gambling and playing it safe is to have a clear characterization of these two attitudes toward a decision problem. If you want to gamble or to play it safe, you know clearly what to do. And if you want to understand decisions already made, by others and even by yourself, one of these two strategies may correctly characterize what has been done. You may be able at least to understand what is happening, even if you cannot claim to know what is correct.

The underlying reason for this unhappy situation is easy to spot. We are dealing with decision problems in the absence of any specific information about the states of the world other than that they are possible. It should not be expected that there is always a clearly correct decision in the absence of specific scientific information. The situation is quite different if there is more information, as we shall now see.

9.8 DECISION MAKING WITH RISK

Making decisions in cases of nearly complete uncertainty about the states of nature is obviously risky business. When decision theorists talk about risk, however, they have in mind *known* or *controlled* risk. The risk is known or controlled by *probabilities*. **Decision making with risk,** therefore, is characterized as making a decision knowing the probabilities of all the possible states of nature. Knowing the probabilities is a type of knowledge that is clearly intermediate between complete certainty and complete uncertainty.

Our study of interval estimation taught us that the most we can learn about probabilities from any sample is that the true probability lies within a specified *interval*. And even that much can only be known with a given confidence, say, 95%. For the moment, however, we will follow standard practice and imagine assigning specific probabilities to the possible states of nature. This amounts to introducing the idealization that the *probabilities* are known exactly and with complete certainty.

Up to now, all the decision strategies we have considered can be applied even if our values are expressed merely in terms of a *ranking* of the possible outcomes. Strategies for decision making with risk are not so inclusive. They can be used only when the values are *measured* to the extent that ratios of differences in value are meaningful. This makes sense because probability can be thought of as a kind of measured knowledge. If you are to combine probabilities with values, the values have to be measured to the same extent as the probabilities. If they were not, the combination would not be meaningful.

EXPECTED VALUE

To combine probabilities and values, we need a new concept, **expected value.** Before explicitly characterizing the expected value of an option, let us look at several ways of approaching it informally. Suppose that you are playing the game with values as given in Figure 9.4 and know that the jar contains 30% red marbles, 30% green, and 40% blue. You wish to bet on red.

One way of thinking about the expected value of an option is to imagine playing the game a large number of times. On the average, a bet on red would win three times in ten plays. So, imagine just ten games. If things went by the averages, you would win $10 on three games, get nothing on three games, and lose $5 on four games. That adds up to a net gain of $10, or $1 per game.

Another way of looking at the situation uses the probabilities more directly. If you play only once, betting on red, you have three chances in ten of gaining $10, three chances in ten of gaining nothing, and five chances in ten of losing $5. But these are exclusive alternatives, so you can add the results. Three-tenths of $10 is $3. Three-tenths of nothing is nothing. And four-tenths of $5 is $2. Three minus two is one. This makes it plausible to say that, in betting on red, your expectation is that you would win $1.

Now, let us look at an explicit statement of the expected value of an option.

> ***Expected Value of an Option:***
> The *expected value* **(EV)** of an option is the weighted sum of the values of its possible outcomes, with the weights being the probabilities of the corresponding states.

One computes a weighted sum of values by first *multiplying* each value by its corresponding weight and then *adding* the resulting products. For example, the expected value of betting on red in the game represented by the matrix in Figure 9.4 is

$$\textbf{EV}(\text{bet on red}) = (.30 \times \$10) + (.30 \times \$0) + (.40 \times -\$5) = \$3 - \$2 = \$1$$

This, of course, is just what we calculated earlier. We can now explicitly state the *expected-value strategy* for decision making in cases of known risk.

> ***Expected-Value Strategy:***
> Choose the option with the greatest expected value.

You should verify for yourself that this strategy would lead you to bet on blue for the problem just considered. Betting on red would be the worst of the three options.

If there happens to be more than one option with the same maximum expected value, then you can simply eliminate all the other possible options and treat the remaining matrix as a case of decision making with uncertainty. Having used your information about the probabilities to determine the expected values, you have no information left that could be used to decide which of several remaining options to choose. In practice, this does not happen very often, so you need not worry much about this eventuality.

IS THE EXPECTED-VALUE STRATEGY THE BEST STRATEGY?

It is worth pausing for a moment to consider whether the expected-value strategy is really the best possible strategy for cases of known risk. Consider a final version of our model decision problem as shown in Figure 9.5. Here, betting on red has the lowest expected value and betting on blue the highest.

What if someone confronted with this problem were to insist on ignoring the probabilities and playing it safe. That means betting on red, which has the highest security level. After all, this person reasons, if you play only once you cannot actually get the expected value of $7 when betting on blue. You are either going to win $15, win $5, or lose $5. There are no intermediate outcomes. Moreover, this person might say, losing $5 is not a satisfactory outcome but losing nothing is. So, betting on red is really the better option.

One response is that we should not think of the expected-value strategy as applying to any particular game but as a general policy to be followed in all sorts of situations. If we always ignored the probabilities and followed a play-it-safe strategy, we would not do as well on the average as we would by using the probabilities and following the expected-value strategy. When faced with a particular decision, however, it is sometimes hard to keep our minds on the long run. After all, we might not be around to benefit from the expected long-term gains.

Another problem is that the dollar amounts attached to the outcomes may not represent a person's real values regarding those outcomes. For example, if you had

FIGURE 9.5

A decision problem in which there is an intuitive conflict between the expected value strategy and the play-it-safe strategy.

	P(R) = .20	**P**(G) = .30	**P**(B) = .50		
	Red is drawn	Green is drawn	Blue is drawn	Security Level	Expected Value
Bet on red	+10	+5	0	0	3.5
Bet on green	+10	+15	−5	−5	4
Bet on blue	−10	+5	+15	−10	7

only $10 to your name, the prospect of losing it all by betting on blue, even if the chance of that happening is only 20%, would be quite serious. But a fifty-fifty chance of winning $5 or $10 by betting on red, with no chance of actually losing anything, would look quite good. However, if $10 represented just a tiny fraction of your cash, then you might well not worry so much about the 20% chance of losing $10 and care more about the expected gain of $7.

In sum, although there is a lot to be said for the expected-value strategy, it does not have the solid appeal of the highest-value strategy, the best-option strategy, or even the satisfactory-option strategy.

9.9 SUMMARY OF DECISION STRATEGIES

All the decision strategies discussed in this chapter are summarized in the tree shown in Figure 9.6. Keeping this diagram in mind will permit you to categorize any decision

FIGURE 9.6

A summary of decision strategies.

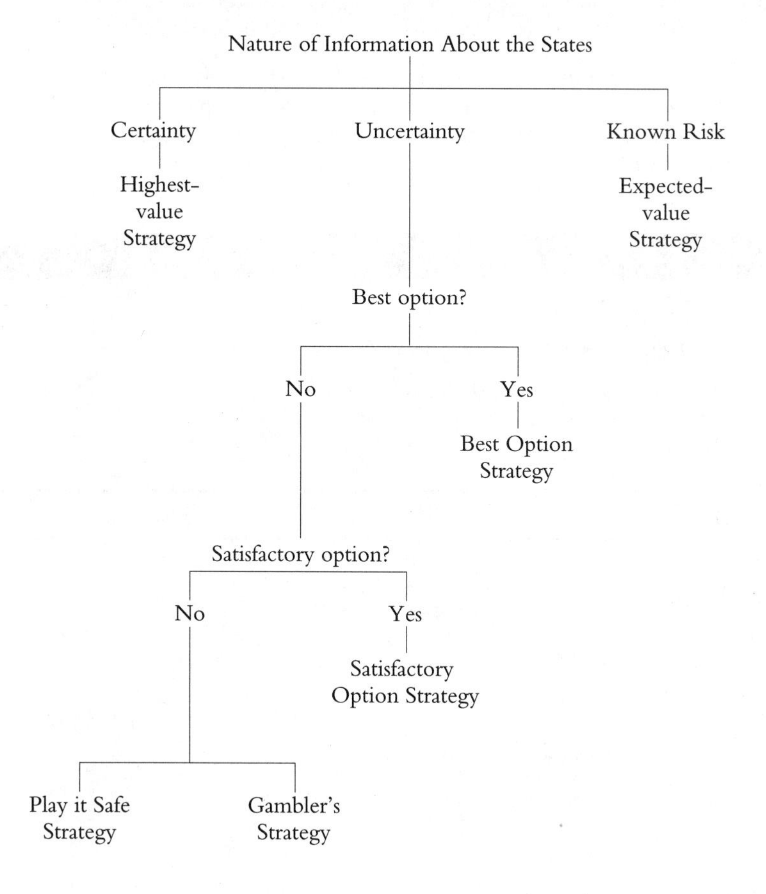

problem and proceed to an appropriate decision strategy. The only complicated part of the tree is the branch for decision making with uncertainty. This branch has several subbranches, depending on whether the matrix exhibits a best option or a satisfactory option.

• EXERCISES

EXERCISE 9.1

Suppose that the values shown in the decision matrix of Figure 9.7 represent a relative ranking of all the possible outcomes of the decision.

A. Suppose it is known that state S_1 will occur no matter which option is chosen. Which option is preferable in this case? Explain briefly.
B. Suppose it is known that state S_2 will occur no matter which option is chosen. Which option is preferable in this case? Explain briefly.
C. Suppose it is known that state S_3 will occur no matter which option is chosen. Which option is preferable in this case? Explain briefly.

EXERCISE 9.2

Suppose it is known "with certainty" that (1) performing option one will lead to the occurrence of state three, (2) performing option two will lead to the occurrence of state two, and (3) performing option three will lead to the occurrence of state one. Which option is preferable in this case? Explain briefly.

EXERCISE 9.3

Now, suppose that there is "complete uncertainty" regarding the outcomes of the decision problem shown in Figure 9.7.

A. Is any option better than any other? Explain briefly.
B. It there a best option? Explain briefly.

FIGURE 9.7

	State 1	State 2	State 3
Option 1	1	9	4
Option 2	5	3	8
Option 3	6	7	2

EXERCISE 9.4

A. Suppose that a value ranking of at least 5 is regarded as a satisfactory payoff for the decision. Is there then a satisfactory option? Explain briefly.
B. Suppose that a value ranking of at least 3 is regarded as a satisfactory payoff for the decision. Is there then a satisfactory option? Explain briefly.

EXERCISE 9.5

A. Determine the security level for each of the options.
B. Which option is preferred if one wishes to "play it safe"? Explain briefly.

EXERCISE 9.6

A. Determine the highest-valued outcome for each of the options.
B. Which option is preferred if one wishes to "gamble"? Explain briefly.

EXERCISE 9.7

Now, suppose that the values attached to the outcomes in Figure 9.7 provide not just a ranking but a measure of the relative value of the outcomes. Suppose further that the states have the following probabilities of occurring, regardless of which option might be chosen:

$\mathbf{P}(S_1) = .2$; $\mathbf{P}(S_2) = .3$; $\mathbf{P}(S_3) = .5$

A. Calculate the expected value for each of the options.
B. Which is the preferred option in this case? Explain briefly.

EXERCISE 9.8

Now, suppose that the probability of the various states depends on which option is chosen. In particular,

$\mathbf{P}(S_1/O_1) = .2$; $\mathbf{P}(S_2/O_1) = .3$; $\mathbf{P}(S_3/O_1) = .5$
$\mathbf{P}(S_1/O_2) = .3$; $\mathbf{P}(S_2/O_2) = .5$; $\mathbf{P}(S_3/O_2) = .2$
$\mathbf{P}(S_1/O_3) = .5$; $\mathbf{P}(S_2/O_3) = .2$; $\mathbf{P}(S_3/O_3) = .3$

A. Calculate the expected value for each of the options.
B. Which is the preferred option in this case? Explain briefly.

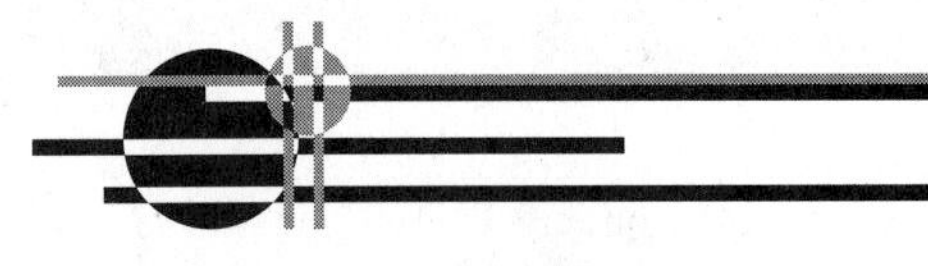

CHAPTER 10
EVALUATING DECISIONS

In this final chapter, we use our model of decision making to analyze and evaluate several real-life decisions. The examples represent types of decisions that must regularly be faced either by individuals or by governments or other groups. They can be used as analog models for evaluating decisions in a wide variety of contexts.

10.1 PROGRAM FOR EVALUATING DECISIONS

Before turning to specific examples of decision making, we pause to set out a simple program for evaluating decisions. Given the model of decision making developed in Chapter 9, the program is straightforward. It follows the form of the other programs we have used.

The Program

Step 1. Available Options. Identify the available options. Make sure they are formulated to be mutually exclusive and jointly exhaustive.

Step 2. States of the World. Identify the possible states of the world that are relevant to the decision. Make sure they are formulated to be mutually exclusive and jointly exhaustive.

Step 3. Outcomes. Construct the resulting decision matrix containing all the possible outcomes of the decision.

Step 4. Values. To the extent that this can be determined from the statement of the problem, construct an appropriate value ranking or measure for the possible outcomes. Record the values in the matrix constructed in Step 3.

Step 5. Strategies. In the light of all the information given, what decision strategy (or strategies) is (are) most appropriate to the problem as formulated in Step 4? Explain.

Step 6. Evaluation. Is there a recommended option that should be (or should have been) chosen? If so, which one, and why? If more than one option could be recommended, explain how so.

Now, let us apply this program to some representative decision problems.

10.2 DECISIONS INVOLVING LOW PROBABILITIES

A frequently encountered decision context requiring scientific information involves the discovery of a causal factor with very low effectiveness. This is the case with many environmental hazards. They are proven causal factors for various diseases, but their effectiveness at producing those diseases in the general population is relatively low. What is one to do? Our earlier discussion of oral contraceptives and breast cancer provides a convenient example.

ORAL CONTRACEPTIVES AND BREAST CANCER

We now know enough not to jump to conclusions merely because something has been shown to be a positive causal factor for some undesirable condition. What matters for decisions is how *effective* a causal factor it is. Once the effectiveness is known, we may find that the risk is outweighed by the benefits of the causal agent. We also know that effectiveness cannot be estimated from *retrospective* data alone. So, even knowing the details of a relevant retrospective study is not much help in making a decision.

As we learned in Chapter 8, researchers in the United Kingdom combined the results of their study with other information on the occurrence of breast cancer and the use of oral contraceptives. In this way, they were able to compare the probability of breast cancer among young women who had used oral contraceptives for more than 4 years with those who had never used oral contraceptives. They estimated the probability of breast cancer among women younger than 36 years old and not using oral contraceptives at about 1 in 500. For similar women using oral contraceptives for more than 4 years, the corresponding probability turned out to be less than 1 in 300. That is an increase of 70% in the chances of developing breast cancer. This may seem alarming, but even a large increase in a low probability is still a relatively low probability. What matters for decisions is not so much the amount of the increase as the size of the resulting probability. Let us see how this works.

Evaluating the Decision

Step 1. Available Options. Contrary to what many people seem to think, including some physicians and public health officials, the choice for most women is not between oral contraceptives and none at all. Formulating the options this way already biases the decision in favor of using oral contraceptives. The realistic options are between oral contraceptives and other types of contraceptives. Nor is the choice between continuous long-term use and no use. Within limits, one can use oral contraceptives intermittently. However, our only data are about use for more than 4 years and no use at all. So, the only options we can consider are using oral contraceptives for more than 4 years and not using oral contraceptives.

Step 2. States of the World. Because the only information at hand concerns the effect of getting breast cancer, the possible states of interest can only be whether one develops breast cancer or not. Ultimately, this is much too narrow a set of relevant states on which to base an overall decision regarding the use of oral contraceptives. In the end, therefore, our evaluation can only apply to the impact of the relative risks of developing breast cancer on a decision to use oral contraceptives for long intervals.

Step 3. Outcomes. There are four possible outcomes: using oral contraceptives and getting breast cancer; using oral contraceptives and not getting breast cancer; not using oral contraceptives and getting breast cancer; and not using oral contraceptives and not getting breast cancer.

Step 4. Values. Values are a personal matter. We can learn a lot about the decision, however, by considering what would, for most people, be a *minimal* positive value in favor of oral contraceptives. Other things being equal, most women prefer oral contraceptives to other available contraceptives or to none at all.

As suggested in Chapter 9, let us measure the values on a scale of 0 to 100. The least-valued outcome would be not using oral contraceptives and, nevertheless, getting breast cancer. Give this outcome value 0. The most-valued outcome, using oral contraceptives and not getting breast cancer, then gets value 100. A value difference of only 1 unit of 100 in favor of oral contraceptives seems appropriately minimal. So, using oral contraceptives and getting breast cancer gets a value measure of 1 and not using oral contraceptives but not getting breast cancer gets measure 99. The completed value matrix is shown in Figure 10.1.

Note that we do not assign a lower value to using oral contraceptives because they are a positive causal factor for breast cancer. Values attach only to the situations that characterize the outcomes themselves—option-state pairs. Any possible causal connections between options and states will be accounted for by differences in the probabilities assigned to outcomes.

Step 5. Strategies. It is instructive to put probabilities to one side for a moment and concentrate just on the value matrix as shown in Figure 10.1. If we, indeed,

FIGURE 10.1

A value matrix for deciding on the use of oral contraceptives. This matrix represents the decision as taking place in a state of complete uncertainty.

	Get Breast Cancer	Do Not Get Breast Cancer
Use Oral Contraceptives	1	100
Not Use Oral Contraceptives	0	99

knew nothing about the relative probabilities of the outcomes, this matrix would represent a problem of decision making with complete uncertainty. As such, it exhibits a clearly best option—using oral contraceptives. This option has the greater value whether or not breast cancer occurs.

Because we *do* know the relative probabilities of the outcomes, the decision problem is not one of uncertainty but of known risk. Our question, then, is whether the addition of this knowledge changes our judgment as to the more appropriate option.

Step 6. Evaluation. Our information is that the probability of getting breast cancer for women younger than 36 having used oral contraceptives for more than 4 years is about $1/300$. The probability for women younger than 36 not using oral contraceptives is about $1/500$. Because the states of getting and not getting breast cancer are exclusive and exhaustive, the corresponding probabilities for the state of not using oral contraceptives are $299/300$ and $499/500$, respectively. A revised matrix, including both values and probabilities and the resulting expected values for both options, is shown in Figure 10.2.

As you can see, the expected value for the option of using oral contraceptives is greater than that for not using oral contraceptives, even though the positive value put on using oral contraceptives is quite small. So, by the expected-value rule, the preferred option is still using oral contraceptives. The additional knowledge of the probabilities does not change the preferred option from what it was assuming no knowledge at all.

The reason for this should be intuitively clear to you by now. With probabilities of $299/300$ and $499/500$ of not getting breast cancer, the expected values for both options will be little different from the values associated with not getting breast cancer. In short, even if the probability of getting breast cancer is 70% greater for long-term users of oral contraceptives, it is still too small to offset a small positive value placed on using the pill rather than other contraceptives. To change this conclusion would require placing a much smaller relative value on using oral contraceptives. A value difference of 1 in 1,000, rather than 1 in 100, for example,

FIGURE 10.2

The decision matrix for the use of oral contraceptives complete with known probabilities. This matrix represents the decision as taking place in a state of known risk.

	Get Breast Cancer	Do Not Get Breast Cancer	Expected Value
Use Oral Contraceptives	1 1/300	100 299/300	99.99
Not Use Oral Contraceptives	0 1/500	99 499/500	98.80

results in the expected value of not using oral contraceptives being a small fraction larger.

It seems fairly clear, then, that deciding not to use oral contraceptives because of the increased risk of breast cancer is not necessarily a good decision for women younger than 36. In general, a decision whether to use oral contraceptives should not be based on a decision problem that focuses on only one specific effect such as breast cancer. We want a broader indicator of the health consequences of using oral contraceptives. Overall life expectancy would be a better measure. Unfortunately, because oral contraceptives have only been in general use since the early 1960s, there is little reliable information on overall life expectancy for those who use them.

10.3 DECISIONS INVOLVING MODERATE PROBABILITIES

Now, let us consider an example of a decision for which the causal factor is of moderate effectiveness. Here, the trade-off between values and probabilities is more difficult to evaluate.

THE SMOKING DECISION

In Chapter 8, we also examined evidence showing that smoking is a *positive causal factor* for coronary heart disease. We now know that this information, by itself, is not sufficient to resolve the decision problem in favor of the choice not to smoke. What matters for the decision problem is the *effectiveness* of smoking as a causal factor for coronary heart disease, which is to say, the relative *probabilities* of the disease for smokers and nonsmokers. In making the decision, a smoker (or potential smoker) must weigh these relative probabilities against the positive enjoyment of smoking (or the difficulty of giving it up).

It would be short-sighted, however, to base a decision on smoking on a single effect such as coronary heart disease or lung cancer. We want a broader indicator of the health effects of smoking, such as overall life expectancy. Figure 10.3 exhibits some representative data on overall life expectancy for smokers and nonsmokers. We will concentrate on two pieces of information: (1) 22% of 25-year-old male nonsmokers die before age 65; and (2) 38% of 25-year-old men who smoke a pack of cigarettes a day die before age 65. We can regard these as estimates from very large samples, so we can ignore the fact that each of these percentages should be a small interval rather than a single number. The data for people who are not 25-year-old men would be similar in predictable ways.

Evaluating the Decision

Step 1. Available Options. To keep the problem simple, we will restrict the options to smoking a pack a day (smoke) or not smoking at all (do not smoke). The resulting decision problem can be understood as applying either to a nonsmoker contemplating taking up smoking or to a smoker contemplating quitting.

FIGURE 10.3

The percentages of 25 year old males expected to die before age 65 as a function of cigarettes smoked per day.

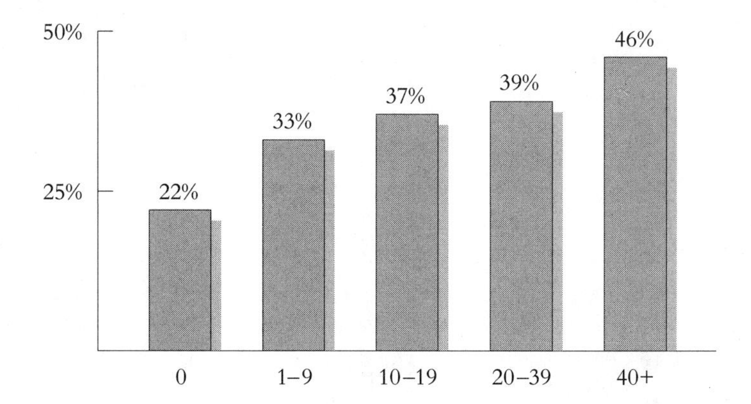

Step 2. States of the World. The information given restricts our attention to just two relevant states of the world: dying before age 65, and living past age 65.

Step 3. Outcomes. Our matrix has only four outcomes: smoking and dying before age 65; smoking and living past age 65; not smoking and dying before age 65; and not smoking and living past age 65.

Step 4. Values. Let us again measure the values on a scale from 0 to 100. The scale is fixed by stipulating that the least preferred outcome has value 0 and that the most preferred outcome has value 100. We will assume that, everything else being equal, the decision maker would prefer smoking to not smoking. We will also assume that, everything else being equal, the decision maker prefers living past 65 to dying before 65. This implies that the least preferred outcome is choosing not to smoke and still dying before 65. The most preferred outcome is smoking and still living past 65. For the moment, we will leave open the values to be assigned to the remaining two outcomes.

Step 5. Strategies. Because we know the probabilities of the outcomes relative to the possible options, this is a case of decision making with known risk.

Step 6. Evaluation. To evaluate the decision, let us first see what the decision matrix looks like if we place a relatively low value on smoking and a high value on living past 65. Suppose that we assign the value 1 to the outcome of smoking and dying before 65. This is equivalent to supposing that our decision maker, caught in the state of dying before age 65, would pay only $1 out of a total fortune of $100 to get from the outcome associated with not smoking to the outcome associated with smoking. Similarly, we will assign the value 99 to the outcome of not smoking and living past 65. This is like supposing that a decision maker who paid $99 to get into the state of living past 65 would be willing to pay only $1

FIGURE 10.4

The completed value matrix for the smoking decision with minimal preferences for smoking over not smoking.

	Die Before Age 65	Live Past Age 65
Smoke	V = 1	V = 100
Do not Smoke	V = 0	V = 99

more to get into the outcome associated with smoking rather than not smoking. In short, we are supposing that smoking rather than not smoking is worth only $1 of $100 to our decision maker. The decision matrix incorporating these values is shown in Figure 10.4.

If this were a case of decision making under uncertainty, the matrix in Figure 10.4 shows the option of smoking as being a *best option.* The fact that by ignoring the relevant evidence we get a matrix favoring smoking may partly explain why both tobacco companies and smokers are so anxious to deny that there is any real evidence of a connection between smoking and health. So long as the connection is denied, smoking looks like a good choice. The trouble with this approach, of course, is that the evidence is undeniable. The connection exists and cannot be wished away. The real decision problem is one of *known risk,* not complete uncertainly. The recommended strategy is not the best-option strategy but the expected-value strategy. The relevant probabilities are that 22% of 25-year-old male nonsmokers and 38% of 25-year-old men who smoke a pack of cigarettes a day die before age 65. Figure 10.5 shows the completed matrix incorporating these probabilities.

To the right of the matrix is the *expected value* of each of the two possible options. Because the expected value of not smoking is clearly higher than that of

FIGURE 10.5

The decision matrix for the smoking decision including known probabilities.

	Die Before Age 65	Live Past Age 65	Expected Value
Smoke	V = 1 P = .38	V = 100 P = .62	62.4
Don't Smoke	V = 0 P = .22	V = 99 P = .78	77.2

smoking, not smoking is the recommended choice. What was the worst option in the absence of statistical information becomes the recommended choice once that information is taken into account.

FURTHER CONSIDERATIONS

In the matrix of Figure 10.5, the difference between a probability of .62 and a probability of .78 is more than enough to offset the 1-point difference in values between the two corresponding outcomes. The only reply that a smoker might make is that the suggested value difference is just too small. A smoker in the state of living past 65 might well demand more than $1 of $100 to move from the outcome involving continuing to smoke to the outcome involving quitting. Likewise, the same smoker caught in the state of getting lung cancer might well pay more than $1 to move up from the outcome involving quitting to the outcome involving continuing to smoke. How much more?

Let us turn the question around. By how much would we have to decrease the value difference between dying before 65 and living past 65 for the two options to have the same expected value? Equivalently, by how much would we have to increase the difference in value between outcomes involving smoking and not smoking to equalize the expected values of the two options. That value difference would mark the break-even point between the two options.

This is a simple problem in high school algebra. We want to determine a particular expected value, call it V, such that the outcome of smoking and dying before 65 has value V. Likewise, the outcome of not smoking and living past 65 will get value (100 – V). Setting the expected value of the two options equal to each other,

$$(.38 \times V) + (.62 \times 100) = (.22 \times 0) + [.78 \times (100 - V)]$$

Solving for V, we get a value of about 14. So, the matrix that makes the two options equally good is as shown in Figure 10.6. If you think smoking is a good decision, you must value living past 65 less than a difference of 86 points on a scale of 100. Similarly, you must value smoking over not smoking more than 14 points on a scale of 100. That seems a high relative value to place on smoking over living into retirement. But we are not here in the business of criticizing a person's values. We are merely pointing out what relative values the decision to smoke represents.

FIGURE 10.6

The "break even" value matrix for the smoking decision.

	Die Before Age 65	Live Past Age 65
Smoke	14	100
Don't Smoke	0	86

Most people do not have much feeling for rating their values. Let us put these numbers into a form that is more easily understood. Suppose that you were giving grades to outcomes. At 100, the outcome of smoking and living past 65 gets an A+. Rating only 86, however, living past 65 and not smoking gets only a B. If you smoke, you are saying that, for you, smoking makes the difference between an A+ life and a B life. Can smoking really be that important?

Sometimes it can. The story is told of a famous scholar who tried hard to give up smoking. Once he stopped smoking, he found he could not write. He decided that being able to do his life's work was worth the risks of smoking. This is an extreme case. Few people can claim such an excuse.

CONFRONTING YOUR VALUES

Decision making with risk is usually presented as a process of using known probabilities together with the values of outcomes to determine which option has the greatest expected value. This works well when the values are given in dollars and cents, as in the case of a lottery. For more qualitative values, such as the value of smoking to a smoker, this approach works less well. In such cases, it is sometimes helpful to put the decision problem in a form that does not require an explicit assessment of values. Rather, values are confronted *indirectly* through the contemplation of the choice to be made.

A simple way to do this is to construct a model of the decision in which each option is represented by a jar containing 100 marbles. You need one jar for each option. Each possible state of the world is assigned a color. So, you need as many different-colored marbles as the problem has states. The probabilities of the states are represented by the relative number of balls of the various colors. A state with a probability of .50 for a given option would be represented by having 50 of the 100 marbles carry the color assigned to that state.

FIGURE 10.7

A marble and jar representation of the smoking decision.

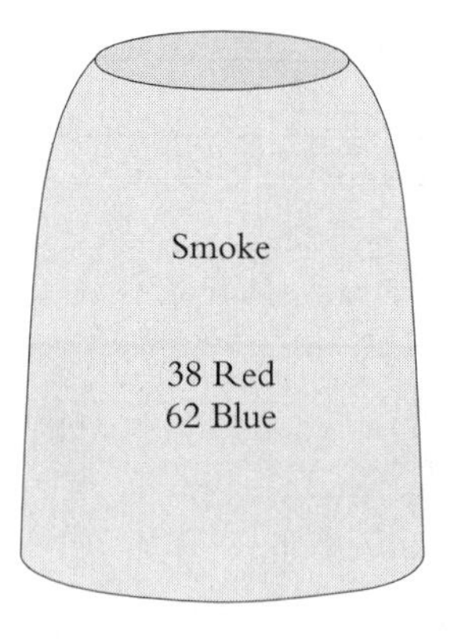

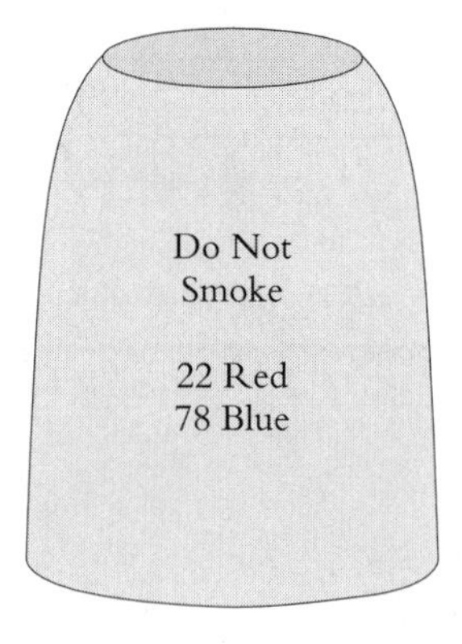

Once all the jars are set up correctly, your decision to choose one of the options is equivalent to deciding which jar to pick. Having picked a jar, you must select one marble at random from that jar. The color of the marble selected tells you which state, and thus which outcome, you have achieved. Because you know the relative numbers of colored marbles in each jar, by picking a jar you are implicitly weighing your desire for the corresponding option against the probabilities of the various states. Imagining reaching in and picking a marble is a graphic way of confronting your true feelings about the decision.

Now, we will apply this device to the smoking decision. Let a red marble represent the state of dying before the age of 65. A blue marble will represent the state of living past 65. The jar that represents the option of smoking will have 38 red marbles and 62 blue ones. The jar representing the option of not smoking has 22 red marbles and 78 blue ones. You have to select a single marble at random from one of these two jars. Selecting a red marble means that you will die before the age of 65. Your choice is pictured in Figure 10.7. Which jar do you choose?

This way of presenting the problem brings you face to face with your values because you have to ask yourself, Is smoking worth facing those additional 16 red marbles in the smoking jar? If you want to smoke, only you can answer that question.

10.4 POLICY DECISIONS WITH UNCERTAINTY

The previous examples focused on decisions by individuals, and the relevant values were those of the individual decision maker. We now evaluate an example in which the decision is a collective political decision. So, the subject is really public policy rather than individual decision making.

GLOBAL WARMING

In Chapter 2, we considered the problem of global warming (or the greenhouse effect). Many scientists believe that the earth is experiencing significant warming due to the generation of carbon dioxide (and other greenhouse gases), mainly from burning fossil fuels such as coal, oil, and gasoline. Even an increase of only a few degrees in the earth's average temperature could have severe effects on the ecology of the earth. It could, for example, result in faster melting of the polar ice caps, thus raising the levels of the oceans and flooding coastal cities such as New York and Los Angeles. It could also turn current agricultural areas into vast deserts.

There have already been several international conferences aimed at reaching an agreement among the major polluting nations on steps that could be taken to lessen the threat of significant warming. Thus far, however, only minor agreements have been reached. Leaders of many governments, including the United States, have questioned whether enough is known to claim with sufficient confidence that global warming is really taking place or that proposed measures could make a significant difference. Reluctance to take significant steps is understandable because any effective measures entail considerable costs. These include unemployment and higher prices for many goods.

Evaluating the Decision

Step 1. Available Options. In practice, the available options are many and complex. For our purposes, we will reduce the complexity to just two options: "do something" and "do nothing". It is to be understood that doing something implies efforts on a scale that entails significant costs. Doing nothing means proceeding as one would if the possibility of global warming were of no serious concern.

Step 2. States of the World. Here again, we will reduce the many possible states to just two: global warming takes place ("warming"), and global warming does not take place ("no warming"). Saying that global warming takes place implies that it is sufficiently severe to have important consequences such as the flooding of major coastal cities or the destruction of farmlands. Otherwise, we would say that significant warming has not taken place.

Step 3. Outcomes. There are, of course, four outcomes: doing something but warming occurs anyhow; doing nothing and warming occurs; doing something and no warming occurs; or doing nothing and no warming occurs. These four possible outcomes are shown in Figure 10.8.

Step 4. Values. Imposing a rough value measure on the matrix of Figure 10.8 is not as difficult as it might seem. The worst outcome is making strenuous efforts to avoid warming and have it occur anyway. In this case, the resources devoted to trying to do something would have been wasted. Give that outcome value 0. The best possible outcome would be to do nothing and not have any significant warming. Here, we get the most desirable state for free. Give that outcome value 100.

Whether warming occurs or not, trying to do something significant to prevent it carries heavy costs. So, in either state of nature, the outcome of doing nothing carries a higher value than doing something. How much greater is not terribly important for evaluating the decision. A jump of 10 points out of 100 when moving from doing something to doing nothing is good enough for our purposes. The completed value matrix is shown in Figure 10.9.

Step 5. Strategies. This decision problem exhibits a value structure similar to that of both decisions examined earlier. The main difference is that, in the present

FIGURE 10.8

The basic decision matrix (excluding values) for a decision about global warming.

	Warming	No Warming
Do Something		
Do Nothing		

FIGURE 10.9

A completed value matrix for the decision about global warming.

	Warming	No Warming
Do Something	0	90
Do Nothing	10	100

case, there is considerable controversy among scientists whether global warming is taking place or would take place any time soon. So, policy makers are inclined to treat the problem as one of decision making under uncertainty.

Step 6. Evaluation. Treating this decision as a case of decision making under uncertainty, doing nothing is a best option! That is because doing something is costly, whatever the eventual state of the world. Is it any wonder that those who benefit the most from continuing to do nothing emphasize the controversy among scientists and the need for continued research?

What would be required to make the decision problem look different to policy makers is undeniable evidence both that doing nothing will lead to warming and that doing something could prevent it. Such evidence, if it were available, would change the decision problem from one of uncertainty either to one of certainty or to one of known risk. Then either a highest-value strategy or an expected-value strategy would apply.

WHOSE DECISION IS IT ANYWAY?

In decision making by individuals, it is the same person who benefits if the outcome is favorable or suffers if the outcome is unfavorable. In policy decisions, those who would benefit if things go well may be different from those who would pay if things go badly. It is very important, therefore, to determine who is making the decision and, consequently, who is assigning values and choosing which decision strategy to follow. This is particularly important if the situation is one of uncertainty and there is no best option. Who decides what is a satisfactory outcome? If there is no satisfactory option, who decides whether to gamble or play it safe? These, however, are questions that have everything to do with politics and little to do with the use of scientific knowledge.

• EXERCISES

Analyze the following decisions following the program set out at the beginning of this chapter.

EXERCISE 10.1

A RAFFLE

A friend stops you on the street saying that his fraternity is having a raffle and you now have the opportunity of buying the very last ticket for only $5. The prize, which has been donated by a rich alumnus, is worth $1,000 cash. Being somewhat suspicious, you inquire as to the number of tickets being sold and are assured there are only 250. And, indeed, the ticket in question has the number 250 on it. Having a spare $5, you pause to consider the decision whether to buy the ticket or not.

EXERCISE 10.2

BUSINESS TRAVEL

An accountant must travel from New York City to Washington, D.C., on official business. By air shuttle, including the cost of time for travel (time is money!), the total cost is $200. Rail fare is less, but because it takes longer, the Metroliner would have a total cost of $220. The train, however, is more reliable. Chances of a serious delay traveling by air are 15%. Chances of being delayed traveling by train are only 5%. In either case, being late would add an additional $200 to the total cost of the trip. Should the accountant go by air or train?

EXERCISE 10.3

THE COST OF MEDICAL TREATMENTS

The financial office of a health maintenance organization (HMO) is considering the relative cost-effectiveness of two different treatments for a fairly common condition. Treatment A costs the HMO $1,000, assuming there are no complications, but $4,000 if there are complications. The probability of complications with this treatment is 10%. Treatment B, however, costs the HMO $1,400 if there are no complications but only $3,000 if there are complications. Moreover, the probability of complications with treatment B is only 1%. Looking solely at their bottom line, which treatment should the HMO recommend?

EXERCISE 10.4

TREATMENTS FOR BREAST CANCER

A woman is diagnosed as having breast cancer. Her physicians inform her that a recently completed randomized clinical trial with 2,000 subjects exhibiting symptoms similar to hers revealed no statistically significant difference in 10-year survival rates for women assigned a radical (Halsted) mastectomy as opposed to a simple removal of the tumor only. In general, the woman definitely prefers outcomes that are less disfiguring. Assuming these are her only options, what should she do?

EXERCISE 10.5

VACATION PLANS

Spring vacation is coming, and you are trying to decide whether to go to Florida with your friends or to go home. Your main worry is about the weather, about which there is total uncertainty. If the weather in Florida turns out to be good, it would be worth the money to go. But if the weather turns out to be bad, you would rather be home with your family—at very little monetary cost to you. However, if you decide to go home, you prefer that the weather in Florida be bad so you will not think that you are missing something. Of course, you do not reveal that preference to your friends. What should you do?

EXERCISE 10.6

FLU EPIDEMIC

Imagine that the Center for Disease Control in Atlanta has issued a bulletin that there is an impending flu epidemic. The flu is serious but only rarely fatal—typically leaving you incapacitated for 30 days. Fortunately, there is a very effective vaccine ready to be used, and it is being made available free to anyone who requests it. Unfortunately, however, this flu vaccine has the side effect that it may cause temporary paralysis, which, though rarely fatal, also has the effect of leaving one incapacitated for 30 days. If one were so unlucky as to get both, one would be incapacitated for 40 days. The officials are wary of making recommendations and are leaving the decision whether to take the vaccine up to individuals. They do, however, provide the following information. In the whole population, the estimated risk of getting flu without a shot is $1/10$; with a shot, the risk is only $1/10{,}000$ (1,000 times less). However, the probability of getting the paralysis without the shot is only $1/100{,}000$; with the shot, it jumps to $1/100$ (1,000 times more). What should one do? (Hints: There may be more than two possible states of the world to consider. Treat very small probabilities as zero and very large probabilities as one.)

EXERCISE 10.7

THE PRISONERS' DILEMMA

Suppose that you and a friend are engaged in some illegal activity and are "busted." The district attorney (DA) puts you in different cells and then comes to you with the following "bargain." The evidence against you both is quite good, but the case would be stronger, he says, if one of you would provide more information. So, the DA promises that if you talk, you will get off with at most 1 year in the state prison—provided your partner does not also talk. However, if you do not talk and your partner does, you are likely to get 4 years. Knowing a bit about decision theory, you realize that there are two other outcomes to consider. So, you ask the DA what happens if neither of you talks or if both of you do. Being an honest person, the DA admits that, without some additional evidence, you will both get off with at most 2 years. If you both talk, however, you will both get 3 years.

Suddenly, you realize that you do not know what your partner might do in this situation. You do not even know what you will do. So, you ask the DA for a half-hour to think about your decision.

Having carefully analyzed the problem, you reflect on the fact that your partner is in exactly the same situation as you are. If he analyzes the problem as you have, the end result for both of you is predictable. What is that result? Can you see any way out of this dilemma?

EXERCISE 10.8

THE TRAGEDY OF THE COMMONS

In the nineteenth century, it often happened that several families shared a small field in common. This field was used for raising supplementary animals. To keep the example simple, let us suppose that the families all raise cows, and that, at the moment, each family has nine cows. They all sell milk and butter to nearby townspeople, each earning roughly $900 annually. Things have been prosperous, and each family has been adding a new cow every year or so for several years. The Commons, however, has about reached its limit. It cannot take much more grazing.

Suppose you are one of these people, and you are considering whether to add a new cow this year. You realize that, if everyone adds a new cow, the yield per cow will go down due to lack of good grass, so everyone's net gain will drop to $800 a year. However, if you add a new cow and no one else does, that will not hurt the field so much, and you can expect your income to go up to $1,000. The other side of this coin, however, is that if everyone else adds a cow and you do not, the yield per cow will go down, and you will net only about $700. What should you do?

Having carefully analyzed the problem, you reflect on the fact that everyone sharing the Commons is in exactly the same situation as you are. If they all analyze the problem as you have, the end result for all of you is predictable. What is that result? Can you see any way to avoid this tragedy?

EXERCISE 10.9

PREVENTATIVE ATTACK

Imagine two countries, A and B, that have a disputed piece of territory between them. Tension is mounting. The ministers of country A meet in emergency session to plot their course of action. They conclude that there are really only two options open to them: to offer to negotiate the dispute with country B, and to attack swiftly in an attempt to take the territory by force. The main uncertainty is over what country B will do. Will country B negotiate in good faith, or will it try to attack first?

The ministers of A agree that the best thing would be to manage to attack while B is preparing to negotiate. That way, they can get most of the territory with minimal losses. The worst possibility would be to have B attack while they are trying to negotiate. In that case, B would get most of the territory. However, if both countries attack simultaneously, being fairly equally matched, they will probably each end up with about half the territory after fighting a short war. If B would negotiate in good faith, they could probably end up agreeing to split the territory without a war. What should country A do?

Country B, of course, is in exactly the same position regarding the disputed territory as country A. What should country B do? How might a war be avoided?

INDEX

E

F

G

H

I

J

K

L

M

Q

R

S

T

U

V

W

Y

Z

Credits

For permission to use copyrighted materials, the author is grateful to the following:

Chapter 2: Section 2.10, "Gene Analysis Upsets Turtle Theory," *New York Times*, March 14, 1989. © 1989 by The New York Times Company. Reprinted by permission. "New View of the Mind Gives Unconscious An Expanded Role," *New York Times*, February 7, 1984. © 1984 by The New York Times Company. Reprinted by permission. "Was That a Greenhouse Effect? It Depends on Your Theory," *New York Times*, September 4, 1988. © 1988 by The New York Times Company. Reprinted by permission. Exercise 2.1, "Einstein's Impossible Ring: Found," by M. Mitchell Waldrop, *Science*, June 24, 1988, Vol. 240, p. 1733. © AAAS. Reprinted by permission. Exercise 2.2, "Why is the World Full of Large Females," by Roger Lewin, *Science*, May 13, 1988, Vol. 240, p. 884. © AAAS. Reprinted by permission. Exercise 2.6, "A Heresy in Evolutionary Biology," by Roger Lewin, *Science*, September 16, 1988, Vol. 241, p. 1431. © AAAS. Reprinted by permission. Exercise 2.7, "Quartz Discovery Supports Theory That Meteor Caused Dinosaur Extinction," appeared in *Sunday Herald Times*, May 17, 1987, p. A10. Reprinted by permission of The Associated Press. Exercise 2.10, "Scientists Put a New Twist on Creation of the Universe," by Jim Dawson, *Minneapolis Star Tribune*, November 18, 1989, p. 1A. Reprinted by permission of the Minneapolis Star Tribune. Exercise 2.12, "Comet Source: Close to Neptune," by Richard A. Kerr, *Science*, March 18, 1988, Vol. 239, p. 1372–3. © AAAS. Reprinted by permission.

Chapter 3: Exercise 3.12, "Clues to the Drift of Continents and the Divergence of Species," by Walter Sullivan, New York Times, May 30, 1982. © 1982 by The New York Times Company. Reprinted by permission.

Chapter 6: Exercise 6.1, "Study: People Tell Lies to Have Sex," appeared in *Minneapolis Star Tribune*, August 15, 1988, p. 1A. Reprinted by permission of The Associated Press. Exercise 6.3, "Poll Shows Men Sinking in the Opinion of Women," appeared in *Minneapolis Star Tribune*, April 26, 1990, p. 1A. Reprinted by permission of The Associated Press. Exercise 6.7, "Homicide is Top Cause of Death from On-Job Injury for Women," appeared in *New York Times*, August 18, 1990, p. 8Y. Reprinted by permission of the Associated Press. Exercise 6.9, "Aggression in Men: Hormone Levels Are a Key," by Daniel Goleman, *New York Times*, July 17, 1990, p. B5Y. © 1990 by The New York Times Company. Reprinted by permission. Exercise 6.11, "AIDS Plague Hits Teen Heterosexuals," by Kim Painter, *USA Today*, July 20, 1989, p. 1A. © 1989, USA Today, Reprinted by permission.

Chapter 8: Exercise 8.1, "British Study Says Pill Increases Breast Cancer Risk," appeared in *Minneapolis Star Tribune*, May 5, 1989, p. 4A. Reprinted by permission of The Associated Press. Exercise 8.2, reprinted by permission from *Vitamin C and the Common Cold*, by Linus Pauling. Copyright © 1970 by W. H. Freeman and Company, Bantam edition. Exercise 8.3, "Study Finds Decaf Coffee May Raise Cholesterol," appeared in *Minneapolis Star Tribune*, November 4, 1989, p. 11A. Reprinted by permission of the Associated Press. Exercise 8.4, "Sharp Cut in Serious Birth Defect is Tied to Vitamins in Pregnancy," by Gina Kolata, *New York Times*, November 24, 1989, p. 1. © 1989 by The New York Times Company. Reprinted by permission. Exercise 8.9, "Drinking in Pregnancy Harmful, Study Says," appeared in *St. Paul Pioneer Post Dispatch*, February 16, 1989, p. 19A. © 1989 by The New York Times Company. Reprinted by permission. Exercise 8.12, "Findings on Aspirin Confirmed in Report," *New York Times*, July 20, 1989, p. 18. © 1989 by The New York Times Company. Reprinted by permission. Exercise 8.17, "Study Casts Doubt on Link Between Media, Teen Suicide," appeared in *Minneapolis Star Tribune*, November 23, 1989, p. 5. Reprinted by permission of The Associated Press. Exercise 8.18, "High-fat Diets in Pregnancy May Lead to Future Tumors for Fetus," appeared in *Minneapolis Star Tribune*, May 25, 1989, p. 10A. Reprinted by permission from Scripps Howard News Service.